The Princeton Review®

LSAT®

DECODED

For PrepTests 52–61

The Staff of The Princeton Review

PrincetonReview.com

Penguin
Random
House

The Princeton Review
24 Prime Parkway, Suite 201
Natick, MA 01760
E-mail: editorialsupport@review.com

ISBN: 978-1-101-91959-0
eBook ISBN: 978-1-101-91963-7
ISSN: 2381-4500

Editor: Aaron Riccio
Production Editors: Kathy Carter and Liz Rutzel
Production Artist: Deborah A. Silvestrini

Printed in the United States of America on partially recycled paper.

10 9 8 7 6 5 4 3 2 1

Editorial

Rob Franek, Senior VP, Publisher
Casey Cornelius, VP Content Development
Mary Beth Garrick, Director of Production
Selena Coppock, Managing Editor
Meave Shelton, Senior Editor
Colleen Day, Editor
Sarah Litt, Editor
Aaron Riccio, Editor
Orion McBean, Editorial Assistant

Random House Publishing Team

Tom Russell, Publisher
Alison Stoltzfus, Publishing Manager
Melinda Ackell, Associate Managing Editor
Ellen Reed, Production Manager
Andrea Lau, Designer

Acknowledgments

Many thanks to Chad Chasteen, Drew Brody, Karen Hoover, Mindy Myers, and Craig Patches for their invaluable work in the creation of this title.

Contents

Register Your

1 Go to **PrincetonReview.com/cracking**

2 You'll see a welcome page where you can register your book using the following ISBN: 9781101919590.

3 After placing this free order, you'll either be asked to log in or to answer a few simple questions in order to set up a new Princeton Review account.

4 Finally, click on the "Student Tools" tab located at the top of the screen. It may take an hour or two for your registration to go through, but after that, you're good to go.

If you are experiencing book problems (potential content errors), please contact EditorialSupport@review.com with the full title of the book, its ISBN number (located above), and the page number of the error. Experiencing technical issues? Please e-mail TPRStudentTech@review.com with the following information:

- your full name
- e-mail address used to register the book
- full book title and ISBN
- your computer OS (Mac or PC) and Internet browser (Firefox, Safari, Chrome, etc.)
- description of technical issue

Book Online!

Once you've registered, you can...

- Access a handy spreadsheet of the LSAT scores accepted by top law schools

- See rankings of the best law schools in the country courtesy of *Best 173 Law Schools*

- Get a list of any updates to the book post-publication

The
Princeton
Review®

Chapter 1
General Information

DECODING THE LAW SCHOOL ADMISSION TEST

This book is designed to help you figure out questions on LSAT PrepTests 52–61 as part of your LSAT preparation. Each chapter tackles a different PrepTest and provides complete explanations for each question of these real Law School Admission Council (LSAC) tests. These explanations also include strategies and tips about how to eliminate certain answers.

Work through each PrepTest on your own, and then review your performance using our explanations. This will help you identify your strengths and weaknesses and better understand the logic of the LSAT. We've also categorized the various questions and labeled their corresponding explanations with tabs, to help you exploit any shortcuts or patterns you find within them.

In the following introduction, we'll look at how to identify those categories from the question stem and provide one key point about each. We'll also look at some efficient and standardized ways to approach each of the three main sections of the test: Analytical Reasoning (Games), Logical Reasoning (Arguments), and Reading Comprehension.

STRUCTURE OF THE LSAT

The LSAT is a tightly timed, multiple-choice test that almost always consists of 99 to 102 questions. By tightly timed, we mean that the test is designed so that the "average" test taker (someone scoring around the fiftieth percentile) should not be able to comfortably complete all the questions in the time allotted.

This experimental section can be Arguments, Games, or Reading Comprehension.

To be more specific, the LSAT is made up of five 35-minute multiple-choice sections and one 35-minute essay. Two of the five multiple-choice sections will be Logical Reasoning (Arguments), one will be Analytical Reasoning (Games), and one will be Reading Comprehension. The remaining section (which is usually one of the first three to be administered) will be an experimental section that will not count toward your score.

As you may have already noticed, the order of these sections changes with each administered PrepTest. This is because the only consistent thing about the format of the LSAT is the 10–15 minute break given between sections 3 and 4, and that the essay will be at the end of the test. Also, bear in mind that the experimental section is not included in LSAC's official PrepTest book. If you're trying to prepare for the pacing of this test, you might consider using one or two sample tests to supplement the others. (For instance, insert the Reading Comprehension section from PrepTest 60 after the first Arguments section in PrepTest 52. Just make sure you keep track of which tests you've already taken.)

Because the essay is unscored, this book does not include samples. However, a scan of your essay is sent to each school that you apply to, so if you're feeling uncomfortable with this section, we recommend checking out some of the successful submissions found in *Law School Essays That Made a Difference*.

WHEN IS THE LSAT GIVEN?

The LSAT is administered four times a year—February, June, September/October, and December. Typically, students applying for regular fall admission to a law program take the test during June or September/October of the previous calendar year. You can take the test in December or February, but many schools will have filled at least a portion of their seats by the time your scores hit the admissions office.

HOW IS THE LSAT SCORED?

The LSAT is scored on a scale of 120 to 180, with the median score being approximately 152. You need to answer about 60 questions correctly (out of 99–102) to get that median score of 152, which means you need to bat about 60 percent. Very few people earn a perfect score, mainly because the test is designed so that very few people can correctly answer all the questions, let alone do so in the time allotted. Along with your LSAT score, you will receive a percentile ranking. This ranking compares your performance with that of everyone else who has taken the LSAT for the previous three years. Because a 152 is the median LSAT score, it would give you a percentile ranking of approximately 50. A score of 156 moves you up to a ranking of about 70. A 164 pulls you up to a ranking of 90. And any score over 167 puts you above 95 percent of all the LSAT takers.

As you can see, small numerical jumps (five points or so) can lead to a huge difference in percentile points. That means you're jumping over 20 percent of all test takers if, on your first practice test, you score a 150, but on the real test, you score a 155. Small gains can net big results. The following table summarizes the number of questions you can skip or miss and still reach your LSAT goal. Notice that 93 percent of those taking the test make more than 15 errors. Take this into consideration as you develop your strategy of exactly how many questions you intend to answer or skip.

Approximate Number of Errors (out of 102)	LSAT Score	Percentile Rank (approximately)
1	180	99++
5	175	99+
8	170	98+
15	165	91+
22	160	80+
32	155	66+
43	150	45+
52	145	27+
62	140	14+
69	135	5+

Because you're working with official PrepTests that have already been administered and graded, be sure to review the "Computing Your Score" pages in the *10 New Actual, Official LSAT PrepTests with Comparative Reading* book. That will give you the most precise assessment of your grade. This also factors in the fact that a very small number of questions were removed from scoring; while you'll still see them referred to in both the LSAC's PrepTest and our explanations, this is only so as to maintain the numbering. No actual question exists for these cases (which means there's also no explanation), and each absence has been factored into its corresponding scoring table.

What Is a Good Score?

A good score on the LSAT is one that gets you into the law school you want to attend. Many people feel that they have to score at least a 160 to get into a "good" law school. That's pure myth. Remember, any ABA-approved law school has to meet very strict standards in terms of its teaching staff, library, and facilities. Most schools use the Socratic method to teach students basic law. Therefore, a student's fundamental law school experience can be very similar no matter where he or she goes to school—be it NYU or Quinnipiac Law School.

GENERAL STRATEGIES

Before we get into specifics, there are several key things you should do when taking any multiple-choice test, especially the LSAT. We recommend that you at least give all of these mantras a shot as you work to develop a test-taking method that works for you—they are the sum of more than 20 years' worth of our experience in researching and preparing hundreds of thousands of test takers to take the LSAT.

Technique #1: Don't Rush

As we showed on the scoring table, you can get into the 98th percentile even with several wrong answers in each section. Most test takers do their best when they don't try to answer every question.

Most test takers believe that the key to success on the LSAT is to go faster. Realize, though, that your accuracy is also a key factor in how well you perform. Generally speaking, the faster you work, the higher the chance of making an error. What this means is that there's a pacing "sweet spot" somewhere between working as fast as you can and working as carefully as you can. That's where official PrepTests come in handy, as they'll help you to find the proper balance for yourself in each of the three sections.

On most LSAT questions, you'll find that you can eliminate two or three answer choices relatively easily. Some test takers simply pick the best-looking answer from the remaining ones and move on; this is poor strategy. It's only once you're down to two or three remaining choices that the real work on this test begins. Don't let the clock force you into bad decisions.

Your mantra: *I will fight the urge to rush and will work more deliberately, making choices about where to concentrate so I can answer questions more accurately and end up with a higher score.*

Technique #2: Fill in Every Bubble

Unlike some tests, the LSAT has no penalty for guessing, meaning that no points are subtracted for wrong answers. Therefore, even if you don't get to work on every question in a section, make sure to fill in the rest of the bubbles before time is called. Even if you do only 75 percent of the test, you'll get an average of five more questions correct by picking a "letter of the day" and bubbling it in on the remaining 25 questions.

Don't wait to start implementing this strategy; you should work through the PrepTests as you plan to work through the actual test. By the time you've gone through a couple of tests, this should be a habit that you employ without even thinking about it. If you're concerned that this won't show your "real" score, remember that your "real" score will come from a bubble sheet that you've (hopefully) completely filled out, so don't hold back. Use this book of explanations to ensure that you know how to solve the questions you might have guessed correctly.

Your mantra: *I will always remember to bubble in answers for any questions I don't get to, giving me better odds of getting a higher score.*

Technique #3: Use Process of Elimination

One solace (perhaps) on multiple-choice tests is the fact that all of the correct answers will be in front of you. Naturally, each will be camouflaged by four incorrect answers, some of which will look just as good as, and often better than, the credited response. But the fact remains that if you can clear away some of that distraction, the right choice is right in front of you. Don't expect that the correct answers will just leap off the page at you. They won't. In fact, choices that immediately catch your eye are often just tricky distractors.

Process of Elimination (POE) may be a very different test-taking strategy from what you are used to. If you look first at the answer choices critically, with an eye toward trying to see what's wrong with them, you'll do better on almost any standardized test than by always trying to find the right answer. This is because, given enough time and creativity, you can justify the correctness of any answer choice that you find appealing. That skill may be useful in certain situations, but on the LSAT, creativity of that sort is dangerous.

Your mantra: *I will always try to eliminate answer choices using Process of Elimination, thereby increasing my chances to get each question right and, therefore, a higher score.*

ANALYTICAL REASONING

In this section, we'll look at the broad structure of the Analytical Reasoning, or Games, section and lay out key strategies for each question type.

Games: A Step-by-Step Approach

Analytical Reasoning is deeply rooted in logic, even if no formal training in that subject is required. To that end, we've devised a series of steps to help methodically work through even the trickiest of games.

Step 1: Diagram and inventory

Your first step will be to determine the appropriate diagram for the game by evaluating both the setup and the clues. You will be given enough information to understand the basic structure of the game. Your diagram is described by the setup and will become the fixed game board onto which you will place the elements—your game pieces. You should make an inventory of the elements next to the diagram, so that you'll have everything in one place and will be able to keep track of it easily. Don't rush through this step, because this is the heart of your process. People often want to start scribbling a diagram as soon as something pops out at them from the setup. Take the time to evaluate the setup thoroughly, and you'll be well equipped for the rest of the process.

Step 2: Symbolize the clues and double-check

After you've drawn your diagram, transform the clues into visual symbols. Your symbols should be consistent with the diagram and with each other. The goal is to change the clues into visual references that will fit into your diagram. Here are the three Cs of symbolization: Keep your symbols clear, consistent, and concise. Never forget that correctly symbolizing every clue is the key to improving accuracy and efficiency.

The most valuable 30 seconds you can spend on any game is double-checking your symbols to make sure that they perfectly match all the information in the clue. Do not merely reread each clue and glance at your symbol again. If you misread the clue once, you might do it again. Instead, work against the grain when you double-check. Number each of your symbols. Then articulate in your own words what each symbol means and carry that back up to the clues you were given. When you find a match, check off that clue. Finally, be sure to go back over the information presented in the setup as well, because some games may include restrictions or extra rules that should be treated like clues. Once you're sure everything is all accounted for, you're ready to move on.

Step 3: Make deductions and size up the game

Now that you're sure you have everything properly symbolized, it's time to make any deductions that you can from the information that was given by the clues.

Look for overlap between the clues and the diagram and among the clues that share the same elements. See if there is anything else that you know for sure. Making deductions is not merely suspecting that something may be true; a deduction is something that you know for a fact. It is something that must always be true or must always be false. Add your deductions to the information you already have.

You'll notice that many deductions give you concrete limitations about where elements are restricted—where they can't go—rather than where they must go. Consider each clue individually to see what it says about the placement of an element. Then look for overlap between different clues.

Step 4: Assess the questions

Not all games questions are on the same level of difficulty. As a result, you should move through the questions from easiest to most challenging.

First, look for what we call Grab-a-Rule questions. Grab-a-Rule questions do not appear on every game, but they are common. They have historically been the first question of a game. These are questions that give you full arrangements of the elements in every answer and ask you which one doesn't break any rules. Remember, if the question does not deal with every element and every space on your diagram, it is not a true Grab-a-Rule.

Next, look for Specific questions. These questions will further limit the initial conditions of the game and provide you with more information. They will usually start with the word "if." Specific questions tend to be fairly quick since the question itself constrains some of the vagueness of the game. Once you've done all the Specific questions, you'll have a diagram with several valid permutations—or "plays"—of the game.

The third style of question you should work is the General questions. These questions are typically open-ended and ask what could happen without placing specific restrictions. These questions usually begin with the word "which." By saving these for later, you can often use your prior work from the Specific questions to eliminate bad answer choices.

The final question type that you may see is Complex questions. Complex questions can change the original game by adding, changing, or deleting a rule. They can also ask which answer choice could be substituted for a rule without changing the game. No matter what form they take, Complex questions should be saved for last since they function differently from the rest of the questions. These questions can also be very time-consuming for little gain. Never forget that the Complex question is worth the same number of points as the Grab-a-Rule. It is always worth considering how much you need to get that one question correct. For most test takers, the best strategy on these questions is to bubble in your letter of the day and move on to the next game. Remember that you can always come back and work a Complex question if you have time.

There is one last thing to know about the questions. No matter what the question type, the question stem will affect how the credited response is reached. The four

You may note that we sometimes refer to questions out of chronological order. This is because we've found that there are efficient ways to use the information from one question to rule out choices in another. You'll definitely want to use our explanations to practice this and refine your notes and diagrams so that the specific premises of a Complex question are not accidentally used in another, independent problem.

question stems are must be true, could be true, could be false, and must be false. The LSAT has a wide variety of phrasing, but every question will ultimately use one of these four stems. Make a habit now of underlining each question stem. This will help you to determine the best approach to the question and the type of answer you'll need.

Step 5: Act
Each question task requires its own strategy. Using the proper strategy leads to saving time on a given question without sacrificing accuracy. Plus, by approaching the questions in an efficient order, you'll find that the work you've done on earlier questions will often help you to find the right answer on a later question.

Step 6: Answer using Process of Elimination
Different question stems require POE to different degrees. Sometimes you'll be able to go straight to the right answer from your deductions, but often you'll need to work questions by finding the four wrong answers. As a last resort, you may need to test answer choices one at a time to find the right one.

The Structure of a Games Section
You will be given four "logic games" in a 35-minute section. Each game will have a setup and a set of conditions or clues that are attached to it. Then five to seven questions will ask you about various possible arrangements of the elements in the game. The four games are not arranged in order of difficulty.

The Four Types of Games Questions
A large part of the six-step method involves being able to quickly identify the four different question types so that they can be worked through in the most efficient way possible. As you compare your test results to our explanations, feel free to use the identifying tabs beside each question to check your process. Additionally, here's a core takeaway for each of the four question types you'll find in the Games section.

Grab-a-Rule
- Compare each of the given rules to the answer choices, looking to eliminate the choices that violate the rules.

Specific
- Work the given information into your notes/diagram and only then compare the answer choices.

General
- Use some of the valid solutions that you have already created for other question types to help narrow down choices.

Complex
- Because these questions mix up the rules, be careful to properly modify the assumptions made in your diagrams, or better still, start them from scratch (if you have the time).

THE LOGICAL REASONING SECTION

Here, we'll break down the process for working through the Logical Reasoning, or Arguments, section and present key strategies for each question type.

Working Arguments: A Step-by-Step Process

In the context of the LSAT, Logical Reasoning revolves around careful analysis, without using outside knowledge that may complicate things. For that reason, it helps to have a specific, formal process for working through even the most complex arguments.

Step 1: Assess the question

Reading the question first will tip you off about what you need to look for in the argument. Don't waste time reading the argument before you know how you will need to evaluate it for that particular question. If you don't know what your task is, you are unlikely to perform it effectively.

Step 2: Analyze the argument

You've got to read the argument critically, looking for the author's conclusion and the evidence used to support it. When the author's conclusion is explicitly stated, mark it with a symbol that you use only for conclusions. If necessary, jot down short, simple paraphrases of the premises and any flaws you found in the argument.

To find flaws, you should keep your eyes open for any shifts in the author's language or gaps in the argument. Look for common purpose and reasoning patterns. The author's conclusion is reached using only the information on the page in front of you, so any gaps in the language or in the evidence indicate problems with the argument. You should always be sure that you're reading critically and articulating the parts of the argument (both stated and unstated) in your own words.

Our explanations clearly identify each question task (Step 1) as well as the conclusion, premise, and common flaws (Step 2). If you're attempting to get a routine down, we suggest comparing your train of thought against ours, even on questions that you got right.

Step 3: Act

Each question task will have different criteria for what constitutes an acceptable answer. Think about that before going to the choices.

The test writers rely on the fact that the people who are taking the LSAT feel pressured to get through all the questions quickly. Many answer choices will seem appealing if you don't have a clear idea of what you're looking for before you start reading through them. The best way to keep yourself from falling into this trap is to predict what the right answer will say or do before you even look at the choices, and write that prediction down on your test!

Step 4: Answer using Process of Elimination (POE)

Most people look for the best answer and, in the process, end up falling for answer choices that are designed to look appealing but actually contain artfully concealed flaws. The part that looks good looks really good, and the little bit that's wrong blends right into the background if you're not reading carefully and critically. The "best" answer on a tricky question won't necessarily sound very good at all. That's why the question is difficult. But if you're keenly attuned to crossing out those choices with identifiable flaws, you'll be left with one that wasn't appealing, but didn't have anything wrong with it. And that's the winner because it's the "best" one of a group of flawed answers. If you can find a reason to cross off a choice, you've just improved your chances of getting the question right. So be aggressive about finding the flaws in answer choices that will allow you to eliminate them. At the same time, don't eliminate choices that you don't understand or that don't have a distinct problem.

The Structure of an Arguments Section

There will be two scored Arguments sections, each lasting 35 minutes, on your LSAT. Each section has between 24 and 26 questions. Tests in the past frequently attached two questions to one argument, but LSAC has more or less phased out this style of question; you will almost certainly see one question per argument. Typically, the argument passages are no more than three or four sentences in length, but they can still be very dense and every word is potentially important, making critical reading the key skill on this section. The arguments are not arranged in strict order of difficulty, although the questions near the beginning of a section are generally easier than those at the end.

The Thirteen Types of Arguments Questions

Our explanations have been tagged with different identifiers for each question type, so as to help you more readily associate the strategies you're practicing with the various questions you'll encounter. Here's a breakdown of the main takeaways for each of the thirteen question types you'll find in the Arguments section.

Main Point

Key Words in Question Stem: "main point," "main conclusion," "argument is structured to lead to which conclusion."

Strategy: Keywords and opinion language can often lead you to the main point. You can confirm you found the main point by asking why the author believes a certain statement is true. The other sentences in an argument are all premises that answer that question. We sometimes refer to this as the Why Test.

Reasoning

Key Words in Question Stem: "X responds to Y by," "claim that…plays what role," "technique/method/strategy of argumentation/reasoning."

Strategy: Try to describe the overall structure and logic to these arguments before matching an answer choice to the argument.

Necessary Assumption

Key Words in Question Stem: "assumption on which the argument depends/ relies," "assumption required."

Strategy: Help these arguments by providing an important assumption. Confirm the credited response to these questions by negating the answer choices. A negated necessary assumption will make the conclusion invalid. We sometimes refer to this as the Negation Test.

Sufficient Assumption

Key Words in Question Stem: "if assumed, allows the conclusion to follow logically," "allows the conclusion to be properly drawn."

Strategy: Help these arguments by finding a credited response that will prove the conclusion is true.

Strengthen

Key Words in Question Stem: "most supports/justifies the argument above," "most strengthens."

Strategy: The best way to strengthen an argument is to fill in any gaps in logic. Identify the argument's weakness and find the answer choice that fixes it the best.

Principle-Strengthen

Key Words in Question Stem: "principle that, if valid, justifies the argument."

Strategy: Help these arguments by providing a guiding principle, or rule, that will prove the conclusion is true based on the set of facts in the argument.

Weaken

Key Words in Question Stem: "most undermines," "calls into question," "casts doubt on."

Strategy: The best way to weaken an argument is to attack it where it is weakest. Find the argument's weakness, and then find the answer choice that exploits that logical mistake.

Flaw

Key Words in Question Stem: "flaw/error in reasoning," "vulnerable to criticism."

Strategy: Describe the logical error made in each of these arguments before looking at the answer choices.

Inference

Key Words in Question Stem: "statements above, if true, support," "must/could be true/false."

Strategy: The credited answer to these questions must be strongly supported by the facts in the passage. Avoid making any assumptions as you find the answer choice that is true.

Point at Issue

Key Words in Question Stem: "committed to disagreeing about."

Strategy: Compare each answer choice to each person's argument individually. The credited response will be one in which the two people take an opposing stance.

Resolve/Explain

Key Words in Question Stem: "puzzling statement," "apparent contradiction," "paradox," "resolution," "explanation."

Strategy: Identify the two sides of the issue before looking at the answer choices. The credited response will be a new piece of information that allows both statements to be true.

Parallel

Key Words in Question Stem: "most analogous," "similar pattern of reasoning."

Strategy: Diagram the main argument and each answer choice, and then choose the answer with the most similar diagram.

Principle-Match

Key Words in Question Stem: "conforms/illustrates…principle/proposition."

Strategy: Match these arguments by applying the principle rule to the argument. The best answer will work with the rule to come to the same conclusion.

READING COMPREHENSION

The rest of this chapter will clarify the components of the Reading Comprehension section and provide key strategies for each question type.

Reading Comprehension: A Step-by-Step Process

Whenever you're reading dense, complicated material, it helps to be methodical and to know what you're looking for. The following method helps to break things down.

Step 1: Prepare the Passage

A. Preview the questions, looking for lead words and/or line references that tell you what parts of the passage will be especially relevant.

B. Work the passage efficiently, focusing on the main claims made by the author.

C. Annotate the passage, circling key words that relate to the question topics or that provide clues to the structure and tone of the author's argument and making brief marginal notes.

D. Define the Bottom Line of the passage as a whole: the main point, purpose, and tone of the text.

Step 2: Assess the Question

Translate exactly what each question is asking you to do with or to the passage.

Step 3: Act

Just as some Games questions require you to make new deductions before you attack the answers, or some Arguments questions are best answered by first identifying or analyzing certain aspects of the paragraph, most Reading Comprehension questions are most accurately and efficiently attacked by doing some work with the passage text before looking at a single answer choice.

Step 4: Answer

Use a combination of your understanding of the question and of the relevant part or parts of the passage to use Process of Elimination on the answer choices. Look for what is wrong with each choice, keeping in mind that one small part of the choice that doesn't match the passage and/or the question task means the choice is bad.

The Structure of a Reading Comprehension Section

In this 35-minute section, you will be given four Reading Comprehension passages of about 60 to 80 lines each. Three of the passages will be written by one author; the fourth will be a combination of two shorter passages from two different sources discussing the same general subject. In each case, between five and eight questions will be attached to each passage. This is probably something you're familiar with from the SAT, the ACT, or any of the other myriad standardized tests you might have taken over the years. These passages are not arranged in any order of difficulty.

The Five Types of Reading Comprehension Questions

Being able to quickly pinpoint strategies for each type of question should help you to more efficiently work through the Reading Comprehension section. These are the main identifiers and strategies to recognize and know.

Big Picture
- Develop your own version of the Bottom Line of a passage by putting the overall point, tone, and purpose of the passage in your own words, and then look for the answer choice that comes closest to it.

Extract-Fact
- The credited response will match something directly stated by the author in the passage, so look to the exact language of the text.

Extract-Infer
- The best answer will always be supported by the text; avoid using outside information or making assumptions.

Structure
- These questions ask about the organization of the passage or paragraph, which means you should compare each choice to the relevant section of the text.

Reasoning

- Identify the argument being made in the passage, and describe it in your own words before looking at the answer choices.

SUMMARY

For all these tips, strategies, and explanations of what to expect on the LSAT, at the end of the day, it all comes down to you and the test. The practice found in those official LSAT PrepTests should help to iron out timing issues and point out any immediate problem spots that need additional focus, and the explanations in this book should help to solidify your test-taking process and raise both your comfort level and familiarity with the test's tricks. But if a mantra or a specific technique isn't working for you, don't feel beholden to it. With ten tests to work through, you have the space to try different things and the time to turn a successful strategy into a muscle memory. Once you know the test and understand the explanations, it's just a matter of doing what you've done here on one more official test. You've got this!

Chapter 2
PrepTest 52:
Answers and
Explanations

ANSWER KEY

Section 1: Arguments 1	Section 2: Games	Section 3: Arguments 2	Section 4: Reading Comprehension
1. C ✓	1. E	1. D	1. E
2. D ✓	2. C	2. D	2. E
3. A ✓	3. B	3. B	3. A
4. C ✗	4. B	4. B	4. D
5. B ✓	5. E	5. D	5. C
6. E ✓	6. B	6. C	6. A
7. A ✗	7. B	7. A	7. D
8. C ✓	8. B	8. A	8. B
9. D ✗	9. E	9. C	9. A
10. A ✗	10. A	10. E	10. C
11. C ✓	11. D	11. B	11. B
12. E ✓	12. C	12. E	12. D
13. E ✓	13. B	13. D	13. C
14. C ✓	14. E	14. C	14. E
15. B ?	15. C	15. D	15. N/A
16. A ✓	16. B	16. C	16. D
17. E ✗	17. D	17. B	17. E
18. B ✓	18. C	18. D	18. B
19. E ✓	19. A	19. A	19. A
20. E ✗	20. E	20. E	20. C
21. C ✓	21. C	21. E	21. A
22. D ✓	22. C	22. E	22. B
23. D ✓	23. E	23. A	23. A
24. E ?		24. C	24. B
25. E ✓		25. A	25. C
			26. D
			27. D

15123

EXPLANATIONS

Section 1: Arguments 1

1. C **Main Point**

This argument disagrees with the compensation system companies use requiring managers to first rank their workers from best to worst, and then reward the top 10 percent in each group and penalize or fire the workers in the bottom 10 percent. The argument concludes that this system is unfair to workers. The premises are that the rankings depend too much on the quality of the workers with whom each worker is grouped. Also, managers often rank workers for the wrong reasons, such as affinity.

A. No. This is a premise.

B. No. This is a premise.

C. Yes. This is a good restatement of the disagreement.

D. No. This is a premise.

E. No. This is a premise.

2. D **Flaw**

The argument presents a causal interpretation of evidence. The psychologist concludes that napping is likely to cause insomnia because two groups of people who nap more suffer more from insomnia.

A. No. The argument does not compare university students to the general population, but rather university students who nap to those who do not.

B. No. The argument does not assume that napping is the only cause of insomnia, just that it tends to cause insomnia.

C. No. The argument uses the term "napping" consistently and does not need to define it.

D. Yes. The argument fails to rule out the possibility that the causal direction might be reversed.

E. No. This is not essential to the argument.

3. A **Parallel**

Diagram the argument. Joe's car is vacuumed → K & L vacuumed it. K & L vacuumed it → Joe took it to K & L to be fixed. The argument demonstrates that the sufficient factor (Joe's car is vacuumed) is valid. Therefore, the result (Joe took his car to K & L to be fixed) must also be true.

A. Yes. Emily's glass is wet → she drank water from it this morning → she took her medication. Emily's glass is wet, so she must have taken her medication.

B. No. There is no either/or option in the original argument.

C. No. This answer choice does not match the structure of the original argument.

D. No. This answer choice demonstrates flawed reasoning and the original argument does not.

E. No. There is no either/or option in the original argument.

4. C **Strengthen**

The editorialist concludes that the president has a duty to keep the corporation's profits high. The premise is that one of the functions of the president is to promote the key interests of the stockholders. The argument would benefit from a connection between the key interests of the stockholders and high profits.

A. No. This answer choice would, if anything, weaken the argument.

B. No. The argument is concerned with the president and what he/she should do, not the board of directors.

C. Yes. This answer choice provides a strong connection between the key interests of the shareholders and keeping the profits high.

D. No. The argument does not imply that profitability is the only interest of the shareholders.

E. No. Like (D), the argument does not imply that advancing the important interests of shareholders is the president's only responsibility.

5. B **Inference**

This is a connect-the-facts inference with conditionals. Live in Biba's neighborhood → permitted to swim at some time each day. Under 6 → can't swim between noon and 5 P.M. Child → can't swim from 5 P.M. until closing.

A. No. You can't prove how many, if any, children live in Biba's neighborhood.

B. Yes. Children under 6 can't swim in the pool from noon until closing. Yet, as the passage says, everyone that lives in the neighborhood must be able to swim at some time during the day. This child would have to be able to swim before noon.

C. No. The argument does not provide any information to determine how crowded the pool will be.

D. No. The argument does not explain who lives in Biba's neighborhood. It could be a neighborhood with no children.

E. No. The pool could be open before noon. Also, it's only children under 6 that are not allowed to swim between noon and 5 P.M.

6. E **Flaw**

The purpose of this argument is to disagree with a claim. Beck concludes that, despite what some of the staff says, they can be confident of their computer program's accuracy because the figures that the program provides are consistent from week to week. Beck equates consistency with accuracy.

A. No. The argument doesn't claim that consistency is more important than accuracy. It equates the two.

B. No. The argument is concerned with only one task: estimating the municipal automotive use.

C. No. The argument takes for granted that, because the output is consistent, the program must be accurate.

D. No. The argument is concerned with only the accuracy of the program. It doesn't make any claims about the program's value in general.

E. Yes. The argument assumes that, because the output is consistent, the program must be accurate.

7. **A** Inference

The argument describes how inertia affects the flow of water pumped through a closed system of pipes. It then equates the effects of inductance in electrical circuits with the effects of inertia in water pipes.

A. Yes. If the effects of inductance are similar to the effects of inertia, and inertia affects the flow of water, then inductance will affect the flow of electrical current.

B. No. Inertia refers to water and pipes, not the flow of electrical current.

C. No. You cannot prove how inductance affects inertia from the information provided.

D. No. You cannot prove anything about electrical engineers from the information provided.

E. No. This choice is too strong. All you can prove is that the inertia causes the decrease in the water flow to be gradual. You cannot prove how long this takes.

8. **C** Principle Strengthen

The purpose of this argument is to disagree with a claim. The journalist thinks that the pharmaceutical companies are not justified in selling a drug in rich nations at one price and in poor nations at another price. The journalist's premise is that many individuals in poorer nations might be better able to pay for new drugs than poorer individuals in nations with higher overall wealth.

A. No. The argument doesn't compare ill people to healthy people.

B. No. This answer choice supports the position that the argument is designed to disagree with.

C. Yes. This answer choice points out that special consideration should be provided to individuals when individuals within a society might not have the same amount of resources as the society does, on average.

D. No. This answer choice is not relevant to the argument.

E. No. The argument does not discuss the fairness of unequal distribution of wealth.

9. **D** Weaken

Robert is trying to solve a problem and Samantha claims that he hasn't solved it. Robert concludes that the school board should adopt a year-round academic schedule because teachers need to cover more new material during the school year than they do now. Samantha claims that the new school schedule won't permit the teachers to cover any more new material because the amount of vacation will be the same as before, just in a different configuration. The students will have six two-week breaks, instead of one three-month break.

A. No. This doesn't address the problem of needing to cover more new material.

B. No. This answer choice does not address the problem of needing to cover more new material.

C. No. It's nice that students show a deeper understanding of the material in year-round schools, but the answer choice does not address the issue at hand: needing to cover more new material.

D. Yes. If the teachers have to spend significantly less class time reviewing material after the short breaks in the year-round schedule than after the long break in the traditional schedule, then teachers will have more class days to cover new material.

E. No. Student preference is not relevant. The disagreement is about the amount of new material that could be covered.

10. **A** **Necessary Assumption**

The argument concludes that the mayor's plan to reduce congestion and raise revenue by charging $10 per day for driving in the downtown area will not be effectively enforced when it is first implemented. The premises are that payment will be enforced by a highly sophisticated system that will not be ready until the end of next year, and that many people will avoid paying the charge without this system in place.

A. Yes. It is essential to the argument that the plan be in place before the system is ready at the end of next year.

B. No. The argument does not discuss the possibility of a budget deficit.

C. No. The argument is concerned with whether the plan will be effectively enforced when it is first implemented, not when it should be implemented.

D. No. The argument does not compare the importance of raising revenue versus reducing traffic congestion.

E. No. Too strong. The argument doesn't need to say that a daily charge is the most effective way to reduce traffic congestion.

11. **C** **Resolve/ Explain**

There is a discrepancy in recovery rates between people treated at large, urban hospitals and people treated at smaller, rural hospitals. People treated at smaller, rural hospitals have a higher rate of recovery. Eliminate any answer choices that help resolve the discrepancy.

A. No. If the patients at smaller hospitals are more likely to get fed according to their dietary needs, they might be more likely to recover from their illnesses.

B. No. If patients at larger hospitals are more stressed than patients at smaller hospitals, that might adversely affect their recovery rate.

C. Yes. This answer choice states that there has been no correlation found between the prestige of a doctor's school and patients' recovery rates. In no way is this relevant to explaining the differing recovery rates of patients treated at larger or smaller hospitals.

D. No. If patients are not observed for as long, there is a greater chance that an unobserved complication might occur, thus adversely affecting the recovery rate for patients treated at larger hospitals.

E. No. If the staff and patients do not get explanations about the administration of their medications, improper administration of these medications is more likely to occur. This would adversely affect the recovery rates of patients treated at larger hospitals.

12. **E** | Weaken |

Perry concludes that lenders who are seeking to reduce their risk should not make loans to worker-owned businesses. This is because worker-owned businesses require workers to spend time on management and investment, which are not directly productive. Worker-owned businesses also have less extensive divisions of labor than do investor-owned businesses. These inefficiencies can lead to low profitability, which would increase risk for lenders. An issue with Perry's argument is that, just because inefficiencies can lead to low profitability, it doesn't mean that they will. Maybe there is something unique about worker-owned businesses that will overcome this problem.

A. No. Businesses with the most extensive divisions of labor can sometimes fail to make the fullest use of their most versatile employees' potential and still be more efficient, on average, than the worker-owned businesses and still be, on average, the safer investment.

B. No. This answer choice is a description of the lenders who do make loans to worker-owned businesses. It does not address the warning against lending to worker-owned businesses.

C. No. The argument is not concerned with start-up loans, nor is it concerned with who actually gets loans.

D. No. This answer choice does not give a reason as to why worker-owned businesses might be a less risky investment than the argument claims.

E. Yes. If the workers work longer hours, the inefficiencies might be compensated for, which means that the inefficiencies won't necessarily lead to low profitability. If they don't lead to low profitability, then the risk will not necessarily increase for lenders.

13. **E** | Main Point |

This argument is designed to disagree with a claim. The argument disagrees with some paleontologists, who believe that certain dinosaurs guarded their young in protective nests long after the young hatched. The evidence cited for the paleontologists' claim is the discovery of fossilized hadrosaur babies and adolescents in carefully designed nests. In disagreeing with these paleontologists, the argument notes that modern crocodiles construct similar nests, even though these crocodiles don't guard their young for long. The argument seems to be leading to the conclusion that the evidence of fossilized nests is not enough to claim that the dinosaurs guarded their young long after the young hatched.

A. No. This answer choice is too strong. The paleontologists do have some evidence, just not enough to fully support their conclusion.

B. No. This answer choice is too strong. The evidence cited is not strong enough for the paleontologists' conclusion. That's not to say that we will never know the extent to which hadrosaurs guarded their young.

C. No. This answer choice is too strong. There is not enough evidence to know that they guarded their young for large periods of time. That's not to say that hadrosaurs couldn't have actually guarded their young for large periods of time.

D. No. This is not the disagreement. The paleontologists are making a claim about a certain species of dinosaurs, not all dinosaurs.

E. Yes. The argument disagrees with the paleontologists as to the strength of the evidence that supports their belief.

14. **C** Resolve/Explain

The apparent paradox is that when researchers tested the hypothesis that studying more increased a student's chances of earning a higher grade, the students who spent the most time studying did not earn grades as high as did many students who studied less. Yet, the researchers concluded that the results supported their hypothesis.

A. No. This doesn't resolve the apparent paradox. The passage says that many students who studied less earned higher grades. This still leaves room for some students who studied less to get lower grades, while still maintaining the seeming paradox.

B. No. If all the students tended to get slightly lower grades as the year progressed, the problem still remains that many students who studied less will have higher grades than the students who spent the most time studying.

C. Yes. This resolves the apparent paradox. If each individual student does better in a given class if he or she studies, then it looks like studying more will increase a student's change of getting a higher grade, even if the students who study the most get lower grades than many who don't study as much. The hypothesis was about an individual's grades, while the statistics were about the students considered in groups.

D. No. This does not resolve the apparent paradox.

E. No. This does not resolve the apparent paradox as well as (C) because it doesn't directly connect studying with an individual's chances of getting a better grade in a given class.

15. **B** Inference

Find the answer choice supported by the passage.

A. No. This answer choice is too strong. The argument talks only about cycling, not about exercise in general. In addition, you can't prove that in every instance the higher the pulse rate, the less psychological benefit produced. What if having a pulse rate of 60 percent of the recommended maximum pulse rate leads to greater benefits than having a pulse rate of 40 percent of the maximum?

B. Yes. The argument demonstrates a correlation between the mood of professional cyclists and how intense the cycling is. When the cycling is at 60 percent of the recommended maximum pulse rate for recreational bikers, the professional cyclists reported being less depressed and angry. Those cycling at 85 percent, on the other hand, reported feeling more depressed and angry.

C. No. This answer choice is too strong. You can't prove anything about pulse rates higher than 85 percent so it is possible that something higher could also improve mood.

D. No. This answer choice is too strong. You can't prove that physical factors contribute as much as psychological factors contribute. The passage does not include information about any psychological factors that may have been at play so you can't make that comparison.

E. No. You can't prove whether moderate cycling benefits professional cyclists physically as much or more than intense cycling.

16. **A** `Parallel Flaw`

This argument is diagrammable: Believe in existence of ETs → believe in existence of UFOs. UFOs don't exist → ETs don't exist. The argument does not support the assumption that the existence of ETs depends on the existence of UFOs.

A. Yes. Believe in existence of unicorns → believe in existence of centaurs. Centaurs don't exist → unicorns can't exist. This is the same argument structure and the same flaw.

B. No. This argument is not flawed. Believe in unicorns → believe in centaurs. Don't believe in centaurs → don't believe in unicorns. The second conditional is the contrapositive of the first.

C. No. This answer choice does not make the switch from belief to actual existence.

D. No. This answer choice does not make the switch from belief to actual existence.

E. No. This answer choice does make the switch from belief to actual existence but its second premise starts with the non-existence of unicorns, which were, in fact, the sufficient condition in the first premise. This does not match the structure of the original argument.

17. **E** `Sufficient Assumption`

The conclusion of the argument is that it is imprudent to appear prudent. The first premise is that people want to be instantly and intuitively liked. The second premise is that people who are perceived to form opinions about others non-spontaneously are generally resented. The argument shifts language from the premise, which discusses behavior that causes resentment, to the conclusion, which discusses prudence. You need an answer that proves the conclusion by tying it to resentment.

A. No. The conclusion isn't about how people need to act in order to be well liked. It is a judgment about appearing prudent, not about spontaneity.

B. No. You need to know why it is imprudent to appear prudent, not how imprudent people generally act.

C. No. If anything, this argument seems to claim that people resent those more prudent than themselves.

D. No. The conclusion is concerned with prudence and imprudence, not about intuitive people.

E. Yes. This gives the argument the connection it needs between imprudence and resentment.

18. **B** `Inference`

Find the answer choice that contradicts evidence in the argument.

A. No. This answer choice could be true. The argument doesn't compare the difference in memory between nonsmokers who have just smoked a cigarette and nonsmokers who haven't recently smoked a cigarette.

B. Yes. The argument states that the short-term memory skills of a nonsmoker who has just smoked are typically significantly worse than those of a smoker who has just smoked. So, this answer choice directly contradicts the argument.

C. No. The argument doesn't compare the memory skills of nonsmokers who have just smoked and smokers who haven't smoked in over eight hours. This answer choice could be true.

D. No. This answer choice could be true. The argument doesn't say anything about periods of heavy smoking. The answer choice is also comparing two individuals, not the typical results.

E. No. The argument doesn't compare the memory skills of smokers who last smoked five hours ago and smokers who have just smoked. This answer choice could be true.

19. **E** **Principle Strengthen**

This argument is designed to disagree with a claim. The educator is against deciding matters in his professional organization by a direct vote instead of having matter decided by officers who are elected by direct vote. The premise is that organizational policy will be more influenced by individuals voting for officers rather than individuals directly voting on issues. A principle that would strengthen it would connect procedures for making organizational decisions with the amount of influence each member has on these decisions.

A. No. This principle would weaken the argument, if anything.

B. No. This principle does not connect the procedures for making decisions with the amount of influence of each member on these decisions.

C. No. This answer choice does not tell us that it would be the officers that would have this time, so it doesn't help the argument.

D. No. This might be true but it does not strengthen the educator's claim that voting to elect officers will give each individual more influence in organizational policy.

E. Yes. This principle strengthens the argument by relating procedures for making decisions and the maximization of the power of each individual to influence the decisions.

20. **E** **Sufficient Assumption**

The conclusion of the argument is that the amygdala exerts a greater influence on the cortex than vice versa. The premise for this conclusion is that the neural connections that carry signals from the cortex to the amygdala are less well developed than the connections carrying signals the other way around. The argument equates how developed the connections carrying signals from one part of the brain to the other are to the amount of influence one part of the brain has on the other.

A. No. The argument is concerned only with the influence the amygdala exerts on the cortex, not the rest of the brain.

B. No. Other brain regions are not relevant and the assumption needs to equate how developed the connections are to the amount of influence.

C. No. This answer choice is too general. The region of the brain that has the most highly developed neural connections to the cortex might be something other than the amygdala.

D. No. The argument is concerned with the influence that the amygdala has on the cortex. It doesn't matter whether some other region controls it.

E. Yes. This connects the degree of development of neural connections with the degree of influence one part of the brain has on another.

21. C | **Weaken**

This argument disagrees with the claim that the difference in vocabulary, tone, and details of the fictional world depicted in the *Iliad* and the *Odyssey* imply that they could almost certainly not be the work of the same poet. A good answer choice will demonstrate how even if two works are different in many ways, the same person may have written both of them.

A. No. Homer might not have actually written the hymns either.

B. No. This doesn't go far enough. If the manuscripts have suffered only minor copying errors and other textual corruptions, the corruptions won't explain away all of the stylistic differences between the two.

C. Yes. You know that the modern writer actually wrote the works described. This counterexample lends plausibility to the possibility that Homer wrote both the *Iliad* and the *Odyssey* despite their many differences.

D. No. The argument rests on comparing the *Iliad* with the *Odyssey*, not looking at each by itself.

E. No. This would support the claim that Homer didn't write both.

22. D | **Principle Match**

Diagram the moralist's two principles. 1. Statement wholly truthful → it's true and made without intended deception. Contrapositive: ~true or made with intended deception → ~not wholly truthful. 2. Intended to deceive or doesn't clarify misinterpretation → lie. Contrapositive: ~lie → ~intended to deceive and clarifies misinterpretation. The best answer choice will provide an example in which at least one of the two principles is fulfilled.

A. No. Neither principle gives criteria to determine that a statement is wholly truthful.

B. No. Neither principle gives criteria to determine that a statement is not a lie, only when it is a lie.

C. No. You don't know whether Siobhan intended to deceive, nor do you know whether she is actually sick. This doesn't fit either principle.

D. Yes. If a statement is intended to deceive, it is a lie. Walter intended to deceive, so he lied.

E. No. If the statement is intended to deceive OR the person doesn't clarify a misinterpretation, the statement is a lie. So the tour guide DID lie, according to the second principle.

23. D | **Principle Match**

This argument contains a principle that states the following: healthy to engage in intellectual development → engaging in that activity does not detract from social development. The argument then presents an application in the evidence about Megan. It draws the conclusion that Megan's amount of reading is not healthy because it reduces the amount of time she spends interacting with other people. The flaw is that the argument equates interacting with others with social development.

A. No. The principle is a universal claim.

B. No. The argument does not discuss health effects.

C. No. As the principle is a conditional statement, it has a contrapositive. The contrapositive does make a claim about what is unhealthy.

D. Yes. The argument equates interacting with other people and social development. It might well be that the plot lines in the books that she reads help with her social development.

E. No. This argument does not contain a necessary/sufficient flaw.

24. **E** **Inference**

Find the answer choice supported by the passage.

A. No. The passage does not provide information about the amount of bacteria in other companies' juices.

B. No. The passage doesn't have any comparison between the amounts of bacteria in the apple juice versus the citrus juices. You can't prove which juice is less likely to contain infectious bacteria.

C. No. Intensive pasteurization is likely to destroy the original flavor, but whether other types of pasteurization do this is not discussed in the passage. So there is not enough information to determine whether McElligott's unpasteurized citrus juices retain more of the original flavor than do any pasteurized citrus juices.

D. No. This answer choice sounds good but is too strong. Intensive pasteurization is the most effective method for eliminating bacteria from juice. Intensive pasteurization is also likely to destroy the original flavor of the juice. The passage does not support, however, that intensive pasteurization is the method most likely to destroy flavor. Another method of eliminating bacteria might be even more likely to destroy the flavor.

E. Yes. McElligott's juice did not undergo intensive pasteurization because it was flash pasteurized. It is also stated that intensive pasteurization is the most effective way to eliminate bacteria from the juice, so a juice that undergoes intensive pasteurization is less likely to contain bacteria than McElligott's apple juice.

25. **E** **Necessary Assumption**

The sociologist is solving a problem. The problem is that widespread acceptance of the idea that individuals are incapable of looking after their own welfare is injurious to a democracy. The sociologist concludes that legislators who value democracy should not propose any law that prohibits behavior harmful only to the person engaging in that behavior. The premise is that the assumptions that appear to guide legislators will often become widely accepted. There is a gap between discouraging the proposal of laws prohibiting actions harmful only to the person engaging in them and the assumptions that appear to guide these legislators. For the argument to work, the assumptions that appear to guide the legislators must involve the idea that individuals are incapable of looking after themselves.

A. No. The argument explicitly discusses legislators who value democracy, not all democratically elected legislators.

B. No. The sociologist doesn't care about what the legislators actually believe about whether people are capable of looking after themselves. He/she is concerned with what the legislators appear to believe about this subject.

C. No. This is a description of how legislators often seem to be guided. The argument is a prescription for how legislators who value democracy often seem to be guided.

D. No. This might be true. However, it doesn't give you the connection you need between what laws legislators should propose and what their underlying assumptions appear to be.

E. Yes. This connects the sociologist's prescription for proposing laws and the perceived assumptions of the legislators.

Section 2: Games

Questions 1–7

Order matters in this game, so put 1 through 8 on top of your diagram. Eight valves—G, H, I, K, L, N, O, and P—are opened one at a time. The clues are all about the relative orders of the inventory and all the valves are included in the clues.

Clue 1:
$$\begin{matrix} K \\ & \searrow \\ & & H \\ & \nearrow \\ P \end{matrix}$$

Clue 2: H—O—L

Clue 3: G—L

Clue 4: N—H

Clue 5: K—I

Deductions: Notice that all the clues have at least one valve in common with at least one other clue. This means you can connect all the clues together into one map of possibilities Notice that H can only be opened 4–6, O can only be opened 5–7, and L can only be opened 7 or 8. The only two valves that can be opened last are L and I.

Here's the diagram:

G, H, I, K, L, N, O, P

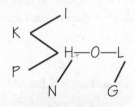

1	2	3	4	5	6	7	8

1. **E** [Grab-a-Rule]

A. No. This violates clue 5.

B. No. This violates clue 2.

C. No. This violates clue 4.

D. No. This violates clue 3.

E. Yes. This choice does not violate any clues.

2. C **General**

This is a general question, so use prior work, deductions, and trying the answers to see which valve cannot be opened fifth.

From the deductions, you can see that K must have at least four valves—H, O, L, and I—opened after it is opened. So, it cannot be opened fifth, making (C) the credited response.

3. B **Specific**

Make a new line in your diagram and add the new information. You are looking for what cannot be true. Place I in 2. This means that K goes in 1. At this point, H cannot go in 4 because it still needs to have N and P opened before it, and there would not be room if H were in 4. This means that (B) must be false and is therefore the credited response.

4. B **Specific**

Make a new line in your diagram and add the new information. You are looking for what cannot be second. Place L in 7. This means that I must go in 8, as L and I are the only valves that can be opened last. I, then, cannot be opened second. This means that (B) must be false and is therefore the credited response.

5. E **General**

Use prior work and your deductions to determine which answer must be true.

From the deductions, you can see that at least H, O, and L must be opened after N, which means that N can be opened fifth at the latest. Therefore no more than four valves can be opened before N is opened, making (E) the credited response.

6. B **Specific**

Make a new line in your diagram and add the new information. Place K in 4. From the deductions, you can see that I and H—O—L take up the last four spaces which leaves G, N, and P to take up the first three spaces, in any order. This means that only (B) could be true, making it the credited response.

7. B **Specific**

Make a new line in your diagram and add the new information. Put G in 1 and I in 3. K has to be in 2 because K—I (clue 5). This eliminates (A).

From the deductions, H must be opened sixth because N and P must be opened before it and O and L must be opened after it. This eliminates (C).

Since H is opened sixth, use the deductions to see that O must be opened seventh because it must be opened after H and before L. This eliminates (D).

If O is opened seventh, L must be opened last (clue 2), which eliminates (E).

This leaves you with (B). It could be true that N is opened fourth, but it doesn't have to be true since P could be opened fourth instead.

Questions 8–12

This is a game in which order does not matter. Six children—J, K, L, S, T, and V—are each being assigned to one of three adults—M, O, or P. Put the adults on top of your diagram and note that each group has two spaces. There are no wild cards.

Clue 1: $J_M \rightarrow L_P$; $\sim L_P \rightarrow \sim J_M$

Clue 2: $\sim K_M \rightarrow V_O$; $\sim V_O \rightarrow K_M$

Clue 3: Place this in the diagram. T cannot be in P's group.

Clue 4: $\boxed{\text{JK}}$ $\boxed{\text{LS}}$ $\boxed{\text{TV}}$

Deductions: There aren't too many deductions to make here because the clues are mostly conditional. Notice the links among the clues: K, J, and T are very important players.

Here's the diagram:

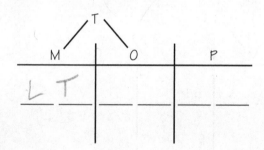

8. **B** Grab-a-Rule

    A.   No. This violates clue 1.

    B.   Yes. This does not violate any of the clues.

    C.   No. This violates clue 2.

    D.   No. This violates clue 4.

    E.   No. This violates clue 3.

9. **E** Specific

Make a new line in your diagram and add the new information. Place L and T with M. Since each adult accompanies two children, M cannot accompany any more children.

According to rule 4, J and K cannot be in the same group, so one must be with O and the other with P.

From clue 2, you can see that V must be accompanied by O because K is not going to be accompanied by M. Since O has V and either J or K, S must therefore be with P making (E) the credited response.

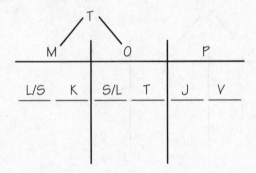

10. **A** [Specific]

Make a new line in your diagram and add the new information. Place J and V with P. P cannot accompany any more children. From clue 2, since V is not with O you know that K must be with M. This leaves L, S, and T left to place. From clue 4, you know that S and L cannot be with the same adult. One must be with M and the other with O. The only spot left is with O, so T must be with O.

M must accompany K, which eliminates (C), (D), and (E). O must accompany T, which eliminates (B), leaving (A) as the credited response.

11. **D** [General]

Use your prior work and deductions to eliminate answer choices that contain children that could be with P. From clue 3, you know that P cannot accompany T, which makes (D) the credited response.

12. **C** [General]

Use your prior work and deductions to eliminate answers that contain children that could be with O.

A.   No. If J and L are with O, then V is not, which means that K is with M (clue 2). T must also be with M since it cannot be with P (clue 3). This leaves S and V to be with P, which does not violate any rules.

B.   No. J and V were seen with O in question 9.

C. Yes. If K and T are with O, then from clue 2, you know that if K is not with M, then V must be with O. If K is with O, it is not with M, so V would also have to be with O, not T. This arrangement does not work.

D. No. L and T were seen with O in question 10.

E. No. If S and V are with O, then T must be with M (clue 3) and since J and K cannot be together, one of them is with M and the other with P. This leaves L to be with P, which does not violate any rules.

Questions 13–17

This is a game with both ordering and grouping elements. The ordered groups—day 1 through day 3—form the core of the diagram. Since two seminars are given each day, divide the days into two rows. Three short seminars—g, o, p—and three long seminars—H, N, T—will be placed in days 1–3 and ordered within those days. Each seminar will be placed only once. There is one wildcard.

Clue 1: Each day must have one short and one long seminar.

Clue 2:
$$\begin{array}{c} g \\ \diagdown \\ \diagup \quad T \\ o \end{array}$$
Keep in mind that g or o could be on the same day as T, as long as T is later.

Clue 3: p—N Keep in mind that p and N can still be on the same day.

Deductions: T must be on either the second day as the second seminar of the day, or on the third day, because both o and g must be before T, and o and g cannot be on the same day. Neither g nor o can be the second seminar of the third day. p cannot be the second seminar of the third day either, so the second seminar of the third day must be a long seminar. N cannot be the first seminar of the first day. H has the fewest restrictions.

Your diagram should look something like this:

	1	2	3
1st	~N	~T	
2nd			H/N/T

S: gop
L: HNT
~T

13. **B** [Grab-a-Rule]

A. No. This violates clue 2.

B. Yes. This does not violate any clues.

C. No. This violates clue 3.

D. No. This violates clue 1.

E. No. This violates clue 2.

14. **E** **Specific**

Draw a new set of rows in your diagram and add the new information. You know that g is on day 1, and because of clue 1, the other seminar on the first day must be a long one. It cannot be T because o must also be scheduled before it (clue 2). It can't be N because p has to be scheduled before it (clue 3). Therefore, the other seminar on the first day must be H. Eliminate (A), (B), (C), and (D), leaving (E) as the only choice that could be true and therefore the credited response.

15. **C** **Specific**

Draw a new set of rows in your diagram and add the new information. Adding to clue 3, you get p—N—o, remembering that p and N might be on the same day, or N and o might be on the same day. This means that (C) must be true and is therefore the credited response.

16. **B** **General**

Use your prior work and deductions to eliminate answer choices that contain seminars that could be the second seminar on day 2.

A. No. H could be the second seminar on day 2 in question 17.

B. Yes. According to clue 3, p—N. If p is the second seminar on day 2, this would force N, a long seminar, onto day 3. Since T cannot happen before the second seminar on day 2, putting p in that position forces T onto day 3 as well, which violates clue 1.

C. No. See question 17. It is possible for o to be the second seminar on day 2.

D. No. N could be the second seminar on day 2 in question 14.

E. No. See question 17. It is possible for g to be the second seminar on day 2.

17. **D** **Specific**

Draw a new set of rows in your diagram and add the new information. Place H on the second day. From clues 1 and 2, you know that T will have to be the second seminar on the third day. In combination with clues 1 and 3, this means that N must be the second seminar of the first day and p must be the first seminar of the first day. These deductions eliminate (A), (B), (C), and (E), leaving (D). Either o or g could be given on the third day with T, making (D) the credited response.

Questions 18–23

This is an ordering game with 1-to-1 correspondence. The inventory consists of six restaurants—F, G, J, K, L, and M—must be placed in order. The numbers 1 through 6 go on top of the diagram. There are no wildcards.

Clue 1: F—G—K

Clue 2: H—G

Clue 3: F—M → L—H; H—L → M—F

Clue 4: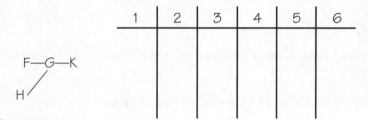

Deductions: Combine clues 1 and 2. This combined clue limits K to spaces 4, 5, and 6. It also limits G to spaces 3, 4, and 5. Neither F nor H can be in spaces 5 or 6. Notice how clue 3 and its contrapositive limit the spaces on the diagram in combination with clues 1 and 2.

Your diagram should look something like this:

18. **C** **Grab-a-Rule**

    A. No. This violates clue 3.

    B. No. This violates clue 4.

    C. Yes. This does not violate any clues.

    D. No. This violates clue 1.

    E. No. This violates clue 2.

19. **A** **Specific**

    Make a new line in your diagram and add the new information. Place F in 4. G—K must be after F (clue 1), so G must be in 5 and K must be in 6. Choice (A) must be true, making it the credited response.

20. **E** **General**

    Make a new line in your diagram and add the new information. Place M in 1 and L in 3. G must be after F and H (clues 1 and 2), which puts G in 5. Either F or H is in 2 and either F or H is in 4. K must be last (clue 1), which makes (E) the credited response.

21. **C** **Specific**

    Use prior work and deductions to eliminate any answer choices that could be false. From combining clues 1 and 2, you know that both F and H must be before G—K. H must be before K, which makes (C) the credited response.

22. C `Specific`

Make a new line in your diagram and add the new information. If K is before L, then so are F, G, and H (clues 1 and 2). This leaves M to place. According to clue 3, since H is before L, then M must be before F. This means that M must be before H and K (clue 4) so you end up with this arrangement:

$$M\text{—}F\text{—}G\text{—}K\text{—}L$$
$$/$$
$$H$$

From this, you can eliminate (A), (B), (D), and (E), leaving (C) as the credited response.

23. E `General`

Use prior work and deductions to eliminate any answer choices that could be true before trying the remaining choices.

A. No. As long as F is before M (clue 3), then F can be first.

B. No. G was fifth in question 20.

C. No. H was third in question 18.

D. No. As long as L is before H (clue 3), it can be second.

E. Yes. From clue 4, you know that M is either before both H and K or after both H and K. Place M in 4. G would then be fifth and K would be sixth. This means that M is before K, and that M must also be before H. But there is no room for H after M, so M cannot be fourth. Choice (E) must be false, so it is the credited response.

Section 3: Arguments 2

1. D `Principle Match`

The passage claims that any museum that owns the rare stamp that features an airplane printed upside down should not display it. This is because a substantial portion of the stamp is red, and ultraviolet light causes red ink to fade. The most important criterion for the conclusion seems to be that if the stamp is displayed, it will be damaged. The author acknowledges that the public will be denied the chance to see the stamp but maintains that the stamp ought to be kept safely locked away.

A. No. The passage does not mention whether the rare objects that a museum possesses should be displayed or not.

B. No. The passage states that if the stamp is displayed, it will be damaged. So, the stamp shouldn't be displayed. It doesn't address what features the museum display cases should have.

C. No. Red ink WAS used on this stamp and the stamp WILL be exposed to ultraviolet light if displayed. This principle doesn't apply.

D. Yes. According to the passage, the stamp would be damaged by display and, therefore, should not be displayed.

E. No. If the primary purpose of a museum is to educate the public, it might be thought that the stamp should be displayed. Yet the passage states that it shouldn't be, as it would be damaged.

2. **D** `Main Point`

The dietician warns that consumers who see a solution to their weight-loss problems in "fake fat" products are likely to be disappointed. This is because the people who either knowingly or unknowingly eat foods containing "fake fat" tend to take in at least as many additional calories as are saved by eating "fake fat" by eating more of the food.

A. No. This is too general. The dietician does not talk about the number of calories people consume, no matter what type of food they eat. The dietician is concerned primarily with fatty foods and their "fake fat" alternatives.

B. No. The dietician addresses only the number of calories consumed, not overall nutrition.

C. No. This is too strong. The dietician claims only that "fake fat" products are unlikely to help in weight loss, not that they will be more likely to contribute to obesity.

D. Yes. Since consumers of "fake fat" products tend to take in at least as many additional calories as are saved when eating these foods, it is unlikely that these foods will help them lose weight.

E. No. The dietician explains that "fake fat" products are designed to give food the flavor and consistency of fatty foods, but the dietician doesn't explain whether or not they are successful in doing so.

3. **B** `Strengthen`

The banking analyst concludes that offering no-charge services to new customers is not an ideal business practice. The premise is that regular, long-term customers are excluded from these special offers and it is these customers who make up the bulk of business for most banks.

A. No. This argument is claiming that a no-fee service for new customers is not an ideal business practice. It does not discuss how much the banks charge for the services, normally.

B. Yes. If this is true, banks would do better to give their best offers and services to their long-term customers instead of focusing on new customers.

C. No. The banking analyst discourages offering no-fee services to new customers but does not discuss what banks should do instead.

D. No. If this were true, it would weaken the conclusion.

E. No. If this were true, it would weaken the conclusion.

4. **B** `Flaw`

The panelist concludes that medical researchers' judgments of the importance of prior research are strongly influenced by the research appearing in popular magazines and newspapers, and, therefore, the judgments do not strongly correspond to the research's true importance. The premise is that medical research that is cited in popular magazines or newspapers is more likely to be cited in later medical research. The panelist fails to consider that there might be a good reason, common to both the citations in popular media and to later medical research, that these medical research articles are cited. Maybe it's the most cutting edge and important medical research that gets cited in popular media, for example.

A.   No. There is no view cited in the premises.

B.   Yes. This would demonstrate that both the later medical research and the popular media have a good reason to cite this research.

C.   No. The argument doesn't talk about how esteemed or well-known the scientists are who completed the medical research that was cited in popular media.

D.   No. The problem isn't the percentage of medical research articles that the popular media are able to review; it is that the panelist doesn't see that there might be a good reason that both the popular media and the later medical research are likely to cite the same research.

E.   No. This is not a circular argument.

5.   D   Reasoning

Lahar concludes that his club should subject meeting agendas to majority vote. He does this through process of elimination. The club's constitution allows three ways to decide on meeting agendas. Lahar claims that unanimous consent is unlikely and that forming a committee to decide this has usually led to groups of people pitted against each other and secret deals. The best option, then, is the one that remains: majority vote.

A.   No. Lahar considers only the options that are allowed under the club's constitution.

B.   No. This is almost right. However, it's not the credited response because the answer choice is too strong. He claims that one procedure is the appropriate method for reaching decisions on meeting agendas, not for reaching every decision.

C.   No. Lahar does acknowledge practical considerations. However, he does not suggest a change to the constitution.

D.   Yes. Lahar eliminates the other two options, leaving only the one that he recommends.

E.   No. Lahar argues against alternatives but he does not argue against the people who have advocated alternatives.

6.   C   Weaken

This argument is designed to disagree with a position. The mayor disagrees with local activists calling for expanded antismoking educations programs, which would be paid for by revenue from greatly increased taxes on cigarettes sold in the city. The mayor thinks that these programs are unnecessary, as there is strong evidence that the taxes by themselves would produce the reduction in smoking that the antitobacco activists are seeking. He bases his conclusion on surveys showing that cigarette sales drop substantially in cities that impose these high tax increases on cigarettes.

A.   No. This strengthens the argument because it makes a link between high taxes and substantially reduced smoking.

B. No. Consumers might be more likely to continue buying cigarettes if the price increase is due to higher taxes, but as long as less people actually buy and smoke the cigarettes, the mayor's argument might still be valid.

C. Yes. If people are buying a lot more cigarettes outside of the city, the rate of smoking in that city might not decrease substantially. This answer choice exploits the language shift from cigarette sales to smoking rates.

D. No. This does not address the tax increase issue that is the crux of the mayor's argument.

E. No. This does not address the mayor's argument.

7. **A** **Necessary Assumption**

Gotera concludes that speech acquisition is entirely a motor control process, not one that is abstract or mental. Gotera bases this conclusion on two facts about infants and children. Infants don't have the motor control required to voluntarily produce particular sounds. Instead, they produce random babbling sounds. Most children cannot voluntarily produce most of the vowel and consonant sounds of their language until they are several years old. Therefore, if children can't voluntarily produce the sounds of their language, they can't really talk. However, that doesn't mean that motor control is the only process involved in speech acquisition. The conclusion is too strong for the evidence that supports it, so it requires an assumption to fill in the gap.

A. Yes. This eliminates the possibility that there might be some additional process that affects speech acquisition that does not involve motor control. This closes the gap.

B. No. It wouldn't matter if infants could intentionally move their tongues, as long as they lack the motor ability to intentionally produce particular sounds. The evidence states that they do lack this ability.

C. No. It wouldn't matter if children babbled until they were 7, as long as they also developed the motor abilities discussed in the argument.

D. No. This might be true. However, it doesn't address the gap between the evidence and the claim that speech acquisition is entirely a motor control process.

E. No. This would weaken the argument. If this were true, then mental development would factor in to speech acquisition, against Gotera's argument.

8. **A** **Flaw**

Caldwell concludes that the government's actions in tearing down a former naval base were not only inefficient but also immoral. Caldwell concludes this because the former naval base had a large number of facilities, such as a swimming pool, housing, etc., that might have been used for the good of the community, benefitting everyone. Thus, Caldwell equates what is moral with benefiting everyone.

A. Yes. Caldwell doesn't allow for the possibility that the action of tearing down the base might still be morally permissible even if it doesn't benefit everyone.

B. No. In fact, Caldwell thinks that the actual consequences are incredibly important to the action's moral permissibility.

C. No. This is too strong. Caldwell is talking about the demolition of a single base, not the actions of the government in general.

D. No. This one is close. However, Caldwell says that the action was not only inefficient but also immoral. Caldwell isn't equating being inefficient with being immoral. So Caldwell is also not presuming that any efficient action is also moral.

E. No. This one is tempting, as well. However, Caldwell doesn't ever claim that tearing down the base or using it for the community are the only options. Other courses of action don't happen to be relevant to Caldwell's point.

9. C   **Necessary Assumption**

The researchers concluded that reducing stress lessens a person's sensitivity to pain, based on an experiment where they played audiotapes to patients before and after surgery. The patients who listened only to music required less anesthesia and fewer painkillers as compared to the patients who listened only to conversation. The gap is between reducing stress and music. The music might have caused the patients to require less anesthesia and fewer painkillers for some other reason than because the music reduced stress.

A. No. It is not essential that the patients listened to the same tape before and after surgery, as long as one group listened to conversation and the other group listened to music.

B. No. This is not essential to the argument.

C. Yes. This makes the connection between music and stress reduction. It eliminates other possible reasons as to why the patients listening to music might have required less anesthesia and fewer painkillers.

D. No. This is not essential to the argument.

E. No. This might be true, but it doesn't give us the connection between music and reducing stress that the argument requires.

10. E   **Point at Issue**

Samuel concludes that communication via computer contributes to the dissolution of lasting communal bonds. His premise is that communication via computer is usually conducted privately and anonymously between people who would otherwise have conducted the communication in person. Tova disagrees with Samuel's conclusion because she disagrees with his claim that communication via computer replaces other forms of interaction and communication. She claims, instead, that it replaces asocial or antisocial behavior.

A. No. Neither discusses the dissolution of social bonds as a general trend of modern life.

B. No. This is too strong. Neither talks about all purely private behavior. They are talking about a specific private behavior: communication via computer.

C. No. Tova doesn't discuss whether face-to-face communication is more likely to contribute to the creation of social bonds.

D.   No. Tova doesn't discuss whether it is desirable to replace social bonds that have dissolved with new ones.

E.   Yes. Samuel thinks that communicating via computer replaces social behavior, whereas Tova thinks that communicating via computer doesn't because it replaces asocial/antisocial behavior.

11.   **B**   **Principle Match**

The passage concludes that we should not immediately spread iron particles over the surface of the ocean in response to the greenhouse effect. Spreading the iron particles would counteract the greenhouse effect by increasing the number of phytoplankton, which would, in turn, decrease the amount of carbon dioxide in the atmosphere. However, the side effects of this strategy haven't been studied yet, so the author of the argument thinks we should hold off on messing with such an important resource as the ocean.

A.   No. The passage doesn't address strategies with known side effects.

B.   Yes. According to the passage, the iron-seeding strategy should not be used yet because the consequences to the ocean, an important resource, are unknown.

C.   No. The passage states that the consequences of the iron-seeding strategy are not known, so there is no way to know if those consequences are more serious than the problem of the greenhouse effect.

D.   No. This is close, but it states that we should not implement a strategy if it requires altering an important resource. The passage doesn't go that far. It just says that research into the side effects should be done before implementing the strategy.

E.   No. The passage doesn't concern itself with whether the iron-seeding strategy has a possibility of exacerbating the greenhouse effect. The worry is in how this strategy might alter the oceans.

12.   **E**   **Flaw**

The problem that this argument tries to solve is that historians always have biases that affect their work, which is the interpretation of historical events. The solution that is proposed is that historians should instead interpret what the people who participated in historical events thought about those events. The flaw is that the solution still requires an interpretation that is susceptible to bias.

A.   No. This might be true. However, the important point is that historians have biases that affect their work, which is what the proposal claims to avoid.

B.   No. Scholars in other disciplines are not relevant to the flaw of this argument.

C.   No. The argument is trying to eliminate the biases. It doesn't matter whether or not these biases have been identified.

D.   No. It doesn't matter, for the purposes of this argument, whether the historians are aware of the effect of their biases. The argument proposes a solution to eliminate the biases whether the historians are aware of them or not.

E.   Yes. If historians still have to interpret what the participants thought about the events, there is still the possibility of biased interpretations.

13. D `Necessary Assumption`

The argument concludes that economic considerations dictate that country X should institute a nation-wide system of air and ground transportation for conveying the seriously injured to specialized trauma centers. The evidence presented for this conclusion is that timely access to the medical care that can be provided only at trauma centers will save many people's lives. These people, who are alive as a result of timely access to trauma centers, would be earning money. That these people are earning money is a twofold benefit to country X: The earnings would result in a large increase in X's GNP, and taxes paid on the earnings would greatly augment government revenues. The argument shifts language from people's lives being saved to the total increase in X's GNP and tax revenues. An increase in X's GNP and tax revenues would require that, as a result of saving these people's lives, there would be more people working in country X than there are right now. If not, the added cost of instituting the nationwide system might not be economically beneficial.

A. No. Country Y is irrelevant. The argument concentrates on country X.

B. No. The argument is concerned with making sure that people have timely access to specialized trauma centers, wherever they may be located.

C. No. It could be more costly, and yet the people would be alive and working, which would increase country X's GNP.

D. Yes. The argument assumes that if more people survived serious injury, they would be adding to the workforce, thereby boosting country X's GNP. If the survivors weren't able to work, or if they replaced other people when they went back to work, the GNP wouldn't increase and neither would tax revenue.

E. No. The issue is whether country X should enable people to get timely treatment in specialized trauma centers, not whether more people should go to specialized trauma centers.

14. C `Inference`

Early urban societies → large-scale farming nearby → irrigation → rivers or lakes. The contrapositive is as follows: ~rivers and ~lakes → ~irrigation → ~large-scale farming → ~early urban society.

A. No. The passage talks about early urban societies, but does not say how many peoples lived in them.

B. No. This answer choice can be diagrammed as follows: societies far from rivers or lakes → farming possible in the absence of irrigation. The passage talks only about early urban societies. Also, it doesn't talk about the possibility of farming without irrigation.

C. Yes. See the contrapositive in the explanation above.

D. No. Even though the passage does not say that urban societies with farms near rivers or lakes necessarily rely upon irrigation, it doesn't say that they don't.

E. No. The passage doesn't mention early rural societies.

15. **D** **Sufficient Assumption**

The economist concludes that countries that put collective goals before individual goals cannot emerge quickly from an economic recession because people's confidence in the economic policies of their country is a precondition for any new investment. This new investment is important because substantial new investment in that country's economy is required for a country's rapid emergence from an economic recession. The gap in the argument is between people's confidence in a country's economic policies and whether the country puts collective goals before individuals' goals.

A. No. This is too strong. There might be some new investment, yet a country might still not emerge quickly from a recession. Emerging quickly from an economic recession requires substantial new investment.

B. No. The economist doesn't discuss whether the recessions themselves affect people's support for their government's policies. Also, this answer choice is talking about the government's policies in general, while the argument focuses on economic policies.

C. No. The economist never claims what would be sufficient for a country to emerge quickly from an economic recession. The economist, instead, tells us that substantial new investments are necessary for a country to emerge from an economic recession and that countries that put collective goals first will fail this necessary condition.

D. Yes. This connects people's confidence, or lack thereof, in their country's economic policies and whether the country puts collective goals before individuals' goals.

E. No. The economist is concerned only with countries that have experienced a recession, not whether they are more likely to experience a recession.

16. **C** **Flaw**

The argument concludes that University Hospital could decrease its average length of stay without affecting quality of care. This conclusion is based on a comparison between the average length of stay for patients at Edgewater Hospital and at University Hospital. Studies show that recovery rates for both are similar for patients with similar illnesses. The argument is problematic because similar recovery rates for patients with similar illnesses at these hospitals does not mean that most patients at both hospitals have similar illnesses. University Hospital might specialize in heart attack patients, while Edgewater might specialize in minor injuries and ailments, for example.

A. No. The argument does not say that quality of care and length of stay are the same thing. Based on the evidence concerning recovery rates at both hospitals, it claims that length of stay can be reduced without affecting the quality of care.

B. No. Wrong flaw. This argument does not confuse something sufficient with something necessary.

C. Yes. If the patients at Edgewater tend to be treated for different illnesses, then the recovery rate information does not support the claim that the average length of stay could be reduced.

D. No. The argument allows for the idea that length of stay might be relevant to recovery rates.

E. No. The connection is between average length of stay, recovery rates, and quality of care. Patients' preferences are irrelevant.

17. **B**   Reasoning

The philosopher disagrees with Graham's position that the best life is a life that is full of activity because a person is truly happy only when doing something. The philosopher gives the example of people sleeping, during which they are not doing anything but are sometimes truly happy. The role of the example is to speak against Graham's reason for his conclusion by undermining the claim that a person is truly happy only when doing something.

A. No. It is a premise of the philosopher's argument.

B. Yes. If the statement is true, Graham cannot claim, as support for his conclusion, that a person is truly happy only when doing something.

C. No. It is not part of Graham's argument.

D. No. This is close, but the claim is an example intended to disprove a premise of Graham's argument, not its conclusion. The best life might still be a life that is full of activity; the philosopher just wants to show that Graham's premise doesn't actually support his conclusion.

E. No. It is a premise of the philosopher's argument, not the conclusion.

18. **D**   Principle Match

Find the answer choice supported by the passage.

A. No. The passage does not provide proof whether Stuart had discussions with Abella about West, only that he was friends with Abella, who studied under West.

B. No. The historian is concerned with defending his claim that West influenced Stuart, not the other way around.

C. No. Stuart's contemporaries didn't use West's terminology but there is no proof in the passage that West did or did not otherwise influence them.

D. Yes. Stuart used West's terminology, which he couldn't have gotten from his own contemporaries since they did not use the same terminology.

E. No. The passage does not provide any information on why West's terminology is now commonplace, just that it is.

19. **A**   Weaken

The theory claims that "drug overdoses" were the cause of the sudden extinction of the dinosaurs. This helps explain why so many dinosaur fossils are found in unusual and contorted positions. The evidence is that angiosperms, which contain psychoactive agents, first appeared at the same time that the dinosaurs became extinct. Most plant-eating mammals avoid eating these agents, which are potentially lethal, because they taste bitter. Also, mammals have livers that help detoxify these agents. Dinosaurs couldn't taste the bitterness, nor could they detoxify the substance. The argument claims that the theory's strongest support comes from the fact that it helps explain the positions of dinosaur fossils. How does it explain the positions of dinosaur fossils? Might there be other reasons as to why the dinosaur fossils were in these positions?

A. Yes. This widens the gap. If fossils of large mammals are also found in these positions, and mammals were less likely to be poisoned by the psychoactive agents, then a key premise is compromised.

B. No. The argument is about whether dinosaurs were poisoned by angiosperms, not how nutritious angiosperms are.

C. No. This would strengthen the argument. If vegetarian dinosaurs fed on angiosperms and then other dinosaurs ate their angiosperm-polluted bodies, then a lot of dinosaurs would have been in contact with the potentially lethal psychoactive agents in the angiosperms.

D. No. The argument is about whether angiosperms poisoned the dinosaurs, not about other poisonous plants.

E. No. The argument allowed for this possibility. It just implied that it was less likely for them to die from eating angiosperms.

20. E Resolve/ Explain

The discrepancy is that continuous maintenance, which dispenses with the need for radical reconstruction, is far less expensive a way to manage an existing transportation infrastructure in the long run. However, continuous maintenance almost never happens; rather, radical reconstruction, which is necessitated by failing to perform continuous maintenance, is usually the way that an existing transportation infrastructure is managed.

A. No. This would make it more, not less, likely that continuous maintenance would be performed.

B. No. This doesn't address why continuous maintenance isn't usually performed, even though it is less expensive in the long run.

C. No. This doesn't address why continuous adequate maintenance isn't usually performed.

D. No. This would make it more, not less, likely that continuous maintenance would be performed.

E. Yes. People feel that they can skip maintenance because the problems don't show up immediately. When they do show up, they are more serious and necessitate radical reconstruction.

21. E Flaw

This argument is designed to solve a problem. The solution proposed for getting over one's fear of an activity is to do it repeatedly. This is supported by the fact that over 50 percent of the people who have parachuted only once reported being extremely frightened by the experience, while less than 1 percent of people who have parachuted 10 times or more reported being frightened by it. This argument has a sampling problem. Who willingly throws themselves out of an airplane 10 times or more? It could be a higher percentage of people who never found it frightening in the first place.

A. No. The argument addresses overcoming the fear of some particular activity by repeating that same activity, not overcoming the fear of many activities by engaging in lots of frightening activities.

B. No. It's true that the argument does not address this sample but this is not a flaw of the argument.

C. No. The argument addresses how to get over fears that people already have, no matter how they have acquired this fear.

D. No. What does it mean to be better off? If it means to be less frightened, then the argument does take this into account by saying that, in fact, repeating the activity will make them less frightened of it.

E. Yes. The sample might not be representative because it might include a higher percentage of people who never found it frightening to jump out of a plane in the first place.

22. **E** **Resolve/ Explain**

The seeming paradox is that although most economists believe that reducing the price of any product generally stimulates demand for it, when most wine merchants reduce the price of domestic wines to make them more competitive with imported wines with which they were previously comparably priced, the sales of the imported wines will increase.

A. No. This still doesn't explain why, when the general rule is that reducing price stimulates demand, the competing wines sales increased when the prices on the domestic wine were reduced.

B. No. The merchants aren't the ones making the economic predictions. They are the observers of what actually happened.

C. No. There is no information about which wine is superior. It doesn't explain why the sales of imported wines increased when domestic wine prices were reduced.

D. No. This does not explain why, if the domestic wines' prices were reduced, the sales of the imported wines increased.

E. Yes. The argument didn't say whether the domestic wines' sales also increased. This allows for the sales of both types of wines to increase, which reconciles the observations with the economists' beliefs.

23. **A** **Inference**

Find the answer choice supported by the passage.

A. Yes. From the last sentence, a dense colony of these bacteria produces for itself an environment in which it can continue to thrive indefinitely. From the second and third sentence, the hydrogen sulfide produced by these bacteria reacts with oxygen, preventing it from harming the bacteria. It provides the bacteria with a source of food because it tends to kill other organisms in the area.

B. No. The passage states that the hydrogen sulfide reacts with and removes oxygen and that it tends to kill other organisms in the area. There is no proof that these two facts are related.

C. No. There is no proof in the passage that most organisms, if killed, can provide a source of food for the bacteria. All you know is that, with a dense colony, enough will be killed to sustain the colony. They could be light eaters.

D. No. There is no proof that, if they have this environment, the bacteria can thrive indefinitely or that it's the only way that they can thrive indefinitely.

E. No. There is no information provided about all colonies of bacteria that might produce hydrogen sulfide as a waste product, just about these particular bacteria.

24. C Parallel

The argument concludes that gloomy books are unlikely to be very popular. This is because they are not a genre that presents a utopian future, and books of the utopian future genre will always find enthusiastic buyers. Utopian future → popular; contrapositive: ~popular → ~Utopian future. Conclusion: ~Utopian future → ~(likely) popular. This argument has a necessary/sufficient problem. Being of the utopian future genre is sufficient for being popular but we don't know that it is necessary. There might well be a group of angst-filled people that like nothing better than to curl up with a gloomy book.

A. No. This argument does not contain the necessary/sufficient switch.

B. No. This argument shifts from people who participate in less violent forms of recreation and enjoy watching more violent sports to people who participate in more violent sports. This is not the same as a necessary/sufficient flaw.

C. Yes. Complicated and dangerous special effects → enormously expensive; ~enormously expensive → ~complicated and dangerous special effects. Conclusion: ~complicated and dangerous special effects → (probably) ~enormously expensive.

D. No. This argument is not flawed.

E. No. This argument is not flawed.

25. A Parallel

The passage claims that we can learn about the past, even though we do not have direct access to it. We can do this by looking at current geology, geography, etc., to find clues about a region's distant history. However, the study of the present becomes less useful the more distant the period we are studying is.

A. Yes. The astronomers are able to use present data about the solar system to find out about the earlier years of the solar system. However, because the origin of the solar system is much more distant, the present data is not very useful in learning about this origin.

B. No. The passage tells us that less will be learned from the present the more distant the period is that we are studying. The oft-studied crime scene is not from a much more distant period.

C. No. This doesn't talk about time relations.

D. No. This doesn't talk about time relations.

E. No. This doesn't relate the pyramids to a much more distant time than the ancient Egyptians.

Section 4: Reading Comprehension

Questions 1–6

In this passage, the author seeks to highlight the originality of Senegalese filmmaker Ousmane Sembène's films. That originality lies in his adaptation of the Western cultural medium of film to the needs, paces, and structures of West African culture. In the second paragraph, the author discusses a number of Sembène's characters and motifs, which can be traced to those found in traditional West African storytelling. The third paragraph notes that the structure of many of Sembène's films is derived from West African dilemma tales. The plots of dilemma tales are debated and decided by audiences. Several of Sembène's films, similarly, offer alternative endings. At the end of the passage, the author discusses how Sembène's films are intended to bring out a basic change in the worldview of the viewer. Here, the author notes the sociopolitical issues that the critics from the first paragraph think are the primary characteristic of Sembène's films. However, the author thinks that the way that Sembène explores these issues in his films reflects African oral storytelling more than the Marxist components of Sembène's ideology.

1. **E**   **Big Picture**

   A. No. This choice starts well but it claims that Sembène's originality lies in his adaptation of traditional archetypal predicaments and open-ended plots, which were discussed only in the last two paragraphs.

   B. No. This choice talks about Sembène's characters being variations on types common to traditional West African storytelling, which is discussed only in the second paragraph.

   C. No. We are never told whether oral narrative traditions were previously considered suitable.

   D. No. We don't know what social and political beliefs are held by most of the Senegalese people.

   E. Yes. This choice mentions why Sembène's films are notable, that they derive elements from traditional West African storytelling, and that these films use these elements to comment critically on contemporary social and political issues.

2. **E**   **Extract Fact**

   A. No. The author does not say that Sembène uses animals as symbols in any of his films.

   B. No. This is close but the author claims that Sembène uses freeze-frames, which suggest continued action. The author does not claim that Sembène uses slow motion.

   C. No. The author does not say that Sembène provides oral narration in any of his films.

   D. No. The author does not claim that Sembène places West African images and Marxist symbols side by side in any of his films.

   E. Yes. This answer choice is supported by the third paragraph.

3. **A**   **RC Reasoning**

   The answer choice should support the author's reading of the dialectical elements as being related to African oral storytelling rather than to the Marxist components of Sembène's ideology.

A. Yes. This choice demonstrates that other people who draw upon the oral traditions of West Africa do use these dialectical elements, and these people haven't read Marxist theory. It lends credence to the author's claim.

B. No. This is too general. The author claims that the binary oppositions are more likely to have come from African oral storytelling, not just some tradition from around the world.

C. No. This weakens the argument. If this were true, then the binary elements would be likely to come equally from his Marxist ideology.

D. No. This is not strong enough. There are other continents besides Europe, North America, and Africa. Also, he still could have gotten the binary oppositions from his Marxist ideology, even if few North American and European filmmakers use binary opposition.

E. No. This is not strong enough. It just says that some films produced by Marxist-principled film-makers don't essentially use binary opposition. They could still produce a lot of films that do.

4. **D** Extract Infer

A. No. The passage doesn't mention how popular Sembène's films are.

B. No. The passage doesn't mention the support of government agencies.

C. No. The passage doesn't mention how the critics in Senegal interpret Sembène's films.

D. Yes. This is discussed in the second paragraph.

E. No. The passage doesn't mention government censorship.

5. **C** Structure

The author uses the phrase "initiatory journeys" to mean journeys that start or bring a basic change, which supports (C).

6. **A** Extract Fact

A. Yes. The passage never says that one of his films exhibits disenchantment with attempts to reform Senegalese government.

B. No. Paragraph two says that he does this a lot, which provides evidence that Sembène exhibits confidence in the aptness of it.

C. No. Paragraph four discusses this.

D. No. The example of the street merchant in the second paragraph shows this.

E. No. The first paragraph talks about his desire to raise awareness.

Questions 7–12

Passage A

The author believes that there is a problem with how academic historians write. Their historiographical approach doesn't leave much to the imagination, which takes the joy out of reading their writing. The first paragraph is an introduction to the problem. The second paragraph discusses a solution to this problem, namely that historians have begun to rediscover stories. The author notes that calling one's historiography a narrative has begun to occur, but that real narrative writing by academic historians is hard to find.

Passage B

The author discusses writing in the legal profession. The first paragraph suggests that, by virtue of the purpose it serves, legal writing is not going to be creative, it will not be humorous, and the author's voice will not be heard in it. The second paragraph notes that a lawyer's writing is influenced by the writing of other lawyers. The lawyers, as a result of educational, professional, and economic constraints, will likely write poorly. It then suggests that attention to narrative might change the quality of writing for lawyers. This would somehow highlight the idea that every case has a story about real people and events. The last paragraph suggests that, even if attention to narrative doesn't change how lawyers will write or how legal writing is taught, awareness of the value of narrative might help legal writing.

7. **D** | Extract Fact |

    A. No. Passage A does not discuss teaching methods to develop writing skills.

    B. No. Passage A does not concern itself with points of view; rather, it is concerned with changing the way history is presented.

    C. No. Passage A claims that historic writing can and should be creatively crafted; passage B at least raises the possibility that legal writing might be creatively crafted.

    D. Yes. Both passages think that more attention to storytelling would benefit the writing in the respective professions that they discuss.

    E. No. Both are entertaining the idea that elements from other disciplines would benefit writing in historical and legal writing, respectively.

8. **B** | Extract Infer |

    A. No. The author of passage A is an active member of the history profession (line 5). The author of passage B is an active member of the legal profession (line 30).

    B. Yes. See the explanation for (A).

    C. No. The author of passage B is a member of the legal profession.

    D. No. We don't know whether or not the author of passage A is also a lawyer.

    E. No. We don't know whether or not the author of passage B is also a historian.

9. **A** | Extract Fact |

    A. Yes. Passage A mentions this in line 10 and passage B mentions this in line 49.

    B. No. Both passages seem to indicate that writing in the respective professions is the opposite of hyperbolic.

C. No. Neither passage mentions that the writing in the respective professions is subversive.

D. No. This is the opposite of what both passages claim is typical for the writing in their respective professions.

E. No. This is the opposite of what both passages claim is typical for the writing in their respective professions.

10. **C**   Structure

A. No. Passage A does not present arguments for an opposing position.

B. No. This is close. However, passage B does make some evaluative claims, albeit weaker than the ones in passage A. It claims, for example, that mere awareness of the value of narrative could perhaps serve as an important corrective.

C. Yes. Passage A notes the titles of papers from the American Historical Association, which are all historiographs. Passage B does not give specific arguments.

D. No. Both offer criticism.

E. No. Passage B does not outline a theory.

11. **B**   Structure

The phrase "scholarly monographs that sap the vitality of history" is being used to describe the typical writing that the author sees as making history books not stimulating for the students who read them, discouraging the students from connecting emotionally. In passage B, the phrases "conformity is a virtue, creativity suspect, humor forbidden, and voice mute" plays the most similar role, as it shows that the writing style of lawyers makes legal writing abstract and disconnected from the human narrative content. This supports (B).

12. **D**   Extract Infer

A. No. This is too strong. The author says that lawyers too often write badly (lines 41–42). This doesn't mean that legal documents are always written poorly.

B. No. The author claims that legal analysis strips the human narrative content from the abstract, canonical legal form of the case (lines 48–50).

C. No. The author claims that lawyers too often write poorly (lines 41–42).

D. Yes. The author claims that legal analysis strips the human narrative content from the abstract, canonical legal form of the case (lines 48–50).

E. No. The author doesn't discuss whether legal writing makes the right connections between the details and relevant legal doctrines.

Questions 13–19

In this passage, the author discusses the work of Susan Riechert on the spider *Agelenopsis aperta* in order to show that traditional theories of animal behavior do not apply to all animals. The first paragraph states the traditional theories of animal behavior, asserting that intra-species animal conflict is highly ritualized and doesn't vary from contest to contest. This intro provides some details about the theory and gives an example. The second paragraph introduces Riechert's work with *Agelenopsis aperta* to demonstrate that, in this population, intra-species conflict does vary greatly from contest to contest. As a result, Riechert argues that evolutionary game theory, developed from classical game theory, better describes what *Agelenopsis apertas* do when fighting, rather than traditional theories. The paragraph discusses the similarities between evolutionary game theory and classical game theory as well as two major differences between them. Evolutionary game theory assumes that instinct and long-term species advantage determine the exhibited strategies, instead of rational thought. Also, the payoffs for evolutionary game theory are defined in terms of reproductive success, instead of an individual's personal judgment. In the third paragraph, Riechart makes some predictions concerning the behavior of *Agelenopsis apertas* in disputes, given certain factors.

13.   C   **Big Picture**

A.   No. This is too general. The passage discusses only evolutionary game theory in terms of its success in analyzing the process of decision making, and only in regards to *Agelenopsis apertas*.

B.   No. This was discussed only in the third paragraph. Also, we don't know that they exhibit an unusually wide variety of behaviors.

C.   Yes. This mentions evolutionary game theory and how it might be used to explain the behavior of *Agelenopsis apertas* in intra-species disputes.

D.   No. This is too strong. The author suggests that the traditional theory might not be as good as evolutionary game theory to explain the fighting behavior of *Agelenopsis apertas*, but doesn't address most species.

E.   No. This is too general. We don't know that scientists in general use evolutionary game theory to predict the behavior of spiders in site selection.

14.   E   **Structure**

The author mentions Galapagos tortoises as an example of the traditional theory, which claims that intra-species conflict is highly ritualized. This supports (E).

15.   N/A   Item removed from scoring.

16.   D   **Extract Infer**

A.   No. This is consistent with the predictions concerning the grassland in paragraph three.

B.   No. This is consistent with the predictions concerning the riparian habitat in paragraph three, as the riparian habitat is 90 percent habitable.

C.   No. The third paragraph predicts that spiders in the riparian habitat, which is 90 percent habitable, will be less likely to escalate fighting than spiders in the grassland habitat, which is 12 percent habitable.

D.   Yes. The third paragraph predicts that spiders in the riparian habitat will be less willing to engage in escalated fighting, not as willing.

E.   No. This is consistent with the predictions in the third paragraph.

17.   **E**   Structure

The third paragraph gives predictions concerning the behavior of spiders in different habitats, based on Riechert's claim that *Agelenopsis apertas*' territorial disputes are better described using evolutionary game theory.

A.   No. The passage does not compare evolutionary game theory and classical game theory.

B.   No. We don't know that evolutionary game theory is controversial, and it isn't discussed in the first paragraph.

C.   No. This is close. However, it makes predictions. The experiment hasn't been done yet.

D.   No. It makes predictions. It does not describe rare phenomena.

E.   Yes. It describes predictions that are based on evolutionary game theory.

18.   **B**   Extract Infer

A.   No. The second paragraph says that variations in conflict behavior may result from a variety of things, not primarily because of the different levels of competition in different habitats.

B.   Yes. The passage states that a spider may engage in escalated fighting during a dispute only if the disputed resource is valuable enough to warrant the risk of physical injury (lines 30–33).

C.   No. *Agelenopsis apertas*' variations in fighting behavior are not compared to those of most other species.

D.   No. The passage never says that *Agelenopsis apertas* are more likely to engage in escalated fighting, just that they may engage in escalated fighting.

E.   No. *Agelenopsis apertas*' proclivities concerning escalated fighting are not compared to those of most other species.

19.   **A**   Big Picture

A.   Yes. The author presents evolutionary game theory as an alternative to the traditional theories of animal behavior.

B.   No. This doesn't address the first paragraph and its discussion of traditional theories.

C.   No. The passage doesn't evaluate the evidence either for the traditional theories or for evolutionary game theory.

D.   No. This is too strong. The data on *Agelenopsis apertas* doesn't refute the traditional theory. And, the only theory that might be considered controversial would be evolutionary game theory.

E.   No. The passage seems to support the new theory.

Questions 20–27

The author disagrees with most people who think that, in general, we have a moral duty to obey the law because it is the law. Instead, the author defends philosophical anarchism, which claims that people who live under the jurisdiction of governments have no moral duty to those governments to obey their laws. In the first paragraph, the author introduces these two points of view and then describes what some commentators take to be two highly counterintuitive implications of philosophical anarchism that cause them to reject this position. In the second paragraph, the author shows that the first implication (that governments do not vary widely in their moral stature) does not follow from philosophical anarchism. In the third paragraph, the author argues that, according to philosophical anarchism, people have many moral duties to one another, against the second supposed implication that people may do as they please without scruple.

20. **C**   **Big Picture**

   A.   No. This is discussed only in the first paragraph.

   B.   No. The author argues in the second paragraph that it is consistent with philosophical anarchism to hold that some governments may be morally better than others.

   C.   Yes. The author presents some supposed implications of philosophical anarchism and then shows that these claims do not logically follow from philosophical anarchism.

   D.   No. The author speaks about philosophical anarchism in general, not about certain philosophical anarchists.

   E.   No. Philosophical anarchism does not hold that one should obey the law because it is the law.

21. **A**   **Extract Fact**

   A.   Yes. The author states this in the first paragraph.

   B.   No. The first paragraph says that most people acknowledge that not all governments have a moral right to govern.

   C.   No. The first paragraph doesn't discuss the connection between being morally bound to obey the law and participating in establishing the law.

   D.   No. The first paragraph says that most people believe that we generally have a moral duty to obey the law. This would make most crimes morally bad.

   E.   No. This was discussed in the third paragraph in reference to what philosophical anarchists believe. Also, there is no discussion about whether the majority of existing laws are to protect others.

22. **B**   **Extract Infer**

   The author defends philosophical anarchists against their critics but does not explicitly endorse this position. This supports (B). Choice (A) is the next best answer but is too strong.

23. **A**   **Structure**

   The author uses the word "counterintuitive" to point out that some commentators think that the implications of philosophical anarchism are "against our intuitions," which supports (A).

24. **B** **Extract Infer**

   A.   No. The last part of the analogy discusses legal penalties, which the anarchists don't recognize as being pertinent to morality.

   B.   Yes. The corporate executive refrains from a practice because she finds out it might be hurting others.

   C.   No. The coworker has hurt someone else but the person does nothing.

   D.   No. This doesn't discuss the possibility of hurting others.

   E.   No. This action does not discuss the reasons for refraining from an action.

25. **C** **Extract Infer**

   A.   No. The author never claims that philosophical anarchism attributes more moral obligations to people than is commonly held.

   B.   No. The author doesn't discuss what morally superior governments recognize.

   C.   Yes. The author discusses this in the third paragraph.

   D.   No. The author defends philosophical anarchism, which states that there is no moral obligation to obey laws, simply because they are the laws.

   E.   No. Philosophical anarchism doesn't recognize laws as such.

26. **D** **Structure**

   The author discusses people's positive moral duty to care for one another to demonstrate that philosophical anarchists think that people have a lot of moral obligations, which supports (D).

27. **D** **Big Picture**

   A.   No. The author doesn't describe the development of philosophical anarchism.

   B.   No. This is close. However, this doesn't talk about the claims of the critics of philosophical anarchism.

   C.   No. The author tries to show that these supposed implications are not necessary implications of philosophical anarchism.

   D.   Yes. The author tries to show that the critics are wrong in thinking that philosophical anarchism has, as its implications, two counterintuitive claims.

   E.   No. The author argues that the supposedly counterintuitive implications are not actual implications of philosophical anarchism and, therefore, are not defects of philosophical anarchism.

Chapter 3
PrepTest 53:
Answers and
Explanations

ANSWER KEY: PREPTEST 53

Section 1:
Arguments 1

1. C
2. B
3. B
4. A
5. E
6. A
7. A
8. D
9. A
10. D
11. D
12. C
13. A
14. D
15. B
16. E
17. B
18. B
19. A
20. C
21. A
22. E
23. D
24. D
25. B

Section 2:
Games

1. B
2. A
3. B
4. B
5. C
6. C
7. A
8. A
9. D
10. C
11. B
12. B
13. E
14. A
15. E
16. A
17. D
18. E
19. A
20. B
21. C
22. E
23. B

Section 3:
Arguments 2

1. A
2. C
3. E
4. A
5. E
6. D
7. A
8. A
9. E
10. B
11. C
12. B
13. B
14. A
15. E
16. B
17. A
18. E
19. A
20. D
21. C
22. B
23. D
24. A
25. C

Section 4:
Reading
Comprehension

1. A
2. C
3. D
4. C
5. D
6. D
7. D
8. A
9. C
10. E
11. D
12. B
13. B
14. A
15. A
16. C
17. D
18. C
19. D
20. C
21. D
22. E
23. A
24. C
25. D
26. E
27. A

EXPLANATIONS

Section 1: Arguments 1

1. **C** **Strengthen**

   The consumer advocate concludes that consumers ought to be skeptical of the claims made in advertisements. The evidence is that, typically, businesses are chiefly motivated by profits, and this motive does not make businesses think that they should present accurate information in their advertisements. The consumer advocate is neglecting to consider other reasons that businesses might not make misleading claims in advertisements, despite their interests in making a profit.

   A. No. This strengthens the connection between maximizing profits and using inaccurate information.

   B. No. This indicates a past history of businesses making inaccurate statements, thus strengthening the conclusion.

   C. Yes. The conclusion claims that consumers OUGHT to be skeptical. It doesn't address whether they actually ARE skeptical or not.

   D. No. This strengthens the claim that advertisements are likely to contain inaccurate information.

   E. No. This eliminates another reason as to why businesses might give accurate information, even though they want to increase profits.

2. **B** **Point at Issue**

   Elaine concludes that museums ought to seek to acquire the best examples of artworks from each period and genre, even if some of the works are not recognized as masterpieces. Her premise is that the purpose of museums is to preserve artworks and make them available to all. Frederick disagrees, claiming that art museums ought to acquire the works of recognized masters, as museums have limited resources and a museum's purpose is to ensure the preservation of the greatest artworks.

   A. No. Frederick does not make any connection between greatest artworks and who deems them as such.

   B. Yes. Elaine claims that they should, while Frederick thinks that museums have a different purpose.

   C. No. Both Elaine and Frederick agree on this.

   D. No. Neither is concerned with the expense of a single piece of art.

   E. No. Neither questions the status of artwork identified as masterpieces.

3. **B** **Weaken**

   The science columnist presents the following evidence: Many human diseases are genetically based, and cats are genetically closer to humans than are any other mammals save nonhuman primates. The columnist claims that this evidence makes is clear why humans and cats have so many diseases in common.

   A. No. The argument doesn't make claims about how many cats (as opposed to humans) actually get the diseases.

B.   Yes. The argument claims only that many human diseases are genetically based, not all. And it doesn't tell us whether the diseases we share with cats are among those. If they are not, the fact that cats are genetically close to humans still doesn't explain why cats and humans share a lot of diseases.

C.   No. The argument doesn't address the diseases cats and nonhuman primates have in common.

D.   No. The argument doesn't address the severity of the diseases shared by humans and cats.

E.   No. The argument already states this.

4.   A   **Main Point**

Because shoe manufacturing, which used to be a major local industry, has experienced severe setbacks and because outdated public policy generally prevents business growth, the argument concludes that this region must find new ways to help business grow.

A.   Yes. This is a restatement of the conclusion.

B.   No. We don't know whether it is still a major source of income or not.

C.   No. This is a premise.

D.   No. This is a premise.

E.   No. This is a premise.

5.   E   **Principle Match**

Modern medicine has enabled more people to live longer and pain-free lives. However, the benefits created by modern medicine have resulted in more and more of the population being older, which gives rise to financial problems for some social welfare programs.

A.   No. This is too strong. The passage doesn't discuss all problems.

B.   No. The passage does not make a recommendation as to what should be done. It describes a situation.

C.   No. This is too strong. The passage doesn't discuss every enhancement of the quality of life.

D.   No. This is too strong. The passage doesn't discuss all social institutions, just some.

E.   Yes. Modern medicine solved the short and painful life-span problem, but in the process it created a financial problem.

6.   A   **Strengthen**

The argument concludes that Jackie will probably like The Cruel Herd's new album. Jackie is a fan of Moral Vacuum's music and, on this album, The Cruel Herd plays a type of music similar to Moral Vacuum's. Also, the witty lyrics are similar to those of some of Moral Vacuum's best. This is an analogy and the answer choice should make the two bands' music even more similar.

A.   Yes. If The Cruel Herd's new musical arranger is Moral Vacuum's musical arranger, the two bands' music should be even more similar.

B.   No. This doesn't make The Cruel Herd sound more like Moral Vacuum.

C. No. This is too general. We don't know that these clubs are popular with Jackie.

D. No. This doesn't make The Cruel Herd sound more like Moral Vacuum.

E. No. This weakens the argument. If Jackie likes the somber and political Moral Vacuum lyrics, then she might not like the witty lyrics of The Cruel Herd.

7. **A** Inference

Connect the facts. Economically feasible → superconducts above –148°C; ~superconduct above –148°C → ~economically feasible. Superconducts above –148°C → alloy of niobium and germanium; ~ alloy of niobium and germanium → ~superconduct above –148°C. Alloys of niobium and germanium superconduct at –160°C or lower. Therefore, ~superconduct above –148°C → ~economically feasible.

A. Yes. Given the information above, this must be true.

B. No. According to the passage, if anything will superconduct above –148°C, it would have to be an alloy of niobium and germanium.

C. No. We know that, if they are going to be economically feasible at all, they must superconduct above –148°C.

D. No. We don't know this.

E. No. This is too strong. Their use might be economically feasible in other areas besides superconducting.

8. **D** Weaken

The doctor concludes that the evidence suggests that, if it's true that night-lights cause nearsightedness, the effect disappears with age. He cites as evidence the results of three separate studies concerning children who had or had not slept with night-lights as infants. The first study involved children who were younger than those in the other studies, and it was only in the first study that a correlation between sleeping with a night-light and nearsightedness was observed. The doctor's language is very tentative, even in his conclusion, so the weakness of the argument must lie in the studies themselves.

A. No. The doctor doesn't claim that sleeping with a night-light definitely causes nearsightedness.

B. No. The doctor doesn't claim that sleeping with a night-light definitely causes nearsightedness, so this is irrelevant.

C. No. The evidence and conclusion concern the possible correlation between infants sleeping with night-lights and nearsightedness, not older children.

D. Yes. This answer choice attacks the studies themselves. If the sample size is not large enough, the studies can't give enough support to the doctor's claim that, if there is a causal relationship, the effect disappears with time.

E. No. There needs to be more than a few children who are still nearsighted to show anything definitively. These few might be nearsighted for other reasons.

9. **A**

The argument concludes that the leatherback turtle is in danger of extinction, based on evidence about nesting female leatherback turtles. This population of turtles has fallen by more than two-thirds in the past 15 years. Any species whose population declines by that amount in that amount of time is in grave danger of extinction. There needs to be a connection between the statistics for nesting female leatherback turtles and the leatherback turtle population as a whole.

A. Yes. This connects the decline of nesting female leatherback turtles to a similar decline in the leatherback turtle population as a whole.

B. No. This is too strong. The argument never claims that the turtles will actually become extinct.

C. No. This is too general. The argument needs a connection between the numbers of nesting female leatherbacks and the leatherback population as a whole. This compares the numbers of females in general with the number of males.

D. No. The argument doesn't address turtles in captivity.

E. No. The argument doesn't attempt to solve the problem; it just points out the problem.

10. **D** Strengthen

There has been a long-standing campaign to get people to eat more vegetables. However, this campaign has had little impact on what people eat. The offered solution to make the campaign more effective is to include information on ways to make vegetables more appetizing, as the argument claims that the probable reason for the campaign's ineffectiveness is that many people dislike the taste of most vegetables. The answer will strengthen the connection between the campaign's ineffectiveness and people's dislike of most vegetables as they now prepare them.

A. No. This weakens the argument. If it doesn't make people who love vegetables eat more of them, then giving people information about how to make veggies tastier won't make people eat more of them.

B. No. This weakens the argument. The campaign urges people to eat more vegetables in order to help prevent cancer. If eating the vegetables once they have been made more appetizing is less likely to prevent cancer, then the campaign will fail in its ultimate goal.

C. No. This weakens the argument.

D. Yes. If knowing how to make the vegetables more appetizing will cause people to eat more vegetables, then the campaign would likely be more effective if it gave out that information.

E. No. The campaign wants people to eat vegetables in general, not specific kinds of vegetables. If the people who disliked broccoli started to eat more Brussels sprouts and green beans, the campaign would still be more effective than it is now, even if these people never learned to like broccoli.

11. **D** Reasoning

The argument concludes that a society that wants to reap the benefits of pure science ought to use public funds to support such research. The argument defines pure science as research with no immediate commercial or technological application and claims that it is a public good. Because of its nature, pure science needs a lot of monetary support and doesn't make profits in the short term. The argument then eliminates another possible funding avenue for pure science by claiming that private corporations will not fund activities that do not yield short-term profits.

A. No. The claim about private corporations is not the conclusion.

B. No. The claim about private corporations does not help define "pure research."

C. No. The claim about private corporations does not address a different goal.

D. Yes. This claim eliminates another possible funding source for pure science, which benefits the public.

E. No. This claim is not an example, so it doesn't illustrate a case.

12. **C**   **Flaw**

Melinda concludes that hazard insurance decreases an individual's risk. Her evidence is that the risk is judiciously spread among many policyholders. Jack disagrees with Melinda's conclusion. Jack concludes that hazard insurance makes sense but that having, say, fire insurance doesn't seem to decrease the risk of his house burning down. Melinda and Jack are talking about different kinds of risk. Melinda is referring to monetary risk and Jack is referring to the risk of some specific event occurring.

A. No. Jack doesn't address this part of Melinda's argument.

B. No. Jack doesn't address other policyholders. He's just interested in one policyholder: himself.

C. Yes. Jack claims that the risk of his own house burning down won't decrease if he has insurance, while Melinda speaks of the monetary risk that such events tend to bring about.

D. No. Both use this term in the same way.

E. No. Both use this expression in the same way.

13. **A**   **Necessary Assumption**

The author disagrees with the doctors who believe that a specific drug reduces the duration of episodes of vertigo, concluding that the drug has no effect on the duration of vertigo. The author cites the three-month shortage of the drug, during which there was no significant change in the average duration of vertigo, as evidence. The answer choice will indicate the drug's effects would have worn off within three months.

A. Yes. This states that the reduction of duration of vertigo supposedly brought about by the drug would have been at least somewhat reversed in three month's time.

B. No. Some doctors claim that there has been a reduction in the duration of vertigo. This weakens the argument.

C. No. This is close but it doesn't go far enough. If no amount of time would have been good to use in judging whether the drug has an effect on the duration of vertigo, then three months would have been just as ineffective as five years to use in judging this.

D. No. This doesn't address the time period wherein some people had to stop taking the drug.

E. No. This weakens the argument, if anything. If there were other significant factors that decrease the duration of vertigo, then stopping the drug for three months wouldn't necessarily cause an increase in the duration of one's vertigo.

14. **D** `Reasoning`

Some people make an analogy between a television and other kitchen appliances. These people suggest that, since we let market forces determine the design of kitchen appliances, we can let market forces determine what appears on television. The argument disagrees with this conclusion, claiming that this view is too simple, and that some government control is needed. It is too simple because television is a major source of political information and it is also a significant cultural force, as it is on for more than five hours a day in most households.

A. No. This claim supports the argument's conclusion.

B. No. This claim is meant to discredit the claim that a television should be thought of as a "toaster with pictures."

C. No. It does not support the claim about kitchen appliances.

D. Yes. This claim helps support the argument's conclusion against those who think there shouldn't be any governmental control. The claim that the television is on for more than five hours a day in the average home is meant to show that the television is so culturally important.

E. No. The claim that television is the primary medium through which many voters obtain information about current affairs partially supports the claim that television is so politically and culturally important, not the other way around.

15. **B** `Necessary Assumption`

The argument concludes that application of highly alkaline crushed limestone to the soil's surface should make the soil more attractive to earthworms. Decomposition of dead plants makes the top layer of soil highly acidic and earthworms, which are vital to soil's heath, prefer soil that is approximately neutral on the acid-to-alkaline scale.

A. No. This is too strong. Aiding the decomposition of dead plants doesn't have to be the most important function performed by earthworms in order for the conclusion to follow.

B. Yes. If the limestone immediately washed off, it wouldn't have a chance to neutralize the top layer's acidity and so limestone application wouldn't make the soil's surface more attractive to earthworms.

C. No. The argument is focused on the interaction between earthworms and the soil.

D. No. The argument is focused on the interaction between earthworms and the soil.

E. No. The argument is focused on a method to make the soil more neutral, in order to make it more attractive to earthworms. It doesn't discuss which type of non-neutral soil is more likely to benefit from earthworms.

16. **E** `Inference`

Pick the answer best supported by the passage.

A. No. The passage doesn't mention the motivations of the statute-makers.

B. No. The passage claims that, in order to have a sound basis for preferring a given set of laws to any others, laws must be viewed as expressions of a transcendental moral code.

C.   No. The passage suggests that the moral rules have the preferred status, not the laws. Also, the last sentence suggests that moral behavior and compliance with laws are at least sometimes distinguishable.

D.   No. This is too strong. The passage doesn't say that there is no stature that the citizens have a moral obligation to obey.

E.   Yes. If the laws are to be seen as expression of a moral code that has precedence over these laws, and that measures the adequacy of these laws, then there shouldn't be an absolute moral prohibition against the violation of statutes. What if, for example, there was a statute that wasn't in accord with the moral code?

17.   **B**   **Principle Match**

The principle concerns correlation versus causation: that is, that persistent correlation does not conclusively prove a causal relationship because this correlation is often due to a common cause. The answer choice will be an example of this.

A.   No. Supply and inflation are the same phenomenon, which is different from them having a common cause.

B.   Yes. The unhealthy lifestyle is likely the common cause for both high blood pressure and being overweight, so we shouldn't necessarily think that being overweight causes high blood pressure. This is an example of the principle in the passage.

C.   No. This doesn't propose a common cause for ice cream consumption and high crime rates.

D.   No. This doesn't propose a common cause for mood and colors worn.

E.   No. This questions a proposed common cause, claiming that the two languages borrowed from each other instead.

18.   **B**   **Flaw**

This is diagrammable. Conclusion: successful salesperson → been in sales for at least three years. Evidence: successful salesperson → establish a strong client base; at least three years developing a client base → eventually make a comfortable living in sales. The argument is confusing something that is sufficient for being a successful salesperson with something that is necessary for being a successful salesperson.

A.   No. The evidence states that they will eventually be successful in sales.

B.   Yes. The argument claims that successful salespeople must have spent at least three years in sales, while the evidence states that, if salespeople spend at least three years in sales, they will eventually make a comfortable living in sales. It is confusing something that is sufficient for being successful in sales with something that is necessary for being successful in sales.

C.   No. This is the contrapositive of the conclusion.

D.   No. The argument claims that salespeople need to spend at least three years in sales, so it allows for the fact that it might take longer than three years to develop a strong client base.

E.   No. The argument doesn't make any claims as to how many salespeople are able to do this.

19. **A** Parallel

The argument concludes that most people who sleep less than six hours a night can probably cause their anxiety levels to fall by beginning to sleep at least eight hours a night. The evidence is a correlation between a drop in anxiety levels of people who have habitually slept less than six hours a night but who start sleeping eight or more hours a night.

A. Yes. This concludes that most small companies that have never advertised on the Internet can probably improve their financial situation by advertising on it. The evidence is a correlation between an improvement in finances and small companies who haven't previously advertised on the Internet starting to do so.

B. No. This is too strong. This concludes that most small companies can probably improve their financial situations by advertising on the Internet, on the basis of evidence that certain small companies improved their financial situations by doing so.

C. No. This is too strong. This concludes that it must be true that any small company that increases Internet advertising will improve its financial situation. The above argument doesn't claim that all people will decrease their anxiety.

D. No. This claims that it is necessary for a small company to start to advertise on the Internet in order to improve their financial situation. The above argument claims that starting to sleep more than eight hours a night is sufficient for a reduction in anxiety.

E. No. This is too strong. This concludes that most small companies that have never advertised on the Internet but start doing so could probably become financially strong. The above argument claims that people's anxiety levels might drop, not that they will become anxiety-free.

20. **C** Assumption Sufficient

The biologist concludes that paleontologists cannot reasonably infer that extinct predatory animals hunted in packs, solely on the basis of skeletal anatomy. The biologist cites the differences between the hunting patterns of lions and tigers, whose skeletons are virtually indistinguishable. Tigers hunt alone, while lions hunt in packs. The credited response will strengthen the analogy between tigers and lions, on the one hand, and the skeletons of extinct predatory animals, on the other.

A. No. The skeletons themselves don't need to be similar. The important part of the analogy is the similarity in the skeletons of creatures and their difference in hunting habits.

B. No. This doesn't address the difference in hunting habits.

C. Yes. The biologist claims that skeletal anatomy alone is an inadequate basis for inferring the hunting behavior of tigers and lions. So, given this answer choice, it is not reasonable to infer that extinct predatory animals hunted in packs, based on skeletal anatomy alone.

D. No. According to the argument, lions and tigers have virtually indistinguishable anatomy. Plus, the argument makes a claim about hunting behaviors based on skeletal anatomy, not the other way around.

E. No. Lions and tigers are not extinct. Also, the argument makes a claim about hunting behaviors based on skeletal anatomy, not the other way around.

21. **A** `Parallel Flaw`

This argument is diagrammable. April rainfall exceeds 5 centimeters → trees blossom in May; ~trees blossom in May → ~April rainfall exceeds 5 centimeters. April rainfall exceeds 5 centimeters → reservoirs full on May 1; ~reservoirs full on May 1 → ~April rainfall exceeds 5 centimeters. Conclusion: ~reservoirs full on May 1 → ~trees blossom in May. The conclusion claims that the reservoirs not being full on May 1 is sufficient to know that the trees will not blossom in May, while the evidence does not support this claim. The argument doesn't flip the terms in the contrapositive of the first premise.

A. Yes. Garlic in pantry → still fresh; → ~still fresh ~garlic in pantry. Garlic in pantry → potatoes on basement stairs; ~potatoes on stairs → ~garlic in pantry. Conclusion: ~potatoes on stairs → ~garlic still fresh.

B. No. Held over burner for two minutes → optimal temperature; ~optimal temperature → ~held over burner for two minutes. Optimal temperature contents liquefy immediately; ~liquefy immediately → ~optimal temperature. Conclusion: held over burner for two minutes → liquefied immediately. This argument is not flawed.

C. No. More than 200 years old → classified "special"; ~classified "special" → ~more than 200 years old. Set with wooden type → more than 200 years old; ~more than 200 years old → ~set with wooden type. Conclusion: ~classified "special" → ~printed with wooden type. This argument is not flawed.

D. No. Mower operates → ~engine flooded; engine flooded → ~mower operates. Foot pedal depressed → engine flooded; → ~engine flooded ~foot pedal depressed. Conclusion: ~foot pedal depressed mower operates. This argument is flawed, but not in the same manner as the original argument.

E. No. Kiln too hot → plates crack; ~plates crack → ~kiln too hot. Plates crack → redo; → ~redo ~plates crack. Conclusion: ~redo → ~kiln too hot. This argument is not flawed.

22. **E** `Flaw`

The doctor concludes that being slightly overweight is sufficient to be healthy. The doctor cites recent research that conclusively shows that people who are slightly overweight are healthier than those who are considerably underweight. He bases an absolute—being healthy—on a comparison: which of two groups of people is healthier.

A. No. The doctor acknowledges the previous medical opinions to the contrary but thinks that the new evidence supports his own conclusion.

B. No. This is never the credited response.

C. No. The doctor never discusses absolute numbers in terms of people's weights.

D. No. The doctor never discusses a property that would be sufficient to make people unhealthy.

E. Yes. Being healthier is a merely relative property, while being healthy is an absolute property.

23. **D** [Necessary Assumption]

The argument solves a problem with killing insects with pesticides. Using pesticides does not address the underlying problem of weaker plants being more vulnerable to damage caused by insect attacks. This is because insects tend to feed on weaker plants, while more robust plants are less likely to be attacked in the first place. More robust plants are also more likely to withstand insects' attacks more successfully. Instead of using pesticides, the argument concludes that a better way to reduce the vulnerability of crops to insect damage is to grow the crops in good soil. The credited response will close the gap between robust plants and growing plants in good soil.

A. No. This doesn't address the robustness of the plants.

B. No. This is too strong. The argument claims that growing crops in good soil will reduce the damage, not eliminate it.

C. No. This is too strong. The argument claims that growing crops in good soil is a better way to reduce the damage. The pesticides just need to be less effective than growing crops in good soil.

D. Yes. This connects growing crops in good soil to their increased robustness.

E. No. This would weaken the argument, as the argument advocates growing crops in good soil as opposed to using pesticides.

24. **D** [Resolve/Explain]

Fact 1: People perceive color by means of certain photopigments in the retina that are sensitive to certain wavelengths of light. Fact 2: Of people who easily distinguish between red and green, 10 to 20 percent in a certain study failed to report distinctions between many shades of red that most subjects were able to distinguish.

A. No. This would explain why 10 to 20 percent could distinguish between red and green, but didn't report distinctions between many shades of red.

B. No. This would explain why 10 to 20 percent failed to report distinctions. They might not have understood the questions.

C. No. This would explain why 10 to 20 percent failed to report distinctions. They could potentially see them but they just failed to notice them because they don't care.

D. Yes. The people in the study were easily able to distinguish red from green, so this evidence doesn't help explain the result of the study.

E. No. This would explain why 10 to 20 percent failed to report distinctions. They might not have had the vocabulary to report such distinctions.

25. **B** [Flaw]

The occultist concludes that astrology is both an art and a science. To create an astrological chart, complicated mathematics and astronomical knowledge are needed, which are scientific components. The synthesis of a multitude of factors and symbols into a coherent statement is the art component. The occultist is making a part-whole mistake. That the parts have certain qualities does not mean that the whole has these qualities.

A. No. The occultist doesn't address all sciences.

B. Yes. The occultist claims that astrology is a science because it has scientific components.

C. No. The occultist doesn't claim that the components cited are the only components of astrology.

D. No. The occultist doesn't claim that astronomical knowledge is scientific just because it is used to create an astrological chart. The occultist states from the onset that astronomical knowledge is scientific.

E. No. The occultist doesn't address all arts.

Section 2: Games

Questions 1 - 5

This is a group game with fixed assignments and a distribution component. The three agencies—F, P, and S—form the core of the diagram and the performers—T, W, X, Y, and Z—are the elements. From the setup, you know that each agency must sign at least one performer and each performer signs with exactly one agency.

Clue 1: X = F. Mark this in your diagram.

Clue 2: ⬛X̷Y̷

Clue 3: Z Y

Clue 4: $T_s \rightarrow W_s$
 $\sim W_s \rightarrow \sim T_s$

Deductions: Combine clues 2 and 3 to see that X and Z can never be together. Then combine this information with clues 1 and 2 to see that neither Y nor Z can sign with F. Combine clues 1, 3, and 4 with the information that each agency must sign at least one performer. If T signs with S, then W must sign with S. You know from clue 1 that X signs with F. Z and Y sign with the same agency, and each agency must sign at least one performer. So, if T signs with S, then Z and Y must sign with P; otherwise, P wouldn't have any performers. From this information, you can see that S can sign at most three performers. Since neither Y nor Z can sign with F, and they have to sign together, and each agency must sign at least one performer, F can sign at most two performers. P can sign at most three performers.

Here's the diagram:

```
                  ~Y
                  ~Z
      TWXYZ    F  |  P  |  S
               X  |  -  |  -
                  |     |
                  |     |
                  |     |
```

1. **B** `Grab-a-Rule`

   Clue 1 eliminates (D). Clue 2 eliminates (E). Clue 3 eliminates (C). Because T signs with S, (A) violates clue 4, leaving (B) as the credited response.

2. **A** `General`

   Clue 4 eliminates (B) because then T alone would have to sign with S. Clues 2 and 3 eliminate (C). Clue 3 eliminates (D). Your deductions eliminate (E), leaving (A) as the credited response.

3. **B** `General`

   From your deductions, you know that (B) is the credited response.

4. **B** `General`

   You have the most information about the performers if T signs with S, so start with (B). If T signs with S, you know that W must sign with S. X signs with F, as per clue 1. From clue 3, you know that Z and Y must sign together. Since each agency must sign at least one performer, Z and Y must sign with P. All the performers have been assigned to agencies; therefore, (B) is the credited response.

   ~Y
   ~Z

F	P	S
X	ZY	TW

5. **C** `Specific`

   Place Z in S. From clue 3, Y must also sign with S; from clue 1, X signs with F. If T also signs with S, then W would have to sign with S, leaving no performers to sign with P. So, you know that T cannot sign with S. So, (C) must be false, making it the credited response.

   ~Y
   ~Z

F	P	S
X	—	ZY

Questions 6–11

This is an order game with 1:1 correspondence between spaces and elements. Place architects G, J, L, M, P, and V in order from 1 to 6.

Clue 1: P—M—L

Clue 2: G—J or L—G; not L—G—J

Clue 3: V—G or P—V; not P—V—G

Deductions: From clue 1, you see that neither L nor M can be in 1 and L cannot be in 2. Also from clue 1, you see that neither P nor M can be in 6 and P cannot be in 5. According to clue 2, G must either be before or after both L and J. And according to clue 3, V must be before or after both P and G.

Here's the diagram:

```
                  ~L                  ~P
                  ~M   ~L        ~P   ~M
        GJLMPV   1 │ 2 │ 3 │ 4 │ 5 │ 6
                  ──┼───┼───┼───┼───┼──
                    │   │   │   │   │
                    │   │   │   │   │
```

6. **C**   Grab-a-Rule

Games Clue 1 eliminates (B) and (E). Clue 2 eliminates (A). Clue 3 eliminates (D), leaving (C) as the credited response.

7. **A**   General

From your deductions, you know that M cannot be either first or sixth, making (A) the credited response.

8. **A**   Specific

Place L in 6. From clue 2, you know that you must have G—J, making (A) the credited response.

```
             ~L                  ~P
             ~M   ~L        ~P   ~M
            1 │ 2 │ 3 │ 4 │ 5 │ 6
            ──┼───┼───┼───┼───┼──
              │   │   │   │   │  L   G—J
              │   │   │   │   │
```

9. **D**   Specific

Combining the question stem with clue 1, we know that J—M and P—M—L. This means that the earliest M can be presented is 3 and the earliest L can be presented is 4. The latest that P and J can be presented is 4. J cannot be presented fifth, which makes (D) the credited response.

```
   ~L                      ~P
   ~M    ~L           ~P    ~M
 ┌──┬──┬──┬──┬──┬──┐
   1   2   3   4   5   6
 ├──┼──┼──┼──┼──┼──┤
                   ~J   ~J   P—M—L
                    J
```

10. **C**   General

From your deductions, you know that neither M nor L can be first. M is not an option, which makes (C) the credited response.

11. **B**   General

Make sure to place the other architects to ensure that a clue is not being violated, as these are only partial lists of architects in the order their designs are presented.

A. No. From your deductions, M cannot be first.

B. Yes.

```
   ~L                      ~P
   ~M    ~L           ~P    ~M
 ┌──┬──┬──┬──┬──┬──┐
   1   2   3   4   5   6
 ├──┼──┼──┼──┼──┼──┤
   V   G   P   J   M   L
```

C. No. From clue 2, you must have either G—J or L—G, but not both. J is sixth and G is fifth, which would result in L—G—J.

D. No. P is fourth and L is fifth, which would violate clue 1, as there is no room for M.

E. No. From clue 3, you must have either V—G or P—V, but not both. V is fourth and G is fifth, which would mean that P would have to be sixth. But L is sixth, so this choice violates clue 3.

Questions 12–17

Place suspects S, T, V, W, X, Y, and Z in order from 1 to 7. In addition, you are determining whether or not the suspects confessed when they were being questioned.

Clue 1: T = 3. Mark this in your diagram.

Clue 2: 4 = no. Mark this in your diagram.

Clue 3: W—S

Clue 4: Z—X; Z—V

Clue 5: W—all no

Clue 6: 2 out of the 4 suspects after T confessed.

Deductions: From clues 5 and 6, you know that W can't be questioned before T. In fact, from clues 3, 4, 5, and 6, you know that W must be questioned sixth and S must be questioned seventh. If W were questioned earlier, there wouldn't be enough people confessing to satisfy clue 6 because the fourth suspect does not confess. From clues 2, 5, and 6, you know that W must confess and S must not confess. The fifth suspect must also confess. From clue 4, you can see that Z must be questioned either first or second. Also from clue 4, you can see that neither X nor V can be questioned first, which means that either Z or Y must be questioned first.

Here's the diagram:

Suspects: STVWXYZ
confess: yes/no

	Z						
	1	2	3	4	5	6	7
S:	Z/Y		T			W	S
c:				no	yes	yes	no

12. **B** [General]

From your deductions, you can eliminate (A), (C), (D), and (E), which leaves (B) as the only answer choice that could be true.

13. **E** [Specific]

If Z was the second suspect to confess, that means that Z cannot be questioned first. From your deductions, you know that Z must be in either 1 or 2, which means that Z is in 2. From the question stem, you know that Z is the second suspect to confess, which means that both Z and the suspect questioned first must have confessed. From your deductions, you know that only Z or Y can be questioned first, which means that Y is in 1 and Y confessed. Choice (E) must then be false and is, therefore, the credited response.

	Z						
	1	2	3	4	5	6	7
S:	Y	Z	T			W	S
c:	yes	yes		no	yes	yes	no

14. **A** [Specific]

Combining the information in the question stem with clue 4, you get Z—V—Y—X. Combining this information with your deductions, you can see that the order is completely determined. Z is in 1, V is in 2, T is in 3 (clue 1), Y is in 4, X is in 5, W is in 6, and S is in 7. From clue 2, Y must not have confessed. From your deductions, you can see that X must have confessed, as the person interviewed fifth must have confessed. We don't know whether Z, V, or T confessed. This information eliminates (B), (C), (D), and (E), leaving (A) as the only choice that could be true.

Z
/\
1 2

	1	2	3	4	5	6	7
S:	Z	V	T	Y	X	W	S
c:				no	yes	yes	no

15. E **General**

From your deductions, you know that Z must be questioned either first or second, so it must be questioned before T. This makes (E) the credited response.

16. A **Specific**

Both X and Y confessed. So, from clue 2, neither X nor Y could be questioned fourth. T is in 3, W is in 6, S is in 7, and Z is in 1 or 2, which means that V must be questioned fourth. Therefore, V cannot have confessed. This makes (A) the credited response.

Z
/\
1 2

	1	2	3	4	5	6	7
S:	Z/Y		T	V		W	S
c:				no	yes	yes	no

17. D **Specific**

Neither X nor V confessed. So, from your deductions, neither X nor V could be questioned fifth. T is in 3, W is in 6, S is in 7, and Z is in 1 or 2, which means that Y must be questioned fifth. Therefore, Y must have confessed, which makes (D) the credited response.

Z
/\
1 2

	1	2	3	4	5	6	7
S:	Z		T		Y	W	S
c:				no	yes	yes	no

Questions 18–23

Rank teams F, G, and H from 1 to 3. Each team has exactly two of m, n, o, p, s, and t as members. Make two slots for each of the members.

Clue 1:

Clue 2: t = 2. Mark this in your diagram.

Clue 3:

Clue 4: p—n

Clue 5: G—H

Deductions: From clue 4, you can see that n cannot be in 1 and p cannot be in 3. From clue 5, you can see that H cannot be in 1 and G cannot be in 3. From clues 5 and 1, you can see that s cannot be in 3. There are no restrictions for o and no restrictions for F.

Here's the diagram:

```
                                      ~p
                          ~n          ~G
     Teams: FGH           ~H          ~s
     members: mnopst    ┌──┬──┬──┐
                         1  │ 2 │ 3
                       ──────────────
                   T:   –    –    –
                   m:   –    t    –
                        –    –    –
```

18. **E**   **Grab-a-Rule**

Clue 2 eliminates (A). Clue 3 eliminates (B). Clue 4 eliminates (C). From your deductions, you know that s cannot be in 3, which eliminates (D). This leaves (E) as the credited response.

19. **A**   **Specific**

H and p must be together. Combining this info with clues 4 and 5, you know H and p must be in 2. So, the second-place team is H, p, and t (from clue 2). From clue 4, n must be in 3. From clue 5, G and s must be in 1. This makes F the third-place team. o and m are in either 1 or 3. Since o could be on the first-place team, (A) is the credited response.

```
                                    ~p
                    ~n              ~G
                    ~H              ~s
                    1      2       3
               T:   G      H       F
               m:   s      t       n
                    o/m    p       m/o
```

20. B   Specific

Place o in 2. From clue 2, the team members of the second-place team are t and o. From clues 1 and 5, G and s must be in 1. From clue 4, p must also be in 1. This leaves n and m to be the two members of the third-place team. F and H are in either 2 or 3. Since n is on the third-place team and F could be the third-place team, (B) is the credited response.

```
                                    ~p
                    ~n              ~G
                    ~H              ~s
                    1      2       3
               T:   G      F/H     H/F
               m:   s      t       n
                    p      o       m
```

21. C   Specific

If t and p are teammates, then they are the two members of the second-place team. From clue 4, you can see that n must be in 3. From clues 1 and 5, you know that G and s must be in 1. You don't know where, precisely, m and o must be; they could go in either 1 or 3. You definitely know where 4 of the individuals are placed, which makes (C) the credited response.

```
                                    ~p
                    ~n              ~G
                    ~H              ~s
                    1      2       3
               T:   G      _       _
               m:   s      t       n
                    m/o    p       o/m
```

22. E   Specific

According to the question stem, m places higher than H. So, m could be on the second-place team and H could be the third-place team, or m could be on the first-place team. Try both. If m is on the second-place team, H is on the third-place team. From clues 1 and 2, the second-place team would be Ftm, as

G would have to be on the first-place team. From clues 1 and 4, s and p would also be on the first-place team. This leaves n and o to be on H. If, however, m is on the first-place team, from clues 2 and 4, t and p would be the members of the second-place team. From clues 1 and 5, Gsm would be in 1. This leaves n and o to be the members of the third-place team.

$$
\begin{array}{c}
\quad\sim p \\
\sim n\quad\sim G \\
\sim H\quad\sim s \\
\end{array}
$$

	1	2	3
T:	G	F	H
	s	t	n
	p	m	o
m:	G	t	n
	m	p	o
	s		

A.   No. F doesn't place first in either possibility.

B.   No. G places first in both possibilities.

C.   No. n places third in both possibilities.

D.   No. o places third in both possibilities.

E.   Yes. In the first possibility, p places first.

23.   **B**   [General]

The question asks for someone who couldn't be with s, so use information from previous questions to eliminate answer choices. In question 22, m is with s in the second possibility, which eliminates (A). Also in question 22, p is with s in the first possibility, which eliminates (D). In question 19, o could have been with s because either m or o could have been in 1 with s, which eliminates (C). This leaves (B) and (E), neither of which you've seen. Try (B). If n is with s, then they would have to be on the second-place team, from your deductions and clue 4. But, from clue 2, you know that t is on the second-place team. From the setup, you know that each team has exactly two members. So, n and s cannot be together, which means (B) is the credited response.

Section 3: Arguments 2

1.   **A**   [Strengthen]

The argument concludes that consumers are generally better off not buying the extended warranties that are offered for sale at many electronics stores. While these warranties extend beyond the manufacturer's warranty, most problems with electronic goods occur within the span of time covered by the manufacturer's warranty. The credited response will eliminate any other reasons—such as cost—that would make the warranties worthwhile for customers.

A. Yes. If the extended warranty is more expensive than the cost to fix the problems the electronic goods are likely to have, then there seems to be no good reason to buy the warranty.

B. No. This weakens the argument, if anything. If the warranties are generally inexpensive, they might be worthwhile to buy, just in case your electronics do have a problem after the manufacturer's warranty expires.

C. No. This is irrelevant.

D. No. This is irrelevant.

E. No. The reason that retail stores sell the warranties doesn't matter.

2. **C**   **Flaw**

The argument concludes that more environmental regulations are not the solution to the environment's problems. This is because, as environmentalists insist, the condition of the environment is worsening, even though environmentalists have been successful in convincing legislators to enact extensive environmental regulations. However, there is no evidence to suggest that these regulations have had no effect; perhaps the condition of the environment is not as bad as it would have been had there been no environmental regulations.

A. No. There is no personal attack.

B. No. This is too strong. The argument maintains that the environmental regulations are not the solution to the problem, but it never claims that the prevention of environmental degradation requires the absence of environmental regulations.

C. Yes. It is certainly possible that the environment would have worsened even more than it did without environmental regulations.

D. No. The importance of reducing regulations versus the importance of the environment is not discussed.

E. No. The argument's author is an opponent of the environmentalists.

3. **E**   **Main Point**

The argument concludes that there are ways in which it makes sense to talk about musical knowledge growing over time. While it is not advocating a developmental view of music, the argument claims that we certainly know more about how to effectively use certain sounds that earlier composers avoided in musical compositions. An example is the interval of the third.

A. No. There were sounds that were avoided, but the argument doesn't discuss sounds that were never used.

B. No. The argument doesn't claim anything about what is more pleasing to modern listeners.

C. No. This is a qualifier to the conclusion but not the conclusion itself.

D. No. The argument doesn't discuss all value judgments in music.

E. Yes. This is a restatement of the main point.

4. **A** Weaken

The argument interprets the evidence concerning the electric insect control device to indicate that this type of electric insect control device may kill many insects but will not significantly aid in controlling the potentially dangerous mosquito population. The evidence is that, during a 24-hour period, the device killed more than 300 insects but killed only 12 mosquitoes. The argument is overlooking the fact that the actual number of mosquitoes killed might not indicate effectiveness against mosquitoes as well as the percentage of mosquitoes killed. The credited response will widen this gap.

A. Yes. If the device killed all of the mosquitoes present in the area, then it is highly effective at killing mosquitoes. The small number killed just means that there weren't many mosquitoes in the area during that 24-hour period.

B. No. The proportion of insects attracted to the device is not relevant.

C. No. This strengthens the argument, if anything. If it is less likely to kill harmful insects, then it will be less likely to kill the potentially harmful mosquitoes.

D. No. This strengthens the argument. If the device kills a lot of mosquito-eating insects, then there will be less of them to help control the mosquitoes.

E. No. This is irrelevant. The argument is concerned specifically with the mosquitoes.

5. **E** Main Point

Connecting the first two sentences of the argument results in the main point. Brain-scanning technology provides information about brain processes but only if researchers can rely on the accuracy of the verbal reports given by the subjects while the scan is going on. If the reports are inaccurate, the data might not contain information about the thoughts reported.

A. No. The argument does not make claims about the likelihood of the technology enabling researchers to understand how the brain enables us to think.

B. No. This raises a potential problem concerning the accuracy of the reports, but it is not the conclusion of the argument.

C. No. The argument does not make claims about how skeptically we should regard the results of brain-scanning research.

D. No. The argument never states this.

E. Yes. This is a restatement of the first two sentences of the argument, where the point of the argument is located.

6. **D** Flaw

The ornithologist disagrees with those who think that a certain bird species subsists primarily on vegetation. The ornithologist estimates that over half of what these birds eat consists of insects and other animal food sources. The ornithologist bases this claim on the observation of hundreds of these birds every morning while concealed in a well-camouflaged blind. The ornithologist has observed the birds at the same time every day. If someone did that to humans, isn't it likely that they would conclude that humans primarily subsist on breakfast cereal and orange juice?

A. No. The ornithologist mentions that he/she was concealed in a well-camouflaged blind.

B.   No. This doesn't matter. As long as they were animal food sources, they support the ornithologist's conclusion.

C.   No. The ornithologist does not adopt a widespread belief; he actually looks to counter one with his own research.

D.   Yes. The ornithologist observed the birds only in the morning. The birds might eat a lot of animals in the morning and then eat exclusively vegetation throughout the rest of the day.

E.   No. The belief cited is about what the birds do eat, not what they have eaten in the past.

7.   A   **Main Point**

The first statement is diagrammable. Students can successfully learn a topic genuinely → curious about the topic; ~genuinely curious → ~successfully learn. Almost no child starts out curious enough about all the topics that a teacher must instill. The argument is structured to conclude something about teachers needing to make students genuinely curious about all of the topics that the students need to successfully learn.

A.   Yes. In order to ensure that students will successfully learn all of the topics that they need to learn, a teacher must make students genuinely curious about those topics for which they hadn't previously developed a sufficient level of curiosity.

B.   No. The evidence does not discuss how rewards relate to curiosity.

C.   No. The argument is making a connection between the teacher's job and the students' curiosity. Focusing on these topics won't ensure that they'll become curious enough to successfully learn these topics.

D.   No. The evidence does not discuss what the students' responsibilities are.

E.   No. The argument connects genuine curiosity and enjoyment of learning.

8.   A   **Necessary Assumption**

The environmentalist argues that the common practice of converting landfills into public parks is damaging human health. The environmentalist cites the fact that household cleaning products are often found in landfills; when bacteria degrade these cleaning products, toxic vapors are produced. There is a gap between damaging human health by converting landfills to public parks and whether, in these landfills, bacteria are actually degrading the cleaning products.

A.   Yes. This makes a connection between the converted landfills and the bacteria that degrade the products, thereby causing toxic vapors to be emitted.

B.   No. This doesn't state that there are bacteria in these converted landfills that will degrade the cleaning products.

C.   No. This doesn't state that there are bacteria in these converted landfills that will degrade the cleaning products.

D.   No. This would weaken the argument. If people weren't exposed to these vapors, the converted landfills wouldn't necessarily be damaging to human health.

E.   No. This is too general. The environmentalist is arguing specifically about the practice of converting landfills into public parks, not about landfills in general.

9. **E** **Weaken**

The argument concludes that regular consumption of camellia tea can result in a heightened risk of kidney damage. This is because studies show that regular drinkers of camellia tea are more likely than people in general to develop kidney damage. The argument is treating a correlation as if one event causes the other. It is overlooking another possible cause for the increased risk of kidney damage.

A. No. The argument is concerned with camellia tea and the risk of kidney damage associated with drinking it, not other popular beverages.

B. No. This is too general. The argument is concerned with the chemicals in camellia tea, not addictive chemicals in general.

C. No. The argument doesn't mention stress levels.

D. No. This doesn't go far enough. As long as more people who regularly drink camellia tea develop kidney damage than those who do not, the conclusion may still hold.

E. Yes. This presents another possible cause for the kidney damage, which makes it less probable that it is the tea that is causing the greater incidence of kidney damage.

10. **B** **Reasoning**

The artist disagrees with those art collectors who claim that an avant-garde work that becomes popular in its own time is successful. Instead, the artist argues that when an avant-garde work becomes popular, it is a sign that the work is not successful. This is because avant-garde artists intend their work to challenge a society's mainstream beliefs and initiate change, and a society's mainstream beliefs do not generally show any significant change over a short period of time.

A. No. The artist argues against these art collectors.

B. Yes. The artist brings up the claims of these art collectors in order to dispute them.

C. No. The premise about the avant-garde artists' intentions does not support the claims of these art collectors.

D. No. The claims of these art collectors do not provide support for the premise about the avant-garde artists' intentions.

E. No. The claims of the art collectors are not part of a counterargument.

11. **C** **Strengthen**

The argument concludes that it is likely that the stresses felt more commonly while traveling cause the insomnia of businesspeople who travel internationally on business. These businesspeople are much more likely to suffer from chronic insomnia than are the businesspeople who don't travel for business. The businesspeople who travel internationally on business frequently experience stresses that are not commonly felt by those who do not travel.

A. No. The argument discusses international travel in general. It doesn't matter whether the borders of the countries visited are contiguous or not.

B. No. This would weaken the argument, if anything. If some businesspeople who travel greatly enjoy the changes in climate and immersion in another culture, then these are not stresses for them.

C. Yes. This eliminates the possibility that there is another reason for the increased insomnia in businesspeople who must travel internationally.

D. No. This would weaken the argument, as it suggests that the changes and disruptions may ameliorate insomnia instead of cause it.

E. No. The argument is concerned with businesspeople who are currently traveling internationally, not those who once did.

12. **B** Principle Strengthen

The argument advocates against climbers trying to climb Mount Everest because the risk of death or injury is very high, and the climb does not seem to actually enable one to gain "spiritual discovery."

A. No. The argument doesn't state that climbing Mount Everest is undertaken primarily for spiritual reasons.

B. Yes. The argument highlights the fact that climbing Mount Everest is dangerous and that climbing Mount Everest is unlikely to result in significant spiritual benefits. This principle would thereby help justify the conclusion that climbers should not attempt the climb.

C. No. The argument doesn't claim that climbing Mount Everest should be legally prohibited.

D. No. The argument doesn't claim that there are other ways to achieve profound spiritual experiences.

E. No. This isn't strong enough. The principle needs to justify the conclusion that mountain climbers should not try to climb Mount Everest.

13. **B** Parallel Flaw

The argument concludes that the universe has an elegantly simple structure, on the basis of evidence that each of the smallest particles in the universe has an elegantly simple structure and that these particles compose the universe. The argument exhibits a part-whole flaw.

A. No. This argument claims that the car is nearly perfectly engineered, on the basis of a characteristic of its parts. This does exhibit the same flaw.

B. Yes. While this argument makes a claim about the desk as a whole on the basis of its parts, it is warranted to do so. If all the parts of the desk are made of metal, then the desk must be made of metal.

C. No. This argument claims that the wall is rectangular because its parts are. However, bricks can make walls of all shapes. So, this exhibits the same flaw.

D. No. This argument claims that the chair is sturdy because all of its parts are. Yet, the chair could be poorly glued or poorly constructed in some other way. So, this exhibits the same flaw.

E. No. The novel might consist of well-constructed sentences but the sentences might not form good prose. So, this exhibits the same flaw.

14. **A** Weaken

The criminologist concludes that a judicial system that tries and punishes criminals without delay is an effective deterrent to violent crime. If potential violent criminals know that being caught means quick punishment, they will hesitate to break the law, whereas long, drawn-out trials may add to criminals' feelings of invulnerability.

A. Yes. If potential violent criminals don't think about their crimes, then they won't be deterred by the prompt punishment.

B. No. This doesn't claim that innocent people actually get convicted, just that some innocent people get arrested for a crime.

C. No. The number of offenses committed by violent criminals doesn't matter.

D. No. This is too general. The argument is allowing for trials.

E. No. This strengthens the argument, as it shows a correlation between prompt punishment and a relatively lower crime rate.

15. **E**   **Necessary Assumption**

The journalist argues against those people who object to mandatory retirement at age 65. The journalist gives two reasons for this. First, the young will become dissatisfied because they won't be able to get decent jobs in the professions for which they were trained. Second, the people over 65 will be depriving others of opportunities and this is not fair.

A. No. The second claim concerns people who have worked 40 or more years.

B. No. The journalist never claims that all young people are highly trained.

C. No. The unfairness that the journalist points out is found in the second reason, while the training was referenced in the first reason.

D. No. The journalist isn't concerned with the feelings of older people.

E. Yes. People might want to retire at 65 anyway. The reasons that the journalist cites for retaining mandatory retirement apply only if at least some people over 65 would still want to work.

16. **B**   **Weaken**

The editorial concludes that teaching preschoolers is not especially difficult. The evidence is that preschoolers develop strict systems that help them to learn and that preschoolers are always intensely curious about new things. The credited response will give another reason to think that, as a result of their tendencies, preschoolers are difficult to teach.

A. No. This strengthens the argument. If preschoolers follow strict routines, they might well be easier to teach.

B. Yes. Since preschoolers are intensely curious about new things, they will have short attention spans. This is a reason to think that teaching preschoolers is difficult.

C. No. The editorial addresses preschoolers, not older children.

D. No. This isn't strong enough. If they ask as many creative questions as do older children, and this doesn't make older children particularly difficult to teach, then the argument's conclusion would still hold.

E. No. This answer choice strengthens the argument. If preschool teachers are reporting lower stress levels, that gives us a reason to think that teaching preschoolers isn't especially difficult.

17. **A**   Flaw

The lawyer concludes that, even if a few items of a body of circumstantial evidence are discredited, the overall body of evidence retains its basic strength. This conclusion is based on the analogy the lawyer makes between a body of circumstantial evidence and a rope. This is a bad analogy because while every strand of the rope is similar, different pieces of a body of circumstantial evidence might be more or less essential to its strength, depending.

A. Yes. This points out the problem with the lawyer's analogy.

B. No. This is the wrong common flaw. The problem in the argument is not a part-whole problem.

C. No. The argument never claims that many items could be discredited and the overall body of evidence would remain strong.

D. No. This is close but the lawyer does indicate similarities between a body of circumstantial evidence and a rope.

E. No. The argument isn't circular.

18. **E**   Principle Match

The ethicist concludes that an argument for preserving nature emphasizing nature's beauty will be less vulnerable to logical objections than one that emphasizes its moral value. This is because it is philosophically disputable whether nature is morally valuable but not disputable that it is beautiful.

A. No. The ethicist wants to change focus as to what makes nature worth preserving. She doesn't want to avoid the issue of what makes nature worth preserving.

B. No. The ethicist does not judge whether the argument that emphasizes the moral value of nature provides a sufficient reason for preserving it.

C. No. The ethicist makes no judgment as to whether nature would be more clearly worth preserving if it didn't have the characteristic of moral worth.

D. No. The ethicist's argument concentrates on the beauty of nature, so this would weaken the thrust of the ethicist's argument.

E. Yes. The ethicist argues that the argument based on natural beauty will be less open to logical objections because everyone agrees that beauty is a characteristic of nature and nature's beauty can be regarded as a basis for preserving nature.

19. **A**   Inference

This is diagrammable. The book will contain essays by Lind, Knight, or Jones but not all three. Contains essay by Knight → contains an essay by Jones. Connecting this with the previous information, contains essay by Knight → contains an essay by Jones and ~contains an essay by Lind. The contrapositive is as follows: contains an essay by Lind or ~contains an essay by Jones → ~contains an essay by Knight.

A.   Yes. This is the contrapositive of the information given in the passage.

B.   No. We know that if it contains one by Knight, it will contain an essay by Jones.

C.   No. We don't know this.

D.   No. We don't know about essays by Jones if the book contains an essay by Lind. The only thing that we know if the book contains an essay by Lind is that it won't contain an essay by Knight.

E.   No. We don't know for sure which essays will be in the book.

20.   **D**   **Necessary Assumption**

The argument concludes that the ability of mammals to control their internal body temperatures is a factor in the development of their brains and intelligence. This conclusion is derived from the facts that the brain is a chemical machine, all chemical reactions are temperature dependent, and any organism that can control this can assure that the reactions occur at the proper temperatures. There is a gap between the evidence, which discusses elements and processes of the brain, and the conclusion, which talks about brains and intelligence.

A.   No. The argument is about organisms that are able to control their body temperatures.

B.   No. This is too strong. Mammals don't have to be the only animals that have the ability to control their internal body temperatures for the conclusion to follow.

C.   No. This is too strong. The argument claims that the ability to control internal body temperatures is a factor; it doesn't need to be the only factor.

D.   Yes. This closes the gap between the proper temperatures of brain processes and intelligence.

E.   No. The argument is about organisms that can control their body temperatures.

21.   **C**   **Inference**

Choose the answer best supported by the passage.

A.   No. The passage does not make any claims about whether the waste should have been initially stored in its current location.

B.   No. The passage claims that the waste should be placed somewhere more secure. It doesn't claim that it should be placed in the most secure location ever.

C.   Yes. The passage claims that keeping the waste at the current location for as long as it takes to find a site certain to contain it safely would pose an unacceptable risk. So, moving the waste would reduce the threat posed.

D.   No. This is too general. The passage discusses a specific instance of moving waste, not all waste moving.

E.   No. This is too strong. The passage does not claim that any site would be safer.

22. **B**

Fact 1: The average number of books read annually per capita has declined in each of the last three years. Fact 2: Most bookstores reported increased profits during this period.

A. No. This would explain why bookstores reported increased profits while the amount read has declined; more people may now buy popular contemporary novels since they can no longer borrow them for free from public libraries.

B. Yes. This does not explain why bookstores reported increased profits during the three-year period. The profits are higher than their own previous profits, not the profits of other stores.

C. No. This would explain where the increase in revenue came from, given that the average amount read has declined.

D. No. If bookstores were making more money per purchase, they could have an increase in profits even though they weren't selling as many books.

E. No. The additional sales from magazines would help explain the bookstores' increased profits, even though the average number of books read by each individual has declined.

23. **D** Parallel

The naturalist concludes that the threats we are creating to woodland species arise from the rate at which we are cutting down trees. Species can survive a change in environment as long as the change is slow enough. So, the change in environment caused by cutting down trees is not by itself causing the threats to woodland species.

A. No. This does not amend the cause of the problem.

B. No. The threat in the first still involved the cutting down of the trees. This argument discards one possibility for another, unrelated one.

C. No. This argument makes a claim about some students. The argument above makes a claim about all species.

D. Yes. This argument claims that the problem isn't from the company's undergoing change, per se, but from the failure to inform employees of what the changes entail.

E. No. This doesn't present an alternative but related reason for the problem.

24. **A** Reasoning

The professor argues that meaningful freedom cannot be measured simply by the number of alternatives available; rather, the extent of the differences among the alternatives is also a relevant factor. He supports his conclusion by the use of an example, in which he compares choosing one of 50 types of cola to choosing from among 5 different types of beverage—wine, coffee, apple juice, milk, and water.

A. Yes. The professor's conclusion is a general principle and the cola versus milk, etc, example supports this principle.

B. No. The conclusion is the general principle.

C. No. There is no analogy. There is an example.

D. No. The professor's argument does not use part-whole reasoning.

E. No. There is only one general principle.

25. **C** [Strengthen]

The principle claims that meetings should be kept short and should address only the issues that are relevant to the majority of the people attending. Moreover, people to whom none of the issues to be addressed are relevant should not have to attend the meeting. The application is that Terry should not be required to attend today's meeting. The credited response will make it clear that none of the issues to be addressed are relevant to Terry, or that the issues that are relevant to Terry won't be relevant to the majority of the attendees.

A. No. The principle doesn't claim that people should come only if they are also presenting.

B. No. This doesn't go far enough. The meetings should be kept short, in the sense that topics not relevant to the majority should not be discussed. But Terry wouldn't necessarily have to make a presentation if he/she attended the meeting.

C. Yes. This supports the application of the principle because, if none of the issues relevant to Terry could be relevant to a majority of those attending the meeting, then the issues relevant to Terry will not be addressed at the meeting. So, Terry should not be required to attend.

D. No. This doesn't make it clear that Terry shouldn't have to go to the meeting. If any of the issues to be addressed are relevant to Terry, he/she might still have to go to the meeting.

E. No. The principle claims that if none of the issues to be addressed are relevant, then a person should not have to attend. If at least one of the issues to be addressed is relevant to Terry, even if the majority of them are not, Terry might still be required to attend.

Section 4: Reading Comprehension

Questions 1–6

The purpose of this passage is to Advocate/Defend. The author critiques the recent work of the Asian American poet Wing Tek Lum, claiming that his book, *Expounding the Doubtful Points*, demands to be understood on its own terms. This is in contrast to most Asian American poetry from Hawaii, which can usually be characterized either as portraying a model multicultural paradise or as exemplifying familiar Asian American themes like generational conflict. In the first paragraph, the author introduces the contrast between most Asian American poetry from Hawaii and the recent work of Wing Tek Lum. In the second paragraph, an example of Lum's poetry is introduced in order to illustrate how, through the presence of immigrants, Lum is able to refer both to the traditional culture of his Chinese homeland and to the flux within Hawaiian society. A laudatory poem to a famous Chinese poet is introduced to illustrate Lum's refusal to offer a stereotypical nostalgia for the past, while still participating in a distinguished literary tradition. In the third paragraph, the author discusses the final poem in Lum's volume. This poem illustrates the complex relationship between heritage and local culture in determining one's identity. In this poem, Lum acknowledges the hope that many immigrants have for their lives in the United States, while cautioning that immigrants should come to terms with the strong cultural emphasis in the United States on individual drive and success so as to form a healthy new sense of identity.

1. **A** [Big Picture]

   A. Yes. The passage highlights how Lum's poetry is striking in its departure from other Asian American poetry from Hawaii. Lum does address his own heritage but combines that with a search for a new local identity.

   B. No. Individual success is addressed only at the end of the last paragraph and only in reference to a caution that Lum raises for immigrants.

   C. No. The passage does not discuss Hawaiian writers in general, only Asian American Hawaiian writers.

   D. No. The poetry of Lum is different from that of other Asian American writers in Hawaii, so it can't illustrate something about Asian American writers in Hawaii as a whole.

   E. No. The author is admiring of Lum's poetry, so the author would not say that Lum's poetry is unsuccessful.

2. **C** [Extract Infer]

   A. No. In the examples cited by the author, Lum does not explain his images in great detail.

   B. No. In the poem cited in the beginning of the second paragraph, Lum addresses how connections to the homeland are necessary but that one needs to have a new sense of family. However, this is only in reference to someone who has, in fact, immigrated. Lum never advocates immigration per se.

   C. Yes. This is exactly what Lum is suggesting in the poem cited in the third paragraph.

   D. No. Lum's poetry attempts to discover and retain a local sensibility while keeping ties to the homeland. This illustrates a dynamic identity, not a static one.

   E. No. Lum says that it's necessary to keep ties to one's homeland in the poem cited at the beginning of the second paragraph.

3. **D** [Structure]

   The author uses the phrase "the flux within Hawaiian society" in order to highlight the continuous changes in that society brought about by the influx of immigrants, which supports (D).

4. **C** [Extract Fact]

   A. No. This is too strong. It is not totally opposed to or against the process of developing a local sensibility.

   B. No. This was a part of the United States' strong cultural emphasis, not a characteristic of Asian American literature from Hawaii.

   C. Yes. This was cited as a characteristic of one of two types of Asian American literature from Hawaii in the first paragraph.

   D. No. This is not discussed in reference to Asian American literature from Hawaii.

   E. No. This is true of Lum's poetry, which is strikingly different from Asian American literature from Hawaii.

5. **D**   `Structure`

The author describes *Expounding the Doubtful Points* as striking in order to emphasize how different Lum's recent work is from the usual Asian American poetry from Hawaii, which supports (D).

6. **D**   `Extract Infer`

A. No. The author does not discuss political ideology at all, so we don't know whether the author would agree with this claim.

B. No. The author does not discuss whether Lum's poetry exhibits appreciation of stylistic contributions, so we don't know whether the author would agree with this claim.

C. No. The culture discussed is exclusively that of Asian Americans in Hawaii, so we don't know whether the author would agree with this claim about people in all cultures.

D. Yes. The author cites this in the discussion of the example in the first part of the second paragraph.

E. No. The author discusses the fact that Lum recognizes the value of tradition, so the author would not claim that Lum's poetry conveys antipathy toward tradition.

Questions 7–14

The purpose of this passage is to Criticize. It concerns the problems with traditional academic study of jurisprudence in England and one legal historian's argument for a change in how jurisprudence is studied. In the first paragraph, the author introduces the topic of common law, which is the basis of the English legal system, and suggests that common law must be understood in a historical context in order to be understood properly. In the second paragraph, the author introduces how academic study of jurisprudence has traditionally regarded common law as static, for the most part, and criticizes this view. The author then gives the reasons for this view of common law, which are partly political and partly theoretical, noting that the political reasons for this view of common law are to prevent the demoralization of the public and the dispiriting of students of the law. In the third paragraph, the author introduces another way to regard common law, attributed to legal historian Peter Goodrich. He argues that common law is most fruitfully studied as a continually developing tradition instead of as a set of rules.

7. **D**   `Big Picture`

A. No. This is too narrow. This is discussed only in the first paragraph.

B. No. The passage claims that both theoretical and political interpretations of common law are, if anything, somewhat similar.

C. No. The academic study of jurisprudence does not treat common law as an oral history of the English people.

D. Yes. This identifies the problem that the author sees with the study of common law, discussed in the first two paragraphs, and mentions the alternative way to regard common law, discussed in the third paragraph.

E. No. This is too narrow and too strong. This topic is discussed only around lines 30–35 and the author never claims that the body of law is actually inconsistent and unfair.

8. **A** Extract
Infer

The author discusses this topic in the second paragraph.

A. Yes. The author criticizes modern jurisprudence's treatment of common law, as it does not acknowledge its history and how that might affect contemporary law.

B. No. The author does not agree that the original forms of common law are irrelevant to modern jurisprudence.

C. No. This is how the academic study of modern jurisprudence views common law, a view with which the author disagrees.

D. No. It's not that they overlook the order and coherence inherent in legal history; it's that they overlook legal history too much.

E. No. This is the opposite of what the author claims at the end of the second paragraph.

9. **C** RC Reasoning

This kind of interpretive theory is one in which common law is either not seen as evolving or rooted in history or, if it is seen as rooted in history, is not seen as making a significant impact on contemporary law.

A. No. This connects modern law with the past, against the interpretive theory discussed at the beginning of the second paragraph.

B. No. This connects modern law with the past, against this interpretive theory.

C. Yes. This acknowledges the history of common law without addressing how it might impact contemporary law.

D. No. This discusses developments that occurred simultaneously, so it isn't relevant to the interpretive theory as stated.

E. No. The theory doesn't discuss civil versus criminal courts.

10. **E** Extract
Infer

Peter Goodrich's theory is discussed in the third paragraph.

A. No. He claims that it should be seen as a continually developing tradition, not a relic.

B. No. He never claims that it is now incoherent.

C. No. The public's beliefs concerning common law are discussed in the second paragraph.

D. No. He believes that it has applicability to modern life. This suggests that it has only a very limited applicability.

E. Yes. He argues that it is a continually developing tradition and that we have to rewrite some of it to adapt common law to contemporary legal circumstances.

11. D `Structure`

The word "political" is used in the second paragraph to discuss the ways in which modern jurisprudence treats common law in order to maintain the efficacy and prestige of the legal system, which supports (D).

12. B `Extract Fact`

The first paragraph of the passage discusses what students of British law are frequently required to study.

A. No. This is not mentioned in the first paragraph.

B. Yes. The passage mentions this in line 5.

C. No. Political philosophy is not mentioned in the first paragraph.

D. No. While the first paragraph does mention archaic Latin maxims, there is no reference anywhere in the passage to histories of ancient Roman jurisprudence.

E. No. Narrative development is mentioned, in a different context, in the final paragraph.

13. B `Extract Infer`

The author criticizes modern academic theories of common law, so the credited response will reflect this.

A. No. The author never claims that most modern academic theories of common law are boring.

B. Yes. The author criticizes them for viewing common law not as evolving and based in history but instead as static.

C. No. The author never claims that practical factors take precedence over theoretical factors in modern academic theories of common law.

D. No. Students have to study past legal disputes, according to the first paragraph. The problem is that they are not taught that these disputes may well influence and affect modern legal disputes.

E. No. The author never claims that modern academic theories of common law treat the study of the law as an art.

14. A `Big Picture`

The author criticizes modern theories of common law and discusses a new interpretation. The credited response will reflect this.

A. Yes. Common law is recognized as coming from history and is the basis for legal decisions, but modern theories of common law don't address its history or this history's relevance to modern law. In the third paragraph, the author introduces Peter Goodrich's new view of the situation.

B. No. The passage is not just a summary. It is, in part, a criticism.

C. No. The only theorist specifically mentioned is Peter Goodrich, and his ideas are not traced through his career.

D.   No. The legal theories discussed are all modern theories.

E.   No. The passage's purpose is the opposite of this.

Questions 15–19

Passage A

The author criticizes the recent tendency to treat research findings as commodities, claiming that this threatens the tradition of collegial sharing of ideas and the role of research as a public good. This is because the market process and values governing commodity exchange are ill suited to the development and revision of new ideas. Businesses are too focused on short-term gains and, because entrepreneurs aren't usually interested in intellectual pursuit for its own sake, they are more likely to buy research and prevent its dissemination to other researchers, thereby tamping down the exchange of ideas.

Passage B

This author is much less critical of the change in the role of science to a market commodity. This passage documents the change and what it means to science. As a result of this change, the assertion of legal claims to intellectual property becomes essential. Also, what counts as discovery—not patentable—and invention—patentable—has become blurred. The author then mentions that industry claims that it should be able to claim as its property any discovery made by those whose research it has supported.

15.   **A**   **Extract Fact**

A.   Yes. Passage A does not discuss the legal aspects of the change in the role of science to a market commodity, while passage B discusses this just after line 55.

B.   No. Both passages discuss the effects of the market on the exchange of scientific knowledge.

C.   No. Both passages discuss this.

D.   No. Neither passage discusses new pharmaceuticals that result from industrial research. Passage B mentions pharmaceuticals but not in the context of industrial research.

E.   No. Both passages discuss industry's practice of restricting access to research findings.

16.   **C**   **Extract Fact**

A.   No. Neither passage discusses commercially unsuccessful research explicitly.

B.   No. These are not placed in opposition in either passage.

C.   Yes. Passage A does this near line 5 and passage B does this in the first sentence of the second paragraph.

D.   No. Only passage B discusses discovery versus invention.

E.   No. Both passages are focused on scientific research and not on other types of inquiry.

17. **D** **Extract Fact**

   A. No. Only passage A refers to theoretical frameworks.

   B. No. Only passage A refers to venture capitalists.

   C. No. Passage A does not refer to either physics or chemistry.

   D. Yes. Passage A refers to this in line 22 and passage B refers to this in line 44.

   E. No. Only passage A refers to shareholders.

18. **C** **Extract Infer**

   A. No. Neither passage mentions the enormous increase in the volume of scientific knowledge being generated.

   B. No. Neither passage discusses the desires of the individual researchers.

   C. Yes. Passage A implies this in the third paragraph, while passage B implies this in the second paragraph.

   D. No. Neither passage discusses moral reservations.

   E. No. Neither passage states that there has been a drastic reduction in government funding.

19. **D** **Extract Infer**

   A. No. Neither passage implies that many scientific researchers have been leaving universities to work in industry.

   B. No. Passage A does not discuss patents and passage B mentions the issues concerning patents without making a judgment.

   C. No. This subject is discussed only in passage B.

   D. Yes. Both passages contrast the new limitations on access to the results of basic research conducted in universities to how it was in the past.

   E. No. Both passages claim that the goals of private industry have only recently become a major motivation for research.

Questions 20–27

The purpose of this passage is to Tell a Story. The author's intent is to inform the reader how to more effectively control an agricultural pest by means of its natural predators, using the cyclamen mite and its predator mite, *Typhlodromus*, as an example. In the first paragraph, the author introduces the subject and the example. In the second paragraph, the author discusses why this predator mite is so effective against cyclamen mites, citing its reproductive cycles and its ability to survive during those times of year when cyclamen mite populations are greatly reduced. These features are stated to be common among predators of agricultural pests in general. In the third paragraph, the author discusses experiments that have verified his/her claims. In the fourth paragraph, the author cites the example as one instance in which using natural predators would be far better than using a pesticide to control an agricultural pest.

20. **C** **Big Picture**

A. No. This is too strong. The passage claims that there are some instances in which pesticides cause more harm but doesn't claim this about all pesticides in all situations.

B. No. The passage does provide experimental verification but never claims that this is essential.

C. Yes. The passage informs the reader that natural predation can be more effective against agricultural pests and uses the relationship between *Typhlodromus* and cyclamen mites as an example of this effectiveness.

D. No. The passage uses the relationship between *Typhlodromus* and cyclamen mites as an example to illustrate its point. This relationship is not the main point of the passage.

E. No. This is too specific. This is discussed only in the second paragraph.

21. **D** **Extract Infer**

The passage discusses the particulars of control of agricultural pests in the second paragraph.

A. No. The passage talks only about seasonal synchrony and doesn't state that the number of predators should surge just prior to a surge in the number of prey.

B. No. The passage mentions demonstration of effectiveness in an experiment but does not claim that this is essential.

C. No. The passage claims that the predator population is able to survive even when the prey population is dormant or has dropped to very low levels.

D. Yes. This is exactly what the passage claims in the first part of the second paragraph.

E. No. The passage is not advocating pesticides as fundamental to long-term predatory control of agricultural pests.

22. **E** **Extract Fact**

The passage discusses this topic in the second paragraph.

A. No. The passage does not discuss *Typhlodromus*'s ability to withstand most insecticides.

B. No. The passage does not discuss the natural predators of *Typhlodromus*.

C. No. The passage does not claim that *Typhlodromus* can live in different climates and regions.

D. No. The passage acknowledges that *Typhlodromus* does not always have a constant supply of cyclamen mites.

E. Yes. The passage claims that *Typhlodromus*'s ability to subsist on the honeydew produced by aphids and white flies when there aren't many cyclamen mites is a feature that makes *Typhlodromus* effective as a predator.

23. **A** RC Reasoning

A. Yes. Parathion killed the predator species but didn't affect the cyclamen mites. Since this pesticide does not affect the predator species, and *Typhlodromus* preys on cyclamen mites, the mites should have been controlled in both treated and untreated plots.

B. No. If there were no *Typhlodromus*, then the cyclamen mite populations of plots in which *Typhlodromus* was absent would likely have been higher than those of the plots in which *Typhlodromus* was preying on the cyclamen mites.

C. No. We don't know this because the key to *Typhlodromus*'s reproductive cycle is that it is faster than that of the cyclamen mites.

D. No. The pesticide does not have any direct effect on *Typhlodromus*.

E. No. We don't know that they would have remained at damaging levels longer in the treated plots.

24. **C** Extract Infer

A. No. The passage never advocates the use of parathion.

B. No. The passage does not discuss the potential impact of predators on beneficial insects.

C. Yes. The passage advocates the use of predators over pesticides when the predators are effective.

D. No. The passage advocates the use of predators over pesticides when the predators are effective.

E. No. The passage does not claim that pesticides generally harm the crops.

25. **D** Structure

The author mentions the egg-laying ability of each kind of mite in order to support the claim that *Typhlodromus* can reproduce at least as quickly as, if not more quickly than, cyclamen mites, which supports (D).

26. **E** RC Reasoning

The author discusses the practical applications in the third and fourth paragraphs.

A. No. This doesn't mention the strawberry plants discussed in the third paragraph.

B. No. This doesn't clearly strengthen his position; we don't know what effect killing both predatory and non-predatory mites would have.

C. No. The passage doesn't mention which climates are preferable to *Typhlodromus*.

D. No. The author is not advocating the use of parathion.

E. Yes. If *Typhlodromus* easily tolerates the same range of climatic conditions that strawberry plants do, then their use in controlling the cyclamen mite population would be as effective in all regions where strawberries are grown.

27. **A**

53

A. Yes. That's exactly what the passage claims in the third paragraph when it states that, in the strawberry fields where there were both cyclamen mites and *Typhlodromus*, the cyclamen mites did not reach damaging levels.

B. No. The passage does not discuss the possibility of cyclamen mites being controlled by another mite species.

C. No. We know from the passage only about its effectiveness in controlling cyclamen mites.

D. No. The passage does not claim that pesticides would be necessary when *Typhlodromus* is relied on to control cyclamen mites in strawberry crops. In the first paragraph, we are told that cyclamen mites do not reach significantly damaging levels until the crops' second year, which suggests that pesticide use before that time would be unnecessary.

E. No. We don't know that strawberry growers have used parathion indiscriminately.

Chapter 4
PrepTest 54:
Answers and
Explanations

ANSWER KEY: PREPTEST 54

Section 1:
Reading
Comprehension

1. A
2. C
3. D
4. D
5. E
6. B
7. E
8. E
9. B
10. B
11. C
12. A
13. C
14. D
15. C
16. E
17. E
18. A
19. A
20. A
21. C
22. C
23. B
24. E
25. E
26. A
27. B

Section 2:
Arguments 1

1. D
2. E
3. A
4. E
5. B
6. C
7. C
8. A
9. A
10. B
11. B
12. D
13. B
14. C
15. E
16. D
17. D
18. C
19. D
20. E
21. A
22. E
23. C
24. A
25. D
26. D

Section 3:
Games

1. C
2. D
3. E
4. C
5. C
6. A
7. A
8. D
9. E
10. D
11. E
12. B
13. A
14. B
15. E
16. B
17. B
18. B
19. A
20. B
21. D
22. C
23. A

Section 4:
Arguments 2

1. E
2. D
3. A
4. D
5. E
6. C
7. D
8. C
9. A
10. D
11. C
12. D
13. A
14. D
15. B
16. A
17. E
18. C
19. B
20. A
21. C
22. B
23. B
24. E
25. C

EXPLANATIONS

Section 1: Reading Comprehension

Questions 1–5

This passage addresses problems created for "traditional legislation and law enforcement" by the international flow of information on the Internet. The first paragraph defines the Internet and states the thesis. The second paragraph explains that a government can enforce control only over something contained within its national borders and it would be forced to enact a restrictive, unpopular policy of denying its citizens access to the Internet if it wanted to prevent or monitor all transmissions. The third paragraph examines the specific difficulties of trying to enforce trademark laws on the Internet. The fourth paragraph discusses the need for regulation regarding Internet transmissions that travel through several jurisdictions.

1. **A**   **Big Picture**

    A.   Yes. It identifies that certain aspects of the Internet make it problematic for existing legal enforcement and regulation.

    B.   No. The passage does not make reference to weakening a government's power over any sort of financial transactions.

    C.   No. This addresses only one sentence at the end of the second paragraph.

    D.   No. The passage never refers to global crime.

    E.   No. The passage never addresses the stability of many nations.

2. **C**   **Structure**

    This paragraph is examining the need for regulation to determine what rights nations have concerning Internet transmissions passing through their borders.

    A.   No. This does not address the purpose of the paragraph.

    B.   No. This does not address the purpose of the paragraph.

    C.   Yes. This is a hypothetical example given so the reader may consider an unresolved regulatory question involving international Internet transmissions.

    D.   No. This paragraph has nothing to do with trademarks.

    E.   No. The origins of the Internet are never discussed.

3. **D**   **Extract Fact**

    The first sentence of the second paragraph states the defining attribute of sovereignty.

    A.   No. Control over business enterprises is not stated.

    B.   No. Authority over communicative exchanges is not stated.

C.   No. Power to regulate trademarks is not stated.

D.   Yes. This is almost the passage's wording verbatim.

E.   No. Authority over all commercial transactions is not stated.

4.   **D**   **Extract Infer**

A.   No. The context in which this word is used suggests no attitude.

B.   No. This relates to the attitude of the "affected citizens."

C.   No. This relates to the attitude of the "affected citizens."

D.   Yes. By using "draconian," the author suggests such a measure would be unthinkably restrictive.

E.   No. The context in which this word is used suggests no attitude.

5.   **E**   **Structure**

A.   No. This paragraph does not question the discussion of sovereignty.

B.   No. Although there is one hypothetical consideration, this paragraph provides no practical illustrations.

C.   No. This paragraph does not summarize but rather moves into a new aspect of the overall topic.

D.   No. This paragraph does not extend the discussion of trademarks.

E.   Yes. By introducing the topic of the need for new regulations to handle issues unique to the Internet, the fourth paragraph extends the thesis from the first paragraph.

Questions 6–12

Passage A

The author provides a general summary of the function, composition, and practical considerations of drilling fluids and drilling muds. The first paragraph explains the function of drilling fluids. The second paragraph identifies common compositions of drilling muds. The third paragraph discusses reasons the composition of some muds may be hard to ascertain.

Passage B

The author discusses drilling muds in the context of their potential environmental hazards. The first paragraph describes the general function and use of drilling mud. The second paragraph describes a relatively harmless mud, water-based mud (WBM). The third paragraph describes a more environmentally damaging mud, oil-based mud (OBM).

6.   **B**   **Big Picture**

A.   No. Passage A does not mention any type of environmental pollution.

B.   Yes. Both passages explain the makeup of drilling muds.

C. No. Passage A does not deal with environmental impact.

D. No. Passage B does not explain why drilling muds are necessary.

E. No. Passage B does not discuss difficulties inherent in drilling regulations.

7. **E**   Extract Fact

A. No. This is not mentioned in passage A.

B. No. This is not mentioned in passage A.

C. No. This is not mentioned in passage A.

D. No. This is not mentioned in passage B.

E. Yes. Both passages acknowledge that barite is a heavy mineral.

8. **E**   RC Except

A. No. Both passages indicate the presence of clay in drilling muds.

B. No. Passage B indicates WBM is allowed to be dumped into the sea.

C. No. Passage B mentions the environmental effects of OBM, which implies that some study of its effects has been conducted.

D. No. Passage B indicates OBM is 30 percent oil and it is regulated.

E. Yes. Neither passage supports the idea that drilling mud is "continuously" discharged into the sea.

9. **B**   Extract Infer

A. No. The "most environmentally damaging" drilling mud is not supported by either passage.

B. Yes. Passage B indicates the potentially dangerous effects of dumping barite into the sea, while passage A indicates that barite is included in some foods and in a normal medical procedure during which humans ingest it.

C. No. No comparison between offshore and land-based drilling is made.

D. No. Neither author argues for tightened regulations of drilling muds.

E. No. Passage A does not refer to offshore drilling at all.

10. **B**   RC Except

A. No. This is stated in the final sentence of the first paragraph of passage B.

B. Yes. Neither passage supports the idea that governments require disclosure of "all" ingredients. Passage A's reference to secret recipes seems to contradict this as a possibility.

C. No. This is stated in the final sentence of the second paragraph of passage A.

D. No. This is implied by the discussion of drilling through rock in the first paragraph of passage A.

E. No. This is stated in the first two sentences of the last paragraph of passage B.

11. **C** RC Reasoning

The difference stated in passage B between OBMs and WBMs is that OBMs are needed for drilling at greater depths.

A. No. It's possible that the cost of OBMs may also increase, depending on which ingredients are affected.

B. No. This by itself does not suggest any need for change in the future.

C. Yes. If in the future companies must drill deeper to access oil reserves, they will likely make greater use of OBMs when drilling.

D. No. This would seem to reduce the likelihood of using OBMs.

E. No. This by itself does not suggest any need for change in the future.

12. **A** Extract Fact

A. Yes. This is stated in the middle of the last paragraph ("they do not disperse as readily").

B. No. This is not stated.

C. No. This is not mentioned specifically as an environmental hazard.

D. No. This is not mentioned specifically as an environmental hazard.

E. No. This is not stated.

Questions 13–19

The passage discusses the African American choreographer, performer, and dance teacher Aida Overton Walker and examines the proliferating appeal of a dance form she helped popularize. This dance form, "the cakewalk," was embraced by many different social and ethnic groups, including upper-class members the dance was originally designed to parody.

The first paragraph introduces Walker and details the African roots of the cakewalk. The second paragraph discusses the European elements that were added to the cakewalk and describes how they originally served to parody those who would later find the dance form appealing. The third paragraph explains the social and cultural conditions that allowed for the cakewalk's increased popularity. The fourth paragraph examines how Walker was able to win over audiences from different social backgrounds and racial groups.

13. **C** Big Picture

A. No. This focuses only on Walker, whereas the focus of the passage was on Walker's popularization of the cakewalk.

B. No. This choice relates to only one particular audience, described in the second-to-last sentence of the passage, with whom Walker achieved success.

C. Yes. This choice discusses Walker's success in terms of the unique social breadth of the cakewalk's appeal.

D. No. This introduces a false distinction between initial versions of the cakewalk and a supposedly definitive version Walker popularized.

E. No. Different social niches adapted the dance to their own demands, while this answer choice says the dance was preserved in its original form.

14. **D** **Structure**

The passage says the socioeconomic flux of the time created a diverse cultural atmosphere that demanded art forms with versatile appeal, which explains why the layering of parody present in the cakewalk facilitated a broad audience.

A. No. "Only" makes this too strong of a claim.

B. No. There is no discussion of performers in this paragraph.

C. No. The "socioeconomic flux" was not a target of parody.

D. Yes. This identifies that the social backdrop influenced the way the popularity of the cakewalk spread.

E. No. This too narrowly focuses on European American versions of the dance, while the paragraph makes no mention of European Americans at all.

15. **C** **RC Reasoning**

The cakewalk was originally intended to mock European Americans by using elements familiar to them, but this aspect contributed to them embracing the dance.

A. No. The passage never ranks any version of the cakewalk as being more popular than another.

B. No. This doesn't demonstrate that the people being parodied became fans of the music themselves.

C. Yes. Popular music was parodied by a particular style of music, but the elements that were included expressly for that purpose contributed to that style's appeal to pop music audiences.

D. No. This has no sense of parody and instead refers to regaining popularity by cashing in on a current trend.

E. No. This choice discusses only appropriation of elements, not parody.

16. **E** **Extract Fact**

A. No. There is no mention of how well known the cakewalk was before Walker.

B. No. There is no evidence that Walker and only a few others performed it professionally.

C. No. The passage discusses only the layering of parody that was instrumental to the popularizing of the dance, not whether Walker diminished the frequency of the parodies with her interpretation of the cakewalk.

D. No. There is no support for any statements concerning what was "commonly known" of the cake-walk's West African roots.

E. Yes. Support for this statement can be found in the second sentence of the second paragraph.

17. **E** `Extract` `Infer`

A. No. A claim about satiric art forms in general cannot be supported by the passage.

B. No. "Mimetic vertigo" was not discussed in relation to common interactions between African Americans and European Americans.

C. No. There is no discussion of European Americans admiring other African American dances.

D. No. There is no discussion of the post-cakewalk influence of African dance forms.

E. Yes. The last sentence of the passage explains that industrialists and financiers saw the cakewalk as a means through which to express their social rank.

18. **A** `Extract` `Infer`

A. Yes. The first sentence of the last paragraph and the last paragraph in general explain that Walker accentuated different aspects of the cakewalk in order to appeal to the "varied and often conflict-ing demands" of different audiences.

B. No. Nothing is known about the size of the audiences to whom previous versions of the dance appealed. Also, Walker accentuated different elements of the dance, satire being only one of those that ingratiated the dance with different audiences.

C. No. This is close, but the claim that she choreographed different versions of the dance is not sup-ported by the evidence that she "addressed within her interpretation" varying aspects that would appeal to different audiences.

D. No. The idea that Walker inserted imitations of others' performances of the dance into her own work is unsupported, and the only discussion of "mimetic vertigo" did not ascribe anything to Walker.

E. No. Neither the idea that the dance needed to be revitalized nor the idea that its mixture of cul-tural elements needed to be disentangled is supported.

19. **A** `Extract` `Fact`

A. Yes. The last sentence of the first paragraph explains that gliding steps and improvisation were traditional African elements retained in the cakewalk.

B. No. The first performer of the cakewalk is never mentioned.

C. No. Other North American dances were not mentioned.

D. No. The specifics of what certain parodies circulating at the end of the nineteenth century added to the cakewalk are never mentioned.

E. No. The duration of the cakewalk's popularity is never stated.

Questions 20–27

The passage discusses group cohesion, saying that in principle a greater degree of group cohesion leads to better decision making because group members are less apprehensive about dissenting, but in practice a very cohesive group can succumb to a phenomenon termed groupthink, which results in poorer decision making due to less critical discussion of problems and alternatives. The first paragraph sums up the conventional wisdom that holds that the less cohesive a group is, the more its members will be dissuaded from disagreeing with the majority opinion. The second paragraph segues into problems associated with too much group cohesion and introduces groupthink. The third paragraph explains and discusses the factors that lead to and facilitate groupthink.

20.   A   **Big Picture**

   A.   Yes. This acknowledges the potential value of group cohesion and the potential detriment of its contribution to groupthink.

   B.   No. This is too narrowly focused on how individuals can prevent groupthink.

   C.   No. This is better but still too narrowly focused on groupthink, with no reference to the lengthy discussion of group cohesion.

   D.   No. The passage generally did endorse a preference for higher cohesion.

   E.   No. This focuses unduly on the prospects of future research helping to prevent groupthink, while the passage was an explanatory discussion of group cohesion.

21.   C   **Extract**
              Infer

   A.   No. Chronic indecision is not a concept supported by the passage.

   B.   No. This is not groupthink because there was legitimate argument over competing options.

   C.   Yes. Because the scenario involved disagreement over competing options, this does not fit the definition of groupthink, which is specifically characterized by a lack of disagreement over alternatives.

   D.   No. "Illusion of unanimity" is one of the telltale signs of groupthink, so this example simply does not qualify as groupthink.

   E.   No. The inefficiencies mentioned as a result of groupthink relate to pressure to conform and unwillingness to disagree, not a failure to study information thoroughly.

22.   C   **RC Reasoning**

The author lists "cohesiveness of the decision-making group" as a necessary precursor to groupthink.

   A.   No. This addresses no relevant influence on groupthink and presumes that most groups will fall victim to it.

   B.   No. This addresses only group cohesion and does not relate it to groupthink in any way.

   C.   Yes. General distrust of other group members indicates low cohesion, which should preclude groupthink from occurring.

D. No. Stubborn resistance to a consensus is the opposite of groupthink.

E. No. Willingly submitting to the majority opinion is a central factor identified as a contributor to groupthink, so this would weaken the author's explanation of groupthink.

23. **B** Extract Fact

A. No. This suggests low group cohesion, which precludes groupthink.

B. Yes. The first sentence of the final paragraph supports this.

C. No. Unusually high stress is not mentioned in the passage.

D. No. This is mentioned in the first paragraph as a characteristic of intimidated members of groups with low cohesion.

E. No. This is the opposite of groupthink.

24. **E** Extract Infer

A. No. It's not possible to support the idea that groupthink occurs in all cohesive groups.

B. No. Just because the passage states that some contributing factors are still unknown, it isn't possible to support the notion that the factors are unique to each case.

C. No. There is no support for the pessimism of "probably fruitless."

D. No. The strength of "cannot influence" is not supported by the information given in the passage.

E. Yes. In the first sentence of the second paragraph the author foreshadows groupthink as a "pitfall" of group cohesiveness, and the researchers in the final paragraph characterize groupthink primarily in negative terms.

25. **E** Extract Fact

A. No. The idea of enforced conformity is not mentioned in the passage.

B. No. The expectations of military decision-making groups are not mentioned.

C. No. The idea of inappropriate conformity is difficult to support and definitely never mentioned in relation to inadequate information.

D. No. No comparison is made between voluntary and enforced conformity.

E. Yes. The second sentence of the first paragraph supports this.

26. **A** Structure

The discussion in the first paragraph of low cohesion revolves around the idea that in principle low cohesion is less desirable than high cohesion in group decision making.

A. Yes. The first paragraph portrays the expectation that higher group cohesion will better promote an environment of healthy dissension.

B. No. Groupthink is not mentioned until later and is exclusively associated with high cohesion.

C.   No. There is no discussion in this paragraph of ways to improve groups' openness regardless of their cohesion.

D.   No. This is specifically contradicted by the last sentence of the passage.

E.   No. The subsequent discussion in the passage centers entirely on the pitfalls of highly cohesive groups.

27.   **B**   Extract
Infer

A.   No. Highly cohesive groups are more likely to have a healthy level of internal disagreement, but the language of "confrontational negotiating styles with adversaries" is too strong to support.

B.   Yes. The last sentence of the first paragraph affirms that cohesion is positively correlated with hearing the honest opinions of all group members. The second sentence of the first paragraph suggests that in groups with low cohesion, members will be pressured to conform.

C.   No. The passage continually affirms that consideration of varied perspectives is a healthy component of decision making.

D.   No. The passage never cites any particular factors as "the key factors in the formation of groupthink."

E.   No. This is contradicted by the last sentence of the passage, which states that high cohesion is a necessary condition of groupthink.

Section 2: Arguments 1

1.   **D**   Flaw

Since a survey of retirees is being used to support the claim that the company has good relations with its employees, the integrity of the survey must be examined.

A.   No. The premise is the results of a survey, and accepting the results of a given survey does not require believing the company's general claim.

B.   No. There is no reason to think the survey's results cannot be verified; rather, there is reason to think the survey's results are insufficient to prove the company's general claim.

C.   No. The word "fairly" is used the same way both times.

D.   Yes. Retirees who enjoyed working for the company may be more likely to respond to the survey than disgruntled former employees, and the retirees' experiences may not be representative of current relations between the company and its employees.

E.   No. There is no mention of changing managing methods at all.

2.   **E**   Necessary
Assumption

You need to prove that some people who are most opposed to animal cruelty actually contribute to animal cruelty. You know that some people who are most opposed to animal cruelty keep pets and feed those pets meat. You need to get from feeding those pets meat to contributing to animal cruelty.

A. No. You are trying to prove a claim about someone's cruelty; love is out of scope.

B. No. You are trying to prove a claim concerning some people who keep pets; people opposed to keeping pets are out of scope.

C. No. You are trying to prove a claim regarding people opposed to animal cruelty who feed their pets meat. People who work in labs, slaughterhouses, and farms are irrelevant unless you know they feed their pets meat.

D. No. A claim about popular pets is out of scope.

E. Yes. Negated, this would say "feeding meat to pets doesn't contribute to animal cruelty," which ruins the only shred of evidence provided in the argument.

3. A **Weaken**

Over the last five years, national publicity campaigns have tried to encourage people to read more fiction, but bookstores are making less money selling fiction. Therefore, the author concludes that those campaigns have been unsuccessful. You must accept that bookstores are selling less fiction, but look for an answer that allows you to believe the campaigns have still been a success.

A. Yes. Here's a potential sign of the campaigns' success.

B. No. This doesn't help defend the fiction campaigns.

C. No. The argument is about fiction, so biographies are out of scope.

D. No. The argument is about fiction, so books on careers and business are out of scope.

E. No. The argument refers only to national campaigns; overseas customers are out of scope.

4. E **Resolve/ Explain**

On one hand, honey is high in sugar and sugar leads to tooth decay; on the other hand, people who eat honey have fewer cavities. There must be something about eating honey that discourages cavities even more than the sugar content promotes tooth decay.

A. No. Even if all their sugar is from honey, they eat a lot of honey and that still suggests they would have tooth decay problems.

B. No. Does dissolving sugar neutralize its effect on tooth decay? Since you aren't told what effect dissolving the sugar has, this can't be the credited response.

C. No. This doesn't tell you anything about people who consume honey.

D. No. You don't know whether honey is an unrefined sugar, so this choice doesn't resolve the paradox.

E. Yes. Here's a positive dental health feature of eating honey.

5. B **Flaw**

Two of the club's bylaws are explained; violating either would get you suspended. Thibodeaux got suspended. The conclusion assumes that since he didn't do one of those two things, he must have done the other. Why do we have to pick from just these two things? There are probably plenty of things that could get you suspended. Breaking either bylaw is sufficient (→) to get you suspended, but that doesn't mean we can assume getting suspended guarantees (→) you had to break one of those two bylaws.

A. No. Missing a monthly general meeting gets you suspended, not being late. This is irrelevant.

B. Yes. This identifies the assumption that there could not have been other ways to get suspended besides the two bylaws initially mentioned.

C. No. This answer is tempting—the argument took for granted that breaking one of two bylaws was necessary for someone to get suspended when in fact it was only sufficient for someone to get suspended. This choice, however, says the argument took for granted that something was sufficient just because it was necessary.

D. No. It is true that the argument doesn't define late, but that is not a logical problem with the reasoning.

E. No. No part of the argument discusses how long one has been an officer, making this choice irrelevant.

6. C **Necessary Assumption**

The argument concludes that in a future world dominated by recycled paper, more filler will have to be used than is used now. What do you know about recycled paper? The first three sentences combine in a chain of reasoning to tell you that recycled paper requires more filler than other paper if you want to make it white. What remains to be established, though, is that in a future world, people will still want their paper to be white.

A. No. Since the argument is based on recycled paper replacing other types of paper, this answer choice is going against the conclusion.

B. No. Harm to the environment is out of scope when you're only trying to prove that more filler will be used.

C. Yes. Negated, this says that the natural gray hue of recycled paper will be a universally acceptable alternative to white. That means far less filler will be used than is used now.

D. No. This idea of a "whiteness threshold" is irrelevant, and the idea goes against the direction of the conclusion by presenting a reason to potentially stop adding filler.

E. No. This does not need to be true. Manufacturing the current amount of worldwide paper with only recycled paper would still prove the conclusion true.

7. C **Inference**

There is a chain of conditional ideas that ultimately results in the idea that if a nation has to single-handedly bear the burden of curbing industrial emissions, it won't, and therefore the world's carbon dioxide problem will run amok. The conclusion is essentially naming the contrapositive. If the world is to avoid these carbon dioxide problems, then nations cannot be made to singlehandedly bear the burden of curbing industrial emissions.

A. No. This goes in the opposite direction of the argument, which suggests that nations need to be more concerned with pollution than with economics for emissions control to occur.

B. No. The argument was concerned with the behavior of nations, not corporations.

C. Yes. This sounds like nations not singlehandedly bearing the burden of emissions control.

D. No. There was no mention of distrust and the idea that it could be eliminated is way too extreme.

E. No. This is close, in the sense that it also sounds like nations would not be singlehandedly bearing the burden, but the idea of needing to form a world government in order to fairly distribute the burden of emissions control amongst many nations is extreme.

8. **A**   Principle Match

A positive aspect of digital technology (being a pattern of electronic signals minimizes waste) is identified, and then a downside of that same aspect is identified (being a pattern of electronic signals makes losing a document easier).

A. Yes. This matches the information perfectly.

B. No. The idea that more problems are created than are benefits is not supported by the passage. The benefit of and problem with digital technology are stated objectively without any evaluation of which is better or worse.

C. No. Nothing is compared and so there is no support for the idea that one thing is more important than another.

D. No. The innovation of digital technology increases the risk of destroying documents. There is no mention of document storage technology.

E. No. This is all positive and lacks any mention of the downside.

9. **A**   Necessary Assumption

The argument concludes the museum will have to raise fees or reduce services. Why? Because the government mandate will increase the minimum wage rate, which in turn will increase the museum's operating expenses. Does the museum employ anyone at minimum wage? You don't know. If it doesn't, the mandate won't force the museum to change its payroll in any way, and therefore the operating expenses won't be changing.

A. Yes. Negating this means the museum has higher paid people on its payroll, so not only might it not be compelled by the mandate to raise any salaries, but any minimum wage salaries it may have to raise could be offset by lowering the higher salaries to retain the same level of operating expenses.

B. No. Since you can't change the premise (fact) that the revenue does not exceed the operating expenses, it doesn't matter whether the revenue fluctuates or not.

C. No. This is the opposite of what you want to assume. Negating this would tell you that everyone at the museum makes minimum wage, which would greatly strengthen the argument. The negation should never strengthen the argument.

D. No. Crowd size doesn't matter when you can't change the fact that expenses outweigh revenue.

E. No. This also relates to revenue intake. Since you can't change the fact that expenses outweigh revenue, this is irrelevant.

10. **B** `Reasoning`

Helen argues that time spent reading a book is an investment in the eventual benefits yielded by reading it. Randi does not disagree with that general idea but says that it applies only to vocational books. Randi argues that the act of reading fiction is as time-wasting as watching a sitcom.

A. No. Helen's "evidence" was nothing more than her own thoughts, so Randi does not question how she gathered them.

B. Yes. Randi thinks Helen's analogy applies only to vocational books and uses an analogy to sitcoms to show there's a difference when it comes to reading fiction.

C. No. Randi agrees with Helen's conclusion as it applies to vocational books, so it is not an absurd conclusion.

D. No. Helen presents an analogy, not an example, and Randi's analogy contrasts with Helen's.

E. No. Helen presents an analogy, not an example, and Randi accepts Helen's analogy when applied to vocational books, so its relevance is never denied.

11. **B** `Main Point`

The argument concludes no hardware store will be opening in the shopping plaza. Why? If someone were going to open a store, there would be publicity. The contrapositive of that states the following: If there's no publicity, no one's opening a store. There is no publicity; therefore, no one's opening a store.

A. No. The argument doesn't attempt to prove anything about some people believing a store will open.

B. Yes. It's an almost verbatim paraphrase of the argument's conclusion.

C. No. This reiterates a premise.

D. No. The idea that it would be "unwise" to open a store is unsupported by the argument, which only tries to prove that a store will not open.

E. No. This reiterates a premise.

12. **D** `Inference`

The important details marked off here are that science's value system does not require scientists to consider harmful consequences when deciding on research and that ordinary morality requires people to take foreseeable consequences into account when making decisions.

A. No. There is no discussion of responsibility for actions, and so there is no evidence for this answer.

B. No. This is close, but the facts actually say ordinary morality would say a scientist is acting immorally by failing to consider the harmful consequences in the first place, whether or not the research ever yields those consequences. Furthermore, if the harmful applications weren't foreseeable, then ordinary morality as described in the argument wouldn't really apply to this particular case.

C. No. The first sentence contradicts the idea that science is morally neutral.

D. Yes. Scientists deciding on research with potentially harmful consequences would be simultaneously following one part of their value system while violating a part of ordinary morality.

E. No. The idea that the effects of scientific knowledge can never be foreseen is extreme and can't be supported.

13. **B** | Sufficient Assumption

The argument concludes that companies offering neither best price nor highest quality will go bankrupt. How can you prove a company will go bankrupt? Not attracting consumers → bankruptcy. In order to prove the conclusion, you need to know that offering neither best price nor highest quality → not attracting consumers. Scan answer choices for those two concepts.

A. No. This contains nothing about attracting consumers, which is your only logical path to proving a business will go bankrupt.

B. Yes. This is the conditional idea you needed.

C. No. You're trying to prove a claim about companies that don't offer the highest quality or lowest price. This is out of scope.

D. No. This has weak language ("some consumers") which is generally useless on Sufficient Assumption questions. This implies that there may still be some other consumers who might patronize a company out of brand loyalty, which actually goes against the direction of what you're trying to prove because it makes a company with mediocre products less likely to go bankrupt if it has consumers with brand loyalty.

E. No. It's irrelevant to this argument to know whether there are other reasons a company may fail; in order to prove your conclusion, you still need to establish that companies with mediocre products fail to attract consumers.

14. **C** | Weaken

The argument concludes that a reduction of the speed limit in 1986 led to a decrease in serious accidents. Why? The number of serious accidents in the five years after 1986 is less than the number of serious accidents in the five years before 1986. You need to accept that the number of serious accidents has gone down, but find an answer choice that lets us believe this is not due to the change in speed limit.

A. No. If more speeding tickets were issued in greater numbers before or after 1986, you could consider whether that means that more people are dangerously speeding (causing more accidents) or whether cops are enforcing the speed limits more, leading people to drive more carefully (causing fewer accidents). Since the number of tickets is constant, however, this gives you nothing.

B. No. More police presence might let you think that "fear of a ticket" was causing the decrease in accidents more so than the reduced speed limits themselves. Less police presence tells you nothing.

C. Yes. This lets you believe fewer cars on the road, not a lower speed limit, led to the reduction in accidents.

D. No. This only changes the relative proportion of hospitalization accidents to fatal accidents, but since they are both lumped together as one under the category of "serious accidents," the proportion of one to the other tells you nothing.

E. No. This would lead you to think that if they had used the same classification for "serious accident" during the whole 1981 to 1990 time period, there would be an even greater discrepancy between the accident-prone early years and the less accident-prone later years.

15. E — Flaw

The argument concludes that humans are not rational. Why? They engage in irrational behavior such as pollution and bad farming. The concept of being rational is defined as having a capacity for well-reasoned behavior. Because humans sometimes behave irrationally, does that mean they have no capacity for rationality?

A. No. There is no inherent contradiction in the definition of rationality as "a capacity for well-considered thinking and behavior."

B. No. The argument does not need to assume humans are aware of irrational behavior. The argument thinks the mere fact that humans do behave irrationally is proof of their lack of rationality.

C. No. It doesn't need to show this since the argument is designed to lump humans in with other animals as being not superior to them.

D. No. The argument is trying to prove humans are no better than other animals; proving humans are not worse is irrelevant.

E. Yes. This addresses the fact that examples of irrational behavior don't necessarily rule out a capacity for rationality.

16. D — Inference

"Must be true" answers normally come from a combination of quantity statements or conditional rules. All good hunters have a high muscle-to-fat ratio. Most wild cats are good hunters (therefore, most wild cats have a high muscle-to-fat ratio). Some domestic cats are good hunters (therefore, some domestic cats have a high muscle-to-fat ratio).

A. No. While possible, this is not provable; you have no evidence about cats that are not good hunters to even consider.

B. No. You can't prove a comparative quantity type claim when nothing in the evidence compared quantities.

C. No. You know good hunter → high ratio, but you can't then assume bad hunter → low ratio. You can never go from knowing A → B to assuming ~A → ~B.

D. Yes. That's one of the two inferences you were able to make.

E. No. It's possible that there are bad hunters with a high muscle-to-fat ratio, and so it's possible that they can't kill heavy prey.

17. D — Reasoning

First, identify the conclusion—legal responsibility is different than moral responsibility—and the premises—drunk driving penalties vary according to the consequences of an action while moral responsibility depends only on the intentions of the action. The claim you are asked about is one of the premises.

A. No. The language that legal responsibility is based solely upon unintended features of an action is not supported by the argument.

B. No. This is close, but it's not clear that the criteria for legal responsibility always include those for moral responsibility. In the drunk driving example, it is possible that the driver's intentions are not a criterion at all when considering legal penalties.

C. No. The conclusion is just that moral and legal responsibility do not always overlap; this answer choice portrays a different, more specific claim as the conclusion.

D. Yes. This choice paraphrases the conclusion but still effectively identifies both ingredients.

E. No. This choice incorrectly represents the conclusion as being only about moral responsibility.

18. **C**   **Principle Match**

The argument concludes it is best not to take a strong position until one has considered all important evidence. Why? Taking a strong position hinders your ability to consider conflicting evidence which compromises your ability to understand an issue fully. So the underlying principle seems to be as follows: Don't take a strong position until you've understood an issue fully.

A. No. The argument made a claim about when you should not take a strong position, so the principle shouldn't address when you should.

B. No. We must accept the premises as true, and this tries to contradict the first sentence by wanting to undo that strong positions are sufficient to make one misinterpret or ignore conflicting evidence.

C. Yes. This paraphrases your prediction well.

D. No. This is incorrectly trying to move backwards through the conditional statements of the premises, which say that as soon as you take a strong position, you are bound to be biased against conflicting evidence, which in turn precludes you from considering that evidence fully.

E. No. The argument made a claim about when you should not take a strong position, so the principle shouldn't address when it is reasonable to take a strong position.

19. **D**   **Flaw**

The argument concludes that if Jennifer plays in the game, the Eagles will win. Why? So far, the team has lost only when Jennifer was not playing. Not only does that correlation fail to prove that Jennifer's absence caused the team to lose each time, it also fails to prove that Jennifer's presence causes the team to win.

A. No. This is close, but incorrect on two counts. First, Jennifer's not playing a game is not a factor that is sufficient to bring about the result of the Eagles losing. However, even if it were, the argument would be inferring that the absence of that factor (Jennifer playing the game) would be sufficient, not necessary, to bring about the opposite result (Eagles winning).

B. No. The logical flaw of this argument relates to correlations being treated as causal factors. The computer-related content was incidental.

C. No. As the argument states, no computer was necessary to uncover the evidence the argument uses to support its conclusion, so flaws relating to computer analysis are irrelevant.

D. Yes. The argument assumes that because the team has never lost while Jennifer was playing, they will never lose when Jennifer plays.

E. No. The conclusion is not about the value of computer analysis; it is that if Jennifer plays, the Eagles will win.

20. **E** Inference

Styrofoam egg cartons are identified as among the easiest to make because they don't need to be thoroughly cleaned, as the egg shells will provide an insulating barrier between the food and the Styrofoam.

A. No. Egg cartons are among the easiest to make, so there could be other food containers that have the same characteristics.

B. No. You have no evidence about anything that cannot be packaged in recycled Styrofoam.

C. No. You have no evidence to justify calling anything a main reason, and presumably the Styrofoam is cleaned for the sake of food that will come into contact with it.

D. No. You have no evidence to support a claim about most egg cartons, only some.

E. Yes. Translate "Not all A are B" statements into "Some A are NOT B." This is saying that some recycled Styrofoam food containers allow food to come into contact with the container. Egg cartons fit this description because the eggs are allowed to touch the Styrofoam.

21. **A** Parallel Flaw

Correlation = Causality flaw. Because most people who have condition A (migraines) had condition B (depression) as children, the argument erroneously concludes that having condition B as a child makes it likely to have condition A as an adult.

A. Yes. Most dogs with A (good tempers) had B (rabies vaccine) as puppies; therefore, it assumes that having B as a puppy makes you likely to have A as an adult.

B. No. This says most dogs with A (vicious tempers) had B (ill treatment) when they were young, but it concludes that if a pet owner's dog has A, then it is likely to have had B when young.

C. No. This says most dogs with A (good behavior) had B (obedience training), but it concludes that if you did not have B you will not have A.

D. No. This does not take a single correlation between two factors and manipulate those two factors.

E. No. This is not a correlation between two different factors; it assigns one factor (being taken from a mother) to a certain time (eight weeks) and concludes that anything after that time will have that factor.

22. **E** Flaw

The argument concludes that if Professor Vallejo is correct, glassblowing did not originate in Egypt. Why? If Professor Vallejo is correct, there is currently insufficient evidence to prove glassblowing originated in Egypt. Do you have any evidence it originated anywhere else? Not that you know of, so you can't prove that glassblowing did or did not originate in Egypt.

A. No. Contradicting majority opinion is not a logical flaw.

B. No. It does not presuppose Vallejo's claim is true because the conclusion is phrased "If Professor Vallejo is correct..."

C. No. It is true that the argument failed to provide this criteria, but this choice doesn't address any logical flaw.

D. No. The phrase that relates the traditional view to the majority view is neither a premise nor the conclusion and therefore has nothing to do with the reasoning process.

E. Yes. The argument assumes that an inability to prove glassblowing did originate in Egypt proves that it did not originate in Egypt.

23. **C**   Parallel

This is a valid argument that establishes the only mattresses in Southgate Mall are at Mattress Madness. All the mattresses at that store are 20 percent off. Therefore, all the mattresses at Southgate Mall are 20 percent off.

A. No. There could be food in Diane's refrigerator that she didn't purchase in the past week.

B. No. There could be food elsewhere in Diane's apartment that was not purchased in the past week.

C. Yes. The only food in her apartment is in the refrigerator and all the food in her refrigerator was purchased this past week. Therefore, all food in her apartment was purchased this past week.

D. No. Diane could have purchased food in the past week and left some of it in her car or at her office.

E. No. Diane could have month-old food sitting in her pantry or somewhere else in her apartment other than the refrigerator.

24. **A**   Strengthen

This argument attempts to solve a problem with methane production by concluding that cows should be given better-quality diets. What is the methane problem? Worldwide, there are over a billion cows (and counting) to meet our meat and milk demands. These cows produce methane gas, which isn't desirable (global warming). Cows produce less methane gas when given higher-quality diets. Does this solve the original problem? It seems as though it might. Does it create any problems of its own? It's not certain. You need to assume that all other relevant factors about cows (environmental impact and meat/milk production) would not be worsened.

A. Yes. This choice rules out the possible concern that a higher-quality diet may lead to less meat/milk production, which would force farmers to keep more cows in order to meet world demand (thus undermining any methane reduction obtained).

B. No. This doesn't make any difference, particularly since it applies uniformly to low- and high-quality diets.

C. No. The willingness of farmers to make this switch is out of scope; the argument is only trying to prove that if you made the switch, you would reduce methane production.

D.   No. The relative proportion of which cows are guiltier of methane emissions is irrelevant, since they all have to be fed anyway.

E.   No. The extent to which methane contributes to global warming is irrelevant when the argument is only trying to prove that changing cow feed would reduce methane.

25.   **D**   **Inference**

Our first sentence says face danger solely to obtain pleasure → ~courage. Our second sentence says courage → persevere in the face of fear. These two ideas don't chain together, so we should be ready for either contrapositive. The first contrapositive: courage → ~solely for pleasure. The second contrapositive: ~overcame fear → ~courage.

A.   No. Avoiding future pain is not a concept ever mentioned, so you will not be able to prove anything about it.

B.   No. The necessary condition to call something courageous is that someone perseveres in the face of fear of one or more dangers involved. This answer choice nearly contradicts that.

C.   No. This is too broad a statement to prove. You're labeling actions as courageous or not courageous, not people. Just because a person derives pleasure from some dangerous activities doesn't mean that he/she couldn't be involved in a situation in which no pleasure is derived from danger, which still leaves open the possibility for acting courageously.

D.   Yes. This just reiterates the conditional of the second sentence, courageous (only if) → persevere in the face of fear.

E.   No. This choice states that everyone else would fear something → this person doesn't. However, that leaves open the possibility that there could be a situation in which this person does fear something that everyone else would not fear. That leaves open the possibility for this person to act courageously by persevering in the face of fear.

26.   **D**   **Sufficient Assumption**

The argument concludes that if the newspaper is right, the public will be safer in future severe weather. What does the newspaper predict? New sirens installed → public safety in severe weather improved. Do you have a way to prove that new sirens will be installed? Replacement parts for old sirens are difficult to obtain → government will install new sirens. Do you have a way to prove that replacement parts for old sirens are difficult to obtain? The local company the government has previously used to buy those parts has since gone out of business. We just need to know that government can't get parts from its normal company → replacement parts are difficult to obtain.

A.   No. Sufficient assumption answers need to tell you that IF a premise obtains, THEN the conclusion follows. Any answer that begins by saying IF the conclusion obtains is useless.

B.   No. You don't need to establish the newspaper was correct. The conclusion is only trying to prove something that follows if the newspaper is correct.

C.   No. This is close to the relationship you wanted, but it needs to be more explicit. It's possible that it is simple for the government to obtain replacement parts from a nonlocal company, in which case the old sirens will be retained and the conclusion will not follow.

54

D. Yes. This is the link you need.

E. No. This is also close, but it needs to be more explicit. It's still possible that the government takes a reckless attitude toward solving the problem of finding replacement parts and does not care that the parts are of inferior quality. If it was easy for the government to obtain those parts, there is no reason to believe the government will be forced to buy and install new sirens.

Section 3: Games

Questions 1–5

This is an In-Out game with all conditional clues. For each rule, you also need to write the contrapositive. You have six elements (the dancers) divided into two categories: men and women. You should represent this characteristic by making one group capital letters and the other group lowercase.

men: f, g, h WOMEN: J, K, L

Clue 1: J → ~L; L → ~J

Clue 2: ~L → J; → ~J → L

Clue 3: ~f → ~J; J → f

Clue 4: J or K or L → g; ~g → ~J and ~K and ~L

Deductions: When a conditional rule has mixed signs (one is positive, the other negative) in an In-Out game, you can always make a placeholder deduction. The first clue tells you that J and L can never both be In. Therefore, you can add a J/L placeholder to the Out column. The second clue tells you that J and L can never both be Out. Add a J/L placeholder to the In column. By combining these first two clues (and their corresponding placeholders), you can see that J and L will always have to be on opposite sides. Therefore, you should actually write one of the placeholders as L/J as a visual reminder that these two placeholders are actually reciprocal ideas. If J is In, then L must be Out. If L is In, then J must be Out. Finally, the last clue says that if any woman is on stage, then g must also be. From your work with the placeholders, you know that either J or L (both women) will always be among the dancers on stage. Therefore, you know that g will always have to be on stage as well.

Here's the diagram:

	In	Out
W: JKL	J/L g	L/J
m: fgh		

1.   **C**   **Grab-a-Rule**

With In-Out games, the Grab-a-Rule question shows you only half the diagram. Either take a second to draw the Out column for each answer choice or just remember that everyone you don't see in an answer choice is Out.

A. No. Your diagram shows a minimum of two people every time, so this is impossible. And it specifically violates clue 2.

B. No. This violates clue 4 since g must be on stage.

C. Yes. This list complies with all of the rules.

D. No. This violates clue 3. Since you don't see f, he must be off stage, which means J must be off stage as well.

E. No. This violates clue 1 since L cannot be on stage with J.

2. **D** General

This answer should derive from the deductions you have in your diagram.

A. No. The only required man you have is g, and this scenario includes him.

B. No. The only required man you have is g, and this scenario includes him.

C. No. Either J or L is required to be on stage every time, and this scenario includes J.

D. Yes. This must be false. Either J or L is required to be on stage every time, and this scenario would leave them both off stage.

E. No. Either J or L is required to be on stage every time, and this scenario includes J.

3. **E** Specific

This question asks you to look at what happens when J is on stage. You know J being on stage means that L must be off stage. You also know that J being on stage means that f must be on stage. Finally, you know that g is always on stage. Your diagram should look like this:

In	Out
Jgf	L

A. No. L is the only dancer who must be off stage, but there are two others who could also be off stage.

B. No. f must be on stage.

C. No. K could also be off stage.

D. No. L must be off stage as well.

E. Yes. Only J, g, and f are required to be on stage for this scenario, so the remaining three dancers would be the complete list of those who could be off stage.

4. **C** Specific

You need a scenario with more women than men, so clearly you cannot have all three men on stage. You know that g must always be on stage, so you will have at least one man and two women. Can you have three women and two men? No, because you can never get all three women on stage together (because of the mutually exclusive relationship between J and L). Therefore, the greatest number of women you can get on stage is two, which means you can have only one man, g. With two women, L and K, and one man, you have three people on stage. Choice (C) is the credited response.

In	Out
gLK	fhJ

5. **C** General

This answer should derive from your deductions. You concluded that g and either J or L will be on stage every time, so you have a minimum of two. You can verify this answer by forcing everyone else Out to ensure that no other clues force someone else In. None do, so two must be the answer. Choice (C) is the credited response.

Questions 6–12

This is a group game with variable assignments. You need to assign a numbered rating (1–4) to each of six columns. Each number must be used at least once but no more than twice. The clues do not suggest that you need a grid; that sort of diagram could work, but it would be more cumbersome than just making column headings out of the CD titles—H, I, N, Q, R, and S.

Clue 1: Each number must be used once or twice.

Clue 2: $H = N + 1$

Clue 3: $H = I$ or $R = I$

Clue 4: Only one CD, if any, is allowed to be rated higher than Q.

Deductions: These rules do lend themselves to normal symbolization. Spend a little time reviewing them in terms of general limitations. The first clue deals with using all the numbers once or twice. Since you have six spaces and four numbers, each time you will use each number once and two of those four numbers a second time. The second clue says that H will always be one higher than N. From this you can deduce that N will never be 4 (since that would mean H is 5), and H will never be 1 (since that would mean N is 0). Mark these deductions on your diagram. The third clue says that either H and I or R and I will always match. Right now, it seems like that matching pair could be any of the four numbers. The fourth clue says that only one CD is allowed to have a higher number than Q. This means that Q must always be fairly high. It couldn't be 1 or 2 or else there would be more than one CD that is higher. Q could be 3 if there were only one 4. Mark off Q's options as 3/4. The last deduction is a hard one, but when you consider that Q could be 3 if there were only one 4, you might realize the relevance of clue 3: H and I or R and

I will always be a matching pair. Can you ever have a matching pair of 4's that doesn't include Q? No. Therefore, you can be sure that I can never be 4. There are no rules pertaining to S, so that is your free agent.

Here's the diagram:

$$
\begin{array}{ccccccc}
 & & & & \sim 1 & & \\
 & \sim 1 & \sim 4 & \sim 4 & \sim 2 & & \\
1234 & H & I & N & Q & R & S \\
\hline
 & & & & \frac{3}{4} & & \\
\end{array}
$$

6. **A** [Grab-a-Rule]

    A.   Yes. This complies with all of the rules.

    B.   No. This breaks clue 4; two CDs are numbered higher than Q.

    C.   No. This breaks clue 3; neither H nor R matches I.

    D.   No. This breaks clue 2; H is three stars higher than N.

    E.   No. This breaks clue 4; two CDs are numbered higher than Q.

7. **A** [Specific]

Write in that H is 2. Since N is always one fewer than H, write in that N is 1. What do the other clues tell us? Either H and I or R and I must be a match, but the question says H must be the only 2. Therefore R and I must be the match. Now you must figure out whether R and I can be 1's, 2's, or 3's. (You already deduced I can never be 4.) 1 is not possible because N is already a 1, so that would give you three 1's. 2 is not possible because H is the only 2 in this scenario. That means R and I must be 3's. Q always has to be 3 or 4, and since you just used both your 3's for this turn, Q will have to be 4. What about free agent S? It can't be 2 because H is the only 2. It can't be 3 because both 3's have been used. So S could be either 1 or 4.

$$
\begin{array}{ccccccc}
 & & & & \sim 1 & & \\
 & \sim 1 & \sim 4 & \sim 4 & \sim 2 & & \\
 & H & I & N & Q & R & S \\
\hline
 & 2 & 3 & 1 & 4 & 3 & \frac{1}{4} \\
\end{array}
$$

    A.   Yes. See the work above; this must be true.

    B.   No. N is 1.

    C.   No. Q is 4.

    D.   No. R is 3.

    E.   No. S could be 4.

8. **D** | Specific

If R and S must match, then R and I cannot match, which means H and I have to match. Start by considering what possibilities you have or don't have for R and S. They can't both be 4 because then Q will be lower than two things. Try making R and S both 3. That means H and I will both have to be 2 (since you deduced H can never be 1 and I can never be 4). If H is 2, then N is 1. Q will be 4, and the scenario looks fine. See what other scenarios are possible by making R and S both 2. That means H and I will both have to be 3 (since H can't be 1). If H is 3, then N is 2. This is a problem. Now you have three 2's, which is illegal. Cross out or erase that scenario; it's impossible. Try making R and S both 1. Taking a lesson from the previous failed scenario, you know H and I cannot be 2 or else N will end up being 1, which would give you three 1's. Make H and I both 3, which means N is 2; Q will again be 4. This scenario works as well. Since you're answering a "must be true" question that has two possible scenarios, look for what is common to both scenarios. The only thing they both have in common is that Q is 4. Find that in the answer choices.

~1	~4	~4	~1 ~2		
H	I	N	Q	R	S
2	2	1	4	3	3
3	3	2	4	1	1

A. No. It could also be 3.

B. No. It could also be 2.

C. No. It could also be 1.

D. Yes. See the work above; this must be true.

E. No. It could also be 3.

9. **E** | Specific

Write in that R and N are 1. If N is 1, then H must be 2. If R and N match, then you can't have R and I match, which means H and I must match. Write in that I must also be 2. You're left with Q and S. Does it matter which is 3 and which is 4? No. Symbolize the two possibilities by saying Q could be 3/4 and S could be 4/3. Since the question is asking for what could be true, the answer is unlikely to deal with any of the ones set in stone (H, I, R, and N). Scan the answer choices first for those dealing with Q or S.

~1	~4	~4	~1 ~2		
H	I	N	Q	R	S
2	2	1	¾	1	⁴⁄₃

A. No. H is 2.

B. No. H is 2.

C. No. I is 2.

D. No. S is 3 or 4.

E. Yes. This could be true.

10. **D** General

Start by eliminating any answer choices you've already seen could be true from your work on questions 8 and 9. Remember that in question 8, you had to make R and S match. However, S is a free agent, so for the sake of the current question you are free to move S to any available position.

A. No. In question 9, you had a scenario in which Q would be the only one with a 3.

B. No. In question 9, you had a scenario in which Q would be the only one with a 4.

C. No. In question 8, you had a scenario in which R and S were both 1's. However, you could make S a 4 or a 2 in that scenario, which would leave R as the only 1. This is possible.

D. Yes. You can prove all the others are possible through your prior work, which is enough to pick (D) as your answer. The problem with R being the only 2 is that then R and I can't be a match, which means that H and I must therefore match. You have to make H and I both 3's (since H can't be 1 and I can't be 4). If H is 3, though, then N must also be a 2, which means R is not the only 2.

E. No. In question 8, you had a scenario in which R and S were both 3's. However, you could make S a 4 or a 1 in that scenario, which would leave R as the only 3. This is possible.

11. **E** Specific

If R is the only 1, then H and I must match. You could potentially make H and I both 2's or both 3's (since I can't be 4). However, if you've learned your lesson from the previous problems, you'll remember that making H a 2 will make N a 1 (which wouldn't let R be the only 1). So, you have to make H and I both 3's. Because H is 3, N must be 2. Q will have to be 4 since you've already used up your 3's. S is the free agent, so think about what options remain. You're out of 3's and for this problem you have to let R be the only 1. Therefore, S could be 2 or 4. Since this is a "could be true" question, it is unlikely to deal with any of the sure things (you know H, I, N, Q, and R). Scan for an answer choice that deals with S.

			~1		
~1	~4	~4	~2		
H	I	N	Q	R	S
3	3	2	4	1	2/4

A. No. H is 3.

B. No. I is 3.

C.   No. N is 2.

D.   No. Q is 4.

E.   Yes. This could be true.

12.   **B**   General

This answer should come from your original deductions. You deduced that both N and I could never be 4. If you hadn't been so clever initially, you would just eliminate any choices you've already seen can be 4 (such as Q and S) and then think about or try out the remaining options.

A.   No. H can get 4 stars.

B.   Yes. This would mean either H or R would also have to be 4, which means Q could be 3 at most, which violates clue 4.

C.   No. Q can get 4 stars.

D.   No. R can get 4 stars.

E.   No. S can get 4 stars.

Questions 13–17

This is a standard 1D order game except that it involves a vertical order rather than a horizontal one. There are six elements and six layers to the cake. The 1:1 ratio is a good sign of an easy game. The assortment of questions is 1 Grab-a-Rule, 3 Specific, and 1 General.

Clue 1:

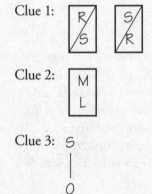

Clue 2:

Clue 3:   S
          |
          O
          |
          M

Deductions: Symbolize the three clues and then chain together the clues that have overlapping elements. Because of the LM block from clue 2, you should attach the L beneath the M—O—S chain from clue 3. Because of clue 1, remind yourself that R cannot go above or below S. Finally, V was not involved in any clues so you should identify it (circle it if you like) as a "free agent"; you are free to use V wherever you want to (other than dividing the LM block).

54

```
        S
        |
        O
        |
       ┌─┐
       │M│
       │L│
       └─┘
```

If you look for deeper deductions, then you should ask yourself, "How limited is the LM block?" It has a couple of things that must come above it. It could go only in 1 and 2, 2 and 3, or 3 and 4. You could draw out that much of each of those scenarios and see if the remaining spaces limit your options of who can go where.

Here's the diagram:

```
LMORSV  ~O~L~M   6  ┌─
           ~M    5  ├─
                 4  ├─
           ~S    3  ├─
         ~O~S    2  ├─
       ~O~M~S    1  ├─
```

13. **A**   Grab-a-Rule

A. Yes. This doesn't break any rules.

B. No. This breaks clue 1.

C. No. This breaks clue 2.

D. No. This breaks clue 3.

E. No. This breaks clue 3.

14. **B**   Specific

In order to avoid putting S on top of O, you have to figure out who can go in between. M and L are out of the running because they're below O. R is impossible because it can't be adjacent to S. All you have left is free agent V. You need to have LM—O—VS. R can fit into three different spots in that sequence: (R)LM(R)O(R)VS

A. No. You could never have R above V; that would make R adjacent to S.

B. Yes. You could put R above O.

C. No. You can't ever break up LM.

D. No. R can be 1, 3, or 4.

E. No. That would make R adjacent to S.

15. **E** `Specific`

If S can't be in 6, what options are left? S has at least three things that must come underneath it, so it would have to be in 5 or 4. If you put S in 4, then O, M, and L are forced in place below it. R can't be touching S, so R would be 6 and V would be 5. If you put S in 5, what can you put in 6? O, M, and L must all be below S. R can't be in 6 because then it would be touching S, so you have to put V in 6. Therefore, by testing the only two places you could put S, you find out that each place requires V to be in a certain spot. There are only two choices for V: fifth and sixth. Choice (E) is the credited response.

~O~L~M	6	R V
~M	5	V S
	4	S O
~S	3	O
~O~S	2	M
~O~M~S	1	L

16. **B** `Specific`

Put L in 3; this forces M to be in 4. Since O and S must still go above those two, O will have to be in 5 and S will have to go in 6. R and V are left to fill spots 1 and 2. Does it matter which takes which? No, so indicate the two possibilities with some slashes. Since this question asks for what could be true, the answer choice will most likely deal with the slashes. Scan the answer choices for those dealing with R or V.

~O~L~M	6	S
~M	5	O
	4	M
~S	3	L
~O~S	2	R/V
~O~M~S	1	V/R

A. No. This is impossible given your diagram.

B. Yes. R could be in 1 and V could be in 2.

C. No. This contradicts what your diagram says must be true.

D. No. This contradicts what your diagram says must be true.

E. No. This contradicts what your diagram says must be true.

17. **B** `General`

Start by figuring out which letters you're sure will never be in the bottom two spots: S and O. You can eliminate any answers that have either of those two elements.

A. No. L has to come before M.

B. Yes. You can see this is possible from your work on question 16.

C. No. L has to come before M.

D. No. L has to come before M.

E. No. S could never be that far down.

Questions 18–23

This is a 1D order game. There are six elements to arrange in order; the one wrinkle of this game is naming one of those six elements the "accepted" bid. However, you can simply deal with this by circling whichever element is the "accepted" bid. The question assortment is 1 Grab-a-Rule, 2 Specific, and 3 General. Having several general questions typically indicates there are some valuable deductions you can make by combining rules. The setup doesn't explicitly say whether to order elements high—low or low—high, but the clues are referring to the bids as fourth or fifth "lowest." Since it would be easier if those labels indicated spots 4 and 5, you should make your diagram go from lowest (1) to highest (6).

Looking at the way the Grab-a-Rule question is set up can also be helpful in determining how the diagram should look.

Clue 1: The accepted bid will always be K or R and in spot 2 or 3. Symbolize this on your diagram and note that "accepted" will be indicated by a circle around the relevant element.

Clue 2:
$$H \diagdown\diagup\begin{matrix} J \\ K \end{matrix}$$

Clue 3: $J_4 \rightarrow$ $J\diagdown\diagup\begin{matrix} S \\ T \end{matrix}$ T—J or S—J $\rightarrow$ ~J_4

Clue 4: $J_4 \rightarrow$ $\begin{matrix} S \\ T \end{matrix}\diagup\diagdown J$ J—S or J—T $\rightarrow$ ~J_4

Clue 5: R/S = 5. Add this to the diagram by putting an R/S placeholder in spot 5.

Deductions: Clue 2 is an ordering clue. H has two things that must come after it, so it can't be fifth or sixth, but since R/S takes up the fifth slot, H can't be fourth either. J and K can't appear until after H appears, so neither J nor K can be first. Because clues 3 and 4 address the idea of whether J is 4, you should investigate those possibilities. Start with a scenario in which J is 4. Clue 3 says that when J is 4, S and T must be higher than J. In this case, S and T must fit in spots 5 and 6. You already have an R/S placeholder in spot 5, so, for this scenario, S must be 5 and T must be 6. What about the remaining spots (1, 2, and 3) and elements (H, K, and R)? From clue 2, H must be before K, so K can't go first and H can't go third. Write H/R in 1 and R/K in 3. All three could theoretically go in spot 2, so either leave it blank or squeeze in H/K/R if you'd rather see all the options listed. How about a scenario in which J is not 4? That means both S and T need to come before it. You also have to use H before you can use J. If three things have to come before J, then J can't be in spots 1, 2, or 3. Your goal is not to put J in 4, so how about spot 5? That's reserved for R/S. It seems the only other place you can put J is 6. There seem to be plenty of options for H, K, R, S, and T in the first five spots, so don't bother to narrow them down. You have made a key deduction—J must always be in either 4 or 6.

Here's the diagram:

18. B   Grab-a-Rule

The first clue says K or R will always be 2 or 3. Scan all the answers for just spots 2 and 3 to find one that doesn't use K or R. Eliminate (C). Clue 2 says H is always to the left of J and K. Scan for any answers that have J or K to the left of H. Eliminate (A). Clue 3 says if J is 4, S and T must come some time after it. Scan the remaining choices to see if they have J in 4. Only (D) does, so check it to make sure both S and T come after J. S doesn't, so eliminate (D). Clue 4 says that when J is not in 4, S and T have to come before J. Check the remaining answer choices; eliminate (E).

19. A   General

Looking at your previous work and deductions, you can see that H cannot be fourth. Is H one of the answer choices? Yes, so (A) is the credited response.

20. B   General

Is there anything you're sure will NEVER be second? Yes. You figured out that J can be only in 4 or 6. Choice (B) is the credited response.

21. D   Specific

If R is the accepted bid, it must be in either 2 or 3. You should try a scenario for each option. The other clue that relates to R is that either R or S is always in spot 5. You know for both scenarios, then, that S will be in spot 5. Since this is a "must be true" question and you know that in both scenarios S will be in 5, you should see if that's the answer.

A. No. There are several options for spot 1.

B. No. R could also be in 2.

C. No. R could also be in 2.

D. Yes. In both possible scenarios, S is fifth.

E. No. J could also be fourth.

22. **C** General

Refer back to your original deductions and look for an answer that is justified by those limitations. You know the most about J, so scan the answer choices for things related to J.

A. No. When J is 6, spots 1 through 5 are pretty open, so it seems as though S might be able to come before H.

B. No. When J is 6, spots 1 through 5 are pretty open, so it seems as though T might be able to come before H.

C. Yes. If J is 4, then you know S and T are 5 and 6, respectively. Otherwise, J is 6. Either way, K will have to come before J.

D. No. When J is 4, S is 5. Otherwise, J is 6, which makes S come before J.

E. No. When J is 4, S is 5 and T is 6. That means K must be lower than S in that scenario.

23. **A** Specific

Four of these answer choices must be true. Put R in 1 and see what follows. S automatically has to go in 5, because the fifth spot is always R or S. The other clue relating to R, clue 1, tells you that K must be the accepted bid and must go in either 2 or 3. K is also mentioned in clue 2, which tells you H must come before K. So, H must be in 2 and K must be in 3. You're down to J and T to fill spots 4 and 6. They each could go in either space, so indicate both possibilities with some slashes. Since the question asks what "could be false," the answer will probably address the slashed elements. Scan the answer choices for either J or T.

A. Yes. J is flexible; it could be in either 4 or 6.

B. No. This must be true; it is not optional.

C. No. This must be true; it is not optional.

D. No. This must be true; it is not optional.

E. No. This must be true; it is not optional.

Section 4: Arguments 2

1. **E** **Strengthen**

The argument concludes that the results of elections in democratic countries do not represent the un-adulterated preferences of the people. Why? Political strategists are hired to manipulate public opinion using advertising techniques. The argument is assuming that these strategists are actually successful at doing what they are hired to do.

A. No. Nondemocratic governments are out of scope.

B. No. It doesn't make a difference whether people know they are being persuaded; you need to establish that they are actually persuaded to think differently.

C. No. The limit advertisers can spend is irrelevant, but this answer does not even go in the right direction of the conclusion because it makes it harder for advertisers to do their brainwashing.

D. No. This goes against the conclusion because it suggests those most likely to vote are those least likely to be exposed to political advertisements via television or print.

E. Yes. You need to know that people's minds have actually been changed, and this answer tells you that political advertisements do often change voters' beliefs.

2. **D** **Reasoning**

Kris compares the chemical industry to the cellular phone industry, arguing that the cellular industry must be regulated just as the chemical industry is. Why? Because just as the chemical industry creates pollution, so too does the cellular phone industry in the form of noise pollution such as unwanted ringing or loud conversations in public. Terry pounces on this comparison, arguing that noise pollution is not truly harmful pollution, just something annoying.

A. No. Nothing in Terry's response has anything to do with doubting the reliability of information. Terry doubts the applicability of an analogy.

B. No. This is almost the same as (A). Terry accepts all of Kris's evidence (premises), but not Kris's conclusion because it unfairly relates two very different things.

C. No. Terry's response involves contrasting two different cause/effect pairs, not rearranging the order of one cause/effect relationship.

D. Yes. Terry argues that it's unfair to compare chemical pollution to noise pollution.

E. No. Nothing in Terry's response relates to "technological progress."

3. **A** **Necessary Assumption**

The researcher argues that countries can decide on the best type of public school system by looking at those of other countries. If every country administers nationwide tests, the country with the best scores on the tests should be copied by others. Necessary assumption questions concerning practical, problem-solving arguments often assume the solution will work without considering possible problems.

A. Yes. By negating this, you would get a statement saying the success of school systems doesn't translate from country to country, which would ruin the argument's plan. This assumption needs to be true.

B. No. This is irrelevant to the scope of the argument, which is about public schools.

C. No. Although a sophisticated outlook on copying other nations' schools would involve discerning the relevant attributes that contribute to differences, the researcher simply advises that other countries wholly adopt the winning school system.

D. No. This doesn't need to be true; it doesn't ruin the plan if most countries don't already administer tests. That doesn't mean they won't administer the test the plan wants them to.

E. No. Different ways of testing could potentially still carry out the plan. Plus, the extreme wording of "as closely as possible" goes too far. You can devise tests that attempt to closely compare similar grade levels without necessarily making it as close as possible.

4. **D** | Flaw

The argument concludes Cynthia is wrong to think her trunk opened because she ran over a pothole. Why? Other times when her trunk has popped open, it was not due to a pothole. But why would it be wrong to think a pothole caused this trunk opening? Ray is apparently thinking that because something else was sufficient to pop open her trunk before, that something else must be a necessary cause every time her trunk opens.

A. No. Other cars are completely out of scope.

B. No. Cynthia's car's engine is out of scope.

C. No. Try to match this answer choice's general language with the specific elements from the argument. It would seem to be saying "presumes that if one event (pothole) causes another (other event?), it (pothole) cannot also cause a third event (trunk opening)." It was never suggested that the pothole could cause another event, so this answer choice doesn't match the argument.

D. Yes. The fact that other things have popped open Cynthia's trunk is not evidence that a pothole could not also pop open her trunk.

E. No. This is describing a "circular argument," which is almost never a correct flaw response. Unless you need the conclusion in order to believe a premise, this is not the credited response.

5. **E** | Inference

The passage establishes that all journalists think lying is wrong. However, the two ideas set off with "yet" and "also" tell us that journalists disagree as to whether one should quote spoken words verbatim and whether it is lying or permissible to fail to identify oneself as a reporter.

A. No. This is contradicted by the first sentence. Reporters disagree as to what constitutes ethical behavior, but they all strive for it.

B. No. This is too broad and strong a claim; you have no way of proving that there is never a way to tell whether or not something counts as lying.

C. No. Although some reporters feel this way, this claim can't be supported because other reporters feel omission is permissible.

D. No. You can't support the idea that lying is permissible in some situations. No reporter thinks lying is ever permissible. Some reporters do certain things they think are permissible, although others might consider them lying.

E. Yes. You can support this with the last sentence: Some reporters consider failing to identify yourself as a reporter lying, while other reporters don't.

6. **C** Resolve/ Explain

On the one hand, wood-frame houses are better equipped to withstand earthquakes than are masonry houses. On the other hand, in a recent earthquake a wood-frame house fell while a masonry house next door did not. You need to find another factor that contributed to this wood-frame house's demise or made this masonry house especially resistant to earthquakes.

A. No. This doesn't tell you anything helpful about these two particular houses.

B. No. This doesn't tell you anything helpful about these two particular houses.

C. Yes. This tells you that the wood-frame house that was destroyed was already compromised by a previous natural disaster.

D. No. This is close to telling you something positive about the masonry house, but you can't assume more expensive means more earthquake resistant.

E. No. This applies to both and therefore doesn't help resolve the confusion as to why the wood-frame house would succumb to the earthquake while the masonry house would withstand it.

7. **D** Necessary Assumption

This argument interprets the evidence of an experiment in which experimenters repeatedly shine a light into a snail's tank and simultaneously shake it. The snail tenses its "foot," a reaction that is known to be caused by turbulent waters. Later, the experimenters shone the light without shaking the tank and the snail still tensed its foot. The argument concludes that the snail learned to associate the shining light with the shaking of the tank. Are there any other ways to interpret the data? What if shining the light is sufficient to make a snail tense its foot? Just because shaking the tank is sufficient to make a snail tense its foot doesn't mean there might not be other things that bring about the same reaction.

A. No. "All" is extreme and you don't need to assume this, since the argument described foot-tensing as the typical reaction of sea snails to ocean turbulence.

B. No. Whether or not the snails are ordinarily exposed to bright light is irrelevant; whether or not they have a reaction to the light is what you want to know about.

C. No. This is close to being necessary to the reasoning but would need to apply to most other members of its species. The argument acknowledges that some sea snails might not react to ocean turbulence by tensing their foot (they might have no reaction or they may have some other atypical response). Because of this, if you negate this answer choice, it is not problematic to say that our experimental snail differs significantly from some other snails because it could simply differ from those few, oddball snails that don't tense their feet in rough waters.

D. Yes. If you negate this, it says "the light itself will ordinarily make a snail tense its foot," which makes the argument's interpretation that the snail has learned to associate the light with the shaking completely groundless.

E. No. If you negate this, it doesn't cripple the argument. Whether it's instinctive or learned, the fact that tensing a foot in turbulent water is a typical snail response is enough for the argument to come to its faulty conclusion that shining the light only mattered because it was associated with shaking the tank.

8. **C** [Parallel Flaw]

Because the whole (the purchasing department) is a certain quality (highly efficient), the argument erroneously concludes that any part of the whole (twelve staff members) have the same quality (high efficiency).

A. No. There is no part/whole logic here at all.

B. No. This is close to a part to whole flaw, assuming that because the parts (individual department members) have a quality (incompetence) that the whole (the department) would have that quality (inadequate for our needs). However, you need whole to part.

C. Yes. Because the whole (supercomputer) is a certain quality (most sophisticated and expensive), then the parts (each of its components) must also have that quality (most sophisticated and expensive).

D. No. Again, this is close to a part (chapter) to whole (book) flaw, but you need a premise about a whole and a conclusion about a part.

E. No. There is no flaw. It lists a condition that is necessary for all employees and correctly concludes that any employee must have met that condition.

9. **A** [Principle Strengthen]

You need to prove that it would not be wrong for the Jacksons just to tell people they have a wrong number and that it would be praiseworthy (that's what laudable means) for the Jacksons to pass along Sara's number. Why isn't the minimal response wrong? The Jacksons never led Sara to believe they would pass along her number. Why is it praiseworthy for the Jacksons to pass along her number? It would be helpful to Sara and not difficult for them.

A. Yes. The first half establishes helpful → laudable, which makes it possible to prove passing along the number is laudable. The second half says wrong → led someone to believe otherwise and the contrapositive of that is didn't lead someone to believe otherwise → not wrong. This also applies to the Jacksons' situation.

B. No. This says being helpful when it is not wrong → laudable. This would prove only that one of the Jacksons' options is laudable, but you also need to prove their other option is not wrong.

C. No. This says helpful and easy → laudable and not wrong. Again, you could prove that passing along the number is laudable, but you also need to show that not passing it along is not wrong. This doesn't present a way to do that.

D. No. This says laudable → difficult and wrong not to do. Without even going further, this won't help you prove something is laudable because that is on the wrong side of the conditional. With the contrapositive, you'll only be able to prove that something is not laudable.

E. No. This says laudable → not wrong to refrain from doing it. The same comments for (D) apply here.

10. **D**   Weaken

Albert argues that there is no need for PAH regulations. Erin concludes that PAH regulations would save thousands of lives. Why? Scientists blame PAH for 10,000 premature deaths each year. How would the regulations solve that problem? The regulations would decrease the amount of PAHs released by automobile exhaust. In order to weaken this claim, you have to accept that scientists blame PAH for thousands of deaths, but look for an answer that lets you believe the proposed regulations would not necessarily save thousands of lives.

54

A. No. The reluctance of car makers toward this regulation doesn't help weaken the idea that it would save lives.

B. No. Other diseases are out of scope. Even if PAHs are linked to no other diseases, they are linked to 10,000 deaths from lung and heart disease, so Erin and the regulations still have a problem worth solving.

C. No. That fewer PAHs are released if fewer people drive seems like an obvious fact. However, since there is no reason to expect that car use will go down, there is no reason to think PAH emissions will go down and so the question of needing these regulations remains.

D. Yes. This makes it seem like a regulation designed to decrease PAH emission from car exhaust will not have much life-saving effect, since most of the PAHs out there are coming from worn-down tires, which the regulation will not address.

E. No. This may suggest that other regulations should target other components of exhaust, but it doesn't weaken the idea that we need regulations to curb PAHs.

11. **C**   Main Point

The conclusion is that Australia's comparatively low rate of carnivorous mammals is probably a consequence of its unusually sparse ecosystems. Why? Carnivorous mammals need more food to survive than do reptiles, so these mammals do not thrive as well in Australia's sparse ecosystems.

A. No. This is background information.

B. No. This is too broad in scope; the conclusion is about Australia specifically.

C. Yes. This is a good paraphrase of the second sentence, and it uses the word "probably" to match the strength of the argument.

D. No. This fails to mention Australia, which establishes the scope of the argument.

E. No. This is a premise.

12. **D**   Inference

The correct answer will be either just a paraphrase of an idea or what you get by synthesizing the new idea with the information that came before it. In this case, the Sapir-Whorf hypothesis is defined. BUT, it says, you can't verify the Sapir-Whorf hypothesis in the normal physical science sense because it is not clear whether you can test the Sapir-Whorf hypothesis for accuracy.

A. No. There's no language in the passage to match this; there is no reason to lean to probably false or probably true. The passage's point is that you don't know.

B. No. There's no language in the passage that matches the strength of "only." All you're told is that physical science hypotheses are verifiable; there could be other kinds of verifiable hypotheses.

C. No. "Should be seriously considered" is a concept that has no matching paraphrase in the passage and thus no support.

D. Yes. This is a paraphrase of the fact that you can't verify the Sapir-Whorf hypothesis.

E. No. Again, the concepts of being taken seriously and "only" are nowhere to be found in the original passage.

13. **A** Resolve/ Explain

On the one hand, wind and rain erosion wear mountains down; on the other hand, the highest mountains are found in areas where the force of erosion is strongest. How can you explain this odd correlation?

A. Yes. This tells you that the mountains aren't defying all odds by growing in windy, rainy places; their height is what causes the weather patterns around them to be windy and rainy.

B. No. This just makes higher mountains even more prone to erosion, which only adds to our confusion.

C. No. The process by which some mountains form beneath the ground is irrelevant to the "apparent conflict" between a mountain's height and its weather conditions.

D. No. This doesn't even address the highest mountain category specifically, so it is very unlikely to resolve any confusion that is specifically about the highest mountain ranges.

E. No. This fact tells you that the highest mountains shrink more than others. You already know that the highest mountains are shrinking due to erosion. This just amplifies the confusion, especially because it doesn't explain the weather aspect of the problem. This is like (B), addressing part of the apparent paradox but making it even more paradoxical.

14. **D** Flaw

When you're reading ideas like "in order to _____, you must _____," think in terms of "necessary condition." For an antenna to work well at all frequencies, it needs to have symmetry and a fractal structure (antenna works equally well → you meet these requirements). The contrapositive of any necessary condition is if you don't meet these requirements → you fail. What necessary/sufficient flaws try to convince you of is if you meet these requirements → you succeed. That's a flaw. The claim that this expert concludes is incorrect only tells you that lacking these features, an antenna won't work equally well. It never claims that if you have these features, the antenna will work well. There could be other things required for it to work equally well.

A. No. This is true, but it does not refer to any logical flaw.

B. No. The conclusion is that a certain claim is incorrect. There is no way that the claim being falsified could be considered a premise, an idea that supports its own refutation. Hence, calling the researchers' claim a premise means this choice is incorrect.

C. No. It concludes the claim is false because of a real-world example that the expert believes disproves the claim.

D. Yes. It assumes that because two things are mentioned as necessary for an antenna to work well, those two things are sufficient to guarantee an antenna will work well.

E. No. This is irrelevant wordplay since the expert doesn't care how many alternatives there are. The fact that the antenna isn't equally good at all frequencies is enough to make his argument.

15. **B** Reasoning

The argument concludes the city is more concerned with apparent bike safety than actual bike safety. Why? If the city wanted actual safety, it wouldn't require helmets; it would make bike lanes and educate drivers about bike safety. Therefore, the claim you are asked about is part of the premises; driver education is brought up to support the idea that there were more helpful things the city could have done toward actual safety.

A. No. There is no claim that the city misunderstands the steps to safety. The argument questions the city's greater concern, not whether it is well informed.

B. Yes. This identifies the statement as part of the premises and the claim as the conclusion concerning the city's motivation for passing the ordinance.

C. No. There is no language about total ineffectiveness. Plus, the conclusion is not about the helmet ordinance; it's about the city.

D. No. It was offered as a measure the city would have taken had it been more concerned with actual safety.

E. No. The city never did educate drivers, so the statement about driver education cannot be an illustration of anything the city has done out of concern for its public image.

16. **A** Flaw

This argument attempts to interpret evidence about building colonies on the moon. Humans currently have the technology, but it's very expensive. As the earth overcrowds, there will be a growing economic incentive to build moon colonies. Therefore, the argument concludes, these colonies will almost certainly be built. Do you agree with the interpretation? It seems fair to accept that there will be growing motivation to build moon colonies, but will it ever be feasible for it to actually happen? Are there any other solutions to the overcrowding problem that are more likely than moon colonies?

A. Yes. This addresses the unjustified overconfidence of the conclusion in accepting the virtual certainty of such an exotic solution.

B. No. Although the argument seems to fail to brainstorm other ways to alleviate overcrowding, since it leaps to accepting moon colonies as an extremely likely scenario, you can't justify that the argument ever stated or implied that moon colonies are the only way to help the problem.

C. No. Flaw answers should bring up an idea that weakens the conclusion. This idea would only strengthen the contention that moon colonies will almost certainly be built.

D. No. What happens after moon colonies are built is out of scope. You're only arguing about whether moon colonies will be built in the first place.

E. No. There is nothing about the preferences of the residents in the argument, so this is out of scope.

17.   **E**   **Principle Match**

Take a second to diagram the conditionals of your rules so that you have a clear sense of what you can prove and what you'll need to prove it. The first principle says violate one of society's general welfare rules → wrong (~wrong → ~violate a rule). The second principle says required by one of society's general welfare rules → right (~right → ~required). When reading the answer choices, start from the bottom of each choice. Find out if you're trying to prove something right or wrong and then read the beginning to determine whether it matches the criteria for proving that label.

A.   No. You don't even have to read this because it's trying to prove something is NOT WRONG. Our two rules (and their contrapositives) never allow you to prove something NOT WRONG. Note that "not wrong" and "right" are not necessarily the same thing.

B.   No. This choice is trying to prove something WRONG, so you need to violate a rule that promotes the general welfare. However, this rule is only not detrimental to the general welfare, so you can't prove Jordan is wrong.

C.   No. This choice is trying to prove something WRONG, so you need to violate a rule that promotes the general welfare. But Elgin is obeying a rule that is detrimental, so this choice is no good.

D.   No. This choice is trying to prove something RIGHT, so you need to perform an action required by a rule of society that promotes its general welfare. However, you don't know that Dahlia's action is required, so even though Dahlia is not violating any rules, you can't prove her action is right.

E.   Yes. This choice is trying to prove something RIGHT, so you need to perform an action required by a rule of society that promotes its general welfare, and Edward is doing so.

18.   **C**   **Necessary Assumption**

The argument concludes that, if maximizing profits is the goal (which sets a conditional scope to this whole argument), then studios should focus on big-budget films. Why? Small-budget films never attract mass audiences. The rest of the discussion contains no premises. Almost always, when a sentence begins with "although," "despite the fact that," or "while," the speaker is addressing opposing arguments or making a concession to the opposite viewpoint. In this case, Teresa is conceding that small-budget films have the positive attribute of being lower cost / lower risk than big-budget films, but she says that that does not guarantee maximal profits. There is a logical flaw there; just because something doesn't guarantee a certain result, it could still be the most likely way of attaining that result. However, this answer is likely to focus on the fact that her argument hasn't connected the premise (sometimes big-budget films attract mass audiences) to the conclusion (if you want highest profits, go with big-budget films).

A.   No. Requiring all big-budget films to succeed is too extreme. When you negate an extreme statement, it does very little. Negating this would say "not all big-budget films are guaranteed to attract a mass audience." That still allows for 99.9 percent of them to be successful, which means the argument is still intact.

B.   No. The conclusion says film studios should concentrate on big-budget versus small-budget films, so that allows for them to simultaneously make both big- and small-budget films. The argument assumes the opposite of this choice.

C. Yes. This conditional statement would look like maximizes profits → attracts mass audiences. The contrapositive would be doesn't attract mass audiences → doesn't maximize profits. That sounds just like the argument.

D. No. This is dealing with neither the premise nor the conclusion, and it moves against the direction of the conclusion by making big-budget films sound like a fiscally dangerous idea.

E. No. You don't need this to be true since the scope of the argument includes only studios that want to maximize profits. *Primary* is an extreme word. When in doubt, avoid any answer choices with strong language on necessary assumption questions.

19. **B**   Flaw

All Tour de France winners have some physiological abnormality. Two common physiological abnormalities are identified. It's assumed there are no others. Hence, because last year's winner didn't have one of those two common abnormalities, he or she must have the other. You could argue, "Why are you limiting yourself to only those two choices?" Because all these answer choices are prefaced in the question stem by "overlooks the possibility that," you need to hear a fact that, if true, weakens the argument.

A. No. The argument would be happy to concede this point; it probably takes for granted that having both traits would be an advantage.

B. Yes. This would weaken the argument. Just because a winner doesn't have a powerful heart, you'd have no reason to assume that winner has exceptional lung capacity since there have been winners before that have had neither.

C. No. Finding out that normal lung capacity and powerful hearts are nearly mutually exclusive doesn't weaken the argument at all since the argument is making the assumption that a cyclist has exceptional lung capacity because his/her heart is not exceptionally powerful.

D. No. Knowing these traits derive from training does nothing to weaken the argument.

E. No. Knowing that the argument is using these terms in relation to average cyclists does nothing to weaken the argument.

20. **A**   Strengthen

The meteorologist concludes his station's weather forecasts are more useful and reliable than those of the competition. Why? Most of the time when his station's forecasts predict rain for the next day, they're right, whereas the competition cannot make the same claim about their forecasts. Since strengthen answers frequently name key assumptions or remove the ability to make possible objections, you should brainstorm some. The claim the meteorologist makes regarding his station's prediction of rain sounds persuasive, but it is phrased in a weird way. It would be better just to hear that his station is more accurate at predicting rain than the competition is. His claim is that when his station's forecasts predict rain, they are normally right. What if they just rarely predict rain unless it's almost a guarantee for the next day and otherwise they predict no rain? That would make them highly accurate whenever they do predict rain, but it wouldn't make them seem like they give the most reliable forecast overall since they will err many times on the side of no rain.

A. Yes. This removes the worry that his station predicts rain only if it's a sure thing. If his station is making a rain prediction more frequently than the competition and his station's rain predictions are more often accurate, then you do know the overall reliability of his station's rain forecasts exceeds that of the others.

B. No. Whether there are full-time or part-time workers making predictions makes no difference to the relevant data of whether those predictions are accurate.

C. No. Popularity does nothing to help prove a claim that one station's weather forecasts are more reliable than those of another.

D. No. This is irrelevant due to the scope of the meteorologist's evidence, which pertains only to predicting rain the following day.

E. No. This is close to addressing our question about how accurate the meteorologist's station is at predicting no rain compared to other stations, but this answer choice would need to apply to the most popular news station, not just any competitor, in order to be relevant to the conclusion (which specifically compares the meteorologist's station to the most popular one in the area).

21. **C**   Resolve/ Explain

You have two rounds of cross-examination, one designed to lead to erroneous testimony and the second designed to lead to accurate testimony. How do you explain that the group with the fewest errors during the first round had the most errors during the second round?

A. No. This doesn't explain why they are less accurate than most during the second round of questioning.

B. No. This doesn't explain why they are less accurate than most during the second round of questioning.

C. Yes. If some witnesses were easy to brainwash, they would agree with many errors during the first round and agree to the correct facts during the second round. The group of witnesses asked about, on the other hand, is steadfastly delivering the same testimony during both rounds. Assuming these witnesses have most facts right but some facts wrong, they will seem more accurate than most in the first round (when everyone else is being persuaded of falsehoods), but they will seem more inaccurate during the second round (when they are insisting on their mistakes instead of being persuaded by accurate information).

D. No. This doesn't explain why they were initially more accurate than most.

E. No. A higher quantity of details doesn't explain why they would seem most accurate during the first round and least accurate during the second round.

22. **B**   Sufficient Assumption

You need to prove the claim that businesses often have compelling reasons to execute a morally preferable act. What were you told about any of those ingredients? Businesses often have a conflict between short- and long-term interests, and the long-term interest is usually served by the morally preferable act. What's new in the conclusion but missing from the premises is the notion of compelling reasons. Since morally preferable act = long-term interest, you probably just need to hear that businesses often have compelling reasons to serve the long-term interest.

A. No. This talks about not having compelling reasons, so this won't help you prove a claim about having compelling reasons.

B. Yes. This is the missing information you need to prove the conclusion.

C. No. Nothing in here addresses compelling reasons.

D. No. Nothing in here addresses compelling reasons.

E. No. Nothing in here addresses compelling reasons.

23. **B** Inference

This passage has a chain of necessary conditions. Remain competitive in global economy (requires) → overcome math education crisis (which requires) → successful teaching (which requires) → getting students to spend significant time outside class studying. Frequently, the "must be true" answer is just the grand contrapositive of the whole chain. In this case, it would be not getting students to study outside class → won't have successful teaching → won't overcome math education crisis → won't remain competitive in global economy. Typically, an answer choice will relate the end of the chain back to the beginning. However, answers can also address any part of the chain.

A. No. This tries to illegally turn all the arrows around and make all these relationships sufficient, but they are just necessary requirements so you don't know that meeting them guarantees you anything.

B. Yes. This just affirms the chain you put together, which allows you to realize that overcoming the math education crisis is dependent upon students studying on their own time outside of class.

C. No. There is no evidence to compare the importance of math to other subjects.

D. No. If you diagram this answer, it looks like students spend time studying outside class (only if) → remain competitive in global economy. That is not what you originally diagrammed. The arrow is pointing the wrong way.

E. No. This is tempting. Getting students to spend time studying outside class is a required condition of remaining competitive in the global economy, so it seems fair to say that meeting this required condition helps us with that goal. However, the concept of helping is different from meeting a required condition. Consider getting your driver's license. Passing the written test is a requirement. However, if you've failed the driving test (which is also a requirement), does the fact that you've passed the written test actually help you get your license?

24. **E** Necessary Assumption

The conclusion is that downtown Petropolis is in a serious state of economic decline. Why? The number of large buildings is an indicator of economic health. Five years ago, Petropolis had over 100 large buildings. Over the past five years, 60 of those have been demolished. Does that mean you have to accept that Petropolis currently has only around 40 tall buildings? Do you actually know how many large buildings Petropolis currently has? What if Petropolis is so economically robust that it demolished all the older buildings in order to make room for building state-of-the-art new buildings?

A. No. Who cares if the demolitions were evenly distributed or in a series of clumps? The way the argument judges the economic health of Petropolis is simply by the quantity of large buildings it has.

B. No. This would be referring to time periods outside the scope of the argument, so it's irrelevant. Negated, this would say that Petropolis had many more than 100 large buildings before, which means it would have had to decline economically at some point to get down to the 100 or so you have at the start of the argument. The negation actually supports the conclusion that Petropolis is declining economically.

C. No. The reasons that a building comes down are irrelevant. You are concerned only with the quantity of large buildings currently in Petropolis because that is how you are told to judge its economic health.

D. No. The argument doesn't need to assume that anything is built in place of the demolished buildings since it is concluding that the area is in economic decline.

E. Yes. This addresses your concern about missing information related to how many buildings may have been built during the same time frame. If you negate this, you find that nearly or potentially more than 60 buildings have been built to replace the ones torn down. That would ruin the argument.

25. **C**   **Parallel**

Paraphrase the reasoning: you know that anyone getting A (free dessert) gets → B (entree) and C (salad); you know that anyone getting B or C gets → D (option of free soft drink). Those two conditionals chain together to say if you get A (free dessert) → you get D (option of free soft drink). Hence, the conclusion is just the contrapositive: no option of free soft drink → no free dessert. So you need A → B and C; B or C → D; thus, ~D → ~A.

A. No. The first sentence gives us our A → B and C. The second sentence says D and ~C → B. This is already too different to continue.

B. No. The first sentence gives us A (class president) B (well liked) and C (well known); if B or C → D (something better to do); however, the faulty conclusion is D → ~A instead of ~D → ~A.

C. Yes. The first sentence gives us A (good azaleas) → B (rich in humus) and C (low in acidity); if B or C → D (can grow blueberries); thus, ~D → ~A.

D. No. The first sentence gives us A (drive to Weller) → B (highway) or C (Old Mill Road). That "or" is already different enough from our original "and," but even beyond that, the second sentence does not combine B and C, so this is way too different.

E. No. The first sentence gives us A (discount) → B (raspberries) and C (ice cream); if B or C → D (coupon); however, the faulty conclusion is ~A → ~D instead of ~D → ~A.

54

Chapter 5
PrepTest 55:
Answers and
Explanations

ANSWER KEY: PREPTEST 55

Section 1:
Arguments 1

1. B
2. A
3. C
4. A
5. B
6. A
7. A
8. D
9. D
10. B
11. E
12. C
13. D
14. E
15. D
16. B
17. D
18. E
19. C
20. A
21. B
22. E
23. B
24. D
25. C

Section 2:
Reading
Comprehension

1. D
2. A
3. A
4. B
5. E
6. E
7. A
8. E
9. B
10. E
11. A
12. C
13. A
14. A
15. D
16. C
17. B
18. C
19. D
20. B
21. A
22. D
23. D
24. B
25. B
26. C
27. D

Section 3:
Arguments 2

1. B
2. C
3. B
4. A
5. A
6. D
7. E
8. E
9. D
10. D
11. B
12. D
13. D
14. B
15. E
16. C
17. A
18. E
19. C
20. B
21. A
22. A
23. C
24. D
25. B

Section 4:
Games

1. D
2. C
3. A
4. B
5. E
6. C
7. D
8. C
9. A
10. E
11. D
12. B
13. D
14. B
15. C
16. C
17. C
18. E
19. E
20. D
21. D
22. C
23. D

EXPLANATIONS

Section 1: Arguments 1

1. **B**   **Parallel Flaw**

   The argument concludes that the editor of a magazine cannot be trusted to pass judgment on matters of spelling and grammar because errors similar to those she has pointed out on a TV program have been found in her own magazine. The flaw here is that the argument fails to consider that her judgment could still be sound with respect to those errors even though her own magazine has committed similar ones.

   A. No. Ethics is compared to spelling in this choice, so it doesn't match the flaw in the original argument.

   B. Yes. Because you have discriminatory hiring practices of your own, you cannot be trusted to pass judgment on the hiring practices of others. This displays the same flaw as the original argument.

   C. No. This choice compares safety to whether something is allowed to be sold, so it doesn't match the flaw in the original argument.

   D. No. This choice claims a coach cannot be trusted to judge swimming practices because he has a lucrative promotional deal, which doesn't match the flaw in the original argument.

   E. No. This choice says a magazine shouldn't run a feature based on concerns about audience and revenue, which doesn't match the original argument.

2. **A**   **Necessary Assumption**

   The argument concludes that if a bean dish's quality is more important than cooking speed, beans should not be presoaked. The reasons given are that soaking reduces cooking time and not presoaking means the beans will be plumper. What's missing in the argument is a link between the quality of the bean dish and plumper beans.

   A. Yes. This links plumper beans to enhanced dish quality.

   B. No. This is out of scope; the argument is concerned only with bean dishes.

   C. No. You know nothing about how appearance and taste contribute to quality here, and you're missing any reference to plumper beans.

   D. No. This is irrelevant; the argument is concerned with only one ingredient, beans.

   E. No. This is close, but you don't know how taste factors into a bean dish's quality. If an answer choice requires additional information to make its connection to the conclusion explicit, it's not the credited response.

3. **C**   **Reasoning**

   Durth concludes that the practice of direct mail advertising is annoying and immoral. Durth bases this conclusion on the fact that most direct mail advertising is tossed without ever being read, thereby wasting paper. Furthermore, this sort of waste would not be tolerated if generated by anyone else.

A. No. Durth never claims that anyone has made the contention that direct mail advertising is immoral, and there is no counterexample presented.

B. No. Durth never raises the issue of what would happen if direct mail advertising became more widespread.

C. Yes. Durth concludes that direct mail advertising is immoral because the amount of wasted paper it creates would be unconscionable if generated by anyone else.

D. No. The conclusion states that direct mail advertising is annoying, so this can't be a premise of the argument.

E. No. Other advertising methods are referenced in the first sentence, but no mention is made as to whether they have any negative effects.

4. **A**   Sufficient Assumption

55

The argument concludes that one cannot accurately predict how effectively a Delta vacuum cleans merely by knowing how powerful the motor is. The reason for this claim is that even among vacuums equipped with identically powerful motors, the dust filtration systems can vary significantly in efficiency. You need to find an answer choice that proves that the nature of the dust filtration system in a given vacuum affects how effectively that vacuum cleans.

A. Yes. This would be enough to prove the conclusion.

B. No. The conclusion focuses on how well a vacuum cleans; this choice doesn't create any link to that.

C. No. This choice suggests that by knowing something about the motor, you know something about the vacuum's cleaning ability, yet the conclusion specifically states that knowing how powerful the motor is doesn't give you an accurate picture of its effectiveness in cleaning. You need an answer that addresses the issue of the dust filtration system.

D. No. You know the motor and the dust filtration system contribute in some way to the cleaning efficacy of a given vacuum, but you don't know that those are the only factors that matter. Because the argument leaves room for other factors to determine how well a vacuum cleans, this choice doesn't help the conclusion to be true.

E. No. You are told in the conclusion that knowing how powerful a motor is isn't enough to predict how well a vacuum will clean. This choice attempts to make knowledge of the motor necessary to assessing how effectively a vacuum cleans, but doing so doesn't make the conclusion any more valid. You still need to address the issue of the dust filtration system.

5. **B**   Inference

Most scientists believe bipedal locomotion evolved in response to early hominids' move from forest life to life in open grasslands. However, because the advantages of bipedalism would apply to hominids in forests as well as to those in grasslands, the question of why bipedalism evolved is not yet settled.

A. No. No comparison is made between forest and grassland environments in terms of how hospitable they were for hominids.

B. Yes. The argument does state that this advantage would apply to hominids in both environments.

C.   No. No mention is made in the argument of bipedal locomotion being a disadvantage.

D.   No. The argument does not take a final stand on the origins of bipedal locomotion.

E.   No. Though the argument does mention both gathering food and detecting and avoiding predators as important activities for early hominids, the argument never addresses which of these was more relevant to their survival.

6.   A   **Principle Strengthen**

The teacher concludes that if pre-university students are to be taught calculus, they must be able to handle the level of abstraction involved. While the teacher acknowledges that learning calculus before going to college may be beneficial, he also notes the potential downside that students may abandon math altogether if they aren't ready for the level of abstraction that calculus entails.

A.   Yes. The teacher concludes that if calculus (new intellectual work) is to be taught to students, they must be able to handle the abstraction involved (meet the cognitive challenges) so that they don't abandon math completely (without losing motivation).

B.   No. This is more extreme than what the teacher proposes. The teacher does not suggest that only the most concrete math should be taught to pre-university students.

C.   No. This is too broad when compared to the teacher's argument. The teacher stipulates that students must be ready for the level of abstraction involved in calculus or else they might abandon math, but there is no mention of the idea that "cognitive tasks that require exceptional effort" *in general* might undermine a student's motivation.

D.   No. This is out of scope. Although the teacher focuses on whether students can handle the level of abstraction needed for calculus, there is no discussion about how to teach students effectively, so there is no need for "the application of mathematics to concrete problems" as a teaching suggestion.

E.   No. This contradicts the teacher's conclusion, since whether students can handle the level of abstraction involved in calculus is a factor in determining whether to teach it to them.

7.   A   **Weaken**

The argument concludes that legislation has increased overall worker safety within high-risk industries. Why? Since 1955, when the legislation gave the government increased control over workplace safety conditions, the likelihood that a worker in a high-risk industry will suffer a serious injury has decreased. To weaken this argument, you'll need to find another explanation for this decrease in injuries, one that isn't linked to the legislation.

A.   Yes. If this is true, then the reason for the reduced risk of injury is technological innovation and not the legislation.

B.   No. This choice does present another possibility—maybe workers became less careless—but since you don't know what happened after 1955, this doesn't go far enough to weaken the argument.

C.   No. This is too broad. The argument is concerned only with the rate of injury within high-risk industries, but this choice refers to work-related injuries in general.

D. No. This choice is concerned with "injuries occurring within industries not considered high-risk," so it's not relevant to the argument, which is focused on high-risk industries.

E. No. This choice doesn't tell you why workplace safety conditions have improved, so it doesn't weaken the idea that the legislation is responsible for the improvement.

8. **D** Inference

The economist suggests that the renewed growing of sunflowers would be good for Kalotopia's unstable farming industry. Sunflower seed was once one of the largest production crops in Kalotopia and sunflower oil can provide both industrial and consumer products at little cost to the environment.

A. No. This is too extreme. The argument makes no predictions about what will happen to Kalotopia's farming industry if sunflowers are not grown there.

B. No. You don't have enough information to know what effect stabilizing Kalotopia's farming industry would have on either the economy or the environment. All you know is that the farming industry is quite unstable and that growing sunflowers would provide it some relief, but it's too much of a stretch to say that this action would stabilize the farming industry.

C. No. There is no information to support this choice. You don't know why the farming industry ceased to grow sunflowers or any other large production crop, so you can't make any judgments about whether it would be better off had it never ceased to grow them.

D. Yes. Sunflowers were once a large production crop in Kalotopia, and the economist suggests that growing them again would give some relief to the farming industry and would provide industrial and consumer products for the general economy.

E. No. The argument makes no mention of other crops that could be grown in Kalotopia, so it's not possible to draw comparative conclusions.

9. **D** Weaken

The argument concludes that a new earthquake prediction method will aid local officials in deciding exactly when to evacuate people in advance of an earthquake. Why? Over the past ten years, several major earthquakes have occurred in the region, all of which were preceded by changes in the electric current in the earth's crust. To weaken the argument, you need to show that this method of using changes in the electric current to detect future earthquakes is either flawed or otherwise unreliable.

A. No. The fact that scientists don't fully understand what causes these changes in the electric current doesn't tell you that the method won't work. Thus, this choice doesn't weaken the argument.

B. No. This choice would actually appear to strengthen the argument by suggesting that this system is based on a correlation for making predictions about earthquakes that is stronger than those of other systems. In any case, it definitely doesn't weaken the argument, since it doesn't point out a problem with the new method.

C. No. This choice is irrelevant—increased earthquake frequency, by itself, doesn't tell you anything about the efficacy of the new earthquake prediction method.

D. Yes. If this is true, then it may not be the case that the new prediction method will aid officials in deciding *exactly when* to evacuate certain towns because they won't know how much time they'll have between the changes detected in the electric current and the onset of the earthquake. Since this choice suggests that the new method may not be entirely reliable, it weakens the argument.

E. No. The fact that there is only one station in the region is irrelevant to whether the new prediction method works; there is no reason to believe that one station won't be sufficient for implementing this new method. Since nothing here suggests that the method won't work, this doesn't weaken the argument.

10. **B** Inference

Pick the answer best supported by the passage.

A. No. This choice goes beyond the scope of the argument, which considers only the case of fax machines. You cannot draw general conclusions about "whenever machines are dependent on other machines of the same type" from the information in the passage.

B. Yes. From the information in the argument, you know that this statement is true of at least one industry, the fax industry, because its manufacturers cooperated to a certain extent by agreeing to adopt a common format for their machines.

C. No. This choice goes beyond the scope of the argument in two ways. First, the only information you have relates to the fax industry, from which you cannot draw conclusions about a "high-tech industry." Second, you don't have enough information to safely conclude that the greater the number of competitors, the greater the amount of cooperation required.

D. No. While this choice may seem to be in line with the argument at first glance, you know only that some cooperation was beneficial in the case of the fax industry. You can't conclude, however, that some cooperation is more beneficial than pure competition, which is never addressed in the argument; perhaps some manufacturers would still have earned greater profits had they not agreed to cooperate.

E. No. This choice is too extreme. There is no information to suggest that cooperation is beneficial "only" in industries whose products must work with other products of the same type.

11. **E** Principle Match

When a critique of teacher performance is accompanied by information suggesting teacher performance is only one factor out of several that play a role in enhancing educational outcomes, the critique leads to enhanced educational outcomes.

A. No. There is no match in the original argument for "earn the respect of their peers."

B. No. There is no match in the original argument for "if they do not see themselves as members of the group being so characterized."

C. No. There is no match in the original argument for the idea that effective self-evaluation is more likely to occur if you convince yourself that you are evaluating someone else.

D. No. There is no match in the original argument for the idea that greater objectivity and reliability can be achieved if one is not a member of the society one is studying.

E. Yes. When criticism of an athlete is accompanied by information suggesting that the criticism is only one part of a larger effort to correct his team's shortcomings, it becomes easier to correct the athlete's mistakes.

12. **C** Necessary Assumption

The argument states that high-quality novels depend on most readers becoming emotionally engaged with the imaginary world described therein; the contrapositive of this idea is that if readers are not emotionally engaged, the novel cannot be of the highest quality. Shifts of narrative point of view within a novel tend to make most readers focus on the author. From this, the argument concludes that shifts of narrative point of view detract from the merit of the work (the novel's quality). The gap here is between readers' focus on the author and their emotional engagement. You need to find a choice that suggests that if readers focus on the author, they will not become emotionally engaged in the imaginary world of the novel.

A. No. This goes in the opposite direction of one of the premises of the argument. This choice says that emotional engagement depends on (note the use of "only if" here) the novel being of the highest quality.

B. No. This more or less restates one of the premises of the argument, but shifts some of the wording as well. The argument discusses most readers becoming emotionally engaged with the imaginary world of the novel, while this choice talks about a novel successfully engaging the imagination of most readers, which isn't quite the same.

C. Yes. This choice bridges the gap as noted above.

D. No. This choice is irrelevant. It may explain why shifts in narrative cause readers to focus on the author, but it doesn't link up with the notions of emotional engagement and novel quality.

E. No. "Literary purpose" is out of scope.

13. **D** Resolve/ Explain

People aged 46 to 55 spend the most money per capita, yet when it comes to advertising products on television, decision-makers focus nearly exclusively on the 25-and-under crowd. Why are people aged 25 and under more highly valued when it comes to advertising products on television when they spend less money per capita than do people aged 46 to 55?

A. No. This is close, but because you don't know which age group is more likely to purchase a company's products, this choice doesn't do enough to explain the discrepancy noted above.

B. No. This choice doesn't tell you anything about the audiences of each type of program, so it doesn't clarify why advertisers place such a high value on the 25-and-under crowd.

C. No. This is out of scope. How executives decide which shows to renew is unrelated to how advertisers place value on television advertising slots.

D. Yes. If decision-makers believe that people aged 46 to 55 will most likely not be persuaded to buy the products advertised, then it makes sense that advertising will be targeted to people aged 25 and under even though they spend less per capita than people aged 46 to 55.

E. No. This choice deals with advertising in print media instead of on television, so it's out of scope.

14. E **Flaw**

The moralist concludes that you should never make an effort to acquire expensive new tastes. He draws this conclusion from the fact that expensive new tastes present a financial drain and are superfluous, as demonstrated by the amount of effort needed to acquire them. Furthermore, you might expose yourself to unpleasant experiences in your pursuit of those new tastes. However, the moralist provides no real evidence with which to assess his argument. Are the costs of acquiring expensive new tastes really as punishing as he depicts them?

A. No. This choice describes circular reasoning, which is not the flaw in this argument. The moralist does not simply restate one of his premises as his conclusion.

B. No. While the moralist does say that acquiring expensive tastes is financially draining, he does not go so far as to say that it leads to financial irresponsibility.

C. No. The moralist does not define the term "sensations"; however, this omission does not represent a flaw in the argument's reasoning.

D. No. The moralist never discusses any causes for the acquisition of expensive tastes.

E. Yes. The moralist claims that you should never try to acquire expensive new tastes because of the costs associated with such a pursuit, yet he never weighs the potential benefits against these costs.

15. D **Inference**

Zack's Coffeehouse schedules free poetry readings nearly every Wednesday. If a poetry reading is scheduled for a given day, then Zack's offers half-priced coffee all day.

A. No. This choice is too extreme. Zack's could offer half-priced coffee on other days, for reasons unrelated to the free poetry readings, so you don't know that Wednesday is the most common day.

B. No. You don't know about "most" free poetry readings given at Zack's; you know only about the ones that occur almost every Wednesday. There could be others scheduled for different days, so those given on Wednesday could represent the minority.

C. No. You know that if there's a poetry reading scheduled, then Zack's offers half-priced coffee all day. However, you can't conclude from this that if Zack's offers half-priced coffee all day, then there is a free poetry reading scheduled.

D. Yes. Since free poetry readings are scheduled most Wednesdays, it follows that Zack's will offer half-priced coffee all day on most Wednesdays.

E. No. Even if there isn't a poetry reading scheduled for a given Wednesday, Zack's could still offer half-priced coffee all day for other reasons.

16. B **Principle Match**

Diagram the two pieces of information given and their contrapositives. Human action performed on basis of specific motivation → intentional. Not intentional → not performed on basis of specific motivation. Not performed on basis of specific motivation and not explainable by normal physical processes → random. Not random → performed on basis of specific motivation or explainable by normal physical processes.

A. No. Tarik's action was not performed on the basis of a specific motivation, but since you don't know whether it could be explained by normal physical processes, you can't conclude that it was random.

B. Yes. Ellis acted on the basis of a specific motivation, so you can conclude the event was intentional.

C. No. Judith's hailing a cab was based on a specific motivation, so you know the event was intentional. However, this conclusion applies only to Judith's action, since the event in question consisted of her action. Because you don't know anything about the driver, you can't draw any conclusions about the driver's becoming distracted from information about Judith's action according to the principle set forth by the philosopher.

D. No. This choice doesn't draw any conclusions about whether the event was random or intentional.

E. No. This choice misapplies the contrapositive of the second statement. Knowing that an action is explainable by normal physical processes isn't sufficient to draw any further conclusions about that action.

17. **D** ◗ Necessary Assumption

The argument claims that it is a mistake to conclude that ancient people did not know what moral rights were just because no known ancient language has an expression that translates to the concept of a moral right. The argument presents as support an analogy of a person who harvests and studies a wild fruit tree without naming it or learning its name; this person, the argument implies, would still have some idea of what the fruit is despite the lack of nomenclature.

A. No. The argument is operating on the idea that you can know something without knowing the name of that thing. This choice, however, takes as its starting point the idea that you know the name of something and that knowledge of the thing itself derives from there.

B. No. Comparing the level of knowledge of people who first discover something to that of people who merely know the name of something isn't relevant to the argument.

C. No. This is too extreme. Even if the name can provide some information about the nature of the thing in question, this does not invalidate the argument's conclusion that you can have some idea about the nature of a thing without knowing the name of the thing.

D. Yes. Try negating this choice. If the person harvesting and studying the fruit has no idea of what the fruit is without knowing its name, this would invalidate the argument's conclusion.

E. No. The argument is claiming that you don't need to know the name of something in order to have an idea of its nature. The idea presented in the answer choice—that you don't need to know what something is in order to name it—is out of scope.

18. **E** ◗ Main Point

The argument disagrees with those who believe that it is absurd to criticize anyone for being critical. The argument's main conclusion is that there is good reason to dissuade people from being too judgmental because often such judgments are not merely negative but also made without a serious effort at understanding.

A. No. This is a premise of the argument.

B. No. The argument's main conclusion goes against this idea.

C. No. This is nearly the same as (B); the argument is concluding the opposite idea.

D. No. This information acts as transitional material between the claim the argument is disagreeing with and the claim the argument is promoting.

E. Yes. This is the main conclusion of the argument.

19. **C** **Reasoning**

The argument claims that the superiority of some painters over others in terms of the execution of their artistic visions must be measured in light of each artist's purposes. The argument then offers the example of Jose Rey Toledo, whose work and artistic skill is not in question though his paintings do not literally resemble what they represent. The claim you are asked about in the question stem serves as a starting point for the conclusion, which delineates the way in which the claim should be appreciated.

A. No. This information is presented as a claim, not a hypothesis. Also, the argument attempts to qualify, not refute, the claim.

B. No. The argument does not object to this generalization; it seeks to qualify how it should be comprehended.

C. Yes. The argument's conclusion is that the idea that some painters are superior to others in the execution of their artistic visions (the claim) must be measured in light of the artists' purposes (understood in the manner specified).

D. No. This claim is not derived from another claim in the argument and it is not used as support for the conclusion.

E. No. The argument does not use the claim to justify the relevance of the Jose Rey Toledo example.

20. **A** **Flaw**

A study of rabbits that, at the time, convinced biologists that parthenogenesis sometimes occurs in mammals has since been shown to be flawed, and no other studies have demonstrated that parthenogenesis is feasible in mammals. Parthenogenesis is also known to occur in a variety of nonmammalian vertebrates. From this information, the argument concludes that parthenogenesis must not be possible in mammals due to something in mammalian chromosomes. However, the argument never provides evidence that proves parthenogenesis is not possible; it bases its conclusion merely on a lack of evidence proving that it is possible.

A. Yes. The argument incorrectly assumes that because parthenogenesis has not been proven true in mammals, it must not be feasible and is therefore false.

B. No. The argument is focused primarily on mammalian species, and it doesn't contain a part-to-whole flaw in its discussion of nonmammalian vertebrate species.

C. No. The argument rules out the possibility of a phenomenon (parthenogenesis) and attempts to provide an explanation (something about mammalian chromosomes) for why the phenomenon doesn't occur. The argument doesn't rule out an explanation or provide an alternative explanation, so this choice doesn't describe the flaw in the reasoning.

D. No. The argument discusses neither necessary nor sufficient conditions for parthenogenesis, so this choice cannot be correct.

E. No. The argument states empirically that the study's methods have been shown to be flawed; this is presented as fact. Why and how the methods came to be viewed as flawed is not discussed in the argument.

21. **B**   Principle Match

The advertiser concludes that those who feel that a given TV show is worth preserving ought to buy the products advertised during that show. Why? TV shows rely on funding from advertisers, without which a show would be canceled. But advertisers don't want to pay to air commercials for their products during a show if many people who watch the show don't actually buy the products advertised. If most people opt not to buy the products advertised during their favorite shows, though, those shows will be canceled.

A. No. This choice is close, but the advertiser does say that "many people" need to take action, not just one individual, if a given show is to be preserved.

B. Yes. Unless many people buy the products advertised during their favorite show, that show will be canceled; therefore all who believe that a show is worth preserving ought to buy the advertised products.

C. No. The argument specifies that "anyone who feels that a TV show is worth preserving" should take action; however, this choice suggests that "everyone" in general should take action, which is stronger than the advertiser's conclusion.

D. No. This discusses what should be done if one feels that a TV show is worth preserving, but it's missing the additional piece that the show will be canceled unless certain actions are taken. "Reduce the likelihood" doesn't have a clear match in the advertiser's original argument.

E. No. The argument never singles out "those who feel most strongly"; it suggests only that anyone who feels a given show is worth preserving should act.

22. **E**   Weaken

A recent study has shown that those who are easily angered are much more likely to have permanently high blood pressure than are those who have more tranquil personalities. In addition, it is a long-established fact that people with permanently high blood pressure are especially likely to have heart disease. From this information, the psychologist concludes that heart disease can result from psychological factors. You want to find an answer choice that suggests an alternative way of interpreting this information.

A. No. How fully someone recovers from heart disease is irrelevant. This choice doesn't present an alternative to the idea that psychological factors can cause heart disease.

B. No. While medication that controls high blood pressure may seem to be an alternative factor, this choice still doesn't tell you that psychological factors aren't involved. The fact that medication may alter a person's moods doesn't rule out the possibility that psychological factors are still at work in causing heart disease.

C. No. This choice would, if anything, strengthen the psychologist's argument by showing that psychological factors, such as having a tranquil personality, can impact the likelihood of developing heart disease, especially given the fact that having permanently high blood pressure makes one more inclined in general toward developing heart disease.

D. No. This is irrelevant; how people react once they learn they have heart disease doesn't tell you anything about what caused it.

E. Yes. If the physiological factors that cause permanently high blood pressure also make people easily angered, then this would weaken the psychologist's argument that heart disease can result from psychological factors, as being quick to anger would stem from a physical, not psychological, basis.

23. **B** **Strengthen**

A business professor put a case-study assignment for her students online, but it turned out that 50 out of 70 students printed it out to read instead of reading it online. From this the argument concludes that books delivered via computer will not make printed books obsolete. You need to find a choice that affirms that what is true for the case-study assignment would also be true for books.

A. No. Knowing that other students in non-business courses behaved in a similar fashion is irrelevant. This doesn't strengthen the argument's conclusion, which applies the example of what happened with the case-study assignment to what will (or won't) happen with books.

B. Yes. You don't know how long the case-study assignment was, but this choice tells you that anything more than a few pages in length is more likely to be printed than read on a computer screen, so this strengthens the idea that printed books will not become obsolete.

C. No. This is irrelevant. You could still have most people read books delivered via a computer even if some people get impaired vision from doing so, so this choice doesn't strengthen the argument.

D. No. This choice is also irrelevant. As long as editors carefully read the scanned versions, it is possible to deliver books that are not error-ridden via computer.

E. No. Books on cassette tape and videos of books are irrelevant.

24. **D** **Flaw**

The advertisement cites the findings of researchers who studied a group of people trying to lose weight. The researchers found that those who lost the most weight got more calories from protein than from carbohydrates and ate their biggest meal early in the day. From this information, the advertisement claims that people who follow its diet, in which breakfast is required to be the biggest meal of the day and more calories are derived from protein than from anything else, will be sure to lose weight. However, there's no proof that the reason those people lost the most weight was that they got more calories from protein and ate their biggest meal early in the day. There could have been other factors at work that were responsible for the weight loss those people experienced.

A. No. Whether certain foods make one feel fuller isn't relevant to the argument; those who lost the most weight could have felt less full while they were losing weight. And even if this possibility were true, it doesn't challenge the notion that the specific regimen followed by those who lost the most weight was responsible for their weight loss.

B.   No. The advertisement claims that the people who lost the most weight followed the regimen outlined. The fact that others had significant weight loss while following a regimen contrary to that of the people who lost the most weight is still consistent with the argument.

C.   No. The fact that people who increased their activity levels lost more weight, on average, than those who did not doesn't provide another factor, since this finding applies to all of the group across the board regardless of eating habits.

D.   Yes. If some people in the group followed the same diet that the advertisement promotes, yet lost no weight, then there would have to be some other factor, other than eating habits, that contributed to the weight loss the advertisement cites in support of its conclusion. However, the advertisement doesn't allow for such a possibility.

E.   No. The information in this choice would be consistent with the advertisement's logic, so it isn't something the advertisement overlooks. Instead, this choice suggests a reason why those who ate their biggest meal early in the day might have lost more weight.

25.   **C**   Inference

Diagram the second sentence. Great art → original ideas; not original ideas → not great art. Great art → influential; not influential → not great art. You also know that some twentieth-century art is great art, which means that some twentieth-century art both involves original ideas and is influential. This is an EXCEPT question, so you are looking for an answer choice that cannot be proven from the information given.

A.   No. This is true. If a work of art is great, then you know it both involves original ideas and is influential.

B.   No. This is also true, as discussed above.

C.   Yes. If you diagram this statement, you get influential → involves original ideas. While in theory this statement could be true, it isn't provable from the information provided in the argument.

D.   No. If you diagram this statement, you get great art → influential and original ideas. This is consistent with the information above.

E.   No. This choice is provable based on the discussion above.

Section 2: Reading Comprehension

Questions 1–6

The author argues that court injunctions intended to protect a company's right to its intellectual property by prohibiting employees from disclosing former employers' trade secrets are probably not entirely effective when it comes to preventing the transfer of information. The first paragraph identifies two basic principles that are incompatible with each other—the company's right to its intellectual property and the individual's right to seek employment and freely use his/her abilities—and discusses how courts have thus far tried, unsuccessfully, to protect both parties' legal rights. The second paragraph details the complications that arise when trying to separate oneself from the expertise acquired from former colleagues and employers. The third paragraph explores the problems inherent in attempting to document "leakage" of trade secrets and explains why these issues render court injunctions less effective in meeting their stated goal.

1. **D** Big Picture

The main point of the passage is that court injunctions are generally not fully effective in preventing the transfer of information between former employees and their new employers.

A. No. The passage never states that there are more effective ways to preserve these rights.

B. No. The passage never advocates for the strengthening of court injunctions; it merely discusses why they are not wholly sufficient for preserving trade secrets.

C. No. Enforcement of court injunctions is never discussed and the word "impossible" is also too strong for this passage.

D. Yes. This is in line with the author's final statement of the passage.

E. No. This is too specific—the effect of court injunctions on the rights of employees to make full use of their talents and previous training is mentioned only in the first paragraph—and too extreme; the author never claims their rights are being "seriously eroded."

2. **A** Extract Infer

Find an answer choice that is supported by information in the passage.

A. Yes. Since the author believes that court injunctions are not truly effective in preserving trade secrets and since no other alternatives are put forth to address the issue, it makes sense that the author would suggest that corporations worried about information leakage would do best to hang on to their current employees.

B. No. This is the opposite of the author's main point, which is that court injunctions are not very effective at accomplishing either aim.

C. No. Nothing in the passage refers to means of redress, and the author seems to believe that proof is necessary to pursue a claim of information leakage, given the difficulty of distinguishing trade secrets from legitimate technological skills developed independently by an employer or employee.

D. No. This goes against what the author claims in the last sentence of the passage. Injunctions can be effective in preventing the disclosure of trade secrets when those secrets are embodied in concrete form.

E. No. This is too extreme. The author suggests that injunctions are not very effective in upholding an individual's right to free employment decisions because of the psychological barriers they generate, so these barriers must have some effect on the employee.

3. **A** Big Picture

The primary purpose of the passage is to show that court injunctions are generally not very effective in preventing the disclosure of trade secrets and may infringe to some degree on an individual's right to free employment decisions.

A. Yes. This matches the ideas expressed above.

B. No. The author never claims that information expressed in concrete form is trivial.

C. No. The passage never calls for new methods to be found to address this issue.

D. No. This is too extreme. Although the author does refer in the last paragraph to a major stumbling block when it comes to attempting to protect trade secrets, he never says the concept is no longer viable.

E. No. This is also too extreme. The author claims that injunctions are highly ineffective, but not that they are unnecessary. He allows for the fact that they do offer some protection in certain situations.

4. **B** Extract Infer

Find an answer choice that is supported by information in the passage.

A. No. This is too extreme. The author never specifies that injunctions should be imposed only when there is strong reason to believe an employee will transfer information.

B. Yes. The author claims both that injunctions are mostly ineffective at protecting trade secrets and that they aren't much better at protecting the rights of employees to seek new employment. See the last couple of sentences in the first paragraph.

C. No. This statement goes too far. The author never proposes to limit employees' right to free employment decisions so as not to compromise employers' trade secrets.

D. No. The author doesn't feel injunctions are all that effective, so the passage doesn't support the notion that there's an increased need for them.

E. No. The passage never mentions companies seeking injunctions as a form of punishment.

5. **E** Extract Infer

The author refers to documents and other concrete embodiments as exceptions to his general claim that injunctions are not very effective in preventing the transfer of materials or information from former employees to new employers.

A. No. The author never compares information transferred via these materials and information transferred via the contributions of an employee in terms of how much damage may arise from each.

B. No. The author never makes any judgments about the relative worth of these materials (as opposed to what an employee may recollect from a previous job).

C. No. The author never suggests that injunctions should focus on the most damaging materials.

D. No. This goes against what the passage says; the author implies that documents and other concrete embodiments are the materials most readily controlled by injunctions.

E. Yes. This is essentially a paraphrase of the final sentence of the passage.

6. **E** Extract Fact

Find an answer choice that is supported by information in the passage.

A. No. The passage never discusses how or whether injunctions affect an employee's chances of being hired by a competitor.

B. No. The author argues that injunctions are mostly ineffective, but he does not state that it is not necessary to protect trade secrets, merely that injunctions aren't achieving this objective.

C. No. The passage does not say that employees usually violate the law unintentionally; it only explains how that might occur. No mention is made of how frequently this actually happens.

D. No. If anything, the passage suggests that an employee's right to free employment decisions does indeed place some limit on what employers can do. Employers can't, for instance, prevent employees from working for a competitor, which is something that employers would likely prefer to avoid.

E. Yes. See the middle of the final paragraph where the author discusses "the further problem of distinguishing trade secrets."

Questions 7–13

Passage A

The author discusses the damaging effects of the invasive species purple loosestrife. The first paragraph explains how purple loosestrife has spread across North America's wetlands and notes some negative effects that have been observed due to the weed's appearance in an area. The second paragraph states that some form of control is needed to stem the spread of purple loosestrife and emphasizes the importance of early detection.

Passage B

The author provides a critique of the rationale underlying purple loosestrife control. The first paragraph lays out the arguments given by those who seek to control the spread of purple loosestrife, most of which revolve around the idea of saving nature from a harmful weed. The second paragraph dissects these arguments and claims that the motivating factor behind purple loosestrife control is economic, not environmental.

7. **A** **Extract Fact**

A. Yes. This is mentioned in the middle of the first paragraph of passage A and in the middle of the second paragraph of passage B.

B. No. This is mentioned only in passage A.

C. No. This is mentioned only in passage B.

D. No. This is mentioned only in passage B.

E. No. This is mentioned only in passage B.

8. **E** **Extract Fact**

A. No. Only passage A answers this question.

B. No. Only passage B refers to hunting, but even there no mention is made of literature that discusses the potential benefits to hunters of purple loosestrife management.

C. No. Only passage B discusses hunting and neither passage discusses farming.

D. No. Only passage B mentions the canvasback.

E. Yes. Each passage provides the answer (wetlands) to this question. See the first two sentences of passage A and the first sentence of the second paragraph of passage B.

9. **B** `Extract Infer`

A. No. Passage B never raises the issue of disturbed versus undisturbed habitats.

B. Yes. The author of passage A would agree with this statement (see the middle of the first paragraph where the author discusses "serious reductions"), while the author of passage B states that none of the furbearing species highlighted in the literature can be considered threatened by purple loosestrife (see the second-to-last sentence of the passage).

C. No. While the author of passage A calls for control and eradication of purple loosestrife, he does not discuss people who advocate for eradication. Furthermore, it is too much of a stretch to say that the author of passage B feels that "most" people who advocate on behalf of eradication measures are not genuine.

D. No. The author of passage B never discusses the amount of biomass that has been displaced by purple loosestrife, so you can't know whether the authors would disagree about this statement.

E. No. Neither passage discusses other non-native plant species.

10. **E** `Extract Infer`

The author of passage B is critical of the arguments made in passage A and displays some doubt as to the true motivation of those who advance such thinking.

A. No. The author does not agree with the argument made in passage A.

B. No. The author does not agree with the argument made in passage A.

C. No. The author is not neutral.

D. No. The author does not appear ambivalent; he has a definite opinion.

E. Yes. The author is skeptical of the idea that purple loosestrife control is primarily environmentally, rather than economically, motivated.

11. **A** `Extract Infer`

A. Yes. Both authors would agree with this statement. See the middle of the first paragraph of passage A, where the author discusses "serious reductions," and the second half of the second paragraph of passage B, which notes the effect of purple loosestrife on the canvasback and implies some decrease in the number of furbearing mammals, though not to the extent that they would be considered threatened.

B. No. The author of passage B would disagree with this statement, since he feels that the harmful effects of purple loosestrife have been overstated or inadequately proven in the literature.

C. No. The author of passage B never mentions herbicides.

D. No. While the author of passage A would clearly agree with this statement, the author of passage B doesn't view purple loosestrife as a dire threat, so he would likely disagree with the strength of this statement.

E. No. Neither passage goes into sufficient detail about how quickly purple loosestrife returns once it has been eliminated from a given area, so you can't determine whether the authors would agree with this statement.

12. **C**   **Structure**

A. No. The claims made in passage B cast doubt on some of the evidence presented in passage A; the author of passage B is the one who is critical, not the other way around.

B. No. Passage B questions the argument that passage A makes.

C. Yes. Passage B is critical of the arguments made in passage A, but passage A does not address any of the concerns that the author of passage B raises with respect to purple loosestrife control.

D. No. While the author of passage B critiques the arguments made in passage A, he does not advocate any policy.

E. No. This is the opposite of what happens in each passage. The claims made in passage A are questioned by the author of passage B, who argues that the situation may not be as urgent as passage A suggests.

13. **A**   **RC Reasoning**

A. Yes. This choice would strengthen the argument in passage A by reinforcing the notion that the spread of purple loosestrife must be controlled in order to protect area wildlife. At the same time, it would weaken the argument made in passage B by showing that a reduction in the size of a species in a given area is likely to signal future endangerment even if the species is not yet listed as threatened or endangered.

B. No. Suburban sprawl is not relevant to either passage's argument.

C. No. This choice would bolster the argument made in passage B, which is the opposite of what the question asks you to do.

D. No. This choice would also support the argument made in passage B, which is the opposite of what the question asks you to do.

E. No. Whether purple loosestrife is a problem in its native habitat is not relevant to either passage's argument.

Questions 14–21

The author argues that the work of Maxine Hong Kingston, whom critics recognize as a major literary figure, is significantly linked to the Chinese American literary tradition through her use of the highly developed Chinese narrative genre "talk-story." In the first paragraph, the author claims that despite the opinion of some critics who have limited the scope of their examinations to written texts, Kingston's work does indeed have some Chinese American antecedents by virtue of her connection to a traditional Chinese oral narrative form known as talk-story. The second paragraph defines what talk-story is and provides a little bit of its history in China; it also explains how this oral heritage has meshed with Western forms of discourse. The third paragraph details Kingston's own outlook on story-telling, in which she views her storytelling process as different from that of print-oriented culture, in which stories are static once they have been captured in print. The fourth paragraph focuses on the precise ways in which Kingston makes use of elements of talk-story in her work, as evidenced in her book *China Men*.

14. **A** [Big Picture]

The main point of the passage is that Kingston's work, through its connection to talk-story, does actually possess considerable literary antecedents within the Chinese American heritage.

A. Yes. This is a decent paraphrase of what was mentioned above.

B. No. This is too specific; the only discussion of Kingston's beliefs about literary artists as performers occurs in the third paragraph.

C. No. This is too broad. The main focus of the passage is Kingston, not critics of ethnic literature in the United States in general.

D. No. This is too specific; what this choice discusses is mentioned only in the final paragraph of the passage.

E. No. The passage never claims that Kingston's writings have renewed an interest in talk-story.

15. **D** [Extract Infer]

A. No. The passage never makes any statements about the appearance of written forms of talk-story in either Chinese or English within the last few years.

B. No. The passage does not state that scholars until very recently held the belief that oral storytelling was a unique oral tradition.

C. No. The passage doesn't go into enough detail to support any claims about how talk-story developed in the United States.

D. Yes. Kingston uses elements of talk-story in her work, and her memory processes are described as contrasting with those of print-oriented culture, in which precise sequences of words are retained. Thus, talk-story does not rely upon memory processes that emphasize the retention of precise sequences of words. See the second sentence of the third paragraph.

E. No. The passage makes no mention of critics who argue that the connection between Kingston's work and talk-story is weak and questionable.

16. **C** [Extract Infer]

The author uses the phrase "personally remembered stories" to refer to the fact that in Kingston's story-telling memory processes, the emphasis is not on precise sequences of words but rather on the relating of stories by performers who continuously reconstruct the essential elements of a narrative.

A. No. The author does not refer to a literary genre here.

B. No. There is no mention made of a thematically organized personal narrative.

C.   Yes. As narratives are passed on and retold, each performer will relate certain elements of the story differently based on his or her recollections of the narrative.

D.   No. This is the opposite of what you're looking for. Kingston separates her memory processes from those that seek to retain in memory precise sequences of words.

E.   No. The issue here isn't one of theme; it's the way in which narratives are recalled and retold.

17.   **B**   RC Reasoning

The final sentence of the last paragraph describes how Kingston uses elements and qualities inherent in the Chinese language to transform her English writing into a written form of talk-story. You need to find an answer that describes a similar sort of transformation.

A.   No. There is no transformation here, merely additional color.

B.   Yes. The cotton cloth is transformed into a product having the qualities of woolen cloth in much the same way as Kingston transforms her English writing into a product having the qualities of Chinese talk-story.

C.   No. There is no judgment made about what is "appropriate" in Kingston's work, so this choice does not match.

D.   No. This describes a substitution, not a transformation.

E.   No. Issues of cost are not relevant to the description of Kingston's work in the last sentence of the passage.

18.   **C**   Extract Infer

Kingston's beliefs about storytelling are discussed in the third paragraph.

A.   No. Since she writes in English, it is unlikely that she believes stories cannot be adequately expressed in English.

B.   No. The passage does not say that Kingston believes any of her stories should be thought of primarily as ethnic literature.

C.   Yes. See the final sentence of the third paragraph.

D.   No. The passage does not attribute to Kingston this sort of judgment about the best way to chronicle Chinese American history.

E.   No. This is too extreme. Again, she writes in English, so it is unlikely that she finds written texts wholly inadequate with respect to capturing the beauty and significance of her stories.

19.   **D**   RC Reasoning

The author claims that the work of Kingston is significantly linked to the Chinese American literary tradition through her use of the highly developed Chinese narrative genre "talk-story." You need to find a choice that will undermine this assertion.

A.   No. This choice is too vague. The author's argument is specifically about Kingston.

55

B. No. Again, this choice is too broad. The author is making a point about Kingston, not about Chinese American writers in general, so it doesn't matter whether her work differs significantly from theirs.

C. No. Native American storytellers are not relevant to the author's argument about Kingston.

D. Yes. Because the author focuses on *China Men* to illustrate Kingston's use of talk-story, the element linking her to the Chinese American literary tradition, it would weaken the author's argument if *China Men* proved to be atypical of Kingston's literary works.

E. No. This choice has no bearing on the author's argument, which isn't focused on the question of authenticity.

20. **B** `Structure`

The author includes details about typical talk-story forms in order to show how Kingston's work embodies elements of the talk-story tradition.

A. No. The author states that Kingston has been recognized as a major literary figure in the first sentence of the passage, but that idea does not resurface in the final paragraph.

B. Yes. This matches what was noted above.

C. No. The passage never claims that critics believe Chinese American literature in general lacks literary antecedents, only that some critics feel that Kingston's work lacks them.

D. No. The last paragraph isn't focused on Kingston's views; it's focused more on the actual elements involved in Kingston's writing.

E. No. There is no alternative view provided in this paragraph, only support for the author's main idea.

21. **A** `Extract` `Infer`

The author takes a fairly academic outlook on talk-story and seems to appreciate its history and complexity.

A. Yes. This is appropriately positive in tone.

B. No. The author expresses no sense of disappointment anywhere in the passage.

C. No. The author does not claim that talk-story is resistant to critical evaluation, only that some critics have overlooked its significance and impact in their examinations of Kingston's work.

D. No. While the author does seem respectful of the tradition, no mention is ever made as to the diversity of talk-story's sources and derivations.

E. No. The author doesn't single out song in particular; it is simply mentioned, along with spoken narrative, as comprising part of talk-story's oral tradition.

Questions 22–27

In the passage, economist Peter Garber challenges the view of Charles Mackay, who in his classic nineteenth-century account argues that the seventeenth-century Dutch tulip market provides an example of a speculative bubble. The first paragraph explains what a speculative bubble is and briefly introduces the opinions of Mackay and Garber. The second paragraph describes what happened in the Dutch tulip market during the seventeenth century and details the evidence that Mackay uses to substantiate his belief that a speculative bubble was responsible for the increase and then rapid decline in rare tulip bulb prices. The third paragraph presents Garber's view that the situation shouldn't really be described as a speculative bubble because the events of the period can be explained in terms of economic fundamentals.

22. **D**   **Big Picture**

The main point of the passage is that Charles Mackay's account of the seventeenth-century Dutch tulip market as an example of a speculative bubble isn't necessarily correct, according to Peter Garber.

A.   No. The only economists mentioned in the passage are Mackay and Garber, so you don't know that this belief is widely held by other economists.

B.   No. The passage makes only brief references to earnings derived in the first and last paragraphs, so this choice is too specific.

C.   No. This is also too specific; when a speculative bubble occurs is discussed primarily in the first paragraph.

D.   Yes. This is a close paraphrase of the main point stated above.

E.   No. This is too specific as well. This detail is discussed only in the final paragraph.

23. **D**   **RC Reasoning**

In the second half of the second paragraph, Garber describes how an initial tulip bulb could command a very high price, drop in value as more bulbs are reproduced from the original, and yet still provide a reasonable return on investment from all the reproduced bulbs now selling at lower cost but in much greater quantities. You need to find an answer choice that displays a similar situation.

A.   No. There is no parallel to the idea of competition in the original example.

B.   No. The idea that the work is now inferior has no match in the original example.

C.   No. The cheap substitute parts do not constitute reproductions of the original parts in the same way that the lower-priced bulbs are reproduced from an original, highly-valued bulb.

D.   Yes. The original copy is the most highly valued, but then the reproduced copies are sold at a lower price.

E.   No. The idea that the airline sold most of its tickets at a higher price doesn't match the original example.

24. **B**   **Extract Infer**

A.   No. There are no claims about the frequency of speculative bubbles attributed to Garber in the passage.

B. Yes. See the last two sentences of the passage.

C. No. Garber makes no statements about what is the case when there is no speculative bubble in a market.

D. No. This is too extreme. You don't know whether Garber thinks that most people who invested were generally rational in all their investments.

E. No. Garber thinks that Mackay mistakenly infers from the rapid decline in tulip prices that a speculative bubble was at work.

25. **B** Extract Fact

Mackay claimed that the seventeenth-century Dutch tulip market provides an example of a speculative bubble.

A. No. Fashionability isn't discussed until the third paragraph, and if anything, Mackay would be more likely to claim that the rapid rise in prices was due to the fashionability of the flowers produced.

B. Yes. This is in line with the idea that the tulip market is an example of a speculative bubble.

C. No. This is too extreme. You don't know that the Netherlands was the only center of cultivation and development of new tulip varieties at the time.

D. No. The concept of what is irrational is not discussed in the context of Mackay's account.

E. No. This choice relates to information in the third paragraph, in which Garber's views are identified.

26. **C** Structure

The main purpose of the second paragraph is to detail the evidence that Mackay uses to substantiate his belief that a speculative bubble was responsible for the increase and then rapid decline in rare tulip bulb prices.

A. No. The passage makes no reference to all experts in the field.

B. No. The mistake that Garber believes Mackay has made isn't revealed until the third paragraph.

C. Yes. The second paragraph lays out Mackay's evidence and reasoning so that Garber can then refute it in the final paragraph of the passage.

D. No. Again, nothing in the second paragraph attempts to undermine anything.

E. No. No factual errors are pointed out. Garber's challenging of Mackay's conclusion is based on the idea that there is an alternative interpretation available for the facts as they are.

27. **D** Extract Fact

The phrase "standard pricing pattern" refers to a general trend in the prices of new flower varieties.

A. No. No mention of other pricing patterns is made.

B. No. No reference is made to any agreed-upon criterion.

C. No. The idea of acceptability is not discussed in the passage.

D. Yes. The increase and eventual decline in bulb prices is the pattern that regularly recurs with new varieties of flowers.

E. No. The pricing pattern is not held up as a model to be emulated.

Section 3: Arguments 1

1. **B** Resolve/Explain

Aristophanes' play depicts a mid-forties Socrates as an atheistic philosopher concerned primarily with issues in natural science, yet the only other surviving portrayals of Socrates, written after his death at age 70, show him as having a religious dimension and a strong focus on ethical issues. Why is there such a disparity between Aristophanes' and others' representations of the same man?

A. No. The fact that Aristophanes' portrayal was unflattering while the other ones were very flattering does not explain why there was a difference to begin with.

B. Yes. Aristophanes' play was written when Socrates was in his mid-forties, so if Socrates changed his views and interests as he got older, it would explain why the other depictions differed from that of Aristophanes.

C. No. This is irrelevant and doesn't explain why the other portrayals differed from Aristophanes' portrayal.

D. No. The fact that Socrates was much more controversial in the years before his death doesn't explain why the later depictions focused on religion and ethics as opposed to natural science. Socrates could have maintained the same philosophical views and interests even while becoming more controversial.

E. No. The influence Socrates had on subsequent philosophers is irrelevant.

2. **C** Flaw

The board member argues that the work in question fails to meet the conditions under which a grant was made. The grant included a stipulation that the work not contain any material detrimental to the J Foundation, the granting organization, yet the board member bases his conclusion on the fact that the resulting work fails to mention any of the J Foundation's laudable achievements. You are never actually told, however, that the work itself contains any material that would be harmful to the foundation's reputation.

A. No. The notion of high intellectual value is never discussed and isn't relevant to the board member's conclusion.

B. No. The argument does not mistake a necessary condition for a sufficient one; there is no necessary/sufficient dynamic in this argument.

C. Yes. The board member claims that because the work does not mention any of the foundation's praiseworthy achievements, it has violated the stipulation that a work not be detrimental to the foundation's reputation.

D.   No. Whether grant recipients usually strive to meet a foundation's conditions is out of scope; you are concerned only with this particular grant and work.

E.   No. The board member never discusses any of the other conditions that may have been attached to the grant, but this is not a flaw in his argument.

3.   **B**   Strengthen

The psychiatrist concludes that people who succeed in breaking their addiction to smoking are more likely to be motivated by the social pressure against smoking than by health concerns. Why? Social pressure against smoking is an immediate concern, and people who break a habit are more likely to be motivated by immediate concerns than by long-term ones. What's missing from the argument here is an affirmation that health concerns don't also present an immediate concern for those looking to quit smoking.

A.   No. While this choice does address health concerns, you still don't know whether this greater health threat presents an immediate or a long-term concern.

B.   Yes. This strengthens the psychiatrist's argument by confirming that it's more likely to be social pressure that motivates people to quit, as opposed to health concerns, because only the social pressure presents an immediate concern.

C.   No. This doesn't tell you anything in terms of immediate or long-term concern.

D.   No. The fact that people succeed only after several attempts is not relevant to the argument.

E.   No. The argument never claims that these are the only two factors that motivate people who succeed in quitting smoking.

4.   **A**   Weaken

Cassie suggests that in order to improve the quality of customer service at their real estate agency, they should reduce client loads. Melvin, however, claims that this is not feasible, though it would be desirable, because it is already too difficult to recruit enough qualified agents; in order to reduce client loads, still more agents would need to be recruited. You are looking to weaken Melvin's argument.

A.   Yes. This choice suggests that by following Cassie's suggestion and reducing client loads, the agency would actually serve its own interests, in that it would then become easier to recruit new agents.

B.   No. What customers have expressed support for is irrelevant, since Melvin agrees that reducing client loads is preferable. His objection is that it can't be done, not that it shouldn't be done.

C.   No. This would strengthen Cassie's argument, but it does nothing to weaken Melvin's since it doesn't address his claim that it's currently not feasible for the agency to reduce client loads.

D.   No. The idea of hiring extra support staff for the main office is irrelevant; Melvin focuses specifically on the fact that client loads cannot be reduced because it is so difficult to recruit new agents. He never discusses whether there is any way to achieve similar benefits aside from reducing client loads.

E.   No. This choice would appear to strengthen Melvin's claim that reducing client loads is not practicable at this time.

5. **A**   Inference

The star-nosed mole, which has poor sight, has tentacles at the end of its nose; these tentacles contain receptors that detect electric fields produced by other animals, thereby allowing the mole to identify and catch its prey.

A.   Yes. Because the argument states that both worms and insects are suitable prey for the star-nosed mole, they must produce electric fields, since that is how the mole catches it prey.

B.   No. This is too extreme. The argument says moles are poor-sighted, but that doesn't mean they don't rely on their eyesight at all for survival.

C.   No. This is also too extreme. Sense of smell is never mentioned in the argument, so you don't know whether the mole relies on it for hunting.

D.   No. You have information only about the star-nosed mole; other animals that hunt are out of scope.

E.   No. This is never addressed in the argument.

6. **D**   Principle Match

The argument describes a pattern of behavior in which a child, denied something it wants, initiates problematic behavior and escalates it until the child's parent gives in to the child's demands so as to halt the misbehavior. This pattern is then repeated over time, with the child engaging in increasing levels of problematic behavior. You are looking for an answer choice that is inconsistent with this pattern.

A.   No. This is consistent with the pattern presented in the argument.

B.   No. This is consistent with the pattern. A parent's giving in to a child's demands because of the latter's bad behavior reinforces the child's negative behavior pattern. Because the child has learned that the parent will tolerate only so much misbehavior before becoming exasperated and yielding, the child manages to influence the parent's behavior as well.

C.   No. This is consistent with the final sentence of the argument.

D.   Yes. The argument does not illustrate the idea that a child can influence a parent's behavior in ways contrary to the child's intended goals; you have an example only of how a child acts to achieve its intended goals.

E.   No. This is consistent with the pattern; the child misbehaves, which the parent doesn't desire, until the parent gives in to the child's demands.

7. **E**   Reasoning

The scientist concludes that even though chemical R did not cause cancer in laboratory rats, you cannot conclude that chemical R is safe for humans. Why? Many substances that are carcinogenic to humans do not cause cancer in rats, probably because rats have short life spans and some substances cause cancer only via long-term exposure.

A.   No. The scientist does not conclude that chemical R is safe for humans.

B.   No. The statement is not used as support for any contention. Plus, the scientist does not go so far as to say that test results from rats cannot be extrapolated to humans at all.

C. No. The statement does not illustrate anything concerning the rats' life spans; it merely provides the results of a study.

D. No. The scientist never puts forth any hypothesis as to whether chemical R causes cancer in humans via long-term exposure.

E. Yes. The statement provides the results of a study, but the scientist claims these results don't constitute sufficient support to say that chemical R is safe for humans.

8. **E** ▸ **Necessary Assumption**

The department store manager concludes that there is no reason to offer customers free gift wrapping this holiday season based on two considerations. First, if most customers take the offer, it will be expensive and time-consuming for the store. Second, if only a few customers accept it, then there is no advantage to offering the service. The manager leaves out the possibility that the number of customers who want free gift wrapping could fall somewhere in between these two extremes.

A. No. Previous holiday seasons are out of scope.

B. No. You don't know that free gift wrapping would slow down shoppers, so this isn't relevant to the argument.

C. No. The manager doesn't suggest that they charge customers for gift wrapping, so this is out of scope.

D. No. The manager simply says that offering free gift wrapping would be expensive, but he doesn't explain why it would be. Therefore, this choice isn't essential to the argument; there could be another reason the service would be expensive to offer.

E. Yes. The manager assumes that the number of customers who would want the service will be either too many or not enough. If you negate this choice, you'll find that it invalidates the manager's conclusion that free gift wrapping shouldn't be offered, which means this assumption is necessary to the argument.

9. **D** ▸ **Weaken**

The argument concludes that behavior modification is more effective than sleeping pills are in helping people to fall asleep. The evidence provided for this conclusion is that those who rely solely on behavior modification fall asleep more quickly than do those who rely just on sleeping pills. The argument doesn't allow for other factors that might explain this difference, so you're looking for an answer choice that suggests another reason, aside from behavior modification, that those people were able to fall asleep more quickly.

A. No. If anything, this might strengthen the argument by suggesting that one potential difference between the two groups of people doesn't actually exist. In any case, this choice certainly doesn't weaken the conclusion.

B. No. This is out of scope; you're not looking to compare those who use behavior modification techniques to fall asleep to those who have no trouble falling asleep.

C. No. The fact that those who use behavior modification have never used sleeping pills doesn't tell you anything about the relative effectiveness of behavior modification (as opposed to sleeping pills).

55

D. Yes. This suggests that the two groups of people are not similar in their inability to fall asleep, which casts doubt on the conclusion that behavior modification is the more effective remedy for chronic sleep trouble.

E. No. The fact that some people prefer to avoid using drugs if other treatments are available still doesn't tell you about the relative effectiveness of behavior modification (as opposed to sleeping pills).

10. **D** Sufficient Assumption

The lawyer concludes that a witness's testimony should be excluded because, although the witness was present when the lawyer's famous client was assaulted, the witness recognizes only the assailant and not the client. You need to find an answer choice that supports the lawyer's conclusion that the witness's testimony should be excluded simply because the witness doesn't recognize the lawyer's client.

A. No. This is irrelevant, as the witness in this argument claims to recognize only one, not both, of the parties involved.

B. No. There is no mention made of other witnesses who can identify the lawyer's client, so it's unclear how this would support his conclusion.

C. No. According to the lawyer, the witness claims not to recognize the client, and it is on that basis that the lawyer wishes to exclude the witness's testimony. Whether it is possible to determine whether the witness did in fact recognize the assailant isn't relevant to the lawyer's conclusion.

D. Yes. You can diagram this as include testimony → witness claims to recognize both parties. The contrapositive would then be: witness doesn't claim to recognize both parties → testimony should be excluded. This is exactly what the lawyer concludes.

E. No. This doesn't help the lawyer's argument. The fact that it is unlikely that anyone would fail to recognize the lawyer's client still leaves some wiggle room for the witness not to recognize the client.

11. **B** Flaw

The biologist rejects the idea that the difficulty of adapting to ice ages was responsible for the evolution of the human brain. The basis for this rejection is that most other animal species adapted to ice ages with no evolutionary changes to their brains. However, the fact that changes did not occur in other species' brains in response to the difficulty of adapting to ice ages does not disprove the possibility that this did impact the evolution of the human brain.

A. No. There is no issue of necessary or sufficient conditions in a given species, since the argument is comparing one species to many other species.

B. Yes. The biologist doesn't consider that the difficulty of adapting to ice ages may have been responsible for the evolution of the human brain even if the same circumstances did not produce that same change in other species' brains.

C. No. The biologist never claims that the difficulty of adapting to ice ages was necessary for the evolution of the human brain.

D. No. The biologist never discusses the extent of the difficulties any species faced during ice ages.

E. No. The biologist is claiming that the difficulty of adapting to ice ages was actually not responsible for the evolution of the human brain, so this choice goes against the logic of the argument.

12. **D** [Inference]

Pick the answer best supported by the passage.

A. No. This contradicts the argument, which states that the rate of increase of retail sales of new book titles has slowed recently, which implies that retail sales are still increasing, just not as much as they were before. Furthermore, this choice goes too far in attributing any sort of responsibility to television for any changes in the amount of per capita reading, as you are presented only with a correlation.

B. No. You don't know what usually happens to library use when television is introduced; the argument is talking only about North America and it doesn't make any predictions.

C. No. This is similar to (A). While the rate at which retail sales have increased has slowed, sales are still increasing, making this choice untrue.

D. Yes. This is supported by the information in the passage, which says that both the number of published titles and the number of copies sold per title increased in the early days of television.

E. No. You know that book sales increased around the time that television was introduced, but you don't know that this was because television expanded the market for books. This is too much of a stretch.

13. **D** [Main Point]

The botanist concludes that the belief that poinsettia plants should not be kept in homes with children or pets is mistaken, as research has definitively shown that these plants pose no risk to either children or pets.

A. No. The botanist never offers an opinion on what child-rearing books should do.

B. No. If anything, this choice is a premise. The botanist never actually says that poinsettias are not dangerously poisonous, though, only that they pose no risk.

C. No. This is stated in the argument, but it is a point that the botanist disagrees with and therefore not the conclusion of the argument.

D. Yes. This is the botanist's conclusion, as noted above.

E. No. This is the botanist's premise.

14. **B** [Strengthen]

A building at an excavation site was composed of three different kinds of stone, two of which do not occur naturally in the region. Most buildings at the site from the same time period contained only limestone, which occurs naturally in the area, as the sole stone component and most were human dwellings. From this evidence, the archaeologist concludes that the building they are studying was probably not a dwelling.

A. No. This doesn't tell you anything new. The argument says that limestone was the only stone component in most buildings that were human dwellings, so to say that most buildings used as dwellings were made of limestone, at least in part, doesn't answer the question of whether these buildings contained any other stone components.

B. Yes. Of the three types of stone contained in the building, limestone is the only one that occurs naturally in the area; therefore, the presence of quartz and granite, which do not occur naturally in the area, in the building being studied would indicate that the building was not a dwelling.

C. No. This choice doesn't connect the type of stone used to the question of whether a building was used as a dwelling or not.

D. No. This doesn't support the archaeologist's conclusion; if only most, but not all, buildings at the site were used as dwellings, then it is still possible that some buildings at the site were not used as such.

E. No. This is irrelevant; the archaeologist is concerned only with the building under study, so a lack of quartz elsewhere wouldn't tell you anything further about his conclusion.

15.   E   **Parallel**

Diagram the argument. Able to file on time → uses accountant and does not need additional documentation. The contrapositive would be: does not use accountant or needs additional documentation → not able to file on time. Uses accountant → will need additional documentation. Therefore, by taking the contrapositive of the first statement and combining it with the second statement, you get the following: uses accountant → will need additional documentation → not able to file on time.

A. No. This argument uses the word "probably" in both the conclusion and one of the premises, so it does not match the tone of the original argument, which is more definitive.

B. No. Away on business → cannot attend the concert. Does not attend the concert → no other opportunity to attend a concern this month. Already the structure doesn't match that of the original argument—you don't have one thing that requires two others—so there's no need to diagram the rest.

C. No. Children content → play video games. Play video games → no other activities planned. Again, the structure doesn't match that of the original argument—you don't have one thing that requires two others—so there's no need to diagram the rest.

D. No. Not seated in first class → seated in business class. Therefore, cannot be seated in first class → seated in business class. This does not match the structure of the original argument.

E. Yes. Relaxing vacation → children behave well and does not start to suspect mischief. The contrapositive would be as follows: children do not behave well or starts to suspect mischief → not a relaxing vacation. Children behave well → starts to suspect mischief. Therefore, children behave well → starts to suspect mischief → not a relaxing vacation. This matches the structure of the original argument.

16.   C   **Inference**

Pick the answer best supported by the passage.

A. No. This is irrelevant; governmental action is never mentioned in the argument.

B. No. This choice goes beyond the scope of the argument, which never discusses threats that are "particularly dreadful" or that are outside the control of those affected.

C. Yes. News media universally tend to report instances of rare threats in featured stories while only prominently reporting unusual instances of common threats. Therefore, people who get information primarily from news media will overestimate the risk of uncommon threats relative to the risk of common threats because uncommon threats are brought to their attention more often.

D. No. This is irrelevant. The argument makes no mention of long-range future threats.

E. No. This is also irrelevant. The argument does not address the amount of resources spent on avoiding any particular type of threat.

17. **A** **Principle Strengthen**

The real estate agent concludes that since prospective buyers are likely to assume that large appliances in a home are included in the purchase, sellers who plan to keep the appliances are morally obliged either to remove them before showing the home or indicate in some way that they are excluded from the sale of the home. You need an answer choice that supports this line of reasoning.

A. Yes. This clearly paraphrases what the real estate agent's conclusion is.

B. No. The argument tells you that legally large appliances are not permanent fixtures, but that even so prospective buyers might assume they are included in the sale of the home.

C. No. The real estate agent never addresses whether sellers are morally obliged to include in the sale of the home appliances that are not permanent fixtures but were in the home when shown. Her argument focuses on what sellers are morally obliged to do so that prospective buyers are not given the wrong impression as to what large appliances are included in the sale of a home.

D. No. The argument never discusses sellers who deliberately mislead prospective buyers. The conclusion could just as easily apply to a seller who unintentionally misleads a prospective buyer.

E. No. The idea that a seller has indicated in some way that a large appliance is included doesn't fit the real estate agent's argument, the focus of which is what sellers are morally obliged to do if they plan to keep a large appliance themselves.

18. **E** **Flaw**

The argument concludes that parents who rigorously organize their children's activities during playtime are incorrect in thinking that doing so will enhance their children's cognitive development. The evidence offered in support of this conclusion comes in the form of an analogy. The argument suggests that structuring a child's playtime will not result in a child who is creative and resourceful, just as dictating to someone what the plot and characters of a novel should be will not result in a good novel. However, the argument jumps from the notion of producing a creative and resourceful child to that of enhancing a child's cognitive development; you want an answer choice that picks up on this gap in the argument.

A. No. The argument concludes that something is not conducive to a certain goal, so this choice is irrelevant.

B. No. This is irrelevant. The issue is not whether children enjoy rigorously organized playtime, but what effect that playtime will have on their cognitive development.

C. No. There is no mention of necessary or sufficient conditions in this argument.

D. No. What is required to write a good novel is not the focus of the argument. While the argument doesn't specify what is indeed needed to write a good novel, this omission does not constitute the flaw in the reasoning.

E. Yes. The argument doesn't take into account the fact that structured playtime may enhance a child's overall cognitive development without enhancing creativity and resourcefulness, as cognitive development encompasses more than just these two aspects of an individual.

19. **C** **Necessary Assumption**

The bureaucrat concludes that an ideal bureaucracy will have an ever-expanding system of regulations. He bases this conclusion on several premises: that the primary goal of an ideal bureaucracy is to define and classify all possible problems and establish regulations for each eventuality; that an ideal bureaucracy provides an appeal procedure for any complaint; that should a complaint reveal an unanticipated problem, regulations will be expanded to address the new issue. In order for the bureaucrat to draw his conclusion, then, he must be assuming that new, unanticipated problems will constantly surface that will require an expansion of existing regulations.

A. No. The bureaucrat's conclusion suggests that it is not possible to define and classify all possible problems because there will always be some unexpected one that requires additional regulations.

B. No. The argument never addresses how each problem that has been defined and classified came to light; it could have been via a complaint or it could have been foreseen in some other way.

C. Yes. Take out some of the extra negatives. This choice says that an ideal bureaucracy will always have at least some complaints about problems that are not covered by that bureaucracy's regulations. This is in line with the bureaucrat's conclusion that an ideal bureaucracy will have an ever-expanding system of regulations.

D. No. This choice doesn't address the part of the conclusion that deals with an ever-expanding system of regulations. Also, no mention is made of an ideal bureaucracy reaching its primary goal; this is not the focus of the argument.

E. No. Try negating this choice—you'll see that it doesn't affect the conclusion. Even if a complaint does not reveal an unanticipated problem that the bureaucracy is capable of defining and classifying, the bureaucrat's argument could still be true.

20. **B** **Main Point**

The argument claims that, contrary to what some microbiologists have concluded, it is unlikely that most types of bacteria hibernate regularly. The evidence offered in support of this view is that bacteria are rather diverse and so what may be true for one common type of bacteria in terms of hibernation isn't necessarily true for most types.

A. No. This is the opposite of the argument's conclusion.

B. Yes. This is in line with the final sentence of the argument and the analysis above.

C. No. The idea that bacteria are extremely diverse is presented as a matter of fact, so the conclusion of the argument isn't conditional in nature.

D.   No. This is stated, but it is not the main conclusion of the argument.

E.   No. The argument never states that only one type of bacteria may hibernate regularly, just that scientists have been studying one type that happens to hibernate regularly.

21.   **A**   Sufficient Assumption

The argument concludes that if students in a course are given several reading assignments but no written assignments, no student in that course will receive a high grade for the course. Why? If a student is not required to hand in written homework based on the reading assignments in a course, the student will not complete all of the reading assignments. This is true even of highly motivated students. The argument jumps, however, from completing all of the reading assignments to receiving a high grade, so you should look for an answer that attempts to link these two things.

A.   Yes. In other words, if a student doesn't complete all the reading assignments in a course, the student can't earn a high grade for that course.

B.   No. This reverses the sequence that you need. You know that a high grade requires completing all the reading, but completing all the reading in itself doesn't guarantee a high grade for the course.

C.   No. This has the same problem as (B). Completing all the reading assignments for a course does not ensure that a student will receive a high grade, regardless of whether he or she is highly motivated.

D.   No. This choice doesn't connect the completion of all reading assignments to getting a high grade, so it doesn't really help the conclusion.

E.   No. You only know from the argument that completing all the reading assignments depends on students being required to hand in written assignments based on the reading. Simply requiring written assignments to be turned in does not ensure that all the reading will indeed be completed.

22.   **A**   Weaken

The argument concludes that the most effective way to lose body fat is to eat a lot of protein and avoid carbohydrates. The evidence offered for this conclusion comes in the form of a study, in which one group ate a high-protein, low-carbohydrate diet while the other ate a low-protein, high-carbohydrate diet. The group that consumed the low-carbohydrate diet had lost more weight after ten days than did the group on the high-carbohydrate diet. In order to weaken the argument, you want to find an alternative explanation for the low-carbohydrate group's weight loss.

A.   Yes. This suggests that people on either diet would have lost weight, but that the increased water retention of the high-carbohydrate group masked the actual weight loss figure for that group.

B.   No. This is irrelevant. The study is concerned with those who ate a high-protein, low-carbohydrate diet, not those who consume large quantities of protein in general.

C.   No. This suggests that body fat is lost because it gets converted to muscle as a result of a high-protein, low-carbohydrate diet. If anything, this choice strengthens the argument, since the conclusion is directed at those who wish to lose body fat.

D.   No. If this were true, then you should have seen the opposite result—greater weight loss in the group that engaged in the exercise regimen. Since the weight loss was greater for those on the low-carbohydrate diet, this would strengthen, not weaken, the argument.

E.   No. This is irrelevant. You don't care what happens after the volunteers go back to their former eating habits.

23.   **C**   Parallel Flaw

The essayist concludes that the human mind is a type of computer because human minds, like computers, have the capacity to represent and perform logical transformations on pieces of information. However, the fact that two things share a particular trait does not mean that one thing is a type of the other thing, so you'll need to find a choice that replicates this particular flaw.

A.   No. The language of this choice is not as strong as that of the original argument, and the idea that there is a biological basis does not match up with the "one is a type of the other" part of the original argument.

B.   No. The conclusion here, which rules out something as being a reasonable criterion, does not match that of the original argument.

C.   Yes. This choice concludes that communities belong to the category of organisms because in communities, as in organisms, the proper functioning of each component depends upon the proper functioning of every other component. This is the same flaw as the original argument.

D.   No. This choice argues that because one thing is necessary to achieve the full benefit of another, those who lack the former will not gain the full benefit and protection offered by the latter. This doesn't match the original argument.

E.   No. The conclusion in this choice claims that two things share something in common, not that one is a type of the other. This doesn't match the original argument.

24.   **D**   Necessary Assumption

The argument concludes that objective evaluation of poetry is possible only if a popular belief—that a poem has whatever meaning is assigned to it by the reader—is false. Why? The aesthetic value of a poem cannot be discussed unless it is possible for at least two readers to agree on the correct interpretation of the poem. Notice that the argument jumps from being able to objectively evaluate a poem to being able to discuss the aesthetic value of a poem. You need to find an answer choice that connects these two things.

A.   No. This is missing the link to objective evaluation and it repeats information given in the premise of the argument.

B.   No. This is too strong. If two readers agree, then it is possible to discuss a poem's aesthetic value, but that doesn't necessarily lead to being able to objectively evaluate a poem. Having two readers agree is only a necessary, not sufficient, condition anyway, which doesn't ensure that it will be possible to discuss a poem's aesthetic value.

C.   No. This is too broad. The argument is concerned with discussion of a poem's aesthetic value, not just simple discussion of the poem.

D.   Yes. You can diagram this choice to read objective evaluation → aesthetic value can be discussed. This connects the conclusion to the premise, which claims that you must have agreement about a poem's correct interpretation in order to discuss a poem's aesthetic value. So you get objective evaluation → aesthetic value can be discussed → at least two readers agree.

E.   No. This choice goes too far. The argument only specifies at least two readers; no judgment is made as to the best way to accomplish aesthetic evaluation of literature.

25.   **B**   Flaw

The dean concludes that the demand by the mathematics department that it be given sole responsibility for teaching the course Statistics for the Social Sciences is unjustified. The dean bases this conclusion on the fact that the course has no more math in it than does high school algebra and on the fact that a course that has math in it does not need to be taught by a math professor, just as a course that approaches its subject from a historical perspective need not be taught by a history professor.

A.   No. The dean makes no connection between expertise and teaching ability.

B.   Yes. The dean claims that the math department's view is unjustified based on his rejection of one possible reason for that view; however, this doesn't actually refute the department's view that it should have sole responsibility for the course.

C.   No. The dean never makes any claims about the extent of student knowledge in either subject area.

D.   No. The issue of teaching capability is never mentioned, so this is not the problem with the dean's argument.

E.   No. The dean refers to history only by way of his analogy. No mention is made as to policies that apply to different types of courses.

Section 4: Games

Questions 1–6

This is a group game with fixed assignments. You must assign each of six law students—G, L, M, R, S, and V—to one of three numbered teams. Each team is assigned two students, and all students must be used exactly once, so there is 1:1 correspondence, making this one of the easier games in the section. Each student on each team must prepare either an opening argument or a final argument, so your diagram will have two tiers, one for each type of argument.

Clue 1:

Clue 2: L_o

Clue 3: G_f or R_p but not both.

Deductions: Note on your diagram that L cannot be in the f tier. A quick scan of the questions shows you that the teams, though numbered, are actually interchangeable, since none of the questions or answer choices refers to team numbers except for question 1. Therefore, you can place L in the o slot of team 1 as a fixed element. From clue 3, you also know that you will have one of G and R in the o tier and one in the f tier. Since they can be on the same team or on different teams, it's best to note this off to the side. Put a G/R placeholder to the side of the o tier and an R/G placeholder to the side of the f tier.

Here's the diagram:

$$\begin{array}{c|c|c|c}
\text{GLMRSV} & 1 & 2 & 3 \\
\hline
^G\!/_R \ \ \text{O:} & \underline{L} & \text{--} & \text{--} \\
^R\!/_G \ {\sim}\text{L} \ \ \text{F:} & \text{--} & & \text{--}
\end{array}$$

1. **D**   Grab-a-Rule

Use the clues to eliminate answer choices. Clue 1 eliminates (C). Clue 2 eliminates (B). Clue 3 eliminates (A) and (E). Therefore, the credited response is (D).

2. **C**   Specific

Place M and G together on team 2, with M in the o slot and G in the f slot. From clue 3, you know that R must be in an o slot. Since the only o slot left is on team 3, R must go there, leaving either S or V to fill the remaining f slots on teams 1 and 3.

$$\begin{array}{c|c|c|c}
 & 1 & 2 & 3 \\
\hline
^G\!/_R \ \ \text{O:} & \text{L} & \text{M} & \text{R} \\
^R\!/_G \ {\sim}\text{L} \ \ \text{F:} & ^S\!/_V & \text{G} & ^V\!/_S
\end{array}$$

A.   No. V must be in the f tier.

B.   No. S must be in the o tier.

C.   Yes. Your diagram shows that this is possible on team 3.

D.   No. S and V must be on different teams.

E.   No. S and V must be on different teams.

3. **A**   General

Use the clues and your previous work to eliminate answer choices.

A.   Yes. This could be possible if M is paired with V in the block from clue 1.

B.   No. This violates clue 1; M must be paired with either G or V.

C.   No. This violates clue 2; L must be in the o tier.

D.   No. This violates clue 1; M must be paired with either G or V.

E.   No. This violates clue 1; M must be paired with either G or V.

4. **B** `Specific`

Place R and V together on team 2; this means, from clue 1, that M and G will have to be together on team 3. Since you don't know which elements are in which tiers, indicate the possibilities with slashes, keeping in mind that R and G can't both be in the f tier as per clue 3. The remaining open slot is the f slot on team 1; the only element left is S, so S and L will be together on team 1. The question asks how many slots are definitively known. You know for certain the locations of L and S; therefore, (B) is the credited response.

		1	2	3
$^G/_R$	O:	L	$^R/_V$	$^M/_G$
$^R/_G$ ~L	F:	S	$^V/_R$	$^G/_M$

5. **E** `Specific`

Place R with L on team 1. Since R is in an f slot, from clue 3 you know that G must occupy an o slot on either team 2 or 3. While there are several possibilities surrounding G, you don't need to work them all out to answer a "must be true" question. Go to the answer choices to see if any of them mention G.

		1	2	3
$^G/_R$	O:	L		
$^R/_G$ ~L	F:	R	~G	~G

A. No. This is a "could be true" answer.

B. No. This is a "could be true" answer.

C. No. This is a "could be true" answer.

D. No. This is a "could be true" answer.

E. Yes. G must be in the o tier on either team 2 or 3.

6. **C** `Specific`

Place S in the o slot of team 2. From clue 3, you know that one of G and R must be in the o tier. However, you still need to leave room for the block from clue 1. The only way to accomplish this is to place G in the o slot on team 3, with M in the accompanying f slot. The remaining open slots are the f slots on teams 1 and 2. R and V are the only elements left, so put R/V and V/R placeholders into those spaces.

		1	2	3
$^G/_R$	O:	L	S	G
$^R/_G$ ~L	F:	$^R/_V$	$^V/_R$	M

A. No. G and L are on separate teams.

B. No. G and S are on separate teams.

C. Yes. This could be possible on team 1.

D. No. M is on team 3 with G.

E. No. R and V must be split between teams 1 and 2.

Questions 7–12

This is an order game; however, since elements may be used more than once, it's not one of the easier games on the section. You have to determine the order in which E-mail messages are received from one of three possible associates—H, J, and L. You are told that at least one but not more than two messages are received from each associate, which means you will have anywhere from 3–6 messages. Your diagram, then, should have columns 1–6 as its core; you can block out the extra spaces if you are told on a question that fewer than six messages are received.

Clue 1: L≠1. Put this in your diagram.

Clue 2: first = last

Clue 3: H J exactly once

Clue 4: J used once in slots 1–3

Deductions: Because L cannot be in slot 1, you know that slot 1 must be either J or H; note this on your diagram. You also know that L cannot be in slot 6; note this on your diagram as well. H and J are tied in to other clues, too, so you'll want to try to establish which of them is in slot 1 for each specific question you do. From clue 2, you know that whoever is in slot 1 will also be in the last slot; since you must use each element at least once, you won't be able to have this repetition until slot 4 at the earliest. This means you'll have at least four slots to work with each time.

Here's the diagram:

$$
\begin{array}{c c}
& \sim L \qquad\qquad\qquad \sim L \\
\text{HJL} & \begin{array}{|c|c|c|c|c|c|} \hline 1 & 2 & 3 & 4 & 5 & 6 \\ \hline \frac{H}{J} & & & & & \\ \hline \end{array}
\end{array}
$$

7. **D** **Grab-a-Rule**

Use the clues to eliminate answer choices. Clue 1 eliminates (A). Clue 2 eliminates (C). Clue 3 eliminates (B). Clue 4 eliminates (E). Therefore, the credited response is (D).

8. **C** **General**

Use the clues and your previous work to eliminate answer choices. In the second scenario in question 9, there was one message in between J's first message and H's first message, so eliminate (A). Because slots 1 and 6 must be the same as each other, it will never be possible to have four messages in between J's first message and H's first message, so eliminate (E) as well. Try to make (C) work. To do so, J will have to be placed in slots 1 and 6, and to accommodate the HJ block, H will have to be in slot 5. Since you're looking to maximize the number of slots between J and H, place another H in slot 4 and L in both slots 2 and 3. This works, so eliminate (B).

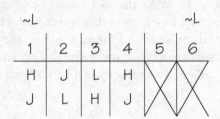

From the work you just did for (C), you can see that in order to get three messages in between J's first message and H's first message, J would have to be in slots 1 and 6, and H would have to be in slot 5. However, you have three slots remaining, only 2 of which can be filled by L. You have already used J twice, so you must use H one more time. However, there's no way to place another H without reducing the number of messages in between J and H to two, so (D) isn't possible. Choice (C) is the credited response.

9. **A**   Specific

Cross out slots 5 and 6 on your diagram. You now know that slots 1 and 4 must be the same as each other (clue 2). Since slot 1 can only be either H or J, try each scenario. If H is in slots 1 and 4, then J must be in slot 2 (clue 3) and L must be in slot 3. If J is in slots 1 and 4, then H must be in slot 3 (clue 3) and L must be in slot 2. Because the question asks for something that must be true, you will need to look at both scenarios when assessing the answer choices.

	~L					~L
	1	2	3	4	5	6
	H	J	L	H	✕	✕
	J	L	H	J	✕	✕

A.   Yes. This is true of both scenarios.

B.   No. This is true of only the second scenario.

C.   No. This is true of only the second scenario.

D.   No. This is true of only the second scenario.

E.   No. This is true of only the second scenario.

10. **E**   General

Use the clues and your previous work to eliminate answer choices.

A.   No. You saw this possibility in question 9.

B.   No. You saw this possibility in questions 9 and 11.

C. No. This is possible, though not worth testing if you've already made the proper deductions to get to (E).

D. No. You saw this possibility in question 11.

E. Yes. You already deduced that because L cannot be in slot 1, it will never be in slot 6, as that would violate clue 2.

11. **D** Specific

You now know that you will use all six slots on your diagram. Place L in slot 5. Again, focus on who will be in slots 1 and 6, as you know it is limited to either H or J. Try each. If H is in slots 1 and 6, then J must be in slot 2 (clue 3) and L must be in slot 3 (clue 4). The final open slot is slot 4, which must be J as both H and L have already been used twice. If J is in slots 1 and 6, then J has been used twice and cannot be used again. However, because L is in slot 5, there is no room to accommodate the HJ block from clue 3. Therefore, this possibility doesn't work—be sure to cross it out or erase it. Use only the first scenario when evaluating the answer choices.

	~L				~L
1	2	3	4	5	6
H	J	L	J	L	H
J				L	J	doesn't work

A. No. You've already proven this cannot be true.

B. No. J must be second.

C. No. L must be third.

D. Yes. This matches your diagram.

E. No. H must be sixth.

12. **B** Specific

You have already seen in question 11 that there can be at least one message between L's first and last messages, so eliminate (A). The only way to have four messages in between L's messages would be to have L be first and sixth; since L cannot be first, this isn't possible. Eliminate (E). In order to have three messages in between L's messages, L would have to occupy only one of slots 1 and 6 and then one of slots 2 and 5; clue 2 makes this impossible. Eliminate (D). Try to put two messages in between L's first and last messages. The only way to accomplish this is to put L in slots 2 and 5. Again, focus on slot 1. If H is in slot 1, then it must also be in slot 6. This leaves no room to accommodate clue 3, however, so it cannot be correct. If J is in slots 1 and 6, the same problem occurs. Therefore, it isn't possible to have two messages in between L's first and last messages; eliminate (C). The credited response is (B).

Questions 13–18

This is an order game with 1:1 correspondence. You must rank six crews—F, G, H, R, S, and T—in order from most to least productive. Your diagram should have six columns numbered 1–6, with 1 as the most productive and 6 as the least productive. The setup also refers to some of the crews as night-shift crews; fortunately, this issue arises only in question 17, so it's less complicated than it seems. Note in your list of elements which crews could be the night-shift crews.

Crews: F, G, H, R, S, T

Night-shift crews: G and T; S and H (one pair only)

Clue 1: F—G

Clue 2: R—S

Clue 3: R—T

Clue 4: S—H

Clue 5: G—T

Deductions: Combine all the range clues into a single composite clue.

Looking at the composite version, you can whittle down the options for a couple of slots on your diagram. Only F or R could be first, so write F/R in slot 1 of your diagram. Only T or H could go last, so add T/H into slot 6 of your diagram.

Here's the diagram:

13. **D** **Grab-a-Rule**

Use the clues to eliminate answer choices. Clue 1 eliminates (C). Clue 3 eliminates (A). Clue 4 eliminates (B). Clue 5 eliminates (E). Therefore, the credited response is (D).

14. **B** Specific

If F is third, then you know from your deductions that R must be first. Based on your composite clue, the only element available for slot 2 is S, since G must follow F and T must follow G. Place S in slot 2 and consider what elements are left. G, H, and T must somehow be placed into slots 4, 5, and 6, but you must consider the limits on each slot. T must come after G, so T cannot go fourth. Put G/H in slot 4. You already know from your deductions that slot 6 can be only T or H. Slot 5 is the only one that can be any of G, H, and T.

	most					least
	1	2	3	4	5	6
	R	S	F	G/H		T/H

A. No. S is second.

B. Yes. This is one of the possibilities noted in your diagram.

C. No. R is first.

D. No. S is second.

E. No. T can be only fifth or sixth.

15. **C** General

Use your deductions and prior work on questions 14 and 17 to eliminate answer choices. Remember that you're looking for what is NOT possible.

A. No. You saw this possibility in questions 14 and 17.

B. No. You saw this possibility in question 14.

C. Yes. R is followed by T, S, and H, so it cannot be fifth.

D. No. You saw this possibility in question 17.

E. No. You saw this possibility in question 14.

16. **C** General

Use your deductions and prior work on questions 14 and 17 to eliminate answer choices.

A. No. If F is second, you know that R is first, but that's as far as the information carries you.

B. No. In question 17, G is fifth in the first scenario, yet that did not determine the rest of the slots.

C. Yes. Try this scenario out. If H is third, then R and S must come before it in slots 1 and 2, respectively. That leaves F, G, and T to follow, in that order, so they will occupy slots 4, 5, and 6, respectively.

most				least	
1	2	3	4	5	6
R	S	H	F	G	T

D. No. If R is third, then you know that F is first and G is second, but that's as much as you know.

E. No. If S is third, you know that R must come first or second, but you don't know exactly which slot R will occupy.

17. C Specific

There are only 2 possibilities for the night-shift crews, so try out each of them. If G and T are the night-shift crews, then G must be fifth and T must be sixth. From your deductions, either F or R must be first. Because H must come after both R and S, neither R nor S can go in slot 4; this means slot 4 must be either H or F. You don't know anything more that's certain in that scenario, so try the other possibility. If S and H are the night-shift crews, then S must be fifth and H must be sixth. Since T must be preceded by both G and R, T will have to be in slot 4. Once again, F or R must be first. Because F must come before G, F cannot be third, which means slot 3 must be either R or G.

most				least	
1	2	3	4	5	6
F/R			H/F	G	T
F/R		R/G	T	S	H

A. No. F, H, or T is fourth.

B. No. Either G or S is fifth.

C. Yes. This is possible in either scenario.

D. No. F, H, or T is fourth.

E. No. T is either fourth or sixth.

18. E General

Use your deductions and prior work on questions 14 and 17 to eliminate answer choices. You've already seen from question 14 that F can be third, so eliminate (C). From question 17, you know that both R and G could be third, so eliminate (A), (B), and (D). Choice (E), therefore, is the credited response.

Questions 19–23

This game combines both order and group components. A shuttle van makes exactly four stops; you must assign one of four possible stops—F, L, M, and S—and one of four passengers—g, j, r, and v—to each stop. Therefore, your diagram will have columns 1–4 as its core with two tiers, one for the stops and one for the passengers. Use upper- and lowercase letters to distinguish between the two types of elements.

Stops: F, L, M, S

passengers: g, j, r, v

Clue 1: L = 1/2

Clue 2: M—r;

M
r

Clue 3: v—j

Clue 4: ; F—j /

F
j

→ S—g /

S
g

; j—F → g—S; g—S → j—F (contrapositive of first conditional)

Deductions: From clue 1, you know that L cannot be in slots 3 or 4; note this on your diagram. From clue 3, j cannot be first and v cannot be last; add this to your diagram as well. Clue 4 gives you a lot of information, so it's worth taking the time to inspect it a bit further. The second part of the clue tells you that if j comes before F, then g must come before S. The contrapositive of the first part of the clue indicates that if g comes before S, then j must come before F. Therefore, those two conditions will always occur together: either j will come before F AND g will come before S, or neither instance will occur.

Here's the diagram:

Stops: FMLS
passengers: gjrv

	1	2	3	4
	~j		~L	~L ~v
S:				
p:				

19. **E**   Grab-a-Rule

Use the clues to eliminate answer choices. Clue 1 eliminates (B). Clue 2 eliminates (D). Clue 3 eliminates (C). Clue 4 eliminates (A). Therefore, the credited response is (E).

20. **D**   Specific

Place M in slot 1. This means L must be in slot 2 (clue 1). The question is asking for which passengers could be in slot 1, but you don't know anything further about the passengers from the information given. Go to the answer choices and eliminate based on the clues and your earlier deductions.

```
              ~v
    ~j      ~L  ~L
    1 | 2 | 3 | 4
S:  M | L |   |
p:    |   |   |
```

A.   No. From clue 2, r could also be in slot 1.

B.   No. v could also be in slot 1.

C.   No. From clue 2, r could also be in slot 1.

D.   Yes. This choice includes all possible passengers for slot 1.

E.   No. j cannot be first.

21.   **D**   Specific

Place F in slot 1. This means L must be in slot 2 (clue 1). From clue 4, you know that g can't be in slot 1 because j will not come before F; g must therefore be either with or after S. You also can't put r in slot 1 because it must be with M or after it. This leaves v as the only possibility for slot 1. For similar reasons, you can't have either r or g in slot 2. This leaves j as the only possibility for slot 2. You don't know anything further about the passengers in slots 3 and 4, so go to the answer choices to see what you can eliminate.

```
              ~v
    ~j      ~L  ~L
    1 | 2 | 3 | 4
S:  F | L |   |
p:  v | j |   |
```

A.   No. g cannot be first.

B.   No. r cannot be first.

C.   No. g cannot be second.

D.   Yes. This is possible.

E.   No. r cannot be second.

22.   **C**   Specific

The starting point for this question is buried at the end. You are told that g is second, so put g into slot 2. The question stipulates that neither L nor S can come after g, so they must be in slots 1 and 2 in either order. For the open space in slot 1, neither j nor r (clue 2) will work, and g is already second. Therefore v must be the passenger in slot 1. Furthermore, since g will not come before S, j cannot come before F (clue 4), though this doesn't tell you anything certain about the remaining open spots in slots

3 and 4. You are asked for what must be true, so go to the answer choices and eliminate based on what you have.

$$
\begin{array}{c|c c|c|c}
 & & & \sim v & \\
 & \sim j & & \sim L & \sim L \\
\hline
 & 1 & 2 & 3 & 4 \\
\hline
S: & L/S & S/L & & \\
p: & v & g & &
\end{array}
$$

A. No. If L is the first stop, this won't be true.

B. No. If S is the first stop, this won't be true.

C. Yes. r must come after S, so this must be true.

D. No. This choice is a "could be true" answer.

E. No. This choice is a "could be true" answer.

23. **D** **Specific**

If g must come before S, then you know that j must come before F (clue 4). Combining this with clue 3, you get v—j—F. You don't know anything more specific, however, so go to the answer choices. You're looking for something that must be false, so eliminate anything that could be true.

A. No. This could be true.

B. No. This could be true.

C. No. This could be true.

D. Yes. From your work above, you know that F must come after v. This choice is definitely false.

E. No. This could be true.

Chapter 6
PrepTest 56:
Answers and
Explanations

ANSWER KEY: PREPTEST 56

Section 1: Games		Section 2: Arguments 1		Section 3: Arguments 2		Section 4: Reading Comprehension	
1.	E	1.	E	1.	C	1.	B
2.	B	2.	A	2.	E	2.	D
3.	C	3.	B	3.	B	3.	A
4.	C	4.	C	4.	A	4.	D
5.	A	5.	E	5.	D	5.	E
6.	E	6.	E	6.	D	6.	A
7.	A	7.	C	7.	E	7.	C
8.	D	8.	D	8.	A	8.	A
9.	B	9.	B	9.	A	9.	C
10.	B	10.	D	10.	C	10.	D
11.	E	11.	B	11.	E	11.	A
12.	D	12.	E	12.	A	12.	A
13.	C	13.	A	13.	A	13.	B
14.	A	14.	D	14.	B	14.	E
15.	A	15.	B	15.	D	15.	C
16.	E	16.	D	16.	A	16.	E
17.	A	17.	E	17.	C	17.	C
18.	A	18.	C	18.	E	18.	D
19.	C	19.	A	19.	E	19.	E
20.	D	20.	E	20.	D	20.	A
21.	E	21.	B	21.	D	21.	B
22.	E	22.	C	22.	B	22.	C
23.	B	23.	E	23.	E	23.	E
		24.	A	24.	D	24.	A
		25.	B	25.	E	25.	B
						26.	E
						27.	C

EXPLANATIONS

Section 1: Games

Questions 1–6

This is an order game with 1:1 correspondence. You must assign six saxophonists—F, G, H, J, K, and L—to each of six hour-long time slots. Your diagram should have columns numbered 1–6 across the top in accordance with the start times of the audition slots.

Clue 1: J—H

Clue 2: G—K

Clue 3: $\boxed{G\,L}\,/\,\boxed{L\,G}$

Clue 4: $\boxed{J{-}L}\,/\,\boxed{L{-}J}$

Deductions: From clue 1, you know that H can't be first and J can't be last. From clue 2, you know that K can't be first and G can't be last. Combining clues 2 and 3, you know that K also can't be second, as both G and L must come before it.

Here's the diagram:

```
                          ~K                    ~G
                  ~H  ~K                         ~J
        FGHJKL     1    2    3    4    5    6
                   |    |    |    |    |    |
                   |    |    |    |    |    |
                   |    |    |    |    |    |
                   |    |    |    |    |    |
```

1. **E** **Grab-a-Rule**

    Use the clues to eliminate answer choices. Clue 1 eliminates (D). Clue 2 eliminates (B). Clue 3 eliminates (A). Clue 4 eliminates (C). Therefore, the credited response is (E).

2. **B** **General**

    Use your deductions and prior work to eliminate answer choices.

    A. No. From your work on question 5, you can see that it's possible for H to audition earlier than L in the second scenario.

    B. Yes. You know this from combining clues 2 and 3 in your deductions above.

    C. No. From your work on question 5, you know that J can also be third or fourth.

D. No. From your work on question 5, you can see that it's possible for F and J to be consecutive in any of the three scenarios.

E. No. From your work on question 5, you can see that it's possible for G and K to be consecutive in the second scenario.

3. **C** General

Use your deductions and prior work to eliminate answer choices.

A. No. From your work on question 5, it's possible for K to be in slot 3 in the first of the three scenarios.

B. No. From your work on question 5, it's possible for K to be in slot 3 in the first of the three scenarios.

C. Yes. From your work on question 5, it's possible for K to be in slot 3 in the first of the three scenarios.

D. No. From your earlier deductions, you know this isn't possible.

E. No. From your earlier deductions, you know this isn't possible.

4. **C** General

Use your deductions and prior work to eliminate answer choices before you attempt to try them all out. From question 5, you can eliminate (B), (D), and (E), as in each instance the element for every slot can't be determined just from the information given. You're left with (A) and (C), so try (A). If H is in slot 4, then J will have to be in slot 1 to allow room for L and G. L would be third, so G would have to be second. Slots 5 and 6 could be either F or K, however, so this choice doesn't satisfy the condition in the question. Eliminate (A). There's no need to test (C) out since it's the only one left, but if you do, you'll find that all the elements fall into place. The order would be F, G, L, K, J, H in slots 1 through 6, respectively. Choice (C) is the credited response.

5. **A** Specific

The question tells you that F can't be first, and you already know from your deductions that neither H nor K can be first either. That leaves G, J, and L as possibilities for the first slot, so you'll have to try each one. Start with G. If G is first, then L will have to be second and J will have to be fourth. This arrangement doesn't seem to present any problems, so leave it for now and move on to the next option. If J is first, then L will be third and G will be either second or fourth. Again, this seems all right, so look at the final possibility. If L is first, then G must be second and J must be third. All of these appear to work, so you can use all three when evaluating the answer choices, as you're looking for something that could be true.

```
  ~K                    ~G
  ~H  ~K                ~J
 ┌───┬───┬───┬───┬───┬───┐
 │ 1 │ 2 │ 3 │ 4 │ 5 │ 6 │
 ├───┼───┼───┼───┼───┼───┤
 │ G │ L │   │ J │   │   │
 │ J │(G)│ L │(G)│   │   │
 │ L │ G │ J │   │   │   │
 └───┴───┴───┴───┴───┴───┘
```

A. Yes. This seems possible in all three scenarios, as only G and J are prohibited from being in slot 6 and they are both already placed elsewhere.

B. No. G is never in slot 5 in any of the three scenarios.

C. No. Slot 3 is already taken in two scenarios, and in the one instance in which it is open—when G is first—H would have to be fifth or sixth because J is fourth.

D. No. J is never in slot 2 in any of the three scenarios.

E. No. J is never in slot 5 in any of the three scenarios.

6. E   **General**

Use your deductions and prior work to eliminate answer choices.

A. No. You don't have prior work that disproves this choice, but you know that G can't be in slot 6. Try to put G in slot 5. If G is fifth, then K must be sixth and L must be fourth. If L is fourth, J will have to be second and H third, leaving F for slot 1. Since it's therefore possible for G to be fifth, this choice doesn't have to be true; eliminate it.

B. No. From your work on question 5, you can see that it's possible for H to be in slot 2 in the second scenario.

C. No. From your work on question 5, you can see that it's possible for H to be sixth in any of the three scenarios.

D. No. From your work on question 5, you can see that it's possible for K to be sixth in any of the three scenarios.

E. Yes. If you've eliminated everything else, go ahead and pick this one; there's no need to test it out. If you're curious, though, here's what happens. From clue 3, you know that L and G must be consecutive, in either order; from clue 2 you know that K must come later than G. Therefore, L will be followed either by K or by both K and G, depending on the order of the block. If both K and G follow L, then L can't be fifth or sixth. If the order is G, L, and K in slots 4, 5, and 6, respectively, then J will have to be in slot 3. However, there's no room for H to follow J, as all the slots are filled, so this scenario doesn't work either. Thus, L can never be later than slot 4.

Questions 7–11

This is a group game with variable assignments. You must assign two of four people—G, H, J, and M—to move each of three pieces of furniture—R, S, and T. Your diagram should have three columns labeled R, S, and T across the top, and each column should have two slots.

Every person must be used at least once, but may be used again as well.

Clue 1: $G_S \rightarrow H_R$; $\sim H_R \rightarrow \sim G_S$; $H_R \rightarrow G_S$; $\sim G_S \rightarrow \sim H_R$

Clue 2: $J_T \rightarrow M_R$; $\sim M_R \rightarrow \sim J_T$

Clue 3: $\boxed{\sout{GJ}}$

Deductions: There's not much you can deduce for certain from the clues. You will need to keep an eye out for potential conflicts with G and J, though, since each is involved in two clues.

Here's the diagram:

$$GHJM \quad \begin{array}{c|c|c} R & S & T \\ \hline \_\_ & \_\_ & \_\_ \end{array}$$

7. A Grab-a-Rule

Use the clues to eliminate answer choices. Clue 1 eliminates (D) and (E). Clue 2 eliminates (C). Clue 3 eliminates (B). Therefore, the credited response is (A).

8. D Specific

Place J and M in the R column. Since R is now full, check to see which clues might be affected. The contrapositive of the first part of clue 1 says that if H isn't in R, then G can't be in S. As G must be used at least once, it will have to be in the T column, so put it there. There's nothing more that you know for certain, so go to the answer choices, keeping in mind that the question asks for what "must be true."

$$\begin{array}{c|c|c} R & S & T \\ \hline JM & \_\_\_ & G\_ \end{array}$$

A. No. This is a "could be true" answer.

B. No. This is a "could be true" answer.

C. No. This is a "could be true" answer.

D.   Yes. Your diagram shows this has to be true.

E.   No. This is a "could be true" answer.

9.   **B**   Specific

Place H in all three columns. Looking at clue 1, you know that G must be in S because H is in R. That means S is now full, and the remaining slots in R and T will have to be occupied by either J or M as each element must be used at least once. Since clue 3 will be satisfied if you place J in T (the only remaining space for M is in R), you can actually have either element in either slot. Put J/M and M/J in the empty slots; the question asks for what "could be true" so your answer will likely involve J or M.

A.   No. G is in S.

B.   Yes. This is possible.

C.   No. H and G are in S.

D.   No. H and G are in S.

E.   No. G is in S.

10.   **B**   General

Use the clues to eliminate answer choices before you resort to testing choices out.

A.   No. This violates clue 3.

B.   Yes. This would leave H and J together in S, which doesn't violate any of the clues given.

C.   No. This violates clue 2.

D.   No. This would leave G and J together in S, which violates clue 3.

E.   No. This would leave G and H together in S, which violates clue 1.

11.   **E**   Specific

Place J and M in column S. From clue 1, you know that if G is not in S, then H cannot be in R, which means H must be in T. Place H in T and put a ~H in R so that you remember that H cannot be there, since elements may be used more than once. That's all you know for certain, so go to the answer choices to see what you can eliminate.

A. No. H cannot be in R.

B. No. H cannot be in R.

C. No. This violates clue 3.

D. No. H must be in T.

E. Yes. This is possible.

Questions 12–16

This is a group game with variable assignments. You must assign three of four varieties of trees—M, O, S, and P—to one of two groups—G or L. Your diagram should have G and L as its core. Elements can be used more than once, but every element does not necessarily have to be used.

Clue 1: Put three slots in each of the G and L groups.

Clue 2: at least one block of MS

Clue 3: O → T; ~T → ~O

Clue 4: Place M in group G.

Deductions: Because you're using three of four elements in each group, it's worth taking the time to figure out how many different possibilities there are; odds are there won't be many.

Begin with clue 3: if O is in a group, T must be there, which means you can't have the MS block in that group. This leaves only two options, then; either you'll have OTM or OTS. What happens if you have the MS block in a group? Then you'll have to have MST, since O requires T and there's not enough room to accommodate both. Therefore, you now know that there are only three possible combinations of elements: OTM, OTS, and MST. You also learn from this that T must be in each group, so put this into your diagram as well.

Here's the diagram:

12. **D** Grab-a-Rule

Use the clues to eliminate answer choices. Clue 2 eliminates (B). Clue 3 eliminates (A) and (C). Clue 4 eliminates (E). Therefore, the credited response is (D).

13. **C** Specific

Use your deductions and prior work to eliminate answer choices.

A. No. This is a "could be true" answer.

B. No. This is a "could be true" answer, as you can see from your work on question 14.

C. Yes. This must be true, as you know from your prior deductions that T must be in both groups.

D. No. This is a "could be true" answer, as you can see from your work on question 14.

E. No. This is a "could be true" answer.

14. **A** [**Specific**]

Place S in both columns. Group G is now filled with MTS while Group L has T, S, and either M or O.

$$
\begin{array}{c|c}
G & L \\
\hline
M\ T\ S & T\ S\ \tfrac{M}{O}
\end{array}
$$

A. Yes. If group L contains O, then this choice could be true.

B. No. At most, you could have two M's and two S's, but M cannot outnumber S.

C. No. There are two S's, but there can be at most one O.

D. No. O cannot be in G.

E. No. L cannot have both M and O.

15. **A** [**General**]

Use your deductions and prior work to eliminate answer choices. Remember that you're looking for what must be false.

A. Yes. This cannot be true, as one of the groups must contain MST in order to satisfy clue 2.

B. No. This is a "could be true" answer, as you can see from your work on question 14.

C. No. From your deductions, you know this statement must be true.

D. No. This is a "could be true" answer, as you can see from your work on question 14.

E. No. This could be true; you could have one group with MST and the other group with MOT.

16. **E** [**General**]

Use your deductions and prior work to eliminate answer choices.

A. No. This cannot be true, as T is in both groups and one of the groups must contain MST in order to satisfy clue 2.

B. No. O can be used at most only once, while S can be used in both groups.

C. No. From your deductions, you know that T must be in both groups.

D. No. From your deductions, you know that T must be in both groups.

E. Yes. This could be true, as you can see from your work on question 14.

Questions 17–23

You must decide which of five executives—Q, R, S, T, and V—will visit which of three manufacturing plant sites—f, h, and m—over the course of three days. Days 1, 2, and 3 will form the core of your diagram, with one tier for the executives and another for the plants. Each executive must be used once, but more than one executive may visit a given site.

Clue 1: f—h

Clue 2:
```
┌───┐
│ ─ │
│ f │
└───┘
```

Clue 3: Q—R, Q—T

Clue 4: S—V, or SV together

Deductions: From clue 1, you know that h can't be on day 1 and f can't be on day 3. From clue 3, you know that neither R nor T can be on day 1 and Q can't be on day 3. Because you must split up the five executives over the course of three days, with no day left empty, you know that the distribution of the executives will either be 1-1-3 or 1-2-2 in no specific order. In the latter case, the day that has just one executive will also have f, in keeping with clue 2.

Here's the diagram:

```
        ~R
        ~T            ~Q
        ~h            ~f
E: QRSTV    ┌────┬────┬────
s: fhm      │ 1  │ 2  │ 3
        ────┼────┼────┼────
      E: ─  │  ─ │  ─ │
        ────┼────┼────┼────
      s: ─  │  ─ │  ─ │
            │    │    │
```

17. **A** Grab-a-Rule

Use the clues to eliminate answer choices. Clue 1 eliminates (D). Clue 2 eliminates (E). Clue 3 eliminates (C). Clue 4 eliminates (B). Therefore, the credited response is (A).

18. **A** Specific

Place R and T on day 2. From clue 3, you know that Q will have to be on day 1. You now have to consider S and V. Since day 3 must have someone, either V alone or both V and S will be on day 3; put V down for certain. Next, think about which plant will be visited each day. From your deductions, you know that f cannot be on day 3, but from clue 2, you also know that f can have only one executive visit. Therefore, f must be on day 1, as both R and T are on day 2. This further limits S to either day 2 or day 3. Since you don't know anything more for certain, go to the answer choices to find something that must be true.

```
        ~R
        ~T              ~Q
        ~h              ~f

         1    2      3
     E:  Q   RT(s)  (V)s
     s:  f    —      —
```

A. Yes. This must be true according to your work.

B. No. This is a "could be true" answer.

C. No. This is a "could be true" answer.

D. No. This is a "could be true" answer.

E. No. This is a "could be true" answer.

19. **C**   Specific

Q and S must be on the same day. From your deductions, you know that Q cannot be on day 3, which means the pair must be on either day 1 or day 2. Try day 1 first. If Q and S are on day 1, then f will have to be on day 2. This means h will be on day 3, leaving m for day 1. There don't appear to be any problems with this scenario, but since you don't know anything more about the other elements, leave it as is. Now try Q and S on day 2. From clue 3, R and T would have to be on day 3, but clue 4 tells you that V would have to be on either day 2 or day 3 as well. Day 1 would then have no executive, which violates the initial conditions in the set-up. Therefore, this scenario doesn't work; cross it out and use the first scenario to eliminate answer choices.

```
        ~R
        ~T             ~Q
        ~h             ~f

         1    2     3
     E:  QS   —     —
     s:  m    f     m
     ·····················
             QS   RTV  — doesn't work
```

A. No. The first site visited is m.

B. No. h is on day 3.

56

C. Yes. This could happen on day 2.

D. No. S is on day 1.

E. No. f is on day 2, so there can only be one executive that day.

20. **D** General

Use your deductions and prior work to eliminate answer choices. Your work from question 18 eliminates (B) and (E). Your work from question 23 eliminates (A). Now try (C). If S and T are with h, they could be on either day 2 or day 3. Try them on day 2; this means Q will have to go on day 1 with f as per clues 1 and 3. Day 3 would then contain V, R, and m. Since this appears to work, you can eliminate (C). Only (D) is left, so there's no need to try it out. The credited response is (D).

21. **E** Specific

Q and V are on the same day as m. From your deductions, you know that Q can be only on day 1 or day 2, so try each possibility. If Q, V, and m are on day 1, then S will also have to be on day 1 as per clue 4. This leaves only one executive, either R or T, for each of days 2 and 3, which will contain f and h, respectively. If Q, V, and m are on day 2, then R and T will have to go on day 3 as per clue 3. Clue 1 tells you that f will have to go on day 1, and since S is the only executive left it will go with f. Finally, h will be on day 3. Use both scenarios to help you eliminate answer choices.

```
      ~R
      ~T              ~Q
      ~h              ~f
            ┌─────┬─────┬─────
            │  1  │  2  │  3
      E: QVS│  R/T│  T/R
      s:  m │   f │   h
            ├─ ─ ─┼─ ─ ─┼─ ─ ─
            │  S  │  QV │  RT
            │  f  │  m  │  h
```

A. No. This does not happen in either scenario.

B. No. Only day 1 has three executives.

C. No. Only day 1 has three executives.

D. No. This does not happen in either scenario.

E. Yes. This is true in the first scenario.

22. **E** General

Use your deductions and prior work to eliminate answer choices.

A. No. Your work for question 19 shows that this doesn't have to be true.

B.   No. Your work for question 18 shows that this doesn't have to be true.

C.   No. Your work for question 18 shows that this doesn't have to be true; S could be on day 3.

D.   No. Your work for question 19 shows that this doesn't have to be true.

E.   Yes. This must be true. f must be on either day 1 or day 2, and as per clue 2 there can be only one executive with it.

23.   **B**   Specific

If S and f are together, they will have to be on either day 1 or day 2. Try each one, keeping in mind that f can have only one executive with it as per clue 2. If S and f are on day 1, then Q will have to be on day 2 with R and T on day 3. You don't know anything more than that, so move on to the next scenario. If S and f are on day 2, then Q will have to be on day 1 with m; V, R, and T will therefore be on day 3 with h. You're looking for something that must be true, so use both scenarios to evaluate the choices.

```
        ~R
        ~T              ~Q
        ~h              ~f

         1    |   2   |   3
    E:   S    |   Q   |  RT
    s:   f    |       |   h
        ------|-------|------
         Q    |   S   |  VRT
         m    |   f   |   h
```

A.   No. This doesn't have to be true in the first scenario.

B.   Yes. This is true in both cases.

C.   No. This isn't true in the second scenario.

D.   No. This isn't true in the second scenario.

E.   No. This isn't true in the second scenario.

Section 2: Arguments 1

1.   **E**   Flaw

The argument concludes that it is not more dangerous to swim in the area at night than during the day based on the fact that all recent shark attacks on swimmers have occurred during the day. However, the argument doesn't consider that there could be another explanation for why the recent shark attacks occur during the day—if swimmers are generally too afraid to swim after dark, there may not be any swimmers in the water for sharks to attack at night.

A. No. This information isn't really relevant. If some sharks are primarily nocturnal hunters, there could still be others that aren't, such as those responsible for the daytime shark attacks.

B. No. There is no reference to any type of source in the argument.

C. No. Anxiety is irrelevant to whether swimmers are actually attacked, so while the argument doesn't take this into consideration, it's not a flaw in its logic.

D. No. The argument makes no assumptions as to whether swimmers are the most knowledgeable about the safest times of day for swimming; it merely contradicts popular opinion.

E. Yes. The reason for the dearth of shark attacks at night could be the absence of night swimmers, which means it could be more dangerous to swim at night than during the day.

2. A **Point at Issue**

Denise believes that reducing crime depends on the certainty of a punishment that is sufficiently severe to act as a deterrent to anyone considering committing a crime. Reshmi believes that ensuring that educational opportunities are readily available to all will most effectively reduce crime by presenting alternatives to those who see criminal activity as the sole means to a comfortable lifestyle.

A. Yes. Both Denise and Reshmi suggest ways to reduce crime that imply that a person has a choice as to whether to commit a crime. Denise offers a deterrent while Reshmi offers an incentive, yet both rely on the idea that someone can choose not to commit a crime.

B. No. Neither of them discusses how important an issue crime is in modern society.

C. No. Denise does mention the idea that punishment should be certain, but Reshmi never addresses any of this, so you don't know whether they would indeed agree.

D. No. Reshmi would likely agree with this statement, but Denise does not address economic factors, so you don't know whether they would indeed agree.

E. No. Denise states that punishment should be certain, but Reshmi never addresses this, so you don't know whether they would indeed agree.

3. B **Weaken**

The argument concludes that Acme Corporation offers unskilled workers excellent opportunities for advancement based on the example of Ms. Garon, who started as an assembly line worker, a position that requires no special skills, and is now the president of the company. However, you don't actually know that Ms. Garon had no special skills when she started. You need to find an answer choice that offers another explanation for how she attained her position as president even though she began as an assembly line worker.

A. No. If anything, this strengthens the argument by implying that Ms. Garon's career is representative of the path Acme employees take.

B. Yes. This suggests that she advanced to her position by virtue of her business degree; therefore, this casts doubt on the argument that unskilled workers have excelled opportunities for advancement at Acme.

C. No. This doesn't tell you whether unskilled workers are among those getting promoted, so it doesn't really impact the argument.

D. No. This is irrelevant. How long she worked at Acme is not important; the reason behind her promotion is, but this choice doesn't address that.

E. No. This is out of scope; there's no link between wages and skills here.

4. **C** **Necessary Assumption**

The argument concludes that during molting, yellow warblers have no competition for the food supply located within the range of their restricted flying. The evidence for this conclusion is that when a warbler molts, which limits its flying distance, its song changes; this in turn affects the behavior of other yellow warblers, who will not enter the smaller core territory of a molting warbler, although they might at other times. The argument assumes that the only competition for the food supply within a warbler's range comes from other yellow warblers and not from anything else.

A. No. Even if the core areas contain enough food to sustain more than one molting warbler, this choice doesn't address the issue of competition for that food.

B. No. This is irrelevant; it doesn't matter whether other birds act in the same fashion when molting.

C. Yes. If you negate this choice, then it invalidates the argument's conclusion by suggesting that yellow warblers do indeed have competition even when molting.

D. No. This weakens the argument somewhat by suggesting that competition would be minimal but not absent entirely.

E. No. This is irrelevant; negating this choice would have no impact on the argument's conclusion.

5. **E** **Flaw**

Chinh concludes that television producers should not pay attention to what the viewing public prefers when making creative decisions; he reasons that great painters do not consider what the museum-going public prefers to see. Lana points out that because television is expressly for the viewing public, Chinh's analogy misses the mark; a television producer is more comparable to a CEO than to an artist.

A. No. Chinh's conclusion is not a restatement of his premise.

B. No. Chinh does not discuss any sample of consumers.

C. No. Chinh does not reverse cause and effect in his argument.

D. No. This isn't the flaw in Chinh's argument. Furthermore, Chinh's premise specifically refers to great painters, not painters in general.

E. Yes. Lana believes the analogy Chinh relies on is problematic, as noted above.

6. **E** **Necessary Assumption**

The dietitian concludes that people looking to maintain cardiac health without lowering sodium consumption should eat fresh, as opposed to canned or frozen, fruit and vegetables. Why? High sodium intake increases the risk of heart disease in some people, and the potassium in plant foods helps to prevent the negative effects of sodium. The dietitian assumes that fresh fruit and vegetables are a better source of potassium than are canned or frozen forms.

56

A. No. The amounts of sodium and potassium relative to each other in a given type of fruit or vegetable aren't essential to the argument.

B. No. This is out of scope; the conclusion is directed at those who do not wish to lower sodium consumption.

C. No. This isn't necessary to the argument. Even if potassium weren't the only mineral that helps to prevent sodium's malign effects, the conclusion would still be valid.

D. No. The side effects of potassium are out of scope so long as it has the desired effect of countering sodium's negative effects.

E. Yes. If you negate this choice, the conclusion would no longer hold true; there would be no reason to recommend fresh over canned or frozen fruit and vegetables.

7. **C**   **Parallel Flaw**

The argument concludes that Dana intentionally killed the plant because she intentionally watered it every other day. As the plant needed dry soil, the frequent watering killed it. However, the argument misapplies the word "intentionally"—there is nothing to suggest that Dana knew frequent watering would kill the plant.

A. No. There is no issue of intent in this argument.

B. No. The conclusion focuses on what Celeste should know, not on what she intended, so this doesn't match the original argument.

C. Yes. This contains the same flaw as the original argument. There is no evidence that the restaurant owner knew that removing that item would disappoint Jerry.

D. No. This argument is not flawed.

E. No. This argument is also not flawed.

8. **D**   **Weaken**

The argument concludes that a boulder in a given area was probably deposited hundreds of miles away from its geological birthplace by a glacier. Why? The boulder is volcanic in origin, unlike the rest of the rock in the area, and the area in question was covered by southward-moving glaciers during the last Ice Age. To weaken this argument, you need to show either that a glacier couldn't have been responsible for transporting the boulder or that some other explanation can account for the boulder's differing makeup.

A. No. This isn't strong enough to weaken the argument. The fact that most boulders haven't been moved that far still allows for the possibility that at least one was moved farther than 100 miles.

B. No. Since the glaciers that supposedly moved the boulder were moving from north to south, knowing that the closest source of volcanic rock is south of the boulder doesn't do anything to weaken the argument.

C. No. This would strengthen the argument by implying that a southward-moving glacier would have passed through a source of volcanic rock, from which the boulder could have originated.

56

D.   Yes. This weakens the argument. If there is no source of volcanic rock north of the boulder, then it doesn't make sense to claim that the boulder was deposited there in the manner described by the argument.

E.   No. This is irrelevant. You are concerned only with this particular boulder, and the boulder could certainly have traveled more than 50 miles according to the argument itself.

9.   **B**   **Reasoning**

Rifka concludes that they do not need to stop and ask for directions because they would only need to stop if they were lost. Craig, however, disagrees, saying that because they are lost, they need to stop. Craig contradicts one of Rifka's unstated premises—that they are not lost—and draws the opposite conclusion—that they need to stop.

A.   No. Craig does reject Rifka's implicit premise that they are not lost.

B.   Yes. Craig denies Rifka's implicit premise that they are not lost and arrives at the conclusion that they should stop, contrary to Rifka's conclusion.

C.   No. Craig does not accept the truth of Rifka's premises because unlike her, he believes that they are lost.

D.   No. Craig doesn't provide a counterexample; he simply disagrees with one of Rifka's premises and conclusion.

E.   No. Craig clearly draws a conclusion that contradicts Rifka's conclusion, so he does not remain noncommittal.

10.   **D**   **Sufficient Assumption**

The critic concludes that neither tragedy nor comedy can be classified as either satirical or romance literature. Why? Major characters in both romance and satirical literature have moral qualities that reflect the worlds in which they are portrayed. But comedy and tragedy require that the moral qualities of major characters change during the course of the action. The critic assumes that characters in both romance and satirical literature do not undergo changes in moral qualities akin to those of characters in tragedies or comedies.

A.   No. The nature of the characters is not relevant to the argument; you need to know whether their moral qualities change.

B.   No. This is out of scope. The critic is specifically concerned with changes to characters' moral qualities, not changes in the vision of the world depicted in a given work.

C.   No. While the critic says that tragedy requires the moral qualities of a character to change throughout the course of the action, you are never told how or to what extent these qualities must change, so this goes too far.

D.   Yes. If in romance and satirical literature characters' moral qualities do not change during the course of the action, the critic's conclusion regarding the classification of comedy and tragedy would be valid.

E.   No. The critic's premises focus specifically on major characters, so this is out of scope.

56

11. **B** Reasoning

Lance claims that every general rule has at least one exception. Frank concludes that Lance must withdraw that conclusion, because if Lance's claim, itself a general rule, is taken as true, then there would exist at least one general rule that has no exceptions, which contradicts Lance's conclusion.

A. No. This choice describes circular reasoning, which Lance's conclusion does not rely on.

B. Yes. Frank demonstrates that by accepting Lance's conclusion as true, a situation then arises that yields a contradiction.

C. No. Frank does not show anything this absolute; this is too extreme.

D. No. Frank's argument does not address the issue of what experience teaches us.

E. No. Frank does not give any examples of real cases; he counters Lance's argument in a theoretical fashion.

12. **E** Flaw

The argument concludes that the energy subsidy has failed to achieve its intended purpose. Why? Even with subsidized energy production, which was intended to help residents of rural areas gain access to electricity, many of the most isolated rural populations still have no access to electricity. Yet the argument doesn't seem to take into account the fact that the subsidy's intended purpose might still be achieved even if only some, not all, rural populations now have access to electricity.

A. No. The argument never claims the subsidy's intended purpose could have been arrived at by other means, only that it has not been fulfilled thus far.

B. No. There is no discussion in the argument of the subsidy benefiting those for whom it was not intended.

C. No. The argument never claims that the subsidy was meant to help other people aside from those in rural areas.

D. No. While the argument doesn't address the possibility raised by this choice, it's not a logical flaw in its reasoning.

E. Yes. The argument incorrectly assumes that for the subsidy to achieve its intended purpose, it would have had to help everyone to whom it was applicable, not just some populations.

13. **A** Resolve/ Explain

It is commonly accepted that heart attacks are most likely to occur on Mondays because, as Monday is the start of the workweek, people feel more stress that day than on other days of the week. However, even unemployed retired people are more likely to have heart attacks on Mondays than on other days. Why is this the case if someone is retired and not tied to a traditional workweek schedule?

A. Yes. This would explain why retirees are just as likely as employed individuals to have a heart attack on a Monday; they keep to the same sort of work schedule even though they are no longer employed.

56

B.   No. This doesn't tell you about either their stress levels or their schedules, so this doesn't help explain the situation.

C.   No. This doesn't explain why they would still be most likely to have a heart attack on a Monday.

D.   No. This explains why heart attacks are more likely to occur on Mondays for people who are employed; however, it doesn't explain the second part of the argument concerning retirees.

E.   No. This makes the paradox worse.

14. **D**   **Strengthen**

The psychologist concludes that people who are especially overconfident are more likely to attempt to start a business in spite of the odds against success than are people who are less confident. The evidence the psychologist cites comes from a survey in which an equal number of entrepreneurs and business managers were asked to answer a bunch of questions and rate how confident they were that their answers were correct. In general, the entrepreneurs were more overconfident than the business managers. You want to find an answer that strengthens the link between being overconfident and trying to start a business.

A.   No. This is irrelevant. The subject matter of the questions doesn't tell you anything about the relationship between overconfidence and starting a business.

B.   No. You don't know whether these entrepreneurs were the ones that were overconfident; if they weren't, then this information isn't applicable to the psychologist's argument.

C.   No. This doesn't strengthen the psychologist's argument, which deals with the relationship between overconfidence and starting a business, not having success in business.

D.   Yes. If what is true of the entrepreneurs in terms of their overconfidence is also found in some of the business managers, it makes it more likely that the psychologist's conclusion about the link between overconfidence and starting a business is valid.

E.   No. Confidence in one's own business acumen is out of scope, since that doesn't tell you whether a person is overconfident or more likely to start a business.

15. **B**   **Flaw**

If Agnes's proposal is approved, the fourth-floor lab must be cleaned out. If Immanuel's proposal is approved, he will continue to work in the second-floor lab because he requires less space. Only if the director supports a proposal will it be approved, which you can diagram as proposal approved → director supports proposal, and the director supports both proposals. The argument therefore concludes that the fourth-floor lab must be cleaned out. However, having the director support a proposal doesn't guarantee that it will be approved; that would entail reading in the opposite direction of the arrow, so there's the flaw.

A.   No. There is no discussion of the relative size of the two labs.

B.   Yes. Having the director's support is a necessary, but not sufficient, condition for any proposal that is approved.

C.   No. The amount of enthusiasm the director expresses for each proposal is not relevant, since the premises require only the director's support and nothing more.

D. No. This is irrelevant. Even if Immanuel does want to move, Agnes's proposal is the one that requires the fourth-floor lab. The argument doesn't address the possibility raised in this choice, but this isn't the flaw in the argument's logic.

E. No. The premises state that if Agnes's proposal is approved, the fourth-floor lab must be cleaned out for her use. You have to take that information as a given. Whether there are other labs that are also suitable is out of scope.

16. **D**   Principle Strengthen

The argument concludes that the Outdoor Sports Company's policy of offering its customers financial incentives to provide the E-mail addresses of their friends is an unethical business practice. Why? It encourages people to exploit their personal relationships for profit, which risks damaging the integrity of those relationships. You need an answer choice that supports this line of reasoning.

A. No. This choice focuses on what is unethical for people to do, but the argument specifically discusses an unethical business practice, so this is out of scope.

B. No. This is too broad. The argument never says that it is unethical to use the information, only that it is an unethical business practice to offer such incentives to gain it.

C. No. This is too strong. The argument says that people risk damaging their relationships, not that a company seeks to deliberately damage those relationships. Also, it is an individual's choice whether to provide E-mail addresses of friends, so a choice that ascribes blame to a company for an individual's willful actions doesn't match the argument.

D. Yes. This matches the language of the argument, which is not extreme. Plus, this choice clearly states that what is unethical is that the company is encouraging behavior that could have damaging effects.

E. No. This doesn't uphold the notion that the company's business practice is unethical; it only addresses the effect an individual's action might have.

17. **E**   Point at Issue

Glen concludes that law's primary role should be to create virtuous citizens because an emphasis on law's purely procedural side produces a concern with personal rights that leads to the individual's indifference to society's welfare. Sara, on the other hand, disagrees with Glen's conclusion, arguing that his outlook would encourage government to decide which modes of life are truly virtuous, which would be more dangerous than the government's being overprotective of individuals' rights.

A. No. The issue of whether citizens are capable of making good choices is never raised in Sara's argument.

B. No. While Glen might agree with this statement, you don't know for certain that Sara would disagree, as she disagrees only with Glen's conclusion, not his premise.

C. No. While Sara might agree with this statement, you don't have enough information to know how Glen would react to it.

D.   No. Sara never addresses law's purely procedural side, so you don't know whether she would agree with this statement. She only claims that if law's primary role were to be the creation of virtuous citizens, the result would be a government that is overprotective of individuals' rights.

E.   Yes. Glen would agree with this, while Sara would disagree.

18.   **C**   **Principle Match**

The argument concludes that it is almost never in a cardholder's interest to skip payments on a credit card because the cost of doing so is much greater to the cardholder in the long run. You need to find an answer choice that similarly shows that the long-term cost of an action is much greater than its short-term benefit.

A.   No. This discusses finding other ways to combat pests, which doesn't match the original argument.

B.   No. This suggests the costs are balanced out or overridden by the benefit, which doesn't match the original argument.

C.   Yes. Constructing new roads, while beneficial in the short term, will result in greater maintenance costs in the long run.

D.   No. Here the costs are only sometimes greater in the long run, which doesn't match the original argument.

E.   No. There is no discussion of short- versus long-term costs or benefits in this choice.

56

19.   **A**   **Inference**

Diagram the two pieces of information that start with "none." Taking literature not taking physics; taking physics not taking literature. Taking rhetoric not taking physics; taking physics not taking rhetoric. You also know that some students taking physics are also taking art.

A.   Yes. Several of the students taking physics are also taking art. Since taking physics not taking literature, this choice follows from the information given.

B.   No. There is no direct connection made between taking literature and taking art. This is possible, but you're looking for something that the information in the passage directly supports.

C.   No. There is no direct connection made between taking literature and taking rhetoric. This is possible, but you're looking for something that the information in the passage directly supports.

D.   No. This choice has the same problem as (C).

E.   No. There is no direct connection made between taking literature and taking art. This is possible, but you're looking for something that the information in the passage directly supports.

20.   **E**   **Principle Strengthen**

The psychologist concludes that psychotherapists should never provide psychotherapy on talk shows. Why? It is expected that psychotherapists who provide psychotherapy on radio or television talks show do so in a manner that is entertaining; however, satisfying this demand is almost always incompatible with providing psychological help that is of high quality.

A. No. This is out of scope. A psychotherapist could potentially be entertaining as long as he or she isn't providing psychotherapy, and there's no discussion of what is "appropriate" in the argument.

B. No. The psychologist doesn't address what is responsible for the quality of the advice; she only states that something is usually incompatible with providing high-quality help.

C. No. The psychologist states that the demand for entertainment in this case is "nearly always incompatible" with providing high-quality care, but this choice creates a lower threshold by stating that psychotherapy should not be provided if there is "any chance" that it is less than high quality.

D. No. This is out of scope; what audiences are seeking isn't relevant to the psychologist's argument, which is concerned with what psychotherapists shouldn't do.

E. Yes. This would support the psychologist's decision, and it matches the strength of the language in the argument.

21. **B** Point at Issue

Tania claims that good art criticism cannot be separated from emotion because art is a passion and a person can be unbiased only about things that are of no interest to him or her. Although Monique's conclusion is implied and not directly stated in the argument, she disagrees with Tania, noting that art is not just a passion and that the best art critics engage with artwork only after shedding all their biases and consulting general principles of aesthetics.

A. No. You don't know whether Tania would agree with this; she only states that art is a passion, but her statement leaves open the possibility that she too thinks it is more than just that.

B. Yes. Tania would disagree with this statement, while Monique would agree with it.

C. No. Neither person makes claims about what art critics should or should not feel toward artworks.

D. No. Monique never addresses the issue of fairness, so you don't know whether she would agree with this choice.

E. No. Neither individual makes any claims about what the most important aspect of art criticism is.

22. **C** Resolve/Explain

Judicial writing is rarely of high literary quality, since the writing styles of works of such quality are more subject to misinterpretation, which would defeat the purpose of judicial decisions. Yet some dissenting opinions have writing of high literary quality even though they are sometimes included in written decisions.

A. No. This doesn't explain why dissenting opinions would have a higher literary quality.

B. No. This doesn't help explain anything because this would seemingly apply to both decisions and dissenting opinions.

C. Yes. If dissenting opinions aren't used to determine laws, then it wouldn't be a problem for them to be written in a style that might allow them to be subject to misinterpretation.

D. No. This is irrelevant. You're not concerned with what judges read, and this doesn't explain why dissenting opinions would have a higher literary quality.

E. No. This wouldn't explain why, if these judicial decisions are more widely read, it would be acceptable for the dissenting opinions contained therein to be written in a style that leaves them more open to misinterpretation.

23. **E**   **Inference**

Diagram the first two statements in the argument. No intervention → squirrel monkeys become extinct; squirrel monkeys do not become extinct → intervention. Tracts of forest preserved → monkeys survive; monkeys do not survive → tracts of forest not preserved.

A. No. This is irrelevant; the argument doesn't discuss habitats other than second-growth forest.

B. No. You don't know what form an intervention by conservationists would take, so this choice goes too far.

C. No. You are told that second-growth forest furnishes squirrel monkeys' favorite insects and fruit; however, it is possible that they could survive on other sources of food that aren't their favorites. The argument never states that their favorite insects and fruit are the only kinds squirrel monkeys eat.

D. No. Intervention by conservationists is a necessary but not sufficient condition for squirrel monkeys to survive. Even if an intervention takes place, they could still become extinct for other reasons.

E. Yes. Combine the first and last diagrammed statements. No intervention → squirrel monkeys become extinct/do not survive → tracts of forest not preserved.

24. **A**   **Strengthen**

The argument concludes that the number of early Byzantine documents sealed with lead seals must have been many times the number of remaining lead seals. Why? Most documents of the era that were sealed with lead remained that way only until the seal was broken, at which point the lead would have been recast and used again. The only way this conclusion could be true would be if most documents of the period that were sealed with lead were actually opened during that time and not kept sealed until much later.

A. Yes. If this is true, then it makes sense to say that there would have been far more documents with lead seals during the early Byzantine era than the number of lead seals that remain today.

B. No. The fact that the documents have been destroyed is irrelevant, but since this choice doesn't tell you whether the documents were opened and when, it doesn't strengthen the argument.

C. No. The amount of lead available is not relevant, since the argument says lead seals tended to be recast.

D. No. This focuses on the documents whose seals would not have been broken; it doesn't matter whether there were at most or more than 40,000 such documents.

E. No. This focuses on how many seals there might have been at any given point during the early Byzantine Empire, but the conclusion focuses on how many documents would have used such seals, so this choice has no bearing on the argument.

25. **B** `Reasoning`

The farmer concludes that it is counterproductive in the long run for farmers to use insecticides. He bases his conclusion on the premise that since insects' resistance to insecticides increases with insecticide use, farmers have to use increasingly greater amounts of costly insecticides to control pests. The proposition asked about in the question stem functions as part of the support for the farmer's conclusion.

A. No. The statement is not the argument's conclusion.

B. Yes. The statement supports the farmer's conclusion and is itself supported by the part of the argument that talks about insects' resistance to insecticides increasing with insecticide use.

C. No. The statement is not the argument's conclusion.

D. No. There is no intermediary conclusion in the argument.

E. No. The argument's conclusion does not offer an explanation for the phenomenon described in the statement.

56

Section 3: Arguments 2

1. **C** `Flaw`

William concludes that Pliny the Elder could not have been correct in claiming that rainbows always occur opposite the sun. He bases this conclusion on the fact that Pliny made some fairly ridiculous and untrue claims in his writings. William fails to consider that Pliny could still be right about rainbows even if a lot of the other stuff he claimed was incorrect.

A. No. William doesn't distort anything that Anna says.

B. No. If anything, William appears to assume that Pliny was sincere in his claims, not that he was in bad faith.

C. Yes. Pliny could have had a few correct assertions, but William discounts this possibility based on the fact that other things Pliny claimed were false.

D. No. William does not accept Pliny's assertions.

E. No. William states that Pliny's writings are incorrect, not that they are outdated.

2. **E** `Inference`

Pick the answer best supported by the passage.

A. No. No mention is made of a need for increased funding.

B. No. There is no discussion of whether investment in pharmaceuticals would siphon off money from other operations.

C. No. The food service industry carries greater risk and might siphon off funds from other operations, but there is no indication that the company will lose money if it chooses to move into this area.

D. No. There is no mention of increasing profits in the argument.

E. Yes. The last sentence of the argument supports this; the food service industry has a higher inherent risk than the pharmaceuticals industry.

3. B **Principle Strengthen**

Mariah concludes that Adam should not judge the essay contest. Her reasons for this, however, are different from those of Joanna, who thinks Adam would be biased because several of his classmates have entered the contest. Mariah believes that Adam should not judge the contest because he has no experience in critiquing essays.

A. No. Mariah discounts Joanna's suspicion of bias, so this choice is not relevant.

B. Yes. Mariah's conclusion that Adam should not be a judge is based on his lack of expertise.

C. No. Mariah is concerned about expertise, and since she seems to believe that Adam would not have a bias, you don't know whether she would consider objectivity more important than expertise.

D. No. Again, Mariah favors expertise, and since she seems to believe that Adam would not have a bias, you don't know whether she would weigh fairness over expertise.

E. No. Since Mariah dismisses the idea that Adam would be biased, this isn't relevant to her conclusion.

4. A **Flaw**

In a recent study, the main ingredient in NoSmoke was shown not to decrease smokers' cravings for cigarettes. NoSmoke has only two ingredients. The argument concludes that if similar results are found for the other ingredient, NoSmoke does not reduce smokers' cravings. However, the argument doesn't consider the fact that it could be the combination of the two ingredients that reduces smokers' cravings.

A. Yes. The argument assumes that if both ingredients individually are unable to reduce smokers' cravings, then NoSmoke as a whole must also be unable to do so.

B. No. The argument does not confuse correlation and cause.

C. No. The sample consists of smokers, so this isn't the flaw in the argument.

D. No. This is out of scope. The manufacturers specifically claim that NoSmoke reduces smokers' cravings for cigarettes.

E. No. The argument makes no allegations of bias.

5. D Main Point

The gardener concludes that the researchers' advice—allow certain kinds of weeds to grow among garden vegetables so as to repel caterpillars—is premature. Why? Those kinds of weeds could deplete the soil of nutrients and moisture that garden crops depend on and might attract other kinds of damaging pests.

A. No. This is not the issue; the gardener doesn't say that the use of insecticides should be eliminated.

B. No. This is a premise.

C. No. This is part of the researchers' advice, with which the gardener disagrees.

D. Yes. This matches the tone of the gardener's conclusion, which is that the researchers' advice is premature.

E. No. The gardener doesn't dispute the fact that certain weeds could have the effect of reducing the presence of caterpillars; he is more concerned about what other unforeseen effects these weeds might have.

6. D Reasoning

The executive concludes that consumer response to the set of advertisements run in the print version of a travel magazine was probably below par. He bases this conclusion on the fact that consumer response to the same set of ads run on the magazine's website was more limited than is typical for website ads.

A. No. The executive bases his prediction of consumer response to the print ads on the response garnered from the website ads, so this choice, especially the part about the cause of the phenomenon, doesn't match the argument.

B. No. The executive uses information about consumer response to ads run on a website to draw a conclusion about the probable consumer response to ads run in print, an event of a different kind.

C. No. The executive does not make a statistical generalization; he is referring only to a specific set of ads.

D. Yes. He uses the evidence from the website ads to draw a conclusion about the results of the print ads, for which no direct information is available.

E. No. Future events are never referred to in the argument.

7. E Resolve/Explain

A pack of ten coyotes, which are known to prey on wild cats and plover, was removed from a small island because the coyotes were supposedly decimating the plover population. However, once they were removed, the plover population decreased significantly, and within two years no plover could be found on the island. Why did the plover population shrink after the coyotes were removed?

A. No. This suggests that the plover population should have recovered after the coyotes were removed.

B. No. This is irrelevant; it doesn't explain why the plover population plummeted.

C. No. By itself, this choice isn't enough to explain why the plover disappeared; you don't know that a disease that commonly infects plover would result in its decimation.

56

D. No. This is irrelevant and doesn't tell you why the plover population decreased.

E. Yes. If the coyotes were removed, then the number of wild cats would no longer be held in check; a greater number of wild cats preying on plover would result in the elimination of the plover population.

8. **A** Strengthen

The economist states that companies have two means by which they can cut personnel costs during a recession—laying off some employees without reducing the wages of remaining employees or reducing the wages of all employees without laying anyone off. While both damage morale, layoffs damage it less since those who are aggrieved have left. From all this the economist concludes that when companies must reduce personnel costs during recessions, they are likely to lay off employees. To strengthen this argument, you need to show that morale is a significant factor in companies' decision making during a recession.

A. Yes. If employee morale is the primary concern, this would strengthen the economist's conclusion that companies will choose the option that damages morale less—laying off employees.

B. No. Increasing wages is outside the scope of the argument.

C. No. Making a profit is outside the scope of the argument, which is concerned with cutting personnel costs.

D. No. The fact that some employees resign when companies resort to reducing wages to cut personnel costs doesn't tie in to the idea of employee morale, as others may not choose to resign.

E. No. Finding qualified employees after a recession is irrelevant to the economist's argument.

9. **A** Necessary Assumption

The argument concludes that chain bookstores' success has been to the detriment of book consumers. Why? The shortage of independent bookstores has prevented the variety of readily available books from growing as much as it otherwise would have. The premises discuss the reduced growth in the variety of available books while the conclusion refers to a detriment to book consumers; this is the gap you need to bridge.

A. Yes. This bridges the gap between detriment and selection; if you negate this statement, the argument is no longer valid.

B. No. If you negate this choice, the argument's conclusion could still be valid, so it's not necessary to the argument.

C. No. The size of the bookstore is out of scope; you want to know about the variety of books available.

D. No. The size of the bookstore is out of scope; you want to know about the variety of books available.

E. No. Whether some consumers prize price over selection is irrelevant to the conclusion.

10. **C** Flaw

The concert promoter notes that some critics claim that his concert series lacks popular appeal. But the income from the sales of t-shirts and other memorabilia at the concerts is equal to or greater than that for similar sales at comparable series, so the concert promoter concludes that those critics are mistaken.

However, the concert promoter compares sales at his concert series to those of comparable series, which doesn't actually address the critics' concerns since the comparable series could also lack popular appeal.

A. No. The concert promoter does not "attack" the critics based on emotional considerations.

B. No. The concert promoter never claims that income from sales of memorabilia is the only indicator of popular appeal; such sales are presented as one means of assessing that appeal.

C. Yes. The concert promoter never provides any evidence to suggest that the comparable series have popular appeal.

D. No. The series is compared to other comparable series, so this doesn't match the argument.

E. No. The concert promoter doesn't make this distinction, but this isn't a flaw in the argument's logic.

11. **E** Inference

Pick the answer best supported by the passage.

A. No. There is no information provided about the percentage of people who wear sunscreen.

B. No. There could be reasons other than sun exposure for people having skin that is prematurely wrinkled.

C. No. No mention is made of when the cause of premature skin wrinkling became known.

D. No. The argument states that sunscreen has protected against UV-B radiation, which causes sunburn, since before ten years ago, so there shouldn't be any lessened risk of sunburn for people now as compared to ten years ago.

E. Yes. Until about ten years ago, sunscreen provided no protection against premature skin wrinkling, so the likelihood of having premature wrinkles would have been the same for both those who wore sunscreen and those who didn't.

12. **A** Principle Strengthen

The advice columnist concludes that sports activity should not be used as a method for coping with stress. She bases this advice on several scientific studies that showed that people who have recently been experiencing major stress in their lives are more prone to suffer serious injuries when playing competitive sports than are other participants. Since risking serious injury is unwise, she advises people to avoid sports activity when under stress. You may have noticed that the argument jumped from competitive sports to sports activity in general; you want to bolster that shift with one of the answer choices.

A. Yes. This supports the advice columnist's conclusion that people recently under stress should avoid engaging in all sports activity on the basis of the idea that they should avoid engaging in competitive sports.

B. No. The advice columnist never states that a method for coping with stress must be subjected to scientific study first.

C. No. This is irrelevant; the argument is specifically concerned with people who have recently been experiencing major stress.

D.   No. The advice columnist's argument seems to be going in the opposite direction.

E.   No. This is irrelevant; the argument is not focused on people with a history of sports injuries.

13.   **A**   **Strengthen**

The argument concludes that tent caterpillars are among the insect species that engage in communal foraging. Why? Tent caterpillars chemically mark the routes between their nests and potential food sources with pheromones, and routes from food sources back to the nest are marked more heavily than are exploratory routes that have not yielded a food source. To strengthen the argument, you need an answer that suggests that these markers are used by other tent caterpillars to find food, thereby supporting the idea that these caterpillars engage in communal foraging.

A.   Yes. If hungry tent caterpillars follow these routes to find food, then the actions of some tent caterpillars serve to aid the whole community, supporting the idea that these insects engage in communal foraging.

B.   No. This would weaken the argument, if anything, as it casts doubt on the idea that the heavily marked routes help convey the location of food to other members of the insect group.

C.   No. This is irrelevant; the argument is concerned with how the paths to these food sources are indicated to others.

D.   No. This doesn't strengthen the argument because it doesn't suggest that tent caterpillars engage in communal foraging, only that their markers aren't useful to other foraging animals.

E.   No. Again, this doesn't tell you anything about tent caterpillars in particular with regard to communal foraging, so it's irrelevant.

14.   **B**   **Parallel Flaw**

Movies starring top actors do well at the box office because of their fame and following. The argument thus concludes that movies with unknown actors are unlikely to do well at the box office. However, you can't conclude that having the opposite quality (unknown vs. well-known) will likely generate an opposite result (bad box office vs. good box office).

A.   No. This argument doesn't involve an opposite quality in the same way that the original argument does.

B.   Yes. This argument mistakenly assumes that because the presence of flower bee balm results in abundant crops, the lack of it will likely produce the opposite effect, meaning crops will not be abundant.

C.   No. There is no opposite aspect to this argument, so it doesn't match the original one.

D.   No. There is nothing in this argument that functions in the way well known/unknown function in the original argument, so this doesn't match.

E.   No. The conclusion of this choice is too extreme—"will achieve success"—when compared to the original argument's conclusion—"are therefore unlikely to do well."

15. **D** — Inference

Pick the answer best supported by the passage.

A. No. Studying details in and of itself isn't what leads to a lessening of our ability to learn from history. A lack of attention to overarching historical trends and movements lessens our ability to learn from history.

B. No. The argument never links these two ideas together in such a mutually exclusive fashion.

C. No. The argument never claims that people should not attend to details at all; this is too extreme.

D. Yes. The shift away from an emphasis on overarching historical trends and movements and toward an emphasis on details of historical events and motivations has lessened our ability to learn from history.

E. No. The argument never states that both approaches should be given equal emphasis; this choice goes too far.

16. **A** — Sufficient Assumption

Diagram the pieces of the argument. No trust → no meaningful emotional connection to another; meaningful emotional connection to another → trust. No meaningful emotional connection to another → isolation; no isolation → meaningful connection to another. Therefore, happiness → trust; no trust → no happiness. If you try to combine this information, you get one longer statement—no isolation → meaningful connection to another → trust—and then the conclusion—happiness → trust. In order for the conclusion to be valid, you need to connect happiness to the longer chain so that you have happiness → no isolation.

A. Yes. If you diagram this, you get isolated → not happy and happy → not isolated.

B. No. This restates information you already know. Meaningful emotional connection to another → trust, but trust is a necessary, not sufficient, condition for happiness. Therefore, this doesn't fully connect the conclusion to the premises.

C. No. This doesn't connect the premises to the idea of happiness in the conclusion.

D. No. The "at least some" part of this choice is weaker than what is needed for the argument.

E. No. This doesn't connect the premises to the idea of happiness in the conclusion.

17. **C** — Flaw

Sirat Bani Hilal is the only Arabic epic poem that is still publicly performed, and unlike most other epics, it is usually sung, not recited. The argument therefore concludes that it is the musical character of the performance that is the main reason for its longevity. However, the fact that *Sirat Bani Hilal* is still performed and is usually sung doesn't mean that the two aspects are necessarily connected; one does not necessarily cause the other.

A. No. The evidence cited here seems possible to corroborate; you can confirm that it is still performed and that it is usually sung.

B. No. There doesn't appear to be any bias with respect to the evidence.

56

C. Yes. The musical character and its longevity are correlated; you don't know for sure that the musical character of *Sirat Bani Hilal* is the actual reason for its longevity.

D. No. This isn't something the argument does; both pieces of information are factual.

E. No. The argument doesn't confuse necessary and sufficient conditions; there's nothing to diagram here.

18. **E** `Necessary Assumption`

The fund-raiser concludes that most charities could probably increase the amount of money they raise through donations by giving donors the right to vote. Why? Charities rarely give their donors the right to vote on their policies, and the inability to directly influence how charities spend contributions makes potential donors feel less of an emotional connection to a given charity. The fund-raiser's conclusion talks about raising more money through donations while the premises discuss donors having an emotional connection to the charity. You need an answer choice that bridges the two.

A. No. The fund-raiser never claims that this is the most effective way to accomplish this goal.

B. No. The fund-raiser offers this as a solution, so charities that have already increased donations are out of scope. Whether other charities have done this before isn't relevant to the argument here.

C. No. This doesn't connect the idea of raising more money through donations; if you negate this, you'll see that the argument's conclusion isn't really affected.

D. No. This leaves out the emotional connection part, so it isn't necessary to the argument.

E. Yes. Try negating this statement and you'll see that the argument becomes invalid. This ties together both the idea of raising more money through donations and fostering an emotional connection between a donor and a given charity.

19. **E** `Main Point`

Leslie concludes that Erich's quest for the treasure is irrational. The basis for this is an analogy that she draws between Erich's quest for this treasure, which is harming his health, and the hypothetical situation she poses to him, in which she asks whether he would risk losing a hand to possess the world, to which his response is no.

A. No. This is a part of the analogy that serves as a premise.

B. No. This idea is part of the support for her conclusion.

C. No. Leslie never says the treasure is of no value, only of lesser value when compared to Erich's health and body.

D. No. Her conclusion isn't that he can be convinced; it's that he's acting in an irrational manner whether he believes it or not.

E. Yes. This is a paraphrase of Leslie's first statement.

20. **D** `Weaken`

The newspaper article concludes that people who take vitamin C supplements tend to be healthier than average. The support for this conclusion is a study that showed that those who regularly consume high doses of vitamin C supplements have a significantly lower-than-average risk of heart disease. To weaken this argument, you need to find a reason other than the vitamin C supplements that could account for the reduced risk of heart disease or show that taking vitamin C supplements doesn't cause one to be healthier than average.

A. No. This is irrelevant; the argument focuses specifically on vitamin C supplements.

B. No. This doesn't weaken the causal relationship that the argument established.

C. No. This doesn't suggest that vitamin C wasn't responsible for the reduction in risk of heart disease.

D. Yes. This introduces a negative effect of high doses of vitamin C supplements, which casts doubt on the argument's conclusion that these supplements are the reason some people are healthier than average.

E. No. This would strengthen the newspaper article's conclusion.

21. **D** Flaw

George asks why a large number of people now take ballroom dancing lessons when throughout the 1980s and early 1990s, few people did. Boris responds that beginning in 1995, people started to learn the merengue and several related ballroom dances, and the popularity of those sparked interest in learning other ballroom dances. However, Boris doesn't actually address George's question of why people suddenly had a renewed interest in ballroom dancing; Boris merely provides some history from the moment that interest was renewed without stating what triggered that renewal.

A. No. Boris doesn't show this, but that's not the flaw in his reasoning.

B. No. George asks why ballroom dancing became popular again in the mid-1990s, so it is not necessary for Boris to explain why it was unpopular before 1995.

C. No. Boris doesn't do this, but that's not the flaw in his reasoning.

D. Yes. Boris doesn't address George's question as to what led to the renewed interest in ballroom dancing.

E. No. The argument isn't concerned with whether all types of ballroom dancing are currently popular; this is irrelevant.

22. **B** Inference

You're looking for an answer that directly contradicts information in the paragraph. Four of the answer choices will be consistent with the information provided, even if they contain ideas that are not directly expressed in the argument.

A. No. This is consistent with the last sentence of the paragraph.

B. Yes. This cannot be true. The second sentences suggests that it is possible for two groups living in different environments to face the same daily challenges, so those challenges cannot be unique to those environments.

C. No. This could be true, as it doesn't contradict anything stated in the passage.

D. No. This could be true, as it is in line with the information found in the second and third sentences.

E. No. This could be true, as you know from the argument that they lived in different environments.

23. **E** | Principle Match

Diagram the two pieces of information you have. Intermittent wind and temperature below 84 degrees → pleasant. Not pleasant → not intermittent wind or temperatures at 84 degrees or higher. High humidity with either no wind or temperatures above 84 degrees → oppressive. Not oppressive → not high humidity and some wind and temperatures at 84 degrees or lower.

A. No. To be pleasant, there must be intermittent wind; however, this says there was no wind.

B. No. To be oppressive, there must be high humidity; however, this says humidity levels were low.

C. No. To be pleasant, the temperature must be below 84 degrees; however, this says the temperature stayed at 84 degrees.

D. No. To be oppressive, the temperature must rise above 84 degrees; however, this says the temperature did not do so.

E. Yes. High humidity and no wind → oppressive.

24. **D** | Parallel

The argument concludes that the local radio station will not win the regional ratings race this year because the station has never finished better than fifth over the past ten years and the station's manager has made no changes in response to the poor ratings. You need to find an argument the conclusion of which is similarly based on trends in the past.

A. No. The conclusion of the argument is stronger than the conclusion here, which uses the word "probably."

B. No. The conclusion of the argument is stronger than the conclusion here, which uses the word "probably."

C. No. This conclusion is based on a conditional requirement (lion → mammal), not on prior trends, so this doesn't match the original argument.

D. Yes. The conclusion about stock prices this coming Monday is based on stock prices from prior Mondays.

E. No. This conclusion is based on a conditional requirement (lifeguard → trained swimmer), not on prior trends, so this doesn't match the original argument.

25. **E** | Necessary Assumption

The chef concludes that she can skip the step of sprinkling the mussels with cornmeal, which is usually done to clean out the sand they may contain. The chef's reason for skipping this step is that the mussels available at seafood markets are farm raised and therefore don't contain sand. In order for the chef's argument to be valid, though, you need to know that the mussels the chef is using are indeed farm raised or from a seafood market; otherwise, skipping the step can't be justified.

A. No. This is irrelevant; as long as any sand is cleaned out before the mussels get to the chef, it doesn't matter.

B. No. This is out of scope; the only contaminant the argument is concerned with is sand.

C. No. The issue of taste is irrelevant to the chef's argument.

D. No. This isn't essential to the argument; if you negate this statement, the chef's conclusion is still valid.

E. Yes. If this isn't true, then the chef isn't justified in skipping the step of sprinkling the mussels with cornmeal based on the information you have in the argument.

Section 4: Reading Comprehension

Questions 1–7

The author argues that the literary works of Amos Tutuola are best understood not as novels but as retellings of folktales. The first paragraph notes the differing critical opinions of Tutuola's work and proposes that these are inaccurate because critics have too readily assumed that the works were written as novels. The second paragraph clarifies the author's view that Tutuola is not a novelist but rather a teller of folktales; it situates Tutuola's works within the African oral tradition. The third paragraph describes the folktale tradition and explains the expectations that an audience brings to the stories, including the expectation that a familiar story will be modified and transformed in its retelling. The final paragraph depicts how Tutuola's works incorporate elements of the folktale tradition.

1. **B**   Big Picture

The main point of the passage is that the literary works of Amos Tutuola are best understood not as novels but as retellings of folktales.

A. No. This is too specific; the focus of the passage is not on Tutuola's style of blending aspects of Yoruba, Nigerian English, and standard English.

B. Yes. This is a paraphrase of the main point expressed above.

C. No. The author never claims that Tutuola is important because he integrates oral traditions into his work. Furthermore, the author feels his works are best understood not as novels but as folktales.

D. No. This point is discussed only in the first paragraph; it is not the focus of the entire passage.

E. No. The author is concerned with evaluating the works of Tutuola, whereas this choice emphasizes the value of the folktale as a genre.

2. **D**   RC Reasoning

Because the last paragraph describes Tutuola's approach to writing folktales, you should look there first to get a sense of what the credited response should do. Since the question stem brings in a modern-day Irish author, you'll most likely need to connect the author to Irish folktales in some way.

A. No. The author's main point is that Tutuola isn't a novelist, so you wouldn't want the Irish author to apply conventions of the modern novel to Irish folktales.

B. No. While Tutuola does utilize elements of African oral tradition, he isn't working within a purely oral art form, so this choice goes too far.

C. No. Tutuola does blend elements of different languages in his works, but nowhere in the passage does the author say that he combines characters from different folktales. Thus, you wouldn't want to see the Irish author combine characters from English and Irish folktales.

D. Yes. This is in keeping with the first sentence of the final paragraph, in which the author says that Tutuola sometimes transfers familiar folktales to modern settings.

E. No. This doesn't match the passage. Tutuola didn't tell original stories using an omniscient narrator; instead he used an omniscient voice to summarize at the end of his recreated folktales.

3. **A** **Extract Infer**

The author seems to feel quite strongly that Tutuola's works should be analyzed not as novels but as folktales that belong to the African oral tradition.

A. Yes. This is a paraphrase of the information above.

B. No. The author never discusses the possibility of a renewed interest in the study of oral traditions.

C. No. The author seems to think that at least some critics' evaluations of Tutuola's work are misguided in that they operate on the assumption that he was writing novels.

D. No. Preserving the original integrity of Tutuola's works when they are translated is never mentioned in the passage.

E. No. The author does not suggest that these works reflect a burgeoning trend in literature.

4. **D** **Extract Infer**

The first paragraph suggests that the basis for some criticism of Tutuola's work is his use of well-known story lines that are retold and embellished.

A. No. The problem isn't that they exhibit too few similarities; it's that some critics are viewing his work through an inappropriate analytical lens.

B. No. None of the criticisms the author refers to deal with Tutuola's mixture of languages.

C. No. Again, the critics who are dismissive of his work have not grasped, according to the author, the notion that Tutuola's works are not actually novels.

D. Yes. Specifically, see the third sentence of the first paragraph.

E. No. The author does not say that Tutuola has ever characterized his own works as novels.

5. **E** **Extract Fact**

A. No. This is mentioned in the first sentence of the final paragraph.

B. No. This is mentioned in the first sentence of the final paragraph.

56

C. No. This is mentioned in the first sentence of the passage.

D. No. This is mentioned in the final sentence of the passage.

E. Yes. The author says that Tutuola makes use of Yoruba as a language, but there is no indication in the passage that Tutuola works with Yoruba folktales.

6. **A** ⬛ Structure

The author refers to the "corpus of traditional lore" as part of his discussion of the differences between the genres of the novel and the folktale. Specifically, he mentions traditional lore as being the source from which tellers of folktales derive their stories, which is contrary to the standards of originality to which novels are held.

A. Yes. The author seeks to distinguish the expectations applied to the literary genre of the novel from those that apply to the literary genre of the folktale.

B. No. The author never weighs in on the inherent value of either genre; he states only that the genre of the folktale is more useful when evaluating Tutuola's works.

C. No. This is out of scope. The passage makes no mention of blending these two distinct genres.

D. No. The author focuses here on elucidating how two literary genres differ, not on how one has direct counterparts in the other.

E. No. The author never says that the distinguishing characteristics of these two literary genres are poorly understood.

7. **C** ⬛ Big Picture

The primary purpose of the passage is to demonstrate why Tutuola's works should be evaluated in the context of the African oral tradition instead of as novels.

A. No. The focus of the passage is on the elements of his work that show his connection to African oral tradition; the passage does not try to illustrate the range of his work.

B. No. This is too broad. The author is primarily concerned with folktale as it related to Tutuola's work.

C. Yes. This is a longer paraphrase of the idea stated above.

D. No. This is done to some extent in the second paragraph, but again, the chief concern of the author is how these two genres relate, or in the case of the novel don't relate, to Tutuola's works.

E. No. The nature of the disagreement among critics is really found only in the first paragraph, so this is too specific.

Questions 8–15

The author argues that while the phenomenon of kin recognition can be explained in part by the idea that natural selection favors species that help their own relatives, thereby increasing total genetic representation of the individual, this idea does not account for kin recognition in every case. The first paragraph states that scientists have begun to examine the question of why kin recognition occurs to begin with; it goes on to explain the inclusive fitness theory, which posits that natural selection favors organisms that help their relatives because doing so increases the total genetic representation of these organisms. The second paragraph provides an example of how the inclusive fitness theory has been applied to instances of cannibalism in certain species and describes how the theory accounts in part for kin recognition in cannibalistic spadefoot toad tadpoles. The third paragraph offers another reason, via a different example, for why organisms recognize kin that goes beyond the premise underlying the inclusive fitness theory, suggesting that kin recognition cannot be solely explained as a means to aid relatives' survival.

8. A   **Big Picture**

The main point of the passage is that while the phenomenon of kin recognition can be explained in part by the idea that natural selection favors species that help their own relatives, thereby increasing total genetic representation of the individual, this idea does not account for kin recognition in every case.

A. Yes. This matches the main point as stated above.

B. No. This is too broad; the author is focused primarily on assessing explanations for why these mechanisms exist to begin with.

C. No. If anything, the tiger salamander example actually lends support to the hypothesis espoused by traditional evolutionary theorists since it demonstrates an organism's prioritizing its own survival. In any case, this isn't what the passage is chiefly concerned with.

D. No. This is too specific.

E. No. This is too strong; in the final sentence of the passage the author implies that kin recognition is not fully explained by the inclusive fitness theory, as the tiger salamander example demonstrates.

9. C   **Extract Fact**

A. No. They develop the ability to recognize kin, not fellow carnivores.

B. No. This is too extreme. The passage doesn't say that they don't feed upon other carnivorous tadpoles.

C. Yes. See the middle of the second paragraph ("causing the tadpole to become larger").

D. No. The spadefoot toad tadpole example is used to support the inclusive fitness theory, not question it.

E. No. The passage doesn't go into sufficient detail about why carnivorousness occurs from an evolutionary standpoint.

10. **D** `Extract Infer`

Find an answer choice that is supported by information in the passage.

A. No. This contradicts the second sentence of the passage; the mechanisms underlying kin recognition appear to be better understood than the reasons for why it evolved.

B. No. This is too extreme. The author does not address whether traditional evolutionary theory needs to be modified in order to explain kin recognition.

C. No. This is irrelevant. The author never brings up issues of social or mental complexity in relation to the organisms whose kin recognition abilities are being analyzed.

D. Yes. The author says that inclusive fitness theory offers a partial explanation for kin recognition in spadefoot toad tadpoles (end of second paragraph, "partial answer"), but goes on to suggest that kin recognition in tiger salamanders does not seem to adhere to the same theoretical evolutionary explanation (final sentence of the passage).

E. No. This is too extreme. The author acknowledges that inclusive fitness theory does not explain all instances of kin recognition.

11. **A** `Structure`

The function of the last sentence of the second paragraph is to note an exception that somewhat tempers the explanatory power of the inclusive fitness theory as it applies to cannibal spadefoot toad tadpoles.

A. Yes. Because the behavior described supports a more traditional evolutionary view of natural selection than it does the inclusive fitness theory, it suggests that one theory alone may not be enough to account for such inconsistencies in behavior.

B. No. There is no comparison made between cannibal spadefoot toad tadpoles and cannibals in other species.

C. No. This behavior presents a problem for the account of kin recognition presented in the second paragraph because it seems to support the more traditional evolutionary view.

D. No. This is too extreme. The author never says the behavior is patently unexplainable.

E. No. This is the opposite intention. The use of the word "interestingly" at the beginning of the sentence implies that this behavior is less common than the behavior described previously.

12. **A** `Extract Infer`

Cannibal spadefoot toad tadpoles nip at other tadpoles first, releasing kin unharmed but eating those that are not their relatives.

A. Yes. See the middle of the second paragraph ("nip at other tadpoles").

B. No. The passage does not go into sufficient detail about whether tadpoles that do not become cannibalistic use or possess this mechanism for kin recognition.

C. No. There is no reason to believe from the passage that this mechanism does not always work; even the fact that cannibal tadpoles will eat their kin when very hungry does not imply that they are unable to recognize kin.

D. No. This contradicts the passage, which specifically states that this mechanism is used by cannibal tadpoles to avoid eating kin.

E. No. This is irrelevant; the passage does not discuss how other species recognize kin.

13. **B** Extract
Fact

This is discussed in the beginning of the passage.

A. No. The author never sets forth a condition for easily explaining these mechanisms.

B. Yes. See the second sentence of the first paragraph.

C. No. The inclusive fitness theory was developed in the 1960s, but the passage doesn't say that this marked the beginning of theoretical investigations into the mechanisms.

D. No. While general understanding of the mechanisms has improved, the passage never claims that this was a necessary precursor to explaining their purpose.

E. No. There simply isn't enough information in the passage about how these mechanisms operate to substantiate this choice.

14. **E** Extract
Infer

Honeybees are discussed at the end of the first paragraph.

A. No. The theory that helped to explain the phenomenon was not developed until the 1960s. The facts surrounding honeybees may well have been known before that time.

B. No. This is too extreme. The passage says only that the inclusive fitness theory has helped to explain the honeybee phenomenon, not that additional assumptions are needed to complete the explanation.

C. No. The passage does not say that most biologists have rejected the traditional view of evolution, and in any event there is no connection made between traditional theory and the honeybee example.

D. No. Again, the passage does not link natural selection to the honeybee phenomenon, and it definitely does not state that natural selection has been called into question.

E. Yes. The passage asserts that inclusive fitness theory has helped to explain previously mysterious phenomena, such as the workings of honeybee society, but since the passage never discounts the traditional view of evolution, the language of "at least supplementing" is appropriate here.

15. **C** RC Reasoning

In the final sentence of the passage, the author states that kin recognition in the case of tiger salamanders can be explained simply as a means of preserving one's own life, not as a way to help relatives survive. To weaken this statement, you need to show that for tiger salamanders, relatives do somehow benefit from kin recognition.

A. No. This is irrelevant, since the author's evaluation is aimed at those tiger salamanders that are cannibalistic.

B. No. What determines whether tiger salamander larvae are carnivorous or omnivorous is not relevant to the author's evaluation of kin recognition.

C. Yes. Since the benefit accrues not only to the individual but also to its offspring, this would undermine the author's assessment of kin recognition in tiger salamanders.

D. No. Again, the assessment made in the final sentence of the passage is concerned with cannibalistic tiger salamanders, not noncannibalistic ones.

E. No. This difference between cannibalistic and noncannibalistic tiger salamanders doesn't impact the author's evaluation of kin recognition.

Questions 16–21

Passage A

The author states that the lack of precise definitions in international law for certain terms is especially problematic for the Roma. The first paragraph discusses several terms in international law that are vaguely defined and notes how some of these terms are applied to different groups. The second paragraph explains how the lack of universally accepted definitions noted in the first group affects one minority group, the Roma, in particular.

Passage B

The author claims that the Roma should be considered a minority in all major European states. The first paragraph presents five criteria that underlie a specific definition of a minority and argues that one of these criteria, the legal one, appears unfair when applied to the Roma. The second paragraph demonstrates how the Roma meet the other four empirical criteria and asserts that the Roma should therefore be considered a minority given that they satisfy these criteria.

16. **E** Big Picture

The author's main point is that the lack of precise definitions in international law for certain terms is especially problematic for the Roma.

A. No. The author does not say that these definitions conflict with each other when applied specifically to the Roma.

B. No. This is mentioned in passage B, not in passage A.

C. No. The author never states that the lack of agreement regarding these definitions stems from their application to the Roma or similar groups.

D. No. This goes beyond the scope of the passage. The author describes the present situation such as it is; he makes no claims about will happen if certain actions are taken.

E. Yes. This is a decent paraphrase of the main point as expressed above.

17. **C** **Extract Infer**

In both passages, the term carries negative implications with it. The first passage mentions "difficulties" for "numerous minority groups" and the second passage characterizes the application of a specific criterion to the Roma as "patently unfair."

A. No. This is neutral, and you need something negative.

B. No. As passage A notes, the lack of clarity in these definitions is responsible for such problematic situations.

C. Yes. As noted above, the word "difficulties" is even used in passage A.

D. No. Passage A never even suggests ways to solve the problems associated with the lack of clear definitions.

E. No. Neither passage suggests that the situation of the Roma is incoherent.

18. **D** **Extract Fact**

A. No. This is mentioned in the final sentence of the passage.

B. No. This is mentioned in the third sentence of the second paragraph.

C. No. This is mentioned in the second sentence of the second paragraph.

D. Yes. Passage B, not passage A, states this.

E. No. This is mentioned in the first sentence of the second paragraph.

19. **E** **Extract Infer**

Find an answer choice that is supported by information in both passages.

A. No. This switches around the passages. The author of passage B disapproves of the latitude granted by international law on this issue; the author of passage A does not address this.

B. No. Neither author states that international law is ineffective when it comes to the Roma, only that there are problems with its application to the Roma.

C. No. The author of passage B never comments on the definition of the term "nation" or on its applicability to the Roma.

D. No. Neither author states a preference for resolving issues on a case-by-case basis rather than through international law.

E. Yes. See the beginning of the second paragraph of passage A and the first paragraph of passage B.

20. **A** **RC Reasoning**

Passage A discusses several terms in international law that lack agreed-upon definitions and shows how this lack negatively impacts the Roma. Passage B posits that the Roma fulfill most of the criteria set forth in one definition of a minority and should therefore be considered as such.

A. Yes. This choice focuses first on a lack of clear-cut criteria, which matches passage A, and then on an argument in favor of a group's classification based on its satisfaction of criteria, which matches passage B.

B. No. Passage A does not focus on effective application of criteria, and passage B is not concerned with a statement of standards.

C. No. The second part of this answer choice, with its emphasis on essential job duties, doesn't match passage B's focus on fulfilling criteria.

D. No. There is no discussion of competency in passage A, so this doesn't match up.

E. No. "Conceptual links" has no parallel in passage A.

21. **B** RC Reasoning

Find an answer choice that is applicable to both passages.

A. No. Passage B does not discuss a vaguely formulated definition; only passage A does.

B. Yes. This choice is supported by the second paragraph of passage A and the first paragraph of passage B.

C. No. Neither passage discusses provisions that apply only to minority groups, so this is irrelevant.

D. No. Passage A never addresses this topic.

E. No. While both passages refer to the nomadic way of life of the Roma, neither author goes so far as to say that the Roma should be considered legitimate citizens of all countries through which they pass.

Questions 22–27

In the passage, the author discusses some attempts at educational reform in the period following the French Revolution and connects these unsuccessful efforts to reforms that followed nearly a century later. The first paragraph notes that even in the aftermath of the French Revolution, the underlying nature of education for French women did not change significantly, although legislators put forth many proposals for reform in the years immediately following the revolution. The second paragraph details two of these proposals and describes the progressive, egalitarian aspects of both proposals as well as their limitations. The third paragraph explains how the ideal of egalitarian education for women found renewed interest in the early 1880s as French legislators looked to these earlier proposals to justify their educational reforms.

22. **C** Extract
Infer

This is discussed in the third paragraph.

A. No. The passage never mentions what items, if any, they proposed to remove from the public school curriculum.

B. No. The legislators were aware of the prior proposals, but it's not certain whether they were unaware of the difficulties faced by earlier legislators who advocated for those proposals.

C. Yes. The legislators sought to create educational equality by founding public secondary schools for women, eliminating education fees, and making school mandatory for all. See the middle of the third paragraph.

D. No. The passage makes no mention of political compromise here.

E. No. If anything, the opposite would be true. As it is, religious authorities are never mentioned in the final paragraph, so this is irrelevant to the French legislators of the early 1880s.

23. E   Structure

See the paragraph breakdown above.

A. No. This choice leaves out the final paragraph, which links the earlier proposals of reform to the ones put forth in the early 1880s.

B. No. The passage does not begin by discussing the movement toward gender equality in France; it focuses specifically on education as it relates to women.

C. No. The final paragraph of the passage does not claim that eventual reform required less of a break with tradition, only that legislators seeking to enact reforms sought to justify their actions by tapping into the tradition and history surrounding the revolutionary period.

D. No. The first paragraph is focused on the education of French women and educational reform, not on the egalitarian aims of the French Revolution, though they are mentioned.

E. Yes. This matches the description above.

24. A   RC Reasoning

Consider the fundamental beliefs underlying the two proposals. From the first proposal, you get the idea that education should be offered to all regardless of gender or economic status (see the second sentence of the second paragraph). From the second proposal, you get the view that men and women should be offered equal education, as both genders possess the same rights (see the second-to-last sentence of the second paragraph). Match these ideals to the proposals in the answer choices.

A. Yes. "Available to all" is in line with the first proposal, and nondiscriminatory practices meshes with the notion that men and women should receive equal education.

B. No. The second proposal's emphasis on improving the quality of housing doesn't match with the second proposal of the passage.

C. No. The first proposal in the passage sought to provide education publicly, so "all who can pay" in this choice doesn't match up.

D. No. The first proposal's emphasis on improving the quality of housing doesn't match with the first proposal of the passage.

E. No. The notion of constructing low-cost housing doesn't match the first proposal's intent to create public schools so that all could be educated.

25. B `Extract Fact`

In the second-to-last sentence of the second paragraph, the author states that this proposal was the only one of its time to call for coeducational schools.

A. No. Teaching is not discussed in relation to the second proposal.

B. Yes. This is a paraphrase of the lines cited above.

C. No. No mention is ever made of lifelong learning.

D. No. This is too extreme. The second proposal championed coeducational schools as a defense against the traditional gender roles that religion reinforced; however, nothing is said about seeking to abolish religious schools altogether.

E. No. This appears to be in line with the second proposal, but this is not what made it distinctive. The call for coeducational schools is what made it distinctive.

26. E `Extract Infer`

The fact that the proposed reforms were introduced shortly after the French Revolution suggests that the proposals echoed some of the goals and sentiments of the time.

A. No. The passage never discusses the excesses of the new government post-revolution.

B. No. The passage doesn't actually say what the proposals had their roots in, so this is out of scope.

C. No. The public's opinion on these proposals is never given.

D. No. There is no mention of education for women serving as a prerequisite for any other reforms, and no discussion of other reforms outside of those relating to education is presented in the passage.

E. Yes. See the last sentence of the first paragraph.

27. C `Extract Infer`

Find an answer choice that is supported by information in the passage.

A. No. While the author does say that neither proposal fully embodied the ideal of egalitarian education, the passage does state in the last sentence of the first paragraph that the proposals were egalitarian to a large extent, which contradicts this choice's claim that they were very modest.

B. No. This is too strong—there is no support in the passage for the phrase "fundamentally unethical."

C. Yes. See the first sentence of the third paragraph.

D. No. The author does make reference to why they did not pass at the time, citing "the immensity of the cultural and political obstacles to egalitarian education for women at the time" in the first sentence of the third paragraph.

E. No. As noted in (D), the reasons the proposals were not adopted had to do not with their lack of comprehensiveness but with the prevailing attitudes and biases of the period in question.

Chapter 7
PrepTest 57:
Answers and
Explanations

ANSWER KEY: PREPTEST 57

Section 1:
Games

1. D
2. B
3. C
4. D
5. C
6. B
7. B
8. E
9. D
10. C
11. B
12. B
13. D
14. A
15. E
16. A
17. B
18. C
19. D
20. E
21. B
22. D
23. E

Section 2:
Arguments 1

1. A
2. A
3. D
4. D
5. E
6. C
7. A
8. E
9. C
10. B
11. C
12. D
13. C
14. E
15. A
16. B
17. E
18. D
19. C
20. D
21. E
22. A
23. B
24. E
25. C
26. B

Section 3:
Arguments 2

1. A
2. C
3. A
4. B
5. A
6. A
7. C
8. C
9. D
10. C
11. A
12. E
13. D
14. D
15. C
16. C
17. D
18. B
19. D
20. E
21. B
22. B
23. C
24. C
25. E

Section 4:
Reading
Comprehension

1. A
2. A
3. D
4. C
5. E
6. E
7. C
8. D
9. B
10. D
11. C
12. B
13. E
14. C
15. C
16. A
17. E
18. E
19. B
20. B
21. C
22. D
23. D
24. E
25. A
26. E
27. D

EXPLANATIONS

Section 1: Games

Questions 1–5

This is a 1D order game. Place six activities—G, H, J, K, L, and M—in order, one at a time.

The game has 1:1 correspondence, and the core of your diagram should be labeled 1 through 6.

Clue 1: $\boxed{\text{H G}}$

Clue 2: K—G

Clue 3: M—L

Clue 4: $\boxed{\text{M J}}$ / $\boxed{\text{J M}}$

Deductions: You can actually combine clues 1 and 2 to get K—$\boxed{\text{H G}}$. From this you can see that H cannot be in 1 or 6, K cannot be in 5 or 6, and G cannot be in 1 or 2. Similarly, you can combine clues 3 and 4 to get (J)M(J)—L, which tells you that neither M nor J can be in 6 and that L cannot be in 1 or 2. You'll notice at this point that the only elements that can go in 6 are G and L, so note that in your diagram.

Because this game doesn't contain any specific questions, it is useful to track where the HG block could go. You have a number of places into which you cannot place H and G. Try out the possibilities to generate some work to help you with the questions. H and G, as noted above, cannot go into 1 and 2, respectively, so try them in 2 and 3. With H in 2 and G in 3, K must be in 1 and L must be in 6. This leaves J and M for 4 and 5 in either order. Next, try H and G in 3 and 4, respectively. This won't allow you to both fit in the other block that contains J and M and satisfy clues 2 and 3. Thus, the HG block cannot go in 3 and 4, so cross that off and mark on your diagram that H cannot be in 3 and G cannot be in 4. Now try H and G in 4 and 5, respectively. This means L is in 6. You don't know exactly where the other block will go, but there is room to accommodate it as long as K is not in 2, which means that either J or M will be in 2. Finally, try the HG block in 5 and 6. There's room to place all the other elements in accordance with the clues, so this possibility also works.

Here's the diagram:

GHJKLM	$\sim$H $\sim$L $\sim$G 1	$\sim$G $\sim$L 2	$\sim$H 3	$\sim$G 4	$\sim$K 5	$\sim$J $\sim$K $\sim$M $\sim$H 6
						G/L
	K	H	G	J/M	M/J	L
		M/J		H	G	L
					H	G

1. **D** Grab-a-Rule

Use the clues to eliminate answer choices. Clue 1 eliminates (E). Clue 2 eliminates (B). Clue 3 eliminates (C). Clue 4 eliminates (A). Therefore, the credited response is (D).

2. **B** General

Use your deductions to eliminate answer choices. You have already seen that you can't place the HG block in 3 and 4, which means that H can't be third. Therefore, (B) is the credited response.

3. **C** General

Use your deductions to eliminate answer choices. The first scenario you have in your diagram eliminates (B). The second scenario eliminates (A) and (E). There are two choices left, so try them out. For (C), in order to put K in 2, look at the last scenario. However, if K is in 2, then there's no room for J and M to be adjacent and have L come after them. Since this choice isn't possible, it's your answer. Choice (C) is therefore the credited response.

4. **D** General

Use your deductions about where the HG block can go to eliminate answer choices.

   A. No. This is possible in the second scenario.

   B. No. This is possible in the third scenario.

   C. No. This is possible in the first scenario.

   D. Yes. In each of the scenarios you looked at, the fifth slot is filled. Since you don't have L in 5 in any of those possibilities, it must not be possible to put L in 5.

   E. No. This is possible in the first scenario.

5. **C** Complex

In order to substitute M with something else, you need an element that doesn't have any additional constraints on it other than what M has. From clue 4, you know that M and J must be consecutive, though the order isn't set. It makes sense, then, to swap out M and replace it with J. You'll need to have a condition for J that copies the original condition for M. This means that J must come before L. The credited response, then, must be (C).

Questions 6–11

Three actors—G, O, and R—will each audition twice over the course of four days, Wednesday through Saturday. The days form the core of your diagram, and on each day at least one actor must audition.

Clue 1: O_1—R_1

Clue 2:

Clue 3: T = S at least once

Deductions: From clue 1 you know that R cannot be on Wednesday and O_1 cannot be on Saturday. You also know that O_1 cannot be on Friday, because if it were, then both R's would have to be on Saturday, which wouldn't be feasible.

Here's the diagram:

6. **B** Grab-a-Rule

Use the clues to eliminate answer choices. Clue 1 eliminates (C). Clue 2 eliminates (E). Clue 3 eliminates (A). Using your diagram, you can eliminate (D) because no one is scheduled for Friday, which violates one of the conditions in the setup. Therefore, the credited response is (B).

7. **B** Specific

Put O on Thursday and Saturday. This means that R will have to go on Friday and Saturday to satisfy clue 1, since O_1 is on Thursday. From your deductions, you know that R cannot go on Wednesday; from the question stem, O cannot be on Wednesday either. That leaves G to go on Wednesday, as you must have at least one actor per day. You still need to address clue 2. Since R is on both Friday and Saturday, the other G must also be on either Friday or Saturday. This means that G will have to be on either Wednesday and Friday or Wednesday and Saturday. Choice (B) is thus the credited response.

8. **E** General

Use your deductions and prior work to eliminate answer choices. Your work from question 7 eliminates (B) and (C). This leaves you with three choices, two of which involve R. From your earlier deductions, you know that R cannot be on Wednesday, so that means it will be impossible for R's last audition to be on Thursday. Therefore, (E) must be the credited response; there is no need to try out (A) or (D).

9. **D** General

Use your deductions and prior work to eliminate answer choices. Your work from question 7 eliminates (E). Your work from questions 6 and 11 eliminates (B). Try the remaining choices. For (A), if O is on Wednesday and Thursday, then R can be on any of Thursday, Friday, or Saturday and G could go on whichever days are necessary to satisfy all the clues. Since this is possible, eliminate (A). For (C), if O is on Wednesday and Saturday, you could place R on Thursday and Friday and G on Thursday and Saturday. This arrangement would take care of all the clues, so this is possible; eliminate (C). Therefore, the credited response is (D). If you put O on Thursday and Friday, then G must be on Wednesday and R must be on Friday and Saturday, which makes it impossible to satisfy clue 3.

10. **C**   General

Use your deductions and prior work to eliminate answer choices.

A.   No. This violates the deduction you made from clue 1 that R cannot be on Wednesday.

B.   No. This would make it impossible to satisfy clue 2.

C.   Yes. Your work from question 7 shows that this is possible.

D.   No. Because of clue 1, there wouldn't be any day available for R_2.

E.   No. This violates the deduction you made from clue 1 that R cannot be on Wednesday.

11. **B**   Specific

Place G on Wednesday and Saturday. From your deductions, you know that R cannot be on Wednesday. In order to satisfy clue 2, then, you have to put R on Saturday. There's nothing else that you know for certain, though, so go to the answer choices to see what you can eliminate.

A.   No. This would violate clue 3 because no one would audition on both Thursday and Saturday.

B.   Yes. This is possible. If O is on both Wednesday and Friday, then R could go on Thursday to ensure that all conditions are satisfied.

C.   No. This would leave you with only R_1 to place on either Thursday or Friday, which means one of those days would be empty, which violates one of the conditions in the setup.

D.   No. R cannot be on Wednesday.

E.   No. R must be on Saturday.

Questions 12–17

Choose five out of seven toy dinosaurs—I, L, P, S, T, U, and V—to include in a display and pick one of four colors—g, m, r, y—for each. Your diagram should have five slots in the In column and two in the Out column. You'll need two tiers, one for the type of dinosaur and one for color.

Clue 1: There are exactly two m's. Place them in your diagram.

Clue 2:
$$\boxed{\begin{array}{c} S \\ r \end{array}}$$
Place this block in your diagram.

Clue 3: I → $\boxed{\begin{array}{c} l \\ g \end{array}}$; ~ $\boxed{\begin{array}{c} l \\ g \end{array}}$ → ~ I

Clue 4: P → $\boxed{\begin{array}{c} P \\ y \end{array}}$; ~ $\boxed{\begin{array}{c} P \\ y \end{array}}$ → ~ P

Clue 5: V → ~U; U → ~V

Clue 6: L and U → at least one not mauve

Deductions: From clue 5 you know that one of the two Out slots will always contain either V or U, so mark that in your diagram. Watch for the interplay between clues 5 and 6, though there's nothing certain you can deduce at the outset.

Here's the diagram:

		In					Out	
D: ILPSTUV	D:	S	_	_	_	_	U/V	_
c: gmry	c:	r	m	m	_	_	_	_

12. B Grab-a-Rule

Use the clues to eliminate answer choices. Clue 2 eliminates (D). Clue 5 eliminates (A) and (E). Clue 6 eliminates (C), since clues 2, 3, and 4 mean that L and U would have to be paired with the two m's. Therefore, (B) is the credited response.

13. D Specific

Place T in the Out column. Because the only other Out spot must be occupied by either U or V, you know that all the other elements must be In. This means I must be In, and from clue 3 it must be green; similarly, P must be In, so from clue 4 it must be yellow. This means the only slots left are where the m's are. Since clue 6 tells you that L and U cannot both be In and mauve, U must be Out and V must be In. Place L and V in the In column with the m's.

	In					Out	
D:	S	L	V	I	P	U	T
c:	r	m	m	g	y	_	_

A. No. This is included.

B. No. This is included.

C. No. This is included.

D. Yes. U is Out.

E. No. This is included.

14. **A**   **General**

Use your prior work to evaluate answer choices. From your work on question 17, you can see that (A) is possible, so (A) must be the credited response. There is no need to test out the remaining answer choices, though if you did, you'd find in each case that you wouldn't have enough elements available to be paired with the m's.

15. **E**   **Specific**

Place T with y in the In column. Since there is only one more spot in the In column that isn't paired with m, you can't have both I and P because of clues 3 and 4; therefore, one of them is In and the other is Out. Place P/I in the In column with y/g below it and I/P in the Out column. The only remaining In spaces now are the m's, so from clue 6 you know that L and V must be In and paired with the m's while U must be Out.

	In					Out	
D:	S	L	V	T	P/I	U	I/P
c:	r	m	m	y	y/g	_	_

A. No. This doesn't have to be true.

B. No. This doesn't have to be true.

C. No. This doesn't have to be true.

D. No. This isn't possible.

E. Yes. This must be true.

16. **A**   **Specific**

If both I and U are In, then I must be green and V must be Out. You don't know whether U is mauve, though, so you'll need to assess the possibilities. Since S and I are definitely In, you'll need to consider U with two of L, T, and P. You could have U, L, and T together or U, T, and P together, but U, L, and P won't work because of clue 4 (P must be green) and clue 6 (both L and U can't be mauve). There are thus two possible scenarios; you'll need to try each one. In the first scenario with U, L, and T, P is Out, T will have to be paired with one of the m's, and either L or U will be with the other m. That means the final empty space will also be either L or U, though you don't know which color will go there. In the second scenario with U, T, and P, L is Out, P must be with y, and U and T must be paired with the m's. The question asks for what must be included in the display, so you'll need to refer to both scenarios when evaluating the answer choices.

57

```
              In              Out
     D: S  L/U  T   I   U/L │  V   P
     c: r   m   m   g   _   │  _   _

     D: S   U   T   I   P   │  V   L
     c: r   m   m   g   y   │  _   _
```

A. Yes. This is true in both scenarios.

B. No. This doesn't have to be true in the first scenario.

C. No. This isn't true in the second scenario.

D. No. This isn't true in the first scenario.

E. No. This isn't true in the second scenario.

17. **B**   Specific

Place g's in the two remaining In color slots. From clue 4, P must be Out; therefore, I, L, and T must all be In, and I has to be with one of the g's. You don't know which of U and V is In, and it's not certain exactly which dinosaurs will be paired with the m's and remaining g. Note that you have L, T, and U/V to place in the In column and use that information to help you eliminate answer choices.

```
              In              Out
     D: S  _   _   I   _  │  V/U  P      In: T L U/V
     c: r  m   m   g   g  │  _   _
```

A. No. You know all the In colors and y is not included.

B. Yes. This is possible. In this case, U would be Out and L and V would be paired with the m's.

C. No. At least one of these must be included.

D. No. At least one of these must be included.

E. No. One of these must be included.

Questions 18–23

You must assign grants from four types of areas—M, T, W, and Y—to each of four quarters. Label the core of your diagram 1 through 4. Place a space in each column to indicate that at least one grant must be awarded in each quarter.

Clue 1: You must use all elements.

Clue 2: maximum number of grants = 6

```
```

Clue 3:

Clue 4: There are exactly two M's.

Clue 5: Place W in 2 in your diagram.

Deductions: Combining clue 5 with clue 3, you know that W can't be in either 1 or 3. From clue 2, you know that the maximum number of grants is six; from clue 4, you know that the minimum number of grants must be five. Therefore, you'll have either five or six total spaces in your diagram, depending on the question.

Here's the diagram:

	~W		~W	
MMTWY	1	2	3	4
	—	W	—	—

18. **C** **Grab-a-Rule**

Use the clues to eliminate answer choices. Clue 2 eliminates (E). Clue 3 eliminates (D). Clue 4 eliminates (A). Clue 5 eliminates (B). Therefore, the credited response is (C).

19. **D** **General**

Use your deductions and prior work to eliminate answer choices.

A. No. Your work from question 21 suggests that this is possible.

B. No. Your work from question 20 suggests that this is possible.

C. No. This is possible. Your list of elements in this case would be M, M, W, T, Y, and Y, and there is room to fit them all without violating any of the clues.

D. Yes. This combined with clue 4 would yield a total greater than six, which would violate clue 2. Therefore, this choice cannot be true.

E. No. Your work from question 20 suggests that this is possible.

20. **E** **Specific**

If Y must be with W, then there are two possible scenarios: either they are together in 2 or else they are together in 4, since from your deductions you know that W cannot be in 1 or 3. Put both scenarios into your diagram. You don't know anything else about the other elements, so go to the answer choices to see what you can eliminate.

~W   ~W

1	2	3	4
$\overline{\sim Y}$	W / Y	$\overline{\sim Y}$	–
–	W	$\overline{\sim Y}$	W / Y

A. No. This is possible.

B. No. This is possible.

C. No. This is possible.

D. No. This is possible.

E. Yes. Y is in either 2 or 4, so from clue 3 you know that there's no way Y can go in 3.

21. **B** **Specific**

This question tells you that you will have only five spaces in your diagram, and from the clues you already know what they are: M, M, W, T, Y. This means you will need to consider where you can place the M's so as not to violate clue 3. They can go in 1 and 3, 2 and 4, or 1 and 4. List each possibility in your diagram to help you eliminate answer choices.

~W   ~W

1	2	3	4
M	W	M	–
T/Y	W	Y/T	M
–	M	–	W
M	W	–	M

A. No. This contradicts what you deduced about the number of spaces you have for this question.

B. Yes. This is possible in the second scenario.

C. No. There is only one W and it must be in 2.

D. No. It is only possible for Y and T to be together in either 4 (first scenario) or 3 (third scenario).

E. No. This would result in either two quarters with two spaces each (first and third scenarios) or else one quarter with 3 spaces (second scenario), both of which violate the condition given in the question stem.

22. **D** General

Use your deductions and prior work to eliminate answer choices.

A. No. Your work from question 20 suggests that this is possible.

B. No. Your work from question 21 suggests that this is possible.

C. No. Your work from question 20 suggests that this is possible.

D. Yes. This would leave no room to place the M's without violating clue 3, so this cannot be true.

E. No. Your work from question 21 suggests that this is possible.

23. **E** Complex

This question asks you to find an answer choice that will allow you to figure out exactly which elements are in each column.

A. No. This doesn't tell you where any of the elements go.

B. No. This doesn't tell you where any of the elements go.

C. No. This tells you that M, T, and Y are in the first quarter, but it doesn't tell you which elements are in 3 and 4.

D. No. This doesn't tell you which elements, aside from W, are in the second quarter.

E.
```
    ~W        ~W
   ┌────┬────┬────┬────┐
   │ 1  │ 2  │ 3  │ 4  │
   ├────┼────┼────┼────┤
   │ M  │ W  │ M  │ W  │
   │    │    │ T  │    │
   │    │    │ Y  │    │
   └────┴────┴────┴────┘
```

Yes. Because W can't be in 3, you know that M, T, and Y must all be in 3. This means the other M has to go in 1. Clue 3 tells you that you must place W in 4 in order to fill that quarter. Therefore this choice allows you to determine the placement of all the elements.

Section 2: Arguments 1

1. **A** Principle Match

The argument concludes that although patients may demand them, doctors should never prescribe antibiotics to treat colds. The reasons behind this conclusion are that colds are caused by viruses, on which antibiotics have no effect, and that antibiotics can have dangerous side effects. You need an answer choice that supports this line of reasoning.

A. Yes. This matches up well with both of the stated premises above.

B. No. There is no mention in the argument of a potential positive effect of antibiotic treatment for colds, so this doesn't match.

C. No. The conclusion argues against prescribing antibiotics because they won't help patients with colds, whereas this choice is concerned with drugs that might have a positive effect.

D. No. There is no mention of uncertainty in the argument.

E. No. No mention is made in the argument of the patient's claims about the effectiveness of antibiotics.

2. **A** **Main Point**

You need to determine what the main point of the argument is. The argument states that there are two kinds of cognitive strategies, "associative" and "dissociative," and that associative strategies, which involve attending closely to physical sensations, require so much concentration that they leave one mentally exhausted for more than a day. Long-distance runners need to enter a race mentally refreshed. It follows, then, that long-distance runners shouldn't make use of associative strategies the day prior to a given race.

A. Yes. This matches what was stated above.

B. No. The evidence presented by the argument doesn't suggest that regular training would eliminate the exhaustion caused by using associative strategies.

C. No. This is irrelevant. Maximizing the benefits of training is not addressed in the argument.

D. No. This is irrelevant. There is no support for the claim that long-distance runners are about evenly divided with respect to which type of strategy they employ during races.

E. No. The argument supports only the idea that dissociative strategies are better than associative ones for the day before a race, not in general.

3. **D** **Resolve/ Explain**

MetroBank made loans to ten small companies in amounts of anywhere from $1,000 to $100,000, and all of these loans had graduated payment plans so that the monthly loan payment increased slightly each month over the five-year term of the loan. However, the average payment that MetroBank received for these ten loans had decreased by the end of the loan period. Why did the average payment received by MetroBank decline when the monthly loan payment amounts were slightly increasing over the five-year term?

A. No. This is irrelevant. The argument is specifically focused on only the ten loans noted above.

B. No. Loans from other banks are not relevant to the argument.

C. No. You are concerned only with MetroBank and its loans, not other banks and their loans, so this doesn't help.

D. Yes. This would explain why, even though the monthly payment amounts were increasing, the average payment received by MetroBank declined: The loans with the biggest monthly payment amounts were paid off sooner, leaving only the smaller monthly amounts and thereby lowering the average payment amount.

E. No. Because the argument is focused only on these ten specific loans, the nature of other loans made by MetroBank is irrelevant to the argument.

4. **D** `Flaw`

The professor concludes that universities these days do not foster fair-minded and tolerant intellectual debate because two students insulted a recent guest speaker and several others applauded those students' attempts to humiliate the speaker. However, the professor is making a very broad generalization about universities based on the behavior of a few students at a single university, so look for an answer choice that describes this flaw.

A. No. The conclusion is the professor's opinion, but the pieces of evidence offered are actual events, so this doesn't match.

B. No. The professor is not advocating tolerance, so there is no inconsistency.

C. No. The professor's argument does not rest on an emotional appeal.

D. Yes. The professor draws his conclusion about universities in general based on the actions of only a few students.

E. No. The flaw isn't that he focuses on the students' behavior; it's that he takes that behavior as being representative of all or most students.

5. **E** `Strengthen`

The argument concludes that health experts might have more success in encouraging people to eat wholesome foods if they emphasized how flavorful those foods are rather than how nutritious they are. The evidence offered to support this conclusion is the fact that studies have shown that most people select which foods to eat primarily on the basis of flavor, with nutrition mostly a secondary concern at best. You want to find an answer that links up emphasizing a given food's flavor with successfully encouraging people to eat that food.

A. No. If anything, this might weaken the argument by implying that health experts wouldn't have greater success if they employed the strategy suggested because most people already think wholesome foods are more flavorful, so calling attention to this fact might not have the desired effect.

B. No. The argument isn't concerned with people choosing between two opposing options.

C. No. This might weaken the argument by suggesting that you could accomplish the same goal by emphasizing nutrition over flavor, but it certainly doesn't strengthen the argument's conclusion.

D. No. This is irrelevant. How people rate foods doesn't strengthen the connection between the suggestion offered to health experts and the studies.

E. Yes. If this is true, it suggests that health experts would be more successful in their quest to get people to eat more wholesome foods if they emphasized flavor as opposed to nutrition.

6. **C** `Flaw`

The argument concludes that business schools can promote more ethical behavior among future businesspeople by promoting among their students the desire to be accepted socially and discouraging the propensity for taking risks. The reasons given in support of this conclusion are that studies have found that people with a high propensity for risk taking tend to have fewer ethical principles to which they adhere in their business interactions than do others, while those individuals with a strong desire to be accepted socially tend to have more such principles than do others. Furthermore, it is generally the case that the more ethical principles to which an individual adheres, the more ethical is that individual's behavior. The flaw here is that you don't know whether anything else is a factor in making individuals more or less prone to ethical behavior. Just because certain elements (such as risk taking or a desire for social acceptance) seem linked to others (the number of ethical principles one consciously adheres to) doesn't mean you can infer a cause-effect relationship.

A. No. This doesn't describe the flaw in this particular argument; there is no jump from "usually" to "always" here.

B. No. The argument never compares this goal to any other in terms of importance.

C. Yes. This is in line with the discussion above.

D. No. There is no mention in the argument of what is "morally wrong," so this is irrelevant.

E. No. This choice describes circular reasoning, which is not the flaw in this particular argument.

7. **A** **Sufficient Assumption**

The essayist concludes that Lessing's claim about literature must be rejected if one considers the imagists' poems legitimate. Why? Lessing contended that an art form's medium dictates the kind of representation the art form must employ in order to be legitimate; for literature, which consists of words read in succession, this entails representing events or actions occurring in sequence. Yet the imagists' poems consist solely of amalgams of disparate images. In order for the conclusion to be valid, you need to know that amalgams of disparate images cannot be considered events or actions occurring in sequence.

A. Yes. This matches what was stated above.

B. No. This is irrelevant; subject matter is never discussed.

C. No. Whether Lessing was aware of the nature of the imagists' poetry is irrelevant to the conclusion.

D. No. This is too broad; the conclusion is about literature, not all art.

E. No. This is too broad; the conclusion is about literature, not all art.

8. **E** **Parallel Flaw**

The psychiatrist concluded that there is no such thing as a multiple personality disorder because in all her years of clinical practice, she had never encountered one instance of this type. The flaw is that this type of disorder could still exist even if the psychiatrist has never personally witnessed a case of it. Note the use of extreme language ("no such thing," "never") in both the conclusion and the premise; you want to be sure to find an answer choice that similarly makes use of strong language.

A. No. This isn't the same flaw as the original argument because it doesn't match in terms of language. The conclusion here is "seldom fatal," which allows for the possibility that Anton might be wrong in his thinking. The original argument does not make this concession, which is why it is flawed to begin with.

B. No. This isn't flawed; the conclusion that there are "probably no groundhogs in the area" is reasonable enough.

C. No. While this choice is flawed, it doesn't match the flaw in the original argument. Sauda does not assume that because she has never witnessed a particular phenomenon, it doesn't exist.

D. No. This isn't flawed; Thomas's conclusion is reasonable because the language, "probably continue," allows room for contradiction.

E. Yes. This is the same flaw as in the original argument: Because Jerod has never seen a deer in his area, he assumes there are no deer in the area. However, it's entirely possible that there could still be deer in his area without his having seen them.

9. **C**   Weaken

The argument concludes that world hunger would not be significantly reduced even if many more people in the world excluded meat from their diet. Underlying this claim is an assumption that the causes of world hunger cannot be solved by greater numbers of people choosing not to eat meat. You want to find an answer choice that suggests that people's decision not to include meat in their diet could somehow impact and help to reduce world hunger.

A. No. This might strengthen the argument by showing that hunger is not generally linked to people's consumption choices.

B. No. This is irrelevant. If disease affects both herds and crops, then there isn't a clear advantage to either, according to this choice.

C. Yes. This shows that not including meat in one's diet has an effect equivalent to feeding more than ten people, suggesting that if more people excluded meat from their diet, a significant reduction in world hunger could be achieved, thereby weakening the argument.

D. No. This is irrelevant. This choice is concerned with people going hungry in times of emergency because they live in a remote area; this is not necessarily the same issue as world hunger, since the original argument isn't limited to emergency situations.

E. No. This would strengthen the argument, if anything, by suggesting that factors other than people's decision to eat meat impact world hunger. It certainly doesn't weaken the argument, though.

10. **B**   Principle Match

The dairy farmer states that on their farm, much concern is shown for cows' environmental conditions in that they have recently made improvements to increase the cows' comfort. These changes are intended to increase blood flow to the udder, thereby increasing milk output and thus profits. You need to find an answer choice that illustrates how the interests of both the farmer (profits) and the cows (comfort) coincide.

A. No. This is too extreme. The argument doesn't support the idea that cows having comfortable living conditions depends on farmers having some knowledge about the physiology of milk production.

B. Yes. This choice is in line with the idea that the interests of the farmer—increased profits—can result in more comfortable conditions for the cows.

C. No. This is irrelevant. The argument doesn't compare cows to other farm animals.

D. No. This is irrelevant. Quality is never mentioned in the argument.

E. No. This is too strong. While the farmer implies that having concern for dairy cows' environment is a way to increase profits, there's no support for the idea that it is the key to maximizing profits.

11. **C** **Point at Issue**

Pat concludes that E-mail promotes a degree of intimacy with strangers that would otherwise take years of direct personal contact to attain because E-mail fosters anonymity, which removes barriers to self-revelation. Amar states that frankness and intimacy are not the same thing because intimacy requires a real social bond, which in turn requires direct personal contact; his implied conclusion is that E-mail therefore doesn't really promote intimacy in the way Pat suggests.

A. No. Amar never mentions barriers to self-revelation, so you don't know whether he would agree or disagree with this statement.

B. No. This is irrelevant. Neither person discusses whether E-mail can increase intimacy among friends.

C. Yes. Pat would seem to agree with this choice, while Amar would disagree.

D. No. Pat never discusses social bonds, so you don't know whether he would agree with this choice.

E. No. Amar doesn't mention either barriers to self-revelation or the use of E-mail, so you don't have enough information to evaluate whether he would agree with this statement.

12. **D** **Sufficient Assumption**

The criminologist concludes that criminal organizations will try to become increasingly involved in the areas of biotechnology and information technology. Why? The ongoing revolutions in these areas promise to generate enormous profits, and the main purpose of most criminal organizations is to generate profits. In order for the conclusion to be properly inferred, you need to know that criminal organizations tend to get involved in those areas where there is the potential for enormous profits.

A. No. You have already been told that the main purpose of most criminal organizations is to generate profits, so this choice doesn't add anything to the argument.

B. No. This is close, but it doesn't go far enough. It's not enough to know that some criminal organizations are or may become aware of these potential profits; you need to know that these groups will try to become involved because of the potential for profits.

C. No. What criminal organizations have done up to now is not relevant to the argument, which is concerned about what they will do in the future.

D. Yes. This connects the conclusion to the premises as noted above.

E. No. The legality of the activities is irrelevant, as you're talking about criminal organizations to begin with.

57

13. C Reasoning

The argument concludes that, contrary to what administrators and teachers may think, the educational use of computers will not enable schools to teach far more courses with far fewer teachers than traditional methods allow. This is because computerized instruction requires more time of instructors, so reducing the number of teachers would likewise require reducing the number of courses offered. The statement asked about in the question stem, therefore, is a belief the argument aims to reject.

A. No. The statement presents the belief of administrators with regard to the educational use of computers as a matter of fact, so there is no "possible explanation" in the argument.

B. No. The argument is not attempting to solve anything.

C. Yes. This is in line with the discussion above.

D. No. The argument's conclusion rejects this statement.

E. No. The argument's conclusion rejects this statement.

14. E Weaken

The argument concludes that foraging leads to the increased brain size of older bees. Why? Older bees, which usually forage outside the hive for food, tend to have larger brains than do younger bees, which usually remain in the hive to tend to newly hatched bees instead of foraging. Foraging requires greater cognitive ability than does tending to newly hatched bees. The argument is assuming a causal relationship (foraging increases brain size) from a correlation (foraging and larger brain size happen to occur together in older bees). In order to weaken the argument, you need to show that this causality isn't true or that some other factor accounts for the size of the brain.

A. No. This doesn't weaken the argument; it could still be true that the act of foraging, regardless of the overall length of time a bee has foraged, contributes to increased brain size.

B. No. This is irrelevant and doesn't provide an alternative explanation as to why the bees' brains increased in size in the first place.

C. No. The distance traveled outside the hive while foraging is not relevant to whether the activity of foraging itself leads to the increased brain size of older bees.

D. No. This doesn't weaken the argument, as this still doesn't provide another explanation for the larger brain size of older bees.

E. Yes. This implies that larger brain size could be due to the age of the bees and not the activity that they engage in, thereby weakening the causal assumption of the argument.

15. A Flaw

Carla concludes that professors at public universities should receive paid leaves of absence to allow them to engage in research because research will both advance human knowledge and improve professors' teaching by keeping them up to speed on the latest developments in their field. David responds by first acknowledging Carla's mention of the possible benefits of research, but then asks why limited resources should be devoted to supporting professors taking time off from teaching. His question indicates that he has missed part of Carla's initial reasoning, in which she explained that engaging in research improves professors' teaching.

57

A. Yes. This accurately states the flaw as noted above.

B. No. This is extreme. David never claims that the sole function of a professor is teaching.

C. No. David never directly addresses the source of funding for professors; he merely says that there are "limited resources."

D. No. David never claims that paid leave has only one function.

E. No. This is irrelevant. Neither person discusses the issue of vacations.

16. **B** **Reasoning**

The software reviewer concludes that, despite the fact that dictation software has been promoted as a labor-saving device, it in fact fails to live up to its billing. The evidence offered by the software reviewer for this opinion is that the laborious part of writing is in the thinking and editing, not in the typing. Furthermore, the time spent proofreading the software's error-filled output generally squanders any time saved in typing. The statement asked about in the question stem, therefore, is the argument's conclusion.

A. No. There are no other conclusions in this argument.

B. Yes. This is in line with the discussion above.

C. No. There are no other conclusions in this argument.

D. No. The statement is the conclusion, not a premise.

E. No. The statement is the conclusion, not a premise, and there are no other conclusions in this argument.

17. E **Weaken**

The poetry journal patron concludes that if the magazine under discussion were to publish an anthology of poems first printed in its pages, it could depend less on donations. The patron cites as evidence *The Brick Wall Review*, which has an agreement with those who publish in it that any poem printed in one of its regular issues can be reprinted without monetary compensation in its annual anthology. *The Brick Wall Review* makes enough money from sales of its anthologies to cover most operating expenses. The patron also notes that most poems published in the magazine at issue are very similar to those published in *The Brick Wall Review*. To weaken the argument, you need to find a choice that attacks the legitimacy of the comparison between the magazine under discussion and *The Brick Wall Review*.

A. No. Whether either publication depends on donations to cover operating expenses is irrelevant.

B. No. While this might appear to suggest that the two publications are not in fact as similar as the patron claims, this still doesn't weaken the argument. It could be that the poems that were rejected by the magazine under discussion were atypical of what the poets themselves normally write and have published in *The Brick Wall Review*.

C. No. The nature of the compensation received by the poets who publish in the magazine in question is not relevant.

D. No. How *The Brick Wall Review* covers operating expenses not covered by income from anthology sales is irrelevant.

E.   Yes. This implies that there are other factors involved in the success of *The Brick Wall Review*'s anthology that could affect whether or how well the magazine in question could replicate *The Brick Wall Review*'s strategy.

18.   **D**   Main Point

You need to supply the conclusion to this argument. You are told that no one with a serious medical problem would rely on the average person to prescribe treatment. Therefore, since a good public servant has the interest of the public at heart, a good public servant would also not rely on the average person to solve a given problem, in keeping with the reasoning underlying the premise above.

A.   No. The outcomes of public opinion surveys are not relevant to the argument.

B.   No. This is irrelevant. The argument isn't concerned with what the average public servant knows.

C.   No. The argument isn't focused on whether public servants need a greater level of knowledge than they already have.

D.   Yes. This is in keeping with the discussion above.

E.   No. What constitutes being a good public servant is not relevant to the argument.

19.   **C**   Parallel

Diagram the statements in the argument. Winning → willingness to cooperate → motivation. Therefore, not motivated → won't win. The conclusion is the contrapositive; you need to find an answer choice that matches this structure.

A.   No. The conclusion here involves a paradox, which does match the structure of the original argument.

B.   No. Improvement → learning → making some mistakes. However, the conclusion states that you will not make mistakes without having some improvement, which isn't the contrapositive of this sequence.

C.   Yes. Retain status → raise more money → increased campaigning. Therefore, no increase in campaigning → won't retain status. This matches the original argument.

D.   No. Repair own bicycle → enthusiastic → mechanical aptitude. Therefore, unable to repair own bicycle → lack mechanical aptitude. This reasoning is flawed, so this choice doesn't match the original argument.

E.   No. Getting ticket → waiting in line → patience. Therefore, don't wait in line → lack patience. This reasoning is flawed, so this choice doesn't match the original argument.

20.   **D**   Weaken

The argument concludes that setting the highway speed limit at 90 kph (55 mph) has reduced the highway accident rate by at least 15 percent. The evidence for this claim is that the highway accident rate peaked a decade ago, at which time the speed limit on highways was set to the current limit. For every year since that time, the highway accident rate has been at least 15 percent lower than that of its peak. The argument assumes that it's the fixed speed limit that is responsible for the lower accident rate; to weaken the argument, then, you need to show that there is another possible explanation, outside of the set speed limit, for why the highway accident rate has decreased.

A. No. This does not provide an alternative explanation for why the highway accident rate has decreased.

B. No. This is not relevant to the argument, which is focused specifically on the highway accident rate. This choice addresses all automobile accidents, which goes beyond the scope of this argument.

C. No. This doesn't go far enough to weaken the argument. Even if most people typically drive faster than the speed limit, that doesn't mean the setting of the limit wasn't responsible for the decreased accident rate.

D. Yes. This weakens the argument by suggesting that changes in automobile design and not the fixed speed limits are responsible for the reduced highway accident rate.

E. No. While this may appear to weaken the argument, it's actually irrelevant. The measures discussed may reduce harm to passengers, but since the conclusion is concerned with the rate of accidents, not injuries or fatalities, this choice has no impact on the argument.

21. **E** **Reasoning**

The editorial disagrees with those who believe that the government's inability to solve long-standing social problems even though it has launched rockets into outer space stems from a case of misplaced priorities. The editorial concludes that such criticism is itself misplaced because rocket technology is much simpler than the human psyche and understanding the human psyche is necessary to solving the great social problems. The statement asked about in the question stem, therefore, is a premise used to support the argument's conclusion.

A. No. It is a premise that supports the argument's conclusion, not an objection to the conclusion.

B. No. The argument never says this fact has misled some social critics.

C. No. The statement is a premise, not the conclusion.

D. No. The statement is used to support the argument's conclusion, which in turn undermines the social critics' reasoning.

E. Yes. The statement is a premise used to support the argument's conclusion undermining the viewpoint of the social critics.

22. **A** **Strengthen**

The archaeologist concludes that, contrary to previous belief, the Clovis point was not invented in North America. The evidence offered for this conclusion is the discovery in Siberia of a cache of Clovis points and the fact that groups of paleohumans, who made Clovis points, left Siberia and crossed the Bering land bridge into North America after the last Ice Age. The archaeologist assumes that the Clovis points found in Siberia must have been made by paleohumans prior to their crossing; you want to find an answer choice that supports this interpretation of facts.

A. Yes. This strengthens the archaeologist's argument that Clovis points were not invented in North America by confirming that those found in Siberia were made before any of those found in North America.

B. No. This doesn't tell you anything further about when the Clovis points found on either side of the Bering land bridge were fabricated, so it's irrelevant.

C. No. The relative effectiveness of Clovis points as hunting weapons is not relevant to the archaeologist's argument.

D. No. Artifacts other than Clovis points are irrelevant, since the conclusion is specifically concerned with Clovis points.

E. No. This weakens the argument by suggesting that the Clovis points found in Siberia might have been made in North America and then brought back to Siberia when some paleohuman groups migrated back.

23. **B** **Inference**

Pick the answer that is contradicted by the passage.

A. No. This could be true. You know that each taxi driver sets a daily income target, which affects the number of hours a driver needs to work, so it's conceivable that the income target is based on that driver's financial needs.

B. Yes. This directly contrasts with the last sentence of the argument. Taxi drivers work fewer hours when they are busiest, which means they work fewer hours when their effective hourly wage is high. This goes against the idea presented by the answer choice.

C. No. This could be true. Nothing in the argument contradicts this idea.

D. No. This could be true. Nothing in the argument contradicts this idea.

E. No. This could be true. Nothing in the argument contradicts this idea.

24. **E** **Necessary Assumption**

The argument concludes that it is wrong to think that the meaning of a poem is whatever the author intends to communicate to the reader by means of the poem. Why? Sometimes one can read a poem and believe that it expresses contradictory ideas, even though it is a great poem. And no one who is writing a great poem intends the poem to communicate contradictory ideas. The missing link here is the assumption that what a reader believes a poem expresses is actually what the author intended the poem to mean. You need an answer choice that connects the poem's meaning to what the reader perceives the poem to be expressing.

A. No. This is irrelevant. Whether readers agree about what the author intends to communicate in a poem is not relevant.

B. No. The notion that the writer of a great poem intends it to express one primary idea is irrelevant.

C. No. Whether readers agree on the meaning of a poem is irrelevant.

D. No. This doesn't bring in the key element of the poem's meaning.

E. Yes. This is in line with the discussion above.

25. **C** Inference

Pick the answer supported by the passage.

A. No. This doesn't have to be true. It's possible that a nonresident who is a former resident of Weston contributed in excess of $100 to Brimley's campaign.

B. No. The only contributions that you know have to be registered are those made by nonresidents who are not former residents of Weston, and according to the last sentence of the argument, Brimley's campaign did not accept any contributions made from those in this particular category.

C. Yes. This must be true. According to the law given in the argument, contributions in excess of $100 made by nonresidents who are not former residents need to be registered with the city council. Since you are told that it is true that Brimley's campaign complied with the law, it must therefore also be true that none of the contributions needed to be registered, given that the campaign accepted contributions only from residents and former residents.

D. No. According to the argument, Brimley did not need to register any contributions with the city council because the campaign did not accept any from those to whom the law would apply. Therefore, you can't know anything about the relative amounts that the campaign might have chosen to register of its own accord.

E. No. According to the argument, Brimley's campaign did not need to register any of the contributions it accepted. However, that does not mean the campaign did not register any with the city council; there could be other reasons for the campaign to register some contributions of its own volition.

26. **B** Flaw

The historian concludes that Flavius was widely unpopular among his subjects based on the fact that a large number of satirical plays were written about him during his administration. However, you are also told that Flavius actively sought to discourage the arts and removed state financial support for them. This calls into question the historian's assertion that Flavius was widely unpopular based merely on the fact that playwrights chose to satirize him; the sample population may not be representative of the larger population of his subjects.

A. No. While the argument does not consider this, this isn't a problem with the historian's logic.

B. Yes. This is in line with the discussion above.

C. No. The historian does provide evidence to support the notion that Flavius was not a fan of the arts: You are told that Flavius removed state financial support for the arts.

D. No. The historian never mentions whether Flavius's attempt to discourage the arts was actually successful, and the fact that a large number of satirical plays were written during his administration would seem to suggest that it was not.

E. No. The argument does not consider this; however, it's neither relevant to the argument nor the problem with the historian's logic.

57

Section 3: Arguments 2

1. **A** Resolve/ Explain

Students who performed the best in a university's history classes had either part-time or full-time jobs, limited social lives, and history classes that met early in the morning. Those students who performed the worst lacked jobs, had very active social lives, and had their history classes early in the morning. You need an answer choice that accounts for the discrepancy in performance given that both the best and worst performers had their classes early in the morning.

A. Yes. This explains the disparity in terms of the differences among the students with respect to their jobs and social lives.

B. No. This doesn't explain why those with full-time jobs performed better than those without jobs.

C. No. This makes the discrepancy worse, since both the best and worst performers had classes that met early in the morning.

D. No. This is irrelevant; you know only that the students in the study were taking history classes, not whether any of them were interested in majoring in history.

E. No. This makes the discrepancy worse, as it suggests that those with full-time jobs shouldn't have performed better than those with active social lives.

2. **C** Flaw

The politician concludes that those who were not persuaded by Kuyler's argument that it would be improper to enter into a contract with the government were right not to have been persuaded. As evidence, the politician states that Kuyler's company has had numerous lucrative contracts with the government. The flaw is that Kuyler could still be correct in terms of the advice given even if Kuyler's company has not followed that advice; there could be differing circumstances, for example. The politician dismisses Kuyler's argument without evaluating its merit as it relates to the situation at hand.

A. No. The politician merely says that everyone was right not to have been persuaded by Kuyler's argument, but this is not the reason the argument is rejected.

B. No. There is no testimony presented here.

C. Yes. This is consistent with the discussion above.

D. No. The politician never discusses Kuyler's reasoning; Kuyler's argument is dismissed because Kuyler's company does not conform to the argument made.

E. No. There is no appeal to popular opinion in the politician's argument.

3. **A** Main Point

The argument concludes that specialization in international trade carries risks. This is because small countries often rely on one or two products for the bulk of their exports. If those products are raw materials, the risk is that the finite supply may be used up; if those products are foodstuffs, the risk is that a natural disaster could wipe out a season's production overnight.

A. Yes. This is stated in the first sentence of the argument.

B. No. This is a premise.

C. No. This is a premise.

D. No. This is a premise.

E. No. This introduces the argument, but it is not its conclusion.

4. **B** Resolve/ Explain

Two groups of adults were asked to write short stories on a particular topic. One group was told that the best stories would be awarded cash prizes, while the other was told no such thing. The stories submitted by those who had been told there would be prizes were ranked on average much lower than those from the other group. You need to find a choice that explains the difference in quality between the two groups.

A. No. This would make the paradox worse—why would one group have had significantly higher average ranking if this were true?

B. Yes. This would account for the lower average ranking of the stories written by those who thought they were competing for prizes.

C. No. This doesn't explain the difference between the two groups; it seems to suggest that the rankings should have been comparable between the two.

D. No. This doesn't account for the differences in average ranking, as both groups were given the same topic to write on and any bias would have been applied equally across the board.

E. No. Again, this doesn't explain why one group's stories were ranked significantly lower than the other's stories, since both groups were treated equally in terms of information about judging standards.

5. **A** Reasoning

Hernandez concludes that staff cars should be replaced every four years instead of every three years because three-year-old cars are still in good condition and this change would result in big savings. Green disagrees, noting that some salespeople with big territories wear out their cars in three years. Hernandez responds to Green's objection by clarifying his reasoning, stating that he was referring to three-year-old cars subjected to normal use.

A. Yes. Hernandez qualifies his statement concerning the condition of three-year-old cars by saying that it applies to those three-year-old cars subjected to normal use.

B. No. Hernandez never criticizes anyone.

C. No. Hernandez does not challenge the accuracy of Green's statement.

D. No. Hernandez does not discuss the size of sales territories.

E. No. Hernandez does not claim that Green used a phrase in an ambiguous manner.

6. A   Weaken

The economist concludes that raising the minimum wage significantly will cause an increase in unemployment. This is because raising the minimum wage significantly makes it more expensive for businesses to pay workers for minimum-wage jobs. Hence businesses could not afford to continue to employ as many workers for such jobs. The economist assumes that there's no way businesses could absorb this extra cost other than by laying off workers. You need to find an answer choice that contradicts this assumption.

A. Yes. This weakens the argument because it suggests that raising the minimum wage significantly does not have to result in an increase in unemployment; businesses simply pass the cost on to consumers.

B. No. This doesn't weaken the argument, as you have no information about the current relationship between minimum wage and a skilled worker's wage.

C. No. This is irrelevant; the argument isn't concerned with what is acceptable in terms of increasing unemployment.

D. No. This comes close, but ultimately doesn't weaken the argument. Even if most workers are earning more than the current minimum wage and would therefore be unaffected by the increase, it's still possible that the economist's prediction could come true if businesses can't otherwise absorb the extra cost of paying their minimum-wage workers more money.

E. No. This is irrelevant; this doesn't address the issue of whether businesses could absorb an increase in the minimum wage without laying off workers.

7. C   Resolve/Explain

Scientists removed all viruses from a seawater sample and then measured the growth rate of the plankton population in the water, expecting that the rate would increase. However, they found that the population actually got smaller. What would explain this result?

A. No. This doesn't explain why, upon removal of the viruses, the plankton population decreased; this seems to suggest that it should have increased as the scientists expected.

B. No. As in choice (A), this seems to suggest that removing the viruses would have allowed the plankton population to expand.

C. Yes. This tells you that removing the viruses actually interfered with the ability of plankton to get enough nutrients, thereby explaining the decrease in the size of the population.

D. No. This isn't strong enough. It doesn't actually state that these bacteria did in fact flourish and that they would have affected the plankton population.

E. No. This doesn't explain why removal of the viruses resulted in a shrinking of the plankton population if it's common for plankton to be infected by viruses.

8. C   Flaw

The city council member concludes that in order to prevent anarchy in their city, they must deny the Senior Guild's request for a temporary exception to the ordinance prohibiting automobiles in municipal parks. This is because, although the Senior Guild's case has merit, the city council member believes that granting one exception will lead to granting many more exceptions to this particular ordinance, some of which will be undeserved, and will ultimately result in granting exceptions to all manner of other city ordinances as well. The flaw in the argument here is that the city council member assumes that granting this one exception will necessarily result in a downward spiral of all manner of other exceptions to city ordinances; however, there's nothing provided to support this belief.

A. No. The city council member doesn't distort an argument and then attack it.

B. No. The decision to deny the request is not based on the source of the request.

C. Yes. The city council member assumes that granting one exception will cause many other exceptions to be granted in the future.

D. No. The premises stated here do not contradict each other.

E. No. The argument does not provide a distinction between these two types of exceptions, but this is not the flaw in the city council member's logic.

9. D Strengthen

The physician concludes that his country suffers significantly fewer ulcers per capita than do two other countries of roughly the same population size. This conclusion is based on the physician's findings that even though all three countries face the same dietary, bacterial, and stress-related causes of ulcers, prescriptions for ulcer medicines in all socioeconomic strata are much rarer in his country than in the other two. The physician assumes that there are no other factors that could account for the difference in prescription rates other than fewer instances of ulcers. To strengthen this argument, you need a choice that either further bolsters the physician's logic or that eliminates a potential alternative explanation for the lower prescription rate.

A. No. Whether the ulcer rates for the two countries to which the physician's country is compared are similar to each other is irrelevant.

B. No. This would weaken the physician's argument by providing an alternative explanation for the lower rate of prescriptions in the physician's country.

C. No. Other countries are not relevant to the physician's conclusion, which is concerned only with the three countries referred to above.

D. Yes. This strengthens the physician's argument by showing that it is equally likely that people in all countries would seek out a prescription if they were suffering from ulcers, supporting the conclusion that the lower rate of prescriptions in the physician's country is due to fewer occurrences of ulcers in that country.

E. No. This is irrelevant. How good the system for reporting the number of prescriptions is doesn't tell you anything about whether the physician's conclusion is justified.

10. C Flaw

The columnist concludes that bicyclists are at least partially responsible for more than half of the traffic accidents involving bicycles. The columnist presents two pieces of evidence for this conclusion. First, the failure of bicyclists to obey traffic regulations is a causal factor in more than a quarter of traffic accidents involving bicycles. Second, inadequate bicycle safety equipment is also a factor in more than a quarter of such accidents. However, the two causes the columnist cites aren't mutually exclusive; it is

57

possible to have both a failure to obey traffic regulations and inadequate bicycle safety equipment as contributors to a given accident. Therefore, it's incorrect to assume that these two factors account for more than half of all traffic accidents involving bicycles.

A. No. The columnist never states what factors are involved in those traffic accidents involving bicyclists in which responsibility is not assigned to the bicyclist.

B. No. The columnist states that each of the two factors is a causal factor in traffic accidents involving bicycles, so there's no confusion here between correlation and causation.

C. Yes. This is in line with the discussion above.

D. No. While the columnist doesn't cite the source of the figures, this isn't the problem with the argument's logic.

E. No. The varying severity of injuries to bicyclists is not relevant to the columnist's argument.

11. A   **Weaken**

Doctors claim they can produce a vaccine that will produce permanent immunity to the viral disease hepatitis E. Why? Many vaccines create immunity by introducing a certain portion of the disease-causing virus's outer coating into the body to stimulate the production of antibodies that will subsequently recognize and kill the whole virus. A suitable portion of the virus that causes hepatitis E has now been isolated. The doctors assume that this particular method of vaccination will work to create permanent immunity; to weaken their claim, you need to look for a reason that this method may not work as planned.

A. Yes. This weakens the argument because it suggests that most people who contract hepatitis E have usually already been exposed to the virus once before and yet still later contracted the disease, implying that exposure to the virus once does not necessarily confer permanent immunity. This suggests that the vaccine the doctors claim to be able to create may not produce permanent immunity.

B. No. The argument is concerned only with whether exposure to one strain can lead to immunity to that particular strain, not to all strains, so this is irrelevant.

C. No. This is irrelevant. While the choice says researchers first isolated the virus that causes hepatitis B before they created the vaccine, that doesn't mean the vaccine was created using the method described in the argument.

D. No. This might appear at first to weaken the doctors' claim, but it's not strong enough. This choice suggests that in some areas the vaccine the doctors hope to produce might not be effective because some people will have already had exposure to the virus that causes hepatitis E, but it's still possible that a vaccine could be produced that would confer permanent immunity on those who hadn't previously been exposed to the virus.

E. No. If anything, this would strengthen the doctors' claim by suggesting that the method described in the argument to create a vaccine (exposure to the virus that causes a given disease) could produce permanent immunity.

12. E — Necessary Assumption

The editorial concludes that what is called "international law" is not effective law. This is because to qualify as effective law, a command must be backed up by an effective enforcement mechanism. Police serve as this enforcement mechanism in any given society, thereby rendering that society's laws effective. But there is no international police force at present. The assumption made by the editorial is that there is no other way to enforce international law other than by having an international police force.

A. No. This is too broad; you need something that specifically relates to international law.

B. No. This is backwards. The argument assumes that an international police force is necessary to making international law effective: international law effective → international police force. This choice, however, claims that an international police force is sufficient to render international law effective: international police force → international law effective.

C. No. The editorial is not focused on differences between international law and the laws of individual societies.

D. No. The editorial claims that police are necessary to enforce the laws of a society, but never assumes that enforcement is the primary purpose of a police force.

E. Yes. Try negating it if you're not sure. If something other than an international police force could effectively enforce international law, then the editorial's conclusion is no longer valid, which means this statement is necessary to the argument.

13. D — Inference

Pick the answer best supported by the passage.

A. No. This is too extreme. You don't know that landscape painting and portraiture are the artistic genres that most naturally lend themselves to the mere reflection of a preexisting external reality.

B. No. The art historian presents this as one way in which an artist controls the composition and subject of a painting, but never claims this is the only way through which an artist can achieve that control.

C. No. Nonrepresentational painting is never mentioned.

D. Yes. The last sentence of the argument states that the artist has more control over the composition and subject of a still-life painting than over those of a landscape painting or portrait. Since you are also told that in a still-life painting, the artist invariably chooses, modifies, and arranges the objects to be painted, you can conclude that in at least landscape painting and portraiture the artist does not always choose, modify, and arrange the objects to be painted.

E. No. There is not enough information about what artists do when painting a portrait to support this claim.

14. D — Principle Match

Food that does not ordinarily contain fat can be labeled "nonfat" only if most people mistakenly believe the food ordinarily contains fat. In that case, the food can be labeled "nonfat" if the label also states that the food ordinarily contains no fat. You need to find an answer choice that violates this food labeling regulation.

A. No. This is consistent with the food labeling regulation described above.

B. No. This is consistent with the food labeling regulation described above. There is no mandate for using the "nonfat" label, only restrictions on how and when it can be used, so the lack of a "non-fat" label on a nonfat food falls within the scope of the regulation.

C. No. This does not contradict the food labeling regulation, as the regulation applies to those foods that do not ordinarily contain fat and you are told that most garlic baguettes contain fat.

D. Yes. This violates the food labeling regulation. Most people are aware that applesauce does not ordinarily contain fat, so there is no need for the "nonfat" label on Lester's Applesauce.

E. No. This is consistent with the food labeling regulation described above. The label indicates that salsa ordinarily is nonfat.

15. **C** Parallel Flaw

The medical ethicist concludes that it is never acceptable to offer experimental treatments to patients who experience no extreme symptoms of the relevant disease. This is because patients who suffer from extreme symptoms of a disease are best able to weigh the risks of an experimental treatment against the benefits of a cure. The ethicist provides no evidence to support the claim that these patients are best able to judge the risks and benefits, nor does the ethicist consider that there could be other factors to support the idea of offering experimental treatments to patients who do not experience extreme symptoms of a given disease. Note also the use of extreme language here ("best able," "never," "no"); you'll need to match that in the answer choices.

A. No. This choice is not flawed.

B. No. The conclusion that the automobile was "likely" not test-driven does not match the original argument.

C. Yes. This choice contains the same flawed reasoning and extreme use of language ("exceptionally qualified," "not," "not") as the original argument.

D. No. The conclusion here uses softer language ("some") than does the conclusion of the original argument, so this doesn't match.

E. No. This choice is flawed, but not in the same way as the original argument. Here, the conclusion is more extreme ("not worthwhile," "unavoidable") than the premise warrants ("almost"), which is structurally different from the original argument.

16. **C** Principle Match

The critic states that as modern methods of communication and transportation have improved, the pace of life has become faster than ever before. This in turn has fostered feelings of impermanence and instability, making people feel as if there is never enough time to achieve what they want or what they think they want. You need to find a principle in the answer choices that addresses the fact that improvements in communication and transportation have led people to feel less permanence and less stability than before.

A. No. You know that the fast pace of modern life has made people feel that there isn't enough time to achieve their goals, but nothing is said about whether it has in fact made it more difficult for people to achieve their goals.

B. No. There is no discussion of whether improvements in communication and technology outweigh feelings of impermanence and instability.

C. Yes. This is in line with the analysis above.

D. No. The critic never addresses what makes it difficult for people to know what they want.

E. No. This is backwards. Technological change has created feelings of impermanence and instability in people, not the other way around.

17. **D** Necessary Assumption

The consumer concludes that Bingham's Jewelry Store, even though it is not a department store, should provide a refund. Why? The watch the consumer purchased from Bingham's stopped working the very next day. If you buy a watch at a department store and use it only in the way it was intended to be used, the department store will refund your money if the watch stops working the next day. The gap here is in how the watch purchased by the consumer was used: In order for the consumer's argument to be valid, the watch must have been used only in the way it was intended to be used.

A. No. This is focused on the seller, whereas the consumer's concern is for the purchaser, so this choice is not relevant.

B. No. How long either watch would work if used only as intended is beyond the scope of the argument, which is concerned only with what compensation there would be if either watch stopped working the day after it was purchased.

C. No. What expectations a purchaser may have of a watch are secondary to whether the watch was used only as it was intended to be used.

D. Yes. This is a paraphrase of the gap stated above.

E. No. This is irrelevant; the consumer never makes a distinction between new and old watches.

18. **B** Flaw

The argument concludes that therapists practicing a new experimental form of therapy are more effective than therapists practicing traditional forms. This is because a study found that patients who were referred to psychotherapists practicing the new form made more progress with respect to their problems than did those referred to psychotherapists practicing traditional forms. The flaw here is that there could be other reasons those patients made more progress than others. Those patients' progress may not be the result of therapists practicing a new form of therapy, so those therapists may not be more effective than those practicing traditional forms.

A. No. The argument never discusses whether therapists trained in the new form of therapy use the same techniques, but this isn't the problem with the argument's logic.

B. Yes. This suggests that it was the nature of the patient's problem, rather than the form of therapy practiced by the therapist, that is responsible for the differing levels of progress.

C. No. The argument does not discuss whether psychotherapists trained in traditional forms of therapy have also trained in the new form of therapy.

57

D. No. The argument doesn't address this, but that isn't the flaw in the argument's reasoning. If there were some systematic difference with respect to a relevant personality attribute, this might actually lend credence to the idea that those therapists practicing the new form of therapy are more effective.

E. No. The argument does not assume that personal rapport has no influence; it merely says that the new form of therapy is what accounts for the difference in progress.

19. **D** ⬤ **Principle Strengthen**

The essayist concludes that one should not support political systems that allow extreme freedom. This is because when people have extreme personal and political freedom, they often make choices for the worst and it is unrealistic to expect people to thrive when they are free to make such unwise choices. Once people see the destructive consequences of extreme freedom, it is possible that they may prefer to establish totalitarian political regimes that allow virtually no freedom. You need an answer choice that supports the essayist's conclusion that political systems that allow extreme freedom should not be supported.

A. No. This is too strong. The essayist says that people "may prefer" to establish a totalitarian regime, not that such a regime will inevitably be established.

B. No. This is not relevant to the essayist's conclusion, which does not discuss whether everyone should be expected to thrive.

C. No. The essayist's conclusion says nothing about what sort of political systems should be supported; it deals only with what sort of political system should not be supported.

D. Yes. This is in line with the essayist's reasoning, as noted above.

E. No. This is not relevant to the essayist's conclusion, which is concerned with political systems that could lead people to desire a more restrictive form of political system.

20. **E** ⬤ **Parallel**

Diagram the argument. Moral action → keeping of an agreement → securing mutual benefit. Not all agreement-keeping actions are moral actions, so then some acts of securing mutual benefit are not moral actions. The conclusion here essentially reinforces the idea that you can't read against the direction of the arrows: Knowing that an action is an agreement-keeping action does not imply that it is a moral one, so while the act of keeping an agreement does have to be an act of securing mutual benefit, that same action could be, but does not have to be, a moral action.

A. No. Calculator → computer → device for automated reasoning. Not all devices for automated reasoning are calculators, so some devices for automated reasoning are not computers. This doesn't have the same structure as the original argument, which places emphasis in the conclusion on the element all the way to the left of the arrows, which in this case would be the calculator (moral action in the original argument).

B. No. Exercise → beneficial → promote health. Not all beneficial things are forms of exercise, so some exercise does not promote health. This is flawed; according to the premises, all exercise must promote health.

C. No. Metaphor → comparison and surprising. This doesn't match the argument above.

D.   No. Architecture → design → art. Not all design is architecture, so some art is not design. This is close, but the conclusion doesn't match up. For the logic to be the same, the conclusion would need to assert that some art is not architecture.

E.   Yes. This is the same logic as the argument above. Book → text → document. Not all texts are books (because you can't read against the arrow), but all texts are documents; therefore, some documents are not books.

21.   **B**   Reasoning

The sociologist concludes that the more technologically advanced a society is, the more marked its members' resistance to technological innovations. This is because the more technologically advanced a society is, the more aware its members are of technology's drawbacks; people realize that sophisticated technologies deeply affect the quality of human relations. The statement that is asked about in the question stem, therefore, is one of the sociologist's premises.

A.   No. The statement is a premise, not a conclusion.

B.   Yes. This is in line with the analysis above.

C.   No. The sociologist never states that the quality of human relations in technologically advanced societies is extremely poor.

D.   No. The sociologist never claims that the more people resist technological innovations, the more difficult it is for them to adjust to those innovations.

E.   No. The statement does not serve as an example and the sociologist never claims that resistance to technological innovations deeply affects the quality of human relations.

22.   **B**   Flaw

The argument concludes that it is false to believe that nonwealthy candidates supported by wealthy patrons in democratic elections not fully subsidized by the government will compromise their views to win such support. Why? The wealthy are dispersed among the various political parties in roughly equal proportion to their percentage in the overall population. The flaw in this reasoning is that you can't presume that the views of the candidates necessarily align with those of the wealthy people who support them, regardless of how those supporters are distributed among political parties. A candidate's views could just as easily not align with any political party and therefore not align with any wealthy supporter, necessitating that the candidate compromise his or her views.

A.   No. The primary function of political parties is not relevant to the argument.

B.   Yes. This paraphrases the problem with the argument noted above.

C.   No. This argument is concerned with democracies in which elections are not fully subsidized by the government, while this choice is focused on government-subsidized elections.

D.   No. The ability of a wealthy person to win an election is not relevant to the argument, which is focused on nonwealthy candidates.

E.   No. This is irrelevant. The argument is concerned with whether candidates might have to compromise their views in order to be elected; it claims they do not need to. Flaws that might be found in a democracy in which candidates do not compromise their views in order to be elected constitute a separate issue.

57

23. **C** Inference

Pick the answer best supported by the passage.

A. No. The argument says that the new clear-coat finishes are more easily scratched than are older finishes and that mitters are easier on most cars' finishes than are brushes. However, you don't know that in the past when all car washes used brushes, more cars had scratched finishes. You don't have enough information to know how much cars with older finishes were prone to scratching by brushes.

B. No. This choice goes too far. From the argument, you don't know specifically why modern "brushless" car washes were introduced.

C. Yes. You are told that the new clear-coat finishes are more easily scratched than are older finishes and that mitters are easier on most cars' finishes than are brushes. Therefore you can conclude that modern "brushless" car washes, which use mitters, usually do not produce visible scratches on cars with older finishes. Note, too, the safe language here ("usually"), which leaves some wiggle room for exceptions.

D. No. The argument tells you nothing about the relative effectiveness of brushes (as opposed to mitters).

E. No. The argument does not state that more cars today have clear-coat finishes than older finishes; you know only that there are many cars today that do have clear-coat finishes.

24. **C** Sufficient Assumption

The argument concludes that, contrary to what is widely believed, lancelets, which are small, primitive sea animals, do have hearts. This is because the contracting vessel that all lancelets have strongly resembles the structure of the heart of certain other sea animals. Moreover, the muscular contractions in the lancelet's vessel closely resemble the muscular contractions of other animals' hearts. The argument makes an analogy assumption: It's valid to draw conclusions about the lancelet's vessel being a heart based on how well it compares to other animals' hearts in terms of structure and muscular contractions. You need an answer choice that confirms this comparison's validity.

A. No. This doesn't focus on the comparison made in the argument.

B. No. Again, this doesn't focus on the specific nature of the comparison being made in the argument.

C. Yes. This tells you that a vessel whose structure and actions resemble those of other animals' hearts can legitimately be considered a heart.

D. No. This doesn't address whether the comparison made in the argument is validly drawn. You already know the lancelet has a contracting vessel; the issue is whether this vessel can be considered a heart based on a comparison between it and other animals' hearts.

E. No. This is irrelevant. The argument is concerned with whether an animal can be considered to have a heart, not whether an animal can have a heart without an artery.

25.   **E**   `Inference`

Pick the answer best supported by the passage.

A. No. You are never told that the current company software is as flexible as the proposed new software package.

B. No. Familiarity is never discussed. You don't know why employees at other companies unofficially continue to use the old software as much as possible.

C. No. The capabilities of the new software package are never discussed.

D. No. The manager never mentions the idea of creating two classes of employees.

E. Yes. This is supported by the last sentence of the argument, in which the manager notes that employees at other companies who have officially adopted the new software unofficially continue to use the old software, and by the first sentence of the argument, in which the manager advocates not completely abandoning the software currently in use at the company.

Section 4: Reading Comprehension

Questions 1–5

The author argues that because of the actions of a church group, the Federal Communications Commission (FCC) must now take into account public views and concerns when holding broadcast licensing proceedings. The first paragraph provides background information on the FCC and describes how the FCC served the broadcasting industry but failed to recognize the rights of viewers and listeners. The second paragraph presents the landmark case that shifted the relationship between the public and the FCC; it explains how in 1964 the United Church of Christ challenged the FCC regarding the renewal of a broadcasting license for a television station that was known to advocate racial segregation.

The third paragraph details how the church appealed the FCC's decision in court on two separate occasions; on the second appeal, the judge went above the FCC and revoked the station's license, opening the door to greater public participation in broadcasting issues. The final paragraph describes the impact of the case and notes that subsequent rulings have further supported the right of the public to question the renewal of radio and television licenses before the FCC.

1.   **A**   `Big Picture`

The main point of the passage is that as a result of the United Church of Christ's actions, the FCC must now hear and take into account public concerns when holding broadcast licensing proceedings.

A. Yes. This matches the main point as stated above.

B. No. The passage never states that the court rulings forced the FCC to abandon particular policies, only that those rulings supported the right of the public to question the performance of radio and television licenses before the FCC when those licenses are up for renewal.

C. No. This is too broad. Government agencies in general are not discussed in this passage.

D. No. The passage never claims that the FCC has become less responsive to the broadcasting industry. It merely states that the public is no longer shut out of broadcast licensing proceedings.

E. No. The FCC did not willingly open its license renewal hearings to the public; it was forced to do so by court rulings.

2. **A** **Structure**

The author mentions the additional topics now discussed at FCC hearings to further support the claim made in the first sentence of the last paragraph, namely, that the United Church case opened up the world of broadcasting to the public. Choice (A), therefore, is the closest match to this idea.

3. **D** **Extract Infer**

A. No. The passage never discusses how the broadcasting industry's economic goals can most easily be met.

B. No. There is no indication that broadcasters actually advised the FCC to bar groups with no economic interest in broadcasting from its hearings.

C. No. This contradicts what the passage says. The judge in the second appeal revoked the station's license without remand to the FCC, implying that the FCC did not have the ultimate authority on this issue.

D. Yes. Evidence for this choice can be found in the second and third sentences of the first paragraph.

E. No. The passage does not discuss other instances of citizens' groups seeking to have their concerns about government agencies addressed, so you don't know whether this was the first time a citizens' group was successful.

4. **C** **Extract Infer**

A. No. You don't know whether, or the extent to which, the FCC would have become aware of the television station's broadcasting policies if the church had not brought its case.

B. No. This is far too broad to be supported by the passage, which is concerned only with the broadcasting industry.

C. Yes. This is supported by the first two sentences of the final paragraph.

D. No. This is too extreme and too broad. The passage provides only one instance in which a regulatory agency did not at first hold public interests above the interest of an individual business, which isn't enough to say that the author would agree with this statement across the board.

E. No. This is also too extreme and too broad. Only one government agency, the FCC, is discussed here, and you cannot extrapolate that the author would distrust all government on the basis of this one example.

5. **E**

The final sentence of the third paragraph states that the judge ruled that the church members were performing a public service by voicing the concerns of the community and should therefore be accorded the right to challenge the renewal of a station's broadcasting license.

A. No. The passage does not provide any information on what legal obligations, if any, broadcasters have with respect to the public.

B. No. The passage does not provide any information about whether the FCC requires broadcasters to consult citizens' groups when making programming decisions.

C. No. The passage does not state that the ruling required the FCC to seek public input in licensing hearings in cases involving clear misconduct by a broadcaster.

D. No. This is too extreme. The ruling did not say that the FCC must obtain information about public preferences, only that it must permit the public the right to question license renewals and provide input.

E. Yes. In effect, the judge's ruling allowed the church members to have standing, which the FCC originally claimed they did not have (see the second-to-last sentence of the first paragraph and the middle of the second paragraph).

Questions 6–12

The author argues that science and the humanities can and should be combined, as they have common objectives. The first paragraph notes that the synthesis of science and the humanities has been hindered by misconceptions that can and should be rectified. The second paragraph discusses the misconceptions that some humanists have about science, namely, that it is concerned only with "bodies in motion." The third paragraph describes the misconception that some scientists have about the humanities, which is that they are useless because they have no immediate and technological function for society's survival. The fourth paragraph returns to the idea that such misconceptions need to be corrected and in their stead a more acceptable position, "scientific humanism," should be developed based on the common elements and goals of each discipline.

6. **E** Big Picture

The main point of the passage is that science and the humanities need to overcome the misconceptions each holds about the other so that collaboration between the two fields can take place.

A. No. The author does not blame one group more than the other for the misunderstandings that hinder collaboration.

B. No. This is perhaps suggested by the author, though in the final paragraph the author deplores the idea that science is only materialistic and the humanities only idealistic. However, it's certainly not the main point the author wishes to convey.

C. No. This is too extreme. The author never claims that technology will cease altogether if reconciliation fails to occur between science and the humanities.

D. No. The author provides no information to indicate that their relationship was once more collaborative than it is now.

E.   Yes. This is a decent paraphrase of the main point as expressed above.

7.   **C**   **Extract Infer**

The misconceptions that humanists have of science are discussed in the second paragraph.

A.   No. The passage states that this is what some humanists, not scientists, believe.

B.   No. This is not a misconception that humanists hold.

C.   Yes. This is supported by the second sentence of the second paragraph.

D.   No. This is what some humanists, not scientists, believe.

E.   No. If anything, some humanists feel that science seeks to explain away human values rather than describe them.

8.   **D**   **Extract Infer**

A.   No. The author does not say that the direction of such an extension goes from science to the humanities; no specific direction is given, only the notion that the two disciplines can work in combination.

B.   No. The author claims scientists share this objective with humanists.

C.   No. The author seems to imply the opposite idea in the middle of the final paragraph of the passage.

D.   Yes. In the fifth sentence of the last paragraph, the author states that "the humanities in fact profit from attempts at controlled evaluation," which suggests that a methodology more commonly used in science has been useful to humanists.

E.   No. The author states that the combination of the two disciplines is "possible, even probable" in the final sentence of the passage.

9.   **B**   **Extract Fact**

In the second sentence of the first paragraph the author says that "the separation is primarily the result of a basic misunderstanding of the philosophical foundations of both science and the humanities." Choice (B) is therefore the best match to this statement and the credited response.

10.   **D**   **Structure**

The last paragraph returns to the idea that the two disciplines need to be reconciled and that the misconceptions each has of the other need to be dispelled so that collaboration can take place.

A.   No. The author states that reconciliation of the two disciplines is "possible, even probable" in the final sentence of the passage.

B.   No. The author does not believe that any of the views mentioned in the second and third paragraphs are correct, though the author does think reconciliation is possible.

C.   No. The author does not support any of the views held in the second and third paragraphs.

D.   Yes. The author presents "scientific humanism" as an alternative to the views presented in the second and third paragraphs.

E.   No. The author does not present examples in the final paragraph to support any of the views in the second and third paragraphs.

11.   **C**   **Extract Infer**

In the fifth sentence of the last paragraph, the author states that "the humanities in fact profit from attempts at controlled evaluation." You need to find an answer choice in line with this idea.

A.   No. This would not represent a modification of the humanist point of view, as according to the author in the second paragraph, some humanists already think the scientist is interested only in the strictly mathematical laws that govern the material world.

B.   No. This is what humanists already believe, so it would not represent a modification of their point of view.

C.   Yes. This paraphrases the author's statement as noted above.

D.   No. The author does not suggest that humanists should insist less on the primary importance of the arts in people's lives.

E.   No. The author does not claim that humanists need to develop ways to show how their discipline supports the practical survival of mankind.

12.   **B**   **Extract Infer**

The author notes that humanists are sometimes perceived as being interested in only emotion and sentiment, lacking direction and discipline.

A.   No. While humanists are said to be concerned with emotions, the author does not claim that they are seen as "wildly emotional."

B.   Yes. If humanists are seen as exhibiting "vagrant fancies," this implies that they are focused only on fleeting notions as opposed to practical concerns.

C.   No. Intransigence is never mentioned.

D.   No. Optimism is never mentioned.

E.   No. The author does not state that humanists can be "inconsistent."

Questions 13–19

Passage A

The author claims that Willa Cather shares Ivan Turgenev's approach to characters. The first paragraph describes the method and approach of Turgenev. The second paragraph discusses Cather's aesthetic in light of Turgenev and highlights the similarities between the two.

Passage B

The author suggests that it is more appropriate to analyze Willa Cather's work from a narrative perspective rather than a novelistic one. The first paragraph describes the literary theory of "narratology." The second paragraph discusses how criticism of Cather's work bolsters the notion that she wrote narratives as opposed to novels.

13. **E** — **Extract Infer**

A. No. The author of passage A would most likely disagree with this choice. The author of passage A does not refer directly to the issue of narrative as opposed to that of the novel, but the elements that are considered key to Cather's aesthetic are found in the second paragraph of passage A. From that description, you can infer that the author of passage A would likely concur with the author of passage B with respect to the latter's claim that Cather's work is better understood as narrative rather than novelistic.

B. No. The author of passage A does not go into sufficient detail about Cather's critics.

C. No. The author of passage A would most likely disagree with this choice, as per the explanation for choice (A).

D. No. The author of passage A would most likely disagree with the idea that Cather embraced the conventions of the realistic novel.

E. Yes. This would be consistent with the second paragraph of passage A.

14. **C** — **Extract Fact**

A. No. Passage B never discusses what narratologists think of Cather's work.

B. No. No mention is made of what Cather thought of the novelists who preceded her.

C. Yes. This is supported by the first sentence of passage B.

D. No. Turgenev and Tolstoy are mentioned only in passage A.

E. No. The opinions of contemporary critics are not discussed.

15. **C** — **Extract Infer**

Cather's impressionistic technique, as described in passage B, contains features such as "unusual treatment of narrative time, unexpected focus, ambiguous conclusions, a preference for the bold, simple, and stylized in character as well as in landscape."

A. No. A "meticulous" inventory would go against the notion of "simple...in landscape."

B. No. You know from passage A that Cather's aesthetic was similar to that of Turgenev, whose method was "to select details that described a character's appearance and actions without trying to explain them." This choice wouldn't be in line with this description.

C. Yes. This would be consistent with both the description above and that given in the second sentence of passage A ("not depicting her characters' emotions directly but telling us how they behave and letting their 'inner blaze of glory shine through the simple recital'").

D. No. This would contradict the idea of "unusual treatment of narrative time."

E. No. This would go against the emphasis the author places on simplification in passage A and would contrast with the notion of "ambiguous conclusions" noted in passage B.

16. **A** Big Picture

The main point of passage B is that it is more appropriate to analyze Willa Cather's work from a narrative perspective rather than a novelistic one.

A. Yes. This matches with the main point stated above.

B. No. This is too specific. The author addresses this only in the second paragraph.

C. No. This is too specific. While it does appear that Cather made a choice to create her characters in the way she did, this isn't the main focus of passage B.

D. No. The author never claims that Cather's narratives served as an impetus for the development of narratology.

E. No. Passage B never states that Cather portrayed her characters by sketching their inner lives.

17. **E** Extract Infer

A. No. Neither passage compares Cather to her contemporaries.

B. No. Passage A does not discuss the issue of narrative.

C. No. Passage A does not discuss narratology.

D. No. Neither passage mentions anything about how or whether Cather influenced later novelists.

E. Yes. This is supported by the comparison in passage A between Turgenev's and Cather's aesthetics and by the second half of the second paragraph of passage B.

18. **E** Extract Infer

A. No. This is consistent with the description of Cather's technique in passage A ("art is the fusing of the physical world of setting and actions with the emotional reality of the character").

B. No. This is consistent with the description of Cather's technique. In passage B, novels are described as having "direct psychological characterization, realistic treatment of time, causal plotting, logical closure." Cather's work, on the other hand, contains features such as "unusual treatment of narrative time, unexpected focus, ambiguous conclusions, a preference for the bold, simple, and stylized in character as well as in landscape."

C. No. This is consistent with the description of Cather's technique. You know from passage A that her aesthetic was similar to that of Turgenev, whose method was "to select details that described a character's appearance and actions without trying to explain them."

D. No. This is not inconsistent with the descriptions of Cather's work.

E. Yes. This would fall under the guise of "direct psychological characterization," making this choice something likely found in a novel but not in Cather's work.

19. **B** **Big Picture**

   A. No. Passage B does not mention any influences on Cather's work.

   B. Yes. This is done in the second paragraph of passage A and the second paragraph of passage B.

   C. No. Passage A does not discuss the critical reception Cather's work received.

   D. No. Only passage B does this.

   E. No. Passage B describes how Cather's work relates to a French literary theory that developed later, but it never indicates that European literature and literary theory impacted her work.

Questions 20–27

The author argues that while fractal geometry has strikingly illustrated how complex forms can be derived from simple processes, some mathematicians question the greater utility of fractal geometry to mathematics because of the field's emphasis on computer images as opposed to theory. The first paragraph introduces the concept of fractal geometry and the property of self-similarity and provides an example of a fractal by describing the Koch curve.

The second paragraph analyzes how self-similarity is built into the construction of the Koch curve; as a result, images of successive stages of the construction process can be generated using computer graphics. The third paragraph discusses how mathematicians' opinions differ as to the significance of fractal geometry and as to how much impact the field will have in the larger world of mathematics.

20. **B** **Big Picture**

   The main point of the passage is that while fractal geometry has strikingly illustrated how complex forms can be derived from simple processes, some mathematicians question the greater utility of fractal geometry to mathematics because of the field's emphasis on computer images as opposed to theory.

   A. No. The last paragraph implies that pre-fractal mathematics has proven more theorems than has fractal geometry, making it unlikely that the latter could render the former obsolete.

   B. Yes. This is an acceptable paraphrase of the main point as stated above.

   C. No. This is too specific. This is mentioned in the passage, but it doesn't encompass the discussion in the third paragraph.

   D. No. The idea that the new mathematical language that fractal geometry has developed is useful because it does not rely on theorems is never stated in the passage.

   E. No. The first two sentences of the final paragraph state that practitioners of fractal geometry consider it a language for describing complex natural forms and that it will permit mathematicians to describe the form of a cloud, so it would be inaccurate to say fractal geometry is not expected to be useful in describing ordinary natural shapes.

21. **C** **Extract Infer**

   You might come up with a phrase such as "well defined" in place of "fully explicit," since the rules for creating the Koch curve are clearly stated in the first paragraph.

A.   No. The Koch curve itself is an example of following the "fully explicit" rules.

B.   No. Nothing in the passage says the rules always have to be simple.

C.   Yes. This comes closest to "well defined."

D.   No. No mention is made of computation.

E.   No. No mention is made of the need for agreement.

22.   **D**   **RC Reasoning**

The concept of self-similarity is explained in the second sentence of the first paragraph ("the reiteration…at progressively smaller scales so that each part, when magnified, looks basically like the object as a whole"). All of the answer choices except choice (D) are consistent with this description. Choice (D) is inconsistent with the concept of self-similarity because there is nothing that suggests that a smaller part of one thing mirrors the whole thing; having several subspecies does not match up to a single part-whole complex. Choice (D) is therefore the credited response.

23.   **D**   **Structure**

The description of the Koch curve in the first paragraph follows the definition of self-similarity as given in the second sentence of that paragraph, so it is meant to illustrate that concept.

A.   No. Traditional geometry isn't discussed in this paragraph.

B.   No. The passage never states that the Koch curve is a natural form.

C.   No. This isn't mentioned until the final paragraph.

D.   Yes. This is in line with the reasoning above.

E.   No. The first paragraph says that no exact definition of fractals has been established.

24.   **E**   **Extract Fact**

Find an answer choice that is supported by information in the passage.

A.   No. The third paragraph notes that it could rival calculus, but the passage never states that it is potentially more important than calculus.

B.   No. Computer speed is never mentioned in the passage.

C.   No. The passage never discusses how fast that field, or for that matter any other field, is growing.

D.   No. While practitioners of fractal geometry make great use of computer-generated graphics, the passage does not say that fractal geometry encourages the use of computer programs to prove theorems.

E.   Yes. This is supported by the last sentence of the second paragraph.

25. **A**

The Koch curve is discussed in the first and second paragraphs.

A. Yes. This is not supported by the passage. The number of protrusions would appear to be linked to the number of times the process is performed, not the length of the initial line segment chosen for the construction.

B. No. This is consistent with the description in the first paragraph of how the Koch curve is constructed.

C. No. This is consistent with the third sentence of the second paragraph.

D. No. This is consistent with the description in the first paragraph of how the Koch curve is constructed.

E. No. This is consistent with the description in the first paragraph of how the Koch curve is constructed. Because the initial line segment is cut into thirds at the beginning of the process, it will determine the lengths of subsequent line segments.

26. **E**

The practitioners referred to in the question consider fractal geometry "a new language for describing complex natural and mathematical forms."

A. No. The passage does not state that the Koch curve is either the most easily generated or the most important of the forms studied by geometers.

B. No. Though the passage does state that practitioners anticipate that fractal geometry will be as useful to mathematicians to describe certain forms as traditional geometry has been to architects, nowhere is it stated that fractal geometry will eventually be used in the same applications as traditional geometry.

C. No. While a worldwide public has become captivated by computer-generated images of fractals, the passage does not claim that this represents the greatest importance of such images.

D. No. This is extreme. There is no evidence for this statement in the passage.

E. Yes. Since you know from the first paragraph that fractals generally exhibit the property of self-similarity, this choice is a decent paraphrase of the lines cited in the question.

27. **D**

Find an answer choice that is supported by information in the passage.

A. No. There is no support in the passage for the claim that the appeal of a theory is limited to those who can grasp its theorems and proofs.

B. No. This is not supported by the passage; important recent breakthroughs in mathematics are not discussed.

C. No. The third paragraph notes that fractal geometry could rival calculus, but the passage never states that fractal geometry has the potential to replace traditional geometry in engineering applications.

D. Yes. The first sentences of the passage tell you that fractal geometry is a mathematical theory and that an exact definition for fractals has not yet been established, while the third paragraph describes what applications its practitioners envision for it.

E. No. While this may appear to be paraphrasing the final sentence of the passage, in fact this claim is not supported. The last sentence of the passage states that in order to achieve a lasting role in mathematics, fractal geometry must become a precise language supporting a system of theorems and proofs. This choice, however, refers to what a theory must do in order to gain enthusiastic support among a significant number of mathematicians, which isn't the same thing.

Chapter 8
PrepTest 58:
Answers and
Explanations

ANSWER KEY: PREPTEST 58

Section 1:
Arguments 1

1. C
2. D
3. E
4. E
5. A
6. A
7. B
8. E
9. E
10. B
11. A
12. D
13. B
14. D
15. D
16. E
17. B
18. C
19. D
20. E
21. C
22. C
23. C
24. E
25. A
26. A

Section 2:
Reading
Comprehension

1. B
2. E
3. E
4. D
5. C
6. E
7. A
8. D
9. C
10. A
11. B
12. A
13. E
14. B
15. A
16. B
17. A
18. E
19. C
20. D
21. E
22. C
23. B
24. A
25. C
26. B
27. D

Section 3:
Games

1. E
2. C
3. E
4. A
5. E
6. C
7. C
8. B
9. C
10. B
11. A
12. B
13. D
14. D
15. B
16. B
17. C
18. C
19. D
20. B
21. E
22. B
23. B

Section 4:
Arguments 2

1. E
2. C
3. A
4. C
5. A
6. D
7. A
8. B
9. A
10. D
11. E
12. A
13. C
14. D
15. B
16. B
17. D
18. E
19. B
20. E
21. D
22. C
23. B
24. B
25. A

EXPLANATIONS

Section 1: Arguments 1

1. C Necessary Assumption

The argument concludes that restrictions on water use will be necessary to meet the freshwater needs of humankind in the not-too-distant future. This is based on the fact that while the water supply is currently adequate, the population will increase over the next few decades. The assumption is that the current water supply will continue to be the water supply in the future.

A.   No. Other natural resources are irrelevant to the argument.

B.   No. This strengthens the conclusion somewhat, but is not necessary for the conclusion to be true. Negating this answer choice doesn't necessarily hurt the conclusion.

C.   Yes. If you negate the answer choice, it says that the freshwater supply WILL increase to meet future demands. This invalidates the conclusion, so this choice must be necessary.

D.   No. Synthesizing water is irrelevant to the argument.

E.   No. The commentator does not seek to increase the freshwater supply; rather, he aims to decrease water consumption. Therefore, this choice is irrelevant.

2. D Principle Match

The psychologist claims that the best way to recall a word or name is to stop trying to think about it.

A.   No. The core of this situation is that one should stop trying in order to achieve the result. This answer choice does not deal with this.

B.   No. This choice deals with how to avoid dwelling on the size of a project by dividing it into small bits, which doesn't match the principle given in the argument.

C.   No. This says one should ignore mistakes, which doesn't match the psychologist's principle.

D.   Yes. Counting sheep is doing something other than trying to fall asleep, which the answer choice claims will make you fall asleep faster. This matches the stated principle.

E.   No. This tells you to focus on people worse off than you are to make yourself feel better. This doesn't match the psychologist's principle.

3. E Strengthen

The argument concludes that the conclusion drawn in the editorial (the Planning Department now spends five times as much money as it did in 2001 to perform the same duties) is not justified. There isn't much evidence that supports the letter-writer's argument, and the only evidence used to support the editorial's claim is that the budget has increased from 2001 to now. The editorial assumes that the Planning Department has the same duties it had in 2001. To justify the position of the letter writer, then, you need a choice that essentially claims those duties have somehow changed since 2001.

A. No. Other departments are irrelevant.

B. No. If this statement were true, it is possible that overall spending could have decreased as well, but then it's unlikely that their budget would have increased fivefold if they were managing to cut spending.

C. No. This is irrelevant. These are the only two years you know about, and for all you know "this year" could be 2002.

D. No. This is irrelevant because the department still had a massive budget increase.

E. Yes. This says that the Planning Department's duties have been increased, which would justify a larger budget and thus strengthen the position expressed in the letter to the editor.

4. **E** | Principle Match

The argument tells you that when a jury is given instructions using technical jargon, jurors tended to side with the judge's opinion. Conversely, when given instructions in nontechnical language, they tended to go against the judge. This suggests that how jurors are given instructions affects the decision they make.

A. No. The argument does not pass judgment on which opinion was more correct, so which set of instructions is more precise is irrelevant.

B. No. It doesn't seem likely that the judge's status would change depending on whether he or she gave technical or nontechnical instructions; thus the judge's influence should not change, either.

C. No. The nonverbal behavior the judge exhibited to the jury that received technical instructions seemed very effective.

D. No. The argument discusses only the results of mock trials, so you have no way of knowing this.

E. Yes. This restates what was stated above: The delivery of the instructions affected the jury.

5. **A** | Weaken

The argument concludes that while there is little firm evidence of medicinal effect, people should always be allowed to prescribe herbal remedies. The evidence is that the patient will not be harmed and may be helped by herbal alternative medicines. The argument assumes that there are no other considerations other than the effectiveness of the remedy itself.

A. Yes. If a patient forgoes effective conventional treatment in favor of herbal remedies, this could definitely bring about negative consequences. Therefore this choice weakens the doctor's argument.

B. No. The argument already claims that there is little firm evidence of medicinal effect. Truth in advertising is irrelevant.

C. No. The doctor is talking only about alternative medicines; this answer choice broadens the focus to all medicines, so it is irrelevant.

D. No. The motives of the purveyors of alternative medicines are irrelevant.

E. No. Whether the benefits are real or derive from a placebo effect is irrelevant.

58

6. **A**

This argument says that government does not violate free-market principles by imposing certain limitations on transactions if it does so in order to prevent economic collapse. As support for this conclusion, the argument uses the analogy of curtailing freedom of speech in certain appropriate situations.

A. Yes. This choice matches the argument: two sets of principles, each limited in its own way under certain circumstances.

B. No. There are no observed facts given in the argument.

C. No. There are no experimental results given in the argument.

D. No. The argument doesn't claim that there is a flaw in an explanation of a phenomenon.

E. No. The entire scenario is a generalization; there is no particular case given.

7. **B** Parallel Flaw

The argument attempts to claim that being the target of a smear campaign can actually benefit a candidate because most elections have been won by candidates who have been attacked via advertising. This is a case in which correlation does not equal causation: The author fails to consider that those candidates may have won elections despite, not because of, these negative attacks.

A. No. This choice displays logical reasoning.

B. Yes. This matches the flaw in the original argument. Many award-winning actors have received negative reviews at some point in their careers, but that doesn't mean those negative reviews caused them to win awards.

C. No. This is fairly logical reasoning.

D. No. This choice doesn't display the same flaw as the original argument; it doesn't attempt to claim that the critics' dislike of horror films is what causes those films to be successful.

E. No. This choice doesn't display the same flawed causal assumption as the original argument.

8. **E** Resolve/ Explain

Fact 1: Residents of Springfield live farther away from work than those of Rorchester, so you would expect a greater demand for public transportation in Springfield. Fact 2: Springfield has half as many bus routes as Rorchester.

A. No. This helps to explain the discrepancy. If the majority of the workforce is employed outside the city limits at the same factory, then it makes sense that there wouldn't be as many bus routes, as most of the workforce would be taking the same routes to work. And public transportation might not extend beyond the city limits, either.

B. No. This helps to explain the discrepancy. If there are more car owners in Springfield, it makes sense that there wouldn't be as great a need for buses.

C. No. This helps to explain the discrepancy. Adding another form of public transportation to the equation might explain why Springfield has fewer bus routes.

58

D. No. This helps to explain the discrepancy. Fact 2 talks only about the number of bus routes. This choice suggests that it is possible for Springfield to have fewer routes yet provide equal coverage.

E. Yes. If anything, this choice exacerbates the contradiction because you would expect a larger population to need more bus routes, not fewer.

9. **E** **Flaw**

The argument concludes that the zero-calorie fat substitute N5 is of no use to people trying to reduce their intake of fat and calories. This is because people who ate foods prepared with N5 ate more food, making up for the calories initially saved by using N5. The argument ignores the fact that half of the goal is still met with N5, namely, reducing fat intake; the phrase "of no use" in the argument's conclusion is too strong.

A. No. How many foods can or cannot be prepared with N5 is irrelevant.

B. No. The side effects of N5 are irrelevant to the argument.

C. No. Whether those who consume N5 pay attention to caloric intake does not seem to matter.

D. No. While possibly a true statement, this is not the flaw in the argument's reasoning because it doesn't deal with fat intake.

E. Yes. This choice tells you that N5 is not completely useless because it solves part of the problem: It reduces fat intake.

10. **B** **Inference**

The music historian claims that the lamentations of some critics are not justified because the things they do not like about postwar bebop recordings can actually be viewed as positives.

A. No. The argument states that they are not only representations of live solos, but also superb artistic works.

B. Yes. This choice fits the music historian's assertion that the critics are wrong.

C. No. The use of the word "always" is too extreme.

D. No. The music historian doesn't claim the next generation's music is of lower overall quality, only that those musicians lack the compactness in live playing that early bebop musicians possessed.

E. No. You have no way of knowing whether difficult recording conditions are a necessary component of short solos, only that it happened in this particular case.

11. **A** **Flaw**

The argument concludes that there is no causal connection between damage to human chromosome number six and adult schizophrenia. The reason for this assertion is that while a recent study found a correlation between the two, there are people who have damage to the chromosome who do not develop schizophrenia and people who have schizophrenia whose chromosome is undamaged. The flaw in this argument is that the term "damage" is fairly broad. It could be that the extent of the damage could be a factor in whether a person develops schizophrenia, a possibility that the extreme language of the conclusion doesn't allow for.

A. Yes. If only some types of damage to chromosome number six can cause schizophrenia, this would explain why some people have damage to the chromosome but not schizophrenia. This choice addresses the flaw in the argument.

B. No. The argument never claims chromosomal damage is the sole cause of schizophrenia. In fact, the argument disputes this, since you are told that some people have schizophrenia yet have no damage to chromosome number six.

C. No. There is no reason to doubt the representativeness of the sample used in this argument.

D. No. The argument does not offer a cause; it merely concludes that damage to the chromosome is not the cause. Thus, the argument does not mistake a cause for an effect.

E. No. The argument claims that in this case correlation does not imply causation, so this choice is backwards.

12. **D**   **Sufficient Assumption**

The city councilperson's conclusion is that the stone edifice qualifies as art. The evidence is that the edifice has caused experts to debate what constitutes art itself and that the purpose of art is to cause experts to debate ideas. The assumption needs to bridge the gap between the object in question and the purpose of art. Essentially, the city councilperson is assuming that if something satisfies the purpose of art, then it can be considered art.

A. No. This is backwards. This choice says if something is art, then it causes debate, but that's the opposite of what was stated above.

B. No. This goes against the assumption you are looking for and would certainly not prove true the city councilperson's conclusion that this edifice is art. Furthermore, whether an expert can be certain that an object is art is not relevant to the argument's conclusion.

C. No. The purpose of this argument is to try to prove that the edifice qualifies as art. Whether the town should purchase it is completely irrelevant.

D. Yes. This choice puts the pieces in the correct order: If something fulfills the purpose of art, then it is art. You know that this edifice fulfills the purpose of art according to the city councilperson; therefore, it must qualify as art.

E. No. Once again, you are not trying to determine whether the city should buy the edifice, only whether the edifice qualifies as art.

13. **B**   **Main Point**

The argument concludes that constantly broadening one's abilities and extending one's intellectual reach will enable one to inspire the perpetual curiosity of others. Why? If a person constantly does the aforementioned things, it makes it impossible for that person to be fully comprehended, rendering him or her a constant mystery to others.

A. No. In the argument, this statement begins with the phrase "it is a given," which implies that this a starting point on which the rest of the argument is based. Therefore, it is not the conclusion.

B. Yes. This almost perfectly restates the conclusion of the argument.

C. No. This is a part of the premise.

D. No. If you compare this choice to (B), you'll notice that they are very similar. The difference is that while both are conditional in nature, the necessary and sufficient terms are flipped. In the argument, the phrase "will enable" means that the information preceding that phrase (constantly broadening one's abilities and extending one's intellectual reach) is sufficient. This choice, however, presents that information as being necessary instead of sufficient.

E. No. This choice uses many of the same words as the argument, but changes their context. The argument is concerned with inspiring curiosity in others. This choice, however, states that the person broadening his or her mind will be curious rather than inspire curiosity in others.

14. **D** **Necessary Assumption**

The argument concludes that film producers tend to make movies that theater managers consider attractive to younger audiences. This is because film producers want their films to be shown as widely as possible. Furthermore, you are told that theater managers will not rent a film if they do not believe it will generate enough revenue, including concession sales, to make a profit. There is a gap in this argument between what film producers want and what theater managers want. You need to show that there is an overlap in the wishes of both groups.

A. No. This strengthens the theater managers' portion of the argument but disregards the position of the film producers.

B. No. It is not necessary that young and old audiences "almost never" agree. This language is too strong.

C. No. This may be true, but it is not necessary to the argument. If you negate this choice, it says that the concession stands are not more profitable than the movies, which does not weaken the conclusion.

D. Yes. If you use the negation test on this choice, it says that theater managers don't think that films targeted to younger audiences are more likely to be profitable than other films. This certainly invalidates the conclusion, because if theater managers don't feel that films targeted to younger audiences are more profitable, there is no reason for film producers to cater to younger audiences in choosing which films to make, given that theater managers use profitability as a factor in deciding which films to rent.

E. No. The entire argument deals with films aimed at younger audiences, so older audiences are irrelevant. This may seem to strengthen the conclusion, but it is not necessary for the conclusion to be true.

15. **D** **Inference**

Almost all advances in genetic research lead to ethical dilemmas. Funding for said research is exclusively provided by government in most cases, with the remainder being funded solely by corporations. Thus it appears you can make a connection between the sources of funding and ethical dilemmas.

A. No. You know that most of the funding for genetic research comes from government sources, but that does not mean that the majority of advances come from that money.

B. No. As with (A), you don't know what percent of government-funded research results in advances, so you cannot prove the word "most" to be true here.

58

C. No. Again, the problem here is similar to those found in (A) and (B). You know that corporations provide some of the money, but you have no idea what percent of advances comes from the research they fund.

D. Yes. You are told all funding comes from either government or corporations and that this funding is necessary for any genetic research. Therefore, any advances made must come from a project funded by one of these two groups. If nearly all advances lead to ethical dilemmas, then at least one of these two funding sources must be connected to these ethical dilemmas.

E. No. Once again, you don't know whether a government-funded program has made any advances in genetic research, so there is no way to say for certain whether there are any ethical dilemmas with which government is associated.

16. **E** **Necessary Assumption**

The conclusion of the argument is that sometimes a business can survive only by becoming a different corporation. The justification is that because corporations must adapt to survive, they are sometimes forced to change their core corporate philosophy. Becoming a different corporation is mentioned only in the conclusion, so you need to link it to the change in core corporate philosophy discussed in the premises.

A. No. There is no mention of becoming a different corporation, so this does not create the link you need. Furthermore, the argument states only that sometimes a company is forced to change its core corporate philosophy, so this choice is also too strong.

B. No. This does not forge the link you want. The argument says extinction results when a business is "no longer efficient," while this choice discusses becoming "less efficient," which is not necessarily the same thing.

C. No. Whether corporations' philosophies are similar or different is irrelevant.

D. No. There is no support for this choice, since the argument says nothing about a business keeping its core corporate philosophy intact, and it does not create the necessary link.

E. Yes. This creates a link between changing core corporate philosophy and becoming a different corporation. Using the negation test, you get that a company CAN change its core corporate philosophy without becoming a different corporation, which definitely invalidates the conclusion.

17. **B** **Resolve/ Explain**

Fact 1: A survey taken ten year ago showed the residents of area L had below-average living conditions relative to the rest of their country; however, most of the residents were generally satisfied with their standard of living. Fact 2: A more recent survey shows that the living conditions in area L are now about the same as those of the rest of the country, yet residents are currently dissatisfied with their living conditions.

A. No. This may be true, but by itself this choice doesn't give any real explanation of why they are no longer satisfied with their living conditions.

B. Yes. The argument leads you to believe that because the standard of living in area L became close to the national average living conditions, the national average remained static while area L's living conditions increased. If, however, area L's standard of living remained static, but the standard in the country as a whole decreased substantially, it would explain why the residents of area L are dissatisfied now even though their living conditions match those of the rest of the country.

C. No. How optimal living conditions are calculated doesn't explain why the residents in area L are now dissatisfied.

D. No. While people in area L were satisfied with their living conditions in the first survey, this is not the same thing as saying they didn't think it needed improving. You don't know whether people saw a need for improvement. And even if they did think conditions needed to improve and thus caused them to improve, this choice still doesn't explain why the residents are now unhappy.

E. No. Even if the residents were not aware they were living in below-average conditions, they were happy. One could argue that ignorance is bliss and so once the residents became aware, it caused them to change their opinions, but the choice itself doesn't state this outright. Plus, you know that their living conditions have changed relative to the national average, so you still need an explanation for why they are unhappy now.

18. **C** | Flaw

The travel agent's conclusion is that passengers are safer on a major airline than on one of the newer low-fare airlines. The travel agent attempts to justify this by stating that though most low-fare airlines have had few, if any, accidents, very few of them have been in existence long enough for their safety records to be reliably established. At the same time, major airlines have been keeping track of safety for many years. The issue with this argument is that the travel agent doesn't actually provide evidence that the major airlines are safe, only that they have been keeping diligent records. What if those records show that they get in a crash every other flight?

A. No. You would expect a major airline to have a higher number of crashes than a low-fare airline because they have more planes flying. The bigger issue is the percent chance a crash will occur on either airline, meaning what percent of the total number flights will result in a crash.

B. No. Major airlines have been keeping records for an adequate length of time. This choice says the time period for both types of airlines is too short.

C. Yes. As stated above, nowhere in the argument does it show that the major airlines have a good safety record, only that they keep track of their safety. This choice accurately describes the flaw in the travel agent's argument.

D. No. The argument discusses the comparison between the airlines and uses the term "safer," which is not the same as the language in this choice, which says "safest." There could be a small airline that does not have low fares, such as a private charter service, that could be safer than the major airlines but does not keep reliable records to indicate such. Nothing in the travel agent's argument, moreover, discounts this possibility, so this doesn't describe the flaw in the travel agent's reasoning.

E. No. The travel agent never claims that flying a major airline eliminates one's chances of getting in an accident, just that it is safer than flying a low-fare airline.

19. **D** | Necessary Assumption

The conclusion of the economist's argument is that if the government were to lower income taxes, the economy would improve. This is based on the several facts. First, the economy's weakness is a result of consumers' reluctance to spend, which has been caused in part by prices going up. Second, this reluctance to spend has been exacerbated by the fact that average income is significantly lower than it was five years ago. The problem with the economist's solution is that it takes into account only part of the problem: falling income. This solution would put more money in the hands of consumers, but you don't know if they will actually spend the money. For the economist's solution to work, then, you need to know that lowering income taxes would override whatever other reasons consumers may have had for not spending money.

A. No. While higher prices have contributed to decreased spending, you have no way of knowing whether the scenario will work in reverse.

B. No. This may happen, but it is not a requirement for the argument. If you negate this choice and say that average incomes will not increase, it doesn't necessarily weaken the argument.

C. No. This choice deals with a factor (lower income) that has already contributed to the economy getting worse. Since the conclusion focuses on improving the economy, this is irrelevant.

D. Yes. This addresses the problem noted above. If you negate this choice, it suggests that consumers will be just as or more reluctant to spend money if this solution—lowering income taxes—is put into effect. If people are more reluctant to spend money, the economy will most likely not improve, which is counter to the economist's conclusion. Therefore this choice must be necessary to the economist's argument.

E. No. Government spending is irrelevant here; the issue is consumer spending.

20. **E** Inference

A person with a type B lipid profile has a greater risk of heart disease than does someone with a type A lipid profile. After being put on a low-fat diet, volunteers with type B profiles lowered their cholesterol levels but remained type B profiles. Type A volunteers, however, showed no benefit from the diet; furthermore, 40 percent of them shifted to type B lipid profiles.

A. No. The opposite of this actually seems to be true, since some of the people in the lower risk group (type A profile) moved to the higher risk group (type B profile) as a result of the diet.

B. No. The argument does not say what anyone's starting cholesterol level was.

C. No. The argument does not discuss anything about the volunteers in terms of their lifestyles, so there's no way to prove that this choice must be true.

D. No. The word "solely" is too strong; you have no way of knowing whether the reduction in cholesterol levels was the only factor or one of many.

E. Yes. This must be true. Those volunteers who began as type A profiles and then shifted to type B as a result of being on the diet increased their risk of heart disease.

21. **C** Principle Match

The principle is that while there should be no restrictions placed on freedom of speech, it can still be considered "bad" to exploit depraved popular tastes for the sake of financial gain.

A. No. The principle says there should be no restrictions, so this choice doesn't match.

B. No. This choice does not address the part of the principle that says it is not okay to exploit depraved popular tastes for financial gain.

C. Yes. This matches the principle stated above. It should be legal to publish whatever sort of book one wants, but it may be morally wrong to do so.

D. No. This choice suggests the government has the right to limit freedom of speech, which goes against the principle stated above.

E. No. To claim that a person should not criticize something would be to limit that person's freedom of expression, which violates the principle.

22. **C** Necessary Assumption

The argument concludes that we may measure the rate at which a society is changing by measuring the amount of deference its younger members show to their elders. The justification for this conclusion is that when a society undergoes slow change, young members find great value in the advice of its older members. However, when a society undergoes rapid change, young people think that little in the experience of their elders is relevant to them and so do not value their advice. There is a gap in this argument between the term "deference" in the conclusion and the notion of valuing advice in the premises.

A. No. Whether a society's younger members can accurately discern rapid societal change is irrelevant to the conclusion.

B. No. This is close; however, the argument is concerned with finding value in the elders' advice, not with whether their experience is practically useful.

C. Yes. This creates the link you need. If you negate this choice, it says that deference does not vary according to the value placed on the advice. This would invalidate the conclusion; therefore, this choice must be necessary to the argument.

D. No. This seems to be supported by the argument and so is not an assumption.

E. No. This choice talks about the advice being practically useful to young people, which is irrelevant.

23. **C** Principle Match

The politician concludes that a tariff should be imposed on imported fruit to make it cost more than domestically grown fruit. If this is not done, domestic growers will go out of business, resulting in their farmland being converted to more lucrative industrial uses. Clearly from these statements, money is not the only motivating factor; the "vanishing of a unique way of life," another consequence of not imposing a tariff, is even more important.

A. No. Economic interest is ancillary to the "unique way of life." If it were only about economics, then fruit would be imported and domestic orchards turned into industrial parks.

B. No. In this scenario that is true, but you cannot generalize from this one case to one of all producers and all consumers.

C. Yes. This says that sometimes social concerns (the unique way of life) are more important than money.

D. No. The interests of citizens of other countries are irrelevant to the argument.

E. No. The politician is not seeking to increase economic efficiency; if anything, the proposed tariff may do the opposite.

24. **E** [Weaken]

The conclusion is that the valley's bear population will increase if the road is kept closed. This is based on the fact that in the Kipper Forest Preserve, most of the bears live in the valley. During the eight years that the main road through the preserve has been closed, the preserve's bear population has nearly doubled. One problem with this argument is that it tells you that the preserve's bear population has doubled and then it concludes that the valley's bear population will also increase. This is flawed: Just because the population of one area has gone up does not mean that the population of the total area will go up. You need to find an answer that addresses this gap.

A. No. Why the population in the preserve increased is irrelevant.

B. No. Once again, why the population in the preserve increased is irrelevant. You are concerned only with whether the total population will increase if the road remains closed.

C. No. This choice also deals with why the population in the preserve has increased, which is irrelevant.

D. No. This doesn't effectively weaken the conclusion. There could be many reasons the bear population in the rest of the valley decreased, reasons that could perhaps be dealt with by keeping the road closed.

E. Yes. This tells you that during the time the main road was closed, the valley's overall bear population remained roughly the same, implying that the increase in the preserve's bear population was not replicated elsewhere in the valley and might have been the result of the bears moving from other parts of the valley into the preserve. Therefore, keeping the road closed could not be expected to increase the valley's bear population further, which weakens the argument's conclusion.

25. **A** [Sufficient Assumption]

The conclusion is that made-to-measure wigs should be dry-cleaned (MMW → DC). This is based on several facts. First, a made-to-measure wig has a price range of medium-priced to expensive (MMW → M-E). Second, handmade foundations are never found on wigs that don't have human hair (HF → HH). Third, any wig that contains human hair should be dry cleaned (HH → DC). So you get this basic setup when mapping out the argument: Conclusion: MMW → DC. Premises: MMW → M-E, HF → HH, HH → DC. You can now see that to get from MMW to DC you have to connect the price range of the wig to the handmade foundation. MMW → M-E → HF → HH → DC. This proves the conclusion and would thus be the answer you want to find.

A. Yes. This is the missing conditional statement that is stated above (M-E → HF). This statement links together the premises and proves the conclusion true.

B. No. This choice mentions a foundation that is not handmade, which isn't what you need.

C. No. This is an inference that can be drawn from both statements regarding human hair in the argument. HF → HH plus HH → DC yields HF → DC. However, this doesn't connect the premise about made-to-measure wigs ranging in price to the conclusion, so it can't be the credited response.

D. No. This choice is backwards. The conditional statement discussed above and stated in (A) has the terms on the correct side of the arrow, while this choice gives you HF → M-E.

E. No. This choice confuses necessity and sufficiency. From the premises you can conclude that any wig with a handmade foundation should be dry cleaned, making the handmade foundation part sufficient. However, this choice uses it as a necessary term (DC → HF), which goes against what you mapped out above.

26. **A** Reasoning

The philosopher's conclusion is that it would be erroneous to deny that animals have rights on the grounds that only human beings are capable of obeying moral rules. The evidence given in support of this conclusion is an example of wolves' behavior: A wolf will not tolerate an attack by one wolf on another if the latter wolf demonstrates submission by baring its throat. The philosopher also mentions that both foxes and domesticated dogs exhibit this sort of behavior, too. The statement that the philosopher rejects is based on the premise that only human beings are capable of obeying moral rules. The argument shows that in certain situations animals do behave morally.

A. Yes. Wolves, foxes, and domesticated dogs are all counterexamples to the premise that the philosopher refutes.

B. No. The philosopher never claims that all animals possess some form of morality, only that wolves, foxes, and domesticated dogs have displayed what could be seen as moral behavior.

C. No. There is no principle stated in this argument; all the evidence given is factual.

D. No. Denying the claim in this argument does not produce any sort of contradiction.

E. No. If anything, the philosopher seems to broaden the application of the concept of morality.

Section 2: Reading Comprehension

Questions 1–7

The author argues that while certain obstacles relating to traditional sources of evidence may have hampered the study of ancient textile production, archaeologists have still learned a great deal about ancient textiles in part because of several advances in the field. The first paragraph details the problems hindering archaeologists from gathering information from traditional sources. The paragraph sets up the rest of the passage by concluding that, despite the obstacles, researchers have still made advances in the field by putting together disparate sources of evidence. The second paragraph is divided into two parts. The first part describes technological advances that have enabled researchers to gain more information from sources than before. The second part mentions philosophical changes that have occurred in the last century that have encouraged the preservation of artifacts. The third paragraph concludes by discussing the reconstruction of ancient textile production methods and how it has enabled scholars in the field to verify hypotheses.

1. **B**   Big Picture

The author's main point is that new technological advances and philosophical changes have allowed researchers to know a great deal about ancient textile production even though little physical or textual evidence exists.

A. No. The scope of this choice is too broad. The passage focuses on the history of textiles and not on women's history.

B. Yes. This is a decent paraphrase of the main point as expressed above.

C. No. This choice is too specific; it focuses too much on the third paragraph and textile replication.

D. No. Changes in the field of archaeology have spurred changes in the research of ancient textiles, not the other way around.

E. No. The author never claims that the most significant findings in the field have come from the reconstruction of ancient production techniques.

2. **E**   Extract
             Infer

At the end of the first paragraph, the author appears content with the advances made in the history of textile production.

A. No. The author does not express an opinion on any hypothesis.

B. No. The author states the opposite of this in both the last sentence of the first paragraph and the entire third paragraph.

C. No. The author seems pleased with the current pace of research.

D. No. The author never mentions increasing the number of researchers.

E. Yes. The author mentions this in the last sentence of the first paragraph.

3. **E**   Extract
             Fact

This is discussed in the third paragraph.

A. No. The author never mentions the re-creation of ancient techniques being used to investigate technical terms.

B. No. The second paragraph states that technological advances have helped trace sources of raw materials, not the re-creation of ancient techniques.

C. No. The author mentions only that stocking museums was a factor in the quest for artifacts. There is no mention of ancient techniques in relation to constructing museum displays.

D. No. The fundamental precept of preserving all objects—born of a philosophical revolution in archaeology—led to this.

E. Yes. The second half of the third paragraph discusses this.

4. **D** `Extract Infer`

The author states that "traditional sources" include archaeological remains and surviving texts; furthermore, the scarcity and poor state of these sources have proven an obstacle to researchers. You need to find a choice that doesn't in some way fall within these categories.

A.   No. The author mentions these as traditional sources in the first paragraph.

B.   No. Cloth is mentioned as a traditional source in the first paragraph.

C.   No. Cloth is mentioned as a traditional source in the first paragraph.

D.   Yes. The re-creations of looms mentioned in the third paragraph represent new advancements and not traditional sources.

E.   No. The first sentence of the passage defines surviving texts as traditional sources.

5. **C** `Big Picture`

The passage begins by describing the obstacles impeding the study of ancient textile production. The second and third paragraphs, however, go on to detail how researchers in this particular field have overcome these hindrances with a variety of advancements.

A.   No. The passage never mentions any controversial methods.

B.   No. The passage does not provide suggestions for studying textile production in the future.

C.   Yes. This is a decent paraphrase of the purpose of the passage as stated above.

D.   No. The author does not reject any commonly held views about the methodologies used to research ancient textile production.

E.   No. The passage catalogs new methods for the research of ancient textile production, not the hypotheses of scientists using these new methods.

6. **E** `Extract Fact`

The only portion of the passage that specifically discusses methodology in the past century is the middle of the second paragraph. It states that what emerged from the philosophical revolution that took place in the field was an emphasis on the scientific pursuit of knowledge of past cultures and the preservation of objects without immediately discernible value. Thus, you'll want to compare the answer choices to that particular part of the passage.

A.   No. The passage never mentions this.

B.   No. The passage never mentions archaeologists adopting other experts' techniques.

C.   No. The passage never mentions restoring artifacts.

D.   No. While the passage does mention this, the discovery of the garment was not part of the philosophical revolution of the past century. The fact that the garment was preserved even though it had no immediately discernible value was an effect of the transformation that had taken place.

E.   Yes. This is mentioned as one of the precepts adopted as a result of the philosophical revolution in the last century and integral to the field's transformation.

58

7. A `Structure`

The first paragraph details how traditional sources of evidence about ancient history have hampered researchers in the field. The paragraph concludes by stating that despite these hindrances, researchers have still made great discoveries. The second and third paragraphs go on to discuss what methods have been used to overcome the obstacles noted in the first paragraph.

A. Yes. The author uses the first paragraph to foster an appreciation for the advances discussed in the second and third paragraphs.

B. No. The first paragraph does not mention any neglected bodies of archaeological evidence.

C. No. The first paragraph does not mention new technology.

D. No. The first paragraph does not discuss findings of archaeological research but rather hindrances to that research.

E. No. The author never argues that other branches of archaeology should adopt the new technologies discussed in the passage.

Questions 8–13

The passage focuses primarily on scientist Philip Emeagwali and his successes in the field of computer science. The author states that these successes were due in part to the inspiration he drew from nature when creating his designs. The first paragraph discusses Emeagwali's pioneering work with massively parallel computers and the inefficiency of supercomputers in predicting oil flow through subterranean oil fields. The second paragraph describes the complexity involved in modeling oil field flow and how Emeagwali was able to successfully address this using a system inspired by the branching patterns of certain tree species. The final paragraph notes Emeagwali's belief that scientists will increasingly look to nature when designing solutions for complex technical problems.

8. D `Big Picture`

The author's conclusion is that Philip Emeagwali has successfully solved many real-world problems because he was willing to reach beyond traditional paradigms and model his computer designs on natural systems.

A. No. This choice lacks the idea that Emeagwali was inspired by natural designs.

B. No. Not only does this choice lack the inspiration Emeagwali derived from natural designs, the passage never says that real-world computational problems could otherwise be solved with little difficulty.

C. No. The passage does not focus on the growing use of Emeagwali's mathematical principles.

D. Yes. This is a good summary of the main point.

E. No. This choice is too narrow. The paradigm shift is mentioned only in the final paragraph.

9. **C**

A. No. The passage never says such systems are becoming obsolete.

B. No. The passage never states that an oil company requested this.

C. Yes. The middle of the first paragraph states that Emeagwali "pioneered" the use of massively parallel computers to predict the flow of oil in oil fields.

D. No. The passage never claims that Emeagwali was the first computer scientist to use nature as a model.

E. No. This is too broad. The passage claims only that Emeagwali was the first to apply massively parallel computers to predict oil flow, not that he was the first to use parallel processing for solving real-world problems in general.

10. **A**

The final paragraph notes Emeagwali's belief that scientists will increasingly look to nature when designing solutions for complex technical problems, so you can use this as a starting point when looking at the answer choices.

A. Yes. The second and third paragraphs detail how Emeagwali considered natural systems good models for the creation of computer systems.

B. No. The first sentence of the last paragraph suggests the opposite of this.

C. No. The passage does not say that Emeagwali thinks computer designs based on natural systems will be more prevalent in the future, only that computer scientists may look to nature more often to find solutions to complex technical problems.

D. No. The passage never mentions using massively parallel computers for mundane computing tasks.

E. No. This choice is too strong. The passage doesn't claim that Emeagwali thinks the mathematical structure is useful primarily for predicting oil flow; you know only that he used that structure for that purpose.

11. **B**

To understand the function of the first two sentences of the second paragraph, you need to read a few lines above them. The final sentence of the first paragraph explains that supercomputers could not accurately model oil field flow because they were too slow and inefficient to predict extremely complex movements. The second paragraph begins by describing the extremely complex movements that need to be modeled. Thus, the author includes these sentences to help the reader understand why supercomputers were not efficient in such situations.

A. No. These sentences do not describe an established paradigm.

B. Yes. This accurately describes the function of these two sentences.

C. No. The passage does not discuss the branching design until much later in the paragraph.

D.   No. The passage does not discuss the mathematical model Emeagwali used until much later in the paragraph.

E.   No. No paradigm shift is described here.

12.   **A**   Reasoning

In this portion of the passage Emeagwali expresses his belief that computer scientists will look to nature for solutions to complex technical problems. You need to find an answer choice that will strengthen this possibility.

A.   Yes. This choice strengthens Emeagwali's statements. If computer scientists now understand the mathematical principles behind natural processes, they will be more likely to look to these processes to solve other problems.

B.   No. This has nothing to do with whether scientists will look to nature for solutions in the future.

C.   No. This has nothing to do with whether scientists will look to nature for solutions in the future.

D.   No. This choice focuses only on Emeagwali. The fact that he uses mathematical principles inspired by natural designs does not automatically mean that other scientists will, so this doesn't strengthen his prediction.

E.   No. This has nothing to do with whether scientists will look to nature for solutions in the future.

13.   **E**   Extract Infer

The second paragraph discusses the use of massively parallel computers to model oil field flow, so that's where you should look to evaluate the answer choices.

A.   No. The end of the first paragraph states that supercomputers were not sufficient for accurately predicting oil field flow.

B.   No. The passage never states whether this had been considered before 1989.

C.   No. This is never mentioned in the passage.

D.   No. The perception of need among oil companies is never mentioned.

E.   Yes. This is mentioned in the middle of the second paragraph.

58

Questions 14–20

This passage is a criticism of the tangible-object theory of copyright, which states that copyright and similar intellectual-property rights can be explained as extensions of the right to own tangible objects. This theory depends on the claim that every work can be manifested in some physical form and that ownership of an object confers certain rights to the owner. The first paragraph explains this theory. The second paragraph describes how the theory works on a practical level and details what the rights of ownership entitle an owner to do with his or her work. The third paragraph discusses how proponents of the theory view it favorably because it justifies property rights without having to resort to the concept of ownership of abstract things such as ideas. The author disagrees with this notion, arguing that conceiving the actual idea is often more crucial than putting it into tangible form. The author then provides an example: A poet dictates a poem to a friend, who writes it down. Based on the tangible-object theory, the friend, not the poet, would own the rights to the work because the friend put it into tangible form.

14.   **B**   **Big Picture**

You need an answer choice that both references the ideas of the tangible-object theory of copyright and acknowledges that this theory is problematic.

A.   No. This describes the theory but does not state that it has drawbacks.

B.   Yes. This gives a basic synopsis of the theory and says that the theory is misguided, so this matches what you are looking for.

C.   No. This idea is talked about only in the second paragraph, so it is too narrow in scope.

D.   No. The author does not claim that this theory limits the circulation of ideas, only that it doesn't allow copyrighting of said ideas.

E.   No. This choice is the opposite of what the third paragraph discusses. The third paragraph says that only tangible objects are covered, not ideas.

15.   **A**   **Extract Fact**

This question restates ideas put forth in the first paragraph, specifically the first two sentences.

A.   Yes. This is exactly what is stated in the second sentence of the first paragraph.

B.   No. This choice is extreme; the author does not claim that only the original creator can hold the copyright for a given work.

C.   No. The discussion of ideas and tangible objects, and the importance of each, does not really occur until the third paragraph.

D.   No. The author does not say that proponents of the tangible-object theory feel this way; rather, this seems to be what the author is arguing.

E.   No. This fact is stated in the second-to-last sentence of the first paragraph, but the tangible-object theory does not depend on this supposition.

16.   **B**   **Extract Fact**

A.   No. The passage does not discuss whether these proponents seek to change any existing laws, so the passage does not answer this question.

B.   Yes. The answer for this comes from the second paragraph. The second sentence introduces the concept of retained rights ("the original owner may retain one or more of these rights."). The third sentence states that the "notion of retained rights is common in many areas of law"; real estate is then used as an example of one area in which this practice is common. The fourth sentence goes on to speak about retained rights in the domain of intellectual property, so there is evidence that retained rights apply beyond the realm of real estate.

C.   No. The passage does not discuss the practical application of this theory with respect to cases, and courts are not mentioned anywhere in the passage.

D. No. The passage does not discuss what sort of protection, if any, current copyright law offers those who have not officially applied for copyright protection.

E. No. The passage does not provide any detail as to whether there are standard procedures governing the transfer of intellectual property.

17. **A** `Extract Infer`

This question is supplying you with a specific situation in which ownership is at issue. Use the theory as the principle governing the situation to determine what would be true. According to the theory and the example the author provides of the poet, the inventor has no grounds for claiming copyright to the invention because the engineer is the one who put it into tangible form.

A. Yes. This is supported by the third paragraph and is analogous to the scenario of the poet and friend mentioned at the end of the third paragraph. Since the inventor had nothing to do with creating the tangible object, he or she has no claim to the invention.

B. No. This is the opposite of what the theory says; the idea seems to be mostly irrelevant to ownership.

C. No. The inventor has no claim to the invention under the theory because he or she did not produce the tangible object.

D. No. Retention of rights is discussed only in relation to transference of ownership, which has not occurred here.

E. No. This is essentially the opposite of (D). Once again, retention of rights is discussed only in relation to transference of ownership, which has not occurred here.

18. **E** `Extract Infer`

You want a statement that is in line with the tangible-object theory as it is described in the passage.

A. No. The only requirement given for copyright protection is that a tangible object be produced. The prestige of the publisher is irrelevant.

B. No. You have no way of knowing whether most legal systems rely on this theory or not.

C. No. The second-to-last sentence of the first paragraph claims only that the owner has the right to copy the work. The owner's motive for copying the work is not discussed and so is irrelevant.

D. No. According to the theory, if the work cannot be manifested as a concrete, tangible object, then it is not deserving of copyright protection.

E. Yes. The entire theory centers on the idea that copyright protection applies only to tangible objects. Thus, the law need not worry about ownership of abstract ideas, as the first sentence of the third paragraph explains.

19. **C** `Extract Infer`

A. No. The word "most" is not supported by the passage. The second paragraph claims that certain rights may be retained, but it does not state how often this actually occurs.

58

B. No. The middle of the second paragraph notes that the notion of retained rights can be found in many areas of law, so you don't know for certain whether this includes intellectual property law. The passage does not provide enough information about current applications of the notion of retained rights to allow you to conclude definitively whether this choice is true.

C. Yes. The second paragraph supports this statement. It states that the right to copy an object for profit can be retained, but that this is not always the case. This in turn suggests that transferring that right is compatible with the tangible-object theory.

D. No. It is impossible to tell from the passage whether this theory is used in any legal system. The passage does draw a parallel between certain aspects of real estate law and the domain of intellectual property, but to claim that intellectual property is sufficiently protected by such provisions is way too strong.

E. No. If you create a tangible form of the computer program, then it is yours and you are free to do anything you want with it, including produce additional copies. However, whether you choose to produce additional copies has no bearing on whether the program is protected by copyright. Thus, this choice contradicts what is stated at the end of the first paragraph.

20. **D** Extract Infer

You are looking for something the author would likely agree with, so keep in mind the fact that the author is critical of the tangible-object theory.

A. No. The author never claims that some theorists are lacking in their understanding of what it means to transfer ownership.

B. No. This seemingly agrees with the tangible-object theory, but since the author is criticizing this theory and in the third paragraph demonstrates why ideas can sometimes be a valid basis for claiming copyright protection, this choice cannot be correct.

C. No. Existing statutes are not discussed in the passage, so it is impossible to determine the author's opinion on them.

D. Yes. This touches on the author's main issue with the tangible-object theory—its inability to address the concept of ownership of an idea.

E. No. The author seems to think that the common standard assumption that things such as live broadcasts can be copyrighted is correct.

Questions 21–27

Passage A

This passage discusses how people experience music. The first paragraph puts forth the general idea that while a simple sound or a single tone is not likely to interest people, a certain complexity of sounds will. The second paragraph compares music to human language; sequential or rhythmical tones are more apt to create an emotional connection in a listener. The third paragraph notes the relaxing effect of certain music and presents a possible explanation for why such music is often continuous and rhythmical in character.

Passage B

This passage is also about the perception of music. The first paragraph discusses musical expectations; that is, music can lead a listener to have certain expectations which, if not met, can create tension in the listener. The second paragraph talks about the mismatch between one's musical expectation and the actual course of the music, noting that the greater the mismatch, the more negative the emotional response. Conversely, if there is no mismatch, the listener will tend to have a more positive emotional response. The last paragraph brings in factors such as the complexity and novelty of the music and the musical preference of the listener and describes how these affect whether a listener experiences a piece of music as pleasurable or uncomfortable.

21. **E**   Extract
              Fact

Both passages talk about positive musical experiences. Use the answers as your lead words and see what each passage says on the topic. You want an answer choice that both passages discuss.

A. No. Passage B does not discuss continuous sound.

B. No. Passage A does not discuss tension.

C. No. Language is discussed only in the first paragraph and only as an analogy to music.

D. No. Improvisation is not mentioned in either passage.

E. Yes. The second sentence of passage A and the entire last paragraph of passage B discuss how complexity is linked to a positive musical experience.

22. **C**   Extract
              Infer

You are asked to determine what the target audience of these passages is interested in.

A. No. Neither passage talks about the actual process of composing music.

B. No. Discontinuous sounds are discussed only in the third paragraph of passage A.

C. Yes. Both passages discuss human emotional responses to music, so this choice makes sense.

D. No. Neither passage discusses teaching people to appreciate music. The phrase "most effective" is also too extreme.

E. No. Passage A is the only place where language is discussed, and the author does not claim that one influenced the other. Instead he uses language as an analogy for music.

23. **B**   Reasoning

You need to find a parallel to the idea that people "...prefer some sort of coherence, a principle that connects the various sounds and makes them comprehensible."

A. No. This is not parallel because this falls under the idea of the "pure tone" mentioned in the second sentence. You need something more complex than this, but not overly so.

B. Yes. A clear and easy-to-follow plot is definitely analogous to the idea of coherence.

C. No. The size of the portion is not relevant here, as the size or length of a musical piece is not discussed.

D. No. Tempo is irrelevant, as the passage doesn't make any claims as to differences in coherence between fast and slow music.

E. No. The taste of food is not analogous; there is no clear connection between the concept of taste and that of coherence.

Big Picture

Passage B is mainly about the expectations a listener brings to a piece of music and how that affects the listener's experience of that music.

A. Yes. This nicely sums up the idea that expectations affect a person's experience of a piece of music based on how well the experience matches the expectation.

B. No. The experience level of the listener is discussed only in the second half of the third paragraph, so this choice is too specific.

C. No. While this is supported by the second paragraph, it is not the main point of the entire passage.

D. No. This is briefly mentioned at the end of the third paragraph; however, it is not the main point of the passage.

E. No. This is discussed only at the end of the first paragraph, so this choice is too specific.

25. **C** **Reasoning**

You are trying to weaken the idea that the relaxing effect of some music is caused by its continuous and rhythmic nature.

A. No. Though the complexity of their rhythms may vary, this choice still claims the traditions are rhythmic, so this will not weaken the explanation.

B. No. It is unclear whether rhythmic speaking and rhythmic music behave the same way. This choice also does not tell you whether rhythmic speaking has a relaxing effect on the listener.

C. Yes. This is a continuous and rhythmic sound that people find unnerving, so this weakens the author's explanation.

D. No. This discusses expectations, which are mentioned only in passage B, so this choice doesn't weaken the author's explanation.

E. No. This tells you only about the complexity of these composers' works, not whether they are continuous and rhythmical, so this doesn't weaken the author's explanation.

26. **B** **Big Picture**

You are asked to come up with a title that applies to both passages.

A. No. Biology is not discussed in either passage.

B. Yes. Psychology is an applicable term because both passages discuss how a person responds to music.

C. No. No other art forms are mentioned in either passage.

D. No. Cultural patterns are not discussed in these passages.

E. No. The process by which a composer conveys meaning is not discussed in either passage.

27. **D** Extract Infer

A. No. The third sentence of passage A contradicts this notion. The author claims that when music becomes too complex it can cause a negative reaction.

B. No. The knowledge level of the listener is discussed only in the third paragraph of passage B, so you have no idea whether passage A's author would agree with this choice.

C. No. Both passages discuss listeners' emotional response to music, but neither claims that this is central to determining artistic value.

D. Yes. Both authors claim that continuity is crucial to a listener's having a positive emotional response to music. In passage A this is discussed in the third paragraph; in passage B it is discussed in the first paragraph.

E. No. Changes in volume are not discussed in either passage.

Section 3: Games

Questions 1–6

This is a 1D order game. You are given five years, 601 through 605, and must determine when each of six monuments—F, G, H, L, M, and S—began construction. For simplicity's sake, label the columns in your diagram 1 through 5.

Clue 1: G—L—F

Clue 2: H = 4/5

Clue 3: M = 1/2/3

Clue 4: Put two spaces in column 1 of your diagram.

Deductions: From clue 1 you know that G can't be in 4 or 5, L can't be in 1 or 5, and F can't be in 1 or 2. You can also deduce that L cannot go in 4, because if it did it would force F into 5, leaving no place for H to go. Similarly, because H is restricted to slots 4 and 5, G cannot be in 3; if it were, both L and F would occupy the only spaces available to H. Thus G can be only in either 1 or 2.

Here's the diagram:

```
                          ~L         ~L   ~L
                    ~F  ~F  ~G  ~G  ~G
    FGHLMS          ~H  ~H  ~H  ~M  ~M

                     1 │ 2 │ 3 │ 4 │ 5
                    ── │ ─ │ ─ │ ─ │ ─
```

1. **E** Grab-a-Rule

Use the clues to eliminate answer choices. Clue 1 eliminates (C). Clue 2 eliminates (B). Clue 3 eliminates (D). Clue 4 eliminates (A). Therefore, (E) is the credited response.

2. **C** General

Use your deductions to eliminate choices. You already know that L can't be in 1, 4, or 5, so that narrows your options to either 2 or 3. Try placing L in 3. If L is in 3, F and H will take slots 4 and 5 in either order, and M, G, and S will be in slots 1 and 2, not necessarily in that order. Since it's possible to place L in 3 and not violate any clues, (C) is the credited response.

3. **E** Complex

Unfortunately, you'll need to try out each answer choice to see whether it determines the placement of every element.

A. No. It is impossible to determine slots 4 and 5 in this scenario.

B. No. It is impossible to determine slots 4 and 5 in this scenario.

C. No. It is impossible to determine where anything else goes except for the given element.

D. No. It is impossible to determine slots 4 and 5 in this scenario.

E.
```
    ~L         ~L   ~L
~F  ~F  ~G  ~G  ~G
~H  ~H  ~H  ~M  ~M

 1 │ 2 │ 3 │ 4 │ 5
MG │ L │ F │ S │ H
```

Yes. If S is in 4, H must be in 5. This means G, L, and F must be in 1, 2, and 3, respectively. The only element left is M, which must occupy the second space in 1.

4. A General

Use your deductions and previous work to eliminate answer choices, then try out whichever choices are left. You are looking for something that must be true.

A. Yes. This is consistent with all your prior work. From your deductions you already know that F cannot be in 1 or 2. Since M is restricted to the first three columns, there is no way that F can precede it without violating a clue.

B. No. Your work from question 3, (E), shows that this does not have to be true.

C. No. Your answer to question 1 shows that this does not have to be true.

D. No. If you put H in 4 and S in 5, it is still possible to fit the remaining elements without violating either clue 1 or clue 3. M and G will be in 1, L will be in 2, and F will be in 3. Therefore, it doesn't have to be true that H comes later than S.

E. No. Your work from question 3, (E), shows that this does not have to be true.

5. E General

This is similar to question 3, but now you are trying to determine only where L is. From your deductions, you know that L can go only in 2 or 3. Any choice that puts an element in one of these spots will force L to go in the other one. Choice (E) puts S in 3, so L must then be in 2. Therefore, (E) is the credited response; there is no need to try out the rest of the choices.

6. C Specific

Since M can go only in the first three years and now has to be after G and L, M must go in 3, with G in 1 and L in 2. Since F and H can't be in 1, the only remaining element that can be with G is S. F and H will occupy slots 4 and 5 in either order.

1	2	3	4	5
~L			~L	~L
~F	~F	~G	~G	~G
~H	~H	~H	~M	~M
GS	L	M	F/H	H/F

A. No. M is in 3.

B. No. G must be in 1.

C. Yes. Though the placement of F and H is not fully determined, you do know that one will be in 4 while the other will be in 5, so this could be true.

D. No. L is in 2.

E. No. S is in 1.

Questions 7–12

This is an In-Out game. You must determine which of seven parents—F, L, M, R, S, T, and V—make up a volunteer group, but no set number of volunteers is given for the group.

Clue 1: R → M; ~M → ~R

Clue 2: M → T; ~T → ~M

Clue 3: ~S → V; ~V → S

Clue 4: ~R → L; ~L → R

Clue 5: T → ~F and ~V; F or V → ~T

Deductions: Clue 3 gives you a V/S placeholder in the In column. Clue 4 gives you an L/R placeholder in the In column.

Here's the diagram:

$$\begin{array}{c|c} & \text{IN} & \text{OUT} \\ \hline \text{FMLRSTV} & \begin{matrix} V/S \end{matrix} \quad \begin{matrix} L/R \end{matrix} & \end{array}$$

7. **C** Grab-a-Rule

Use the clues to eliminate answer choices. Clue 1 eliminates (D). Clue 2 eliminates (B). Clue 4 eliminates (A). Clue 5 eliminates (E). Therefore, (C) is the credited response.

8. **B** Specific

If V is In, then T is Out (clue 5). If T is Out, then M is Out (clue 2), which means R is also Out (clue 1). If R is Out, then L is In (clue 4).

$$\begin{array}{c|c} \text{IN} & \text{OUT} \\ \hline \text{VL} & \text{TMR} \end{array}$$

A. No. R must be Out.

B. Yes. You don't know where F and S are, so they could both be In.

C. No. M must be Out.

D. No. T must be Out.

E. No. T must be Out.

9.   **C**   **Specific**

If T is Out, then both M and R are Out. If R is Out, L must be In, and at least one of V and S must be In as well from your earlier placeholder deduction.

IN	OUT
L V/S	TMR

A.   No. You don't have enough information to determine where F is.

B.   No. L is In, so this must be true.

C.   Yes. You have already determined that R is Out, so this cannot be true.

D.   No. You don't have enough information to determine which of V and S is In.

E.   No. You don't have enough information to determine which of V and S is In.

10.   **B**   **Specific**

If M is In, then T is In and F and V are Out. If V is Out, S must be In. You still don't know, however, which of L and R is In.

IN	OUT
S L/R MT	FV

A.   No. F is Out.

B.   Yes. This is possible.

C.   No. V is Out.

D.   No. S is In.

E.   No. T is In.

11.   **A**   **Specific**

If F is In, then T is Out, which means that M is Out and R is Out. If R is Out, then L is In. You still don't know, however, which of V and S is In.

```
         IN    |   OUT
    _____
      V         |
   FL /         |   TMR
      S         |
                |
```

A. Yes. L is definitely In.

B. No. This could be true, but it doesn't have to be true.

C. No. This could be true, but it doesn't have to be true.

D. No. If both V and S are In, you could have four volunteers.

E. No. If only one of V and S is In, you could have three volunteers.

12. **B**   General

You're essentially looking for two elements that can never be Out together. Use your prior work to eliminate answer choices.

A. No. Question 8 suggests that it's possible to have both T and F Out.

B. Yes. If M is Out, then R must be Out. However, if R is Out, then L must be In, so you get conflicting results, which suggests that it's not possible for L and M to be Out at the same time.

C. No. Question 10 suggests that it's possible to have both L and V Out.

D. No. Question 8 suggests that it's possible to have both R and S Out.

E. No. Question 8 suggests that it's possible to have both S and T Out.

Questions 13–17

There are five planes from two different airlines: P and Q from airline F, and R, S, and T from airline G. For each position you must determine three things: which plane is taking off, which airline the plane belongs to, and whether it is an international or domestic flight. Since the plane/airline relationship is given to you, use subscripts to indicate the airline and make the type of flight the second tier of your diagram.

Clue 1: This tells you the game has 1:1 correspondence with respect to the planes.

Clue 2: i/d

Clue 3:
```
┌───┐
│ P_F │
│   │
│ i │
└───┘
```

Clue 4: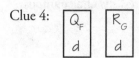

Clue 5: i—d

Clue 6: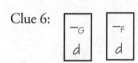

Deductions: Since all international flights depart before all domestic ones and G domestic flights are before F domestic flights, you get a new range clue:

$$\boxed{\begin{array}{c} P \\ {}_F \\ \hline i \end{array}} - \boxed{\begin{array}{c} R \\ {}_G \\ \hline d \end{array}} - \boxed{\begin{array}{c} Q \\ {}_F \\ \hline d \end{array}}$$

This tells you that P cannot be in 4 or 5, Q cannot be in 1 or 2, and R cannot be in 1 or 5. The only two elements not in the chain are S and T, both of which are owned by G. Therefore, regardless of whether they are domestic or international, they will leave before Q, which is domestic. Thus, Q must be in 5.

Here's the diagram:

		~R			~P
F: PQ	~Q	~Q		~P	~R
G: RST	1	2	3	4	5
Plane:	–	–	–	–	Q
i/d:	–	–	–	–	d

13. **D**   **Grab-a-Rule**

Use the clues and your deductions to eliminate answer choices. From your deductions, you know that Q must be in 5; this eliminates (A), (B), and (C). Choice (E) can be eliminated as well, since you know that P must come before R (clue 5). Therefore, (D) is the credited response.

14. **D**   **General**

From your deductions you know that Q can never be in 2. From your work on question 17, you know that P, R, and T can all be in 2. From your work on question 13, you know that S can also be in 2. Therefore, four of the elements could be second; (D) is thus the credited response.

15. **B**   **Specific**

Add S to the P—R—Q range clue to get S—P—R—Q. While T can still go anywhere, you now know that S can be only in 1 or 2 based on this chain. Remember that you're looking for something that must be false.

A.   No. This is possible based on the chain.

B. Yes. Three planes must depart after S, so the last place it can go is 2, making this choice impossible.

C. No. This is possible since T is unrestricted.

D. No. This is possible since T is unrestricted.

E. No. This is possible since T is unrestricted.

16. **B** | General

Use your prior work and deductions to eliminate answer choices.

A. No. Your work from question 17 shows that this does not have to be true.

B. Yes. From your deductions, you know that Q must be fifth.

C. No. Your work from question 17 shows that this does not have to be true.

D. No. Your work from question 17 shows that this does not have to be true.

E. No. Your work from question 17 shows that this does not have to be true.

17. **C** | Specific

Place S in 3. Looking at your deductions, you know that P is now restricted to either 1 or 2. Try each possibility. If P is in 1, then R and T occupy 2 and 4 in either order. If P is in 2, then T must be in 1 and R must be in 4. You're looking for something that must be false, so use both scenarios to eliminate what can be true.

| | | | ~P | |
| ~R | | | ~P | ~R |
~Q	~Q			
1	2	3	4	5
P	R/T	S	T/R	Q
_i_	–	–	–	_d_
T	P	S	R	Q
–	_i_	–	_d_	_d_

A. No. This is possible in the first scenario.

B. No. This is possible in the first scenario.

C. Yes. This is not possible because you already know that Q is in 5. If S is in 3, then there is only one remaining slot open after it. Thus, it is impossible for S to precede both R and T.

D. No. This is possible in the second scenario.

E. No. This is possible in either scenario.

58

Questions 18–23

This is an In-Out game. A student must choose at least three of seven potential courses—H, L, M, P, S, T, and W. Because you are told that at least three courses must be selected, your Out column will have at most four spaces.

Clue 1: H → ~S and ~M; M or S → ~H

Clue 2: M → ~P and ~T; P or T → ~M

Clue 3: W → ~P and ~S; P or S → ~W

Deductions: From the clues, you get three placeholders in the Out column: (S & M)/H, (P & T)/M, and (P & S)/W. This tells you that you have a minimum of three courses not taken (H, M, W), which means that there are three definite spaces in each column and one floater space. Ultimately, then, if the In column has three spaces, the Out column will have four; if four elements are In, then three will be Out. Note this on your diagram.

Here's the diagram:

18. **C**   Grab-a-Rule

Use the clues to eliminate answer choices. Clue 1 eliminates (A). Clue 2 eliminates (B) and (E). Clue 3 eliminates (D). Therefore, (C) is the credited response.

19. **D**   General

From your earlier deductions about the Out column, you know that a minimum of three elements must be Out. This means that the maximum number that could be In is four. Therefore, (D) is the credited response.

20. **B**   Specific

You know there are two elements Out from the question, and the answer choices give you two more, so you know you'll have four spaces total in the Out column for this question. P and W occupy two of those. For each answer choice, then, consider who is left In and check whether that arrangement violates any clues.

A. No. If P, W, H, and L are Out, then M, S, and T are In, which violates clue 2.

B.

Yes. If P, W, H, and M are Out, then L, S, and T are In, which does not violate any clues.

C. No. If P, W, H, and S are Out, then L, M, and T are In, which violates clue 2.

D. No. If P, W, L, and M are Out, then H, S, and T are In, which violates clue 1.

E. No. If P, W, S, and T are Out, then H, L, and M are In, which violates clue 1.

21. **E** Specific

If M is selected, then H, P, and T must all be Out. The remaining elements are L, S, and W. From clue 3 you know that S and W cannot both be In. Since you must have a minimum of three courses In, one of them will be In while the other will be Out. You still have one spot left to fill, so L must be In.

$$\text{IN } (\tfrac{3}{4}) \mid \text{OUT } (\tfrac{4}{3})$$

$$\text{M } \underline{\text{L}} \ \underset{W}{\overset{S}{\_}} \mid \text{P T H } \overset{W}{\_}_{S}$$

A. No. This is possible but it doesn't have to be true.

B. No. This is false.

C. No. This is possible but it doesn't have to be true.

D. No. This is false.

E. Yes. This must be true.

22. **B** General

This question is essentially asking you for a pair of elements that can never be Out together. Use your prior work and deductions to eliminate answer choices.

A. No. Your work from question 21 shows that it's possible for both H and S to be Out together.

B. Yes. If you put both L and T Out there are only two more potential spaces in the Out column. Since L is not involved in any of the placeholders you noted in your deductions, it uses up the extra fourth space (meaning you'll have three spaces in the In column). Because T is already Out, you know you also need to have either P or M Out to satisfy the (P&T)/M placeholder. But since you'll also need to have, at minimum, one element each from the (S&M)/H and (P&S)/W placeholders, you'd end up with five elements, rather than four, in the Out column. Therefore, it's not possible to put both L and T Out at the same time.

C. No. Your work from question 18 shows that it's possible for both L and W to be Out together.

D. No. Your work from question 20 shows that it's possible for both M and P to be Out together.

E. No. Your work from question 21 shows that it's possible for both T and W to be Out together.

58

23. **B** Complex

This question asks you to replace clue 2 with one of the answer choices and achieve the same result. So you are looking for a choice that says if M is selected, P and T are not; if at least one of P or T is selected, then M is not.

A. No. This does not connect M to either P or T.

B. Yes. If M can be only with L, S, and W, then that means it cannot be with either P or T, which is what clue 2 says.

C. No. This does tell you that P cannot be with M, but it allows T and M to be In together, which goes against the original clue.

D. No. This tells you that T cannot be with M, but it allows P and M to be In together, which goes against the original clue.

E. No. If you symbolize this as a conditional, you get P and T → ~M and M → ~P/~T, which is not the same as the original clue.

Section 4: Arguments 2

1. **E** Resolve/ Explain

Fact 1: Automated flight technology can guide an aircraft reliably from navigation to landing. Fact 2: Even when functioning correctly, this technology does not completely guard against human error.

A. No. According to Fact 2, you are concerned only with trying to explain the situation when the technology is functioning correctly.

B. No. This would not explain why the technology isn't a perfect safeguard against human error.

C. No. The argument states that it is not a perfect safeguard against human error even when it is functioning correctly. You are not concerned with instances during which it malfunctions.

D. No. This choice does not explain why correctly functioning flight technology does not prevent such errors.

E. Yes. If automated flight technology responds directly to human commands, then that would explain how it could function correctly and still make errors. If a human makes an error, then the flight technology would simply carry out that error.

2. **C** Weaken

The author concludes that a person can invariably keep his/her hands warm by putting on an extra layer of clothing. The author supports this by stating that by keeping your vital organs warm you can warm your hands as well. However, just because extra clothing can keep your hands warm does not mean it always will, so you want to look for an answer choice that exploits this gap in the argument.

A. No. The question requires you to attack the ability of an extra layer to keep one's hands warm, not the importance of keeping one's hands warm.

B.   No. The way in which one adds extra layers of clothing to keep one's hands warm is irrelevant.

C.   Yes. This choice exploits the strong language in the conclusion by showing there are times when an extra layer of clothing will not keep one's hands warm.

D.   No. Despite being less effective at warming the hands than turning up the heat, an extra layer still could keep the hands warm. Thus, this choice does not weaken the conclusion.

E.   No. Although the physical effort required to put on an extra layer of clothing may not be enough to warm the hands, other factors (such as the body warmth the extra layer may help contain) could help warm the hands, so this doesn't weaken the argument.

3.   **A**   Main Point

The author concludes that the reason music with a simple recurring rhythm exerts a strong primordial appeal is that it reminds us of the womb. Why? The first sound heard in the womb is the comforting sound of the mother's heartbeat which, along with the womb's warmth and security, birth takes away.

A.   Yes. This almost perfectly restates the conclusion.

B.   No. This is a premise.

C.   No. This is provided as one of the reasons that people are comforted by the womb; thus it is a premise, not the conclusion.

D.   No. This choice is too broad. The author specifically discusses the appeal of music with simple recurring rhythms. The fact that people seek the warmth and security that was taken away at birth serves to explain why such music is appealing.

E.   No. The fact that the mother's heartbeat is a simple rhythmic sound is a reason that people like music with a similar sound; thus it is a premise of the argument.

4.   **C**   Principle
Match

The author states that even though people can detect whether a sentence in their language is grammatical, they are not able to specify the particular grammatical rules. You must find a similar case in which people are able to identify a particular concept without being able to state the rules that guide that concept.

A.   No. This choice describes a case in which people are able to perform one sort of action but are not able to perform a completely separate kind of action.

B.   No. This choice deals with two separate groups of people. The argument deals with a single group of people who can perform one action but cannot cite the particular rules guiding their action.

C.   Yes. This choice is similar to the principle underlying the original argument in that it deals with people who are able to identify a particular concept but are unable to cite the rules guiding that concept.

D.   No. While the first part of this choice is similar to the original argument in that it deals with a single group of people in relation to a concept, the latter half differs from the argument in that it discusses the same people not being fully able to recall the details of that concept.

E.   No. This choice concerns people who know the rules of chess but may not be able to play chess very well. This does not match the principle underlying the original argument.

5. A   **Flaw**

The company president concludes that when somebody is finally selected for the consultant position, the company will surely have selected one of the best possible management consultants. The reason the president gives for this belief is that they are interviewing only applicants who have worked for the top 1 percent of firms worldwide. The problem, however, is that the best consultants might not necessarily have worked at those top firms.

A. Yes. This choice addresses the assumption that the best consultants work for the top firms. Perhaps the best consultants do not work for the best firms, in which case hiring someone who has worked for one of those firms wouldn't guarantee that the company has hired one of the best consultants.

B. No. The sample size is never mentioned.

C. No. This choice describes a part-to-whole flaw, while the argument actually contains a whole-to-part flaw. The company president assumes that what is true of the top firms (the whole) is true of each consultant working in those firms (the part).

D. No. The argument mentions only interviewing and selecting people. It never actually mentions the hiring process.

E. No. The company president does not assume that the consultants will be highly competent at every task.

6. D   **Inference**

The passage details techniques used by beginner and expert chess players. Beginners tend to decide each move by considering the consequences. An expert player, however, typically makes use of pattern-recognition techniques in which the player recalls relevant prior experience to help determine the next move.

A. No. The author never states who is better at thinking through the consequences. This information goes beyond the passage.

B. No. While the author states that pattern-recognition techniques are what the experts use, he never claims that they are what should be used. Moreover, the author never states whether beginning chess players have the ability to use such techniques.

C. No. How to improve one's chess skills is never mentioned in the passage.

D. Yes. The passage states that expert players primarily use pattern-recognition techniques in which players recall previous experiences.

E. No. This choice is irrelevant; the passage does not discuss how to improve one's chess skills.

7. A   **Resolve/ Explain**

Fact 1: The best way to dry kernels in order to make popcorn is to dry the corn in the sun while the corn is still in the field. Fact 2: Even though this is the best way, the farmer dries them on a screen in a warm, dry room. You need to find a choice that explains why he doesn't make use of the best method in practice.

58

A. Yes. This choice explains why the farmer does not use the sun-drying method. Drying corn in the field is not possible because the region's cloudy season coincides with the time during which he would generally dry popcorn.

B. No. This choice would give the farmer even more incentive to dry the kernels in the field. You need an answer choice that explains why he doesn't.

C. No. The passage states that drying popcorn on its stalks in the field is the best method. Even if there are other ways to dry the kernels, this doesn't explain why the farmer does not choose the best method.

D. No. This choice does not explain why the farmer does not dry popcorn in the sun.

E. No. What happens when popcorn is dried too much is irrelevant.

8. **B**   Flaw

The factory manager concludes that the factory must be refurbished in order to make its products more competitively priced and thus survive. The support for this conclusion is that the factory's manufacturing equipment is outdated and inefficient, which results in higher prices for the automobile parts it produces. However, the manager states that this is only one reason the parts are expensive. The flaw is that the manager shifts from noting one way to make products more competitively priced to stating that it is the only way to achieve this goal.

A. No. The fact that prices may change over time is irrelevant to the argument.

B. Yes. This choice identifies the manager's flawed assumption that because refurbishing the factory could make products more competitively priced, it is therefore the only way to achieve this result.

C. No. There is no reverse causation flaw in this argument.

D. No. The argument does provide a reason for the expensive products—outdated and inefficient manufacturing equipment.

E. No. The factory manager does make a definite recommendation; he concludes that the factory must be refurbished.

9. **A**   Inference

The passage states that some pythons hatched in Africa and some pythons recently hatched in North America have a deadly liver disease. The passage further states that the disease is difficult to detect in its early stages and that all pythons with the disease die within six months of contracting it.

A. Yes. The passage tells you that some pythons hatched in North America have the deadly liver disease. You know the disease is difficult to detect and all pythons with the disease will die within six months. You can link these two pieces of information together and infer that some pythons hatched in North America will seem okay but will die within six months.

B. No. The passage states that a greater proportion of African-hatched pythons have the disease, but you do not necessarily know that this is due to a higher susceptibility rate to the disease among African-hatched pythons. There could be any number of other reasons that the disease is more prevalent among African-hatched pythons.

C. No. The passage states that pythons die within six months of contracting the disease, not that they die within the first six months of life.

D. No. The first sentence states that the reason for the large number of inexpensive pythons was the arrival of a major shipment of pythons from Africa.

E. No. The passage never discusses the conditions of pythons hatched in areas other than Africa and North America.

10. **D** Weaken

The author concludes that most people need to take vitamin pills. The support for this conclusion is that although nutritionists believe the daily requirement for vitamins can be reached by eating five servings of fruits and vegetables daily, most people eat far less than this amount. However, the author does not consider that there are perhaps other ways of obtaining the daily requirement for vitamins.

A. No. The premises tell you that most people do not even consume five servings of fruits and vegetables to begin with, so this is irrelevant.

B. No. The different levels of nutrients in fruits and vegetables are irrelevant. The argument already states that most people do not eat enough fruits and vegetables to meet the daily vitamin requirement.

C. No. Regardless of what the agreed-upon amount is, the passage states that people do not eat enough fruits and vegetables to fulfill their daily vitamin requirement.

D. Yes. This choice directly weakens the conclusion by showing that it may be possible to acquire the amount of vitamins needed each day from sources other than vitamin pills or fruits and vegetables.

E. No. This is irrelevant; the argument is not concerned with fiber.

11. **E** Necessary Assumption

The researcher concludes that armadillos do not move rapidly into new territories because many of the ones he had tagged the previous spring were found near the location of their tagging the following spring. There is a gap in this argument between finding the tagged armadillos in the same location at one point in time and asserting that they never moved into new territories at all.

A. No. This may support the conclusion by affirming the sample size, but it is not something that is essential for the conclusion to work.

B. No. This may weaken the argument by questioning the sample size, but it is not something the researcher assumes.

C. No. This is not necessary to the argument. Even if predators did kill some of the armadillos that had been tagged, the conclusion could still work.

D. No. Even if the tags could be removed by the armadillos, it would not change the fact that most of the armadillos the researcher recaptured were found near the location of their tagging the previous spring.

E.   Yes. This choice links the idea of finding the armadillos in the same location of their tagging to their remaining in that location since the time they were tagged. If you negate this choice—a large majority of the recaptured armadillos DID move to a new territory in the intervening summer—the conclusion would certainly fall apart. Thus, this statement is necessary to the researcher's argument.

12.   **A**   **Reasoning**

Sahira concludes that governments are justified in subsidizing artists. Her support is that in order to make a living from art, artists would have to create work that would gain widespread popularity instead of their best work. Sahira assumes that an artist's best work would not gain widespread popular acclaim. Rahima responds to Sahira by questioning this assumption.

A.   Yes. This choice describes how Rahima responds to Sahira's argument.

B.   No. Rahima does not support Sahira's argument.

C.   No. Rahima disagrees with Sahira's premises. The passage makes no mention of how Rahima feels about Sahira's conclusion that governments are justified in subsidizing artists.

D.   No. Rahima actually disagrees with Sahira's premises.

E.   No. Rahima never points out a contradiction in Sahira's argument. Rather, Rahima takes issue with an assumption in Sahira's argument.

13.   **C**   **Inference**

The passage states that small adult frogs are unable to live in arid climates, but large adult frogs can. This is due to the animals' moisture requirements, the most important factor in determining where frogs can live. You can link this information to the fact that the Yucatán peninsula has an arid climate in the north and a wet climate in the south to support the notion that large adult frogs would be able to live in more places on the peninsula than would small adult frogs.

A.   No. The passage never mentions the ability of small and large adult frogs to coexist.

B.   No. If anything, the passage suggests the opposite. Because small adult frogs are limited to wet areas, frogs in such areas probably weigh less on average than do frogs in arid regions.

C.   Yes. Because moisture requirements are the most important factor in determining where frogs can live and because the passage states that large adult frogs can survive in arid climates (as opposed to small adult frogs), this choice is supported. Large adult frogs can survive in both arid and wet climates, so they can live in more of the peninsula than small adult frogs can.

D.   No. The passage never mentions the ratio of large adult frogs to small adult frogs in the south.

E.   No. The passage indicates that small adult frogs cannot survive in the north.

14.   **D**   **Flaw**

The editorial concludes that the government should address the rising crime rate. The editorial bases this on the premise that 77 percent of people feel that crime is increasing and 87 percent think tougher sentences should be handed out. However, the editorial makes a leap from a premise that states that people *feel* the crime rate is increasing to a conclusion that assumes that the crime rate actually is increasing.

A. No. Just because more people are concerned about the sentencing of criminals than are concerned about crime itself does not mean the survey is inconsistent.

B. No. The editorial does not make this connection.

C. No. No other surveys are considered, but this is not the flaw in the editorial's argument.

D. Yes. This choice correctly points out the editorial's presumption that the crime rate is rising simply because people think the crime rate is rising.

E. No. The editorial never states that tougher sentences are the most effective means of lowering the crime rate.

15. **B** Inference

Find an answer choice that can be supported by the facts given in the passage.

A. No. The language in this choice is too strong.

B. Yes. The passage states that human cognition alone cannot verify computer-dependent proofs and such proofs can never provide the degree of certainty that might otherwise be achieved from verifying by human calculation.

C. No. This choice is too strong. Just because a computer is used does not mean it had to be used, as noted in the last sentence of the passage. You know only that the degree of certainty is reduced in the case of proofs that rely crucially on computers.

D. No. The passage states that if something cannot be verified by human cognition, then one cannot be certain of it. Verification through human cognition is a necessary component of certainty. This choice, however, claims that corroboration via human calculation is the only thing needed for certainty.

E. No. The passage discusses only computers. Thus, whether it is feasible for other artificial devices to supplement the abilities of humans is unknown.

16. **B** Principle Match

Madden concludes that more problems are created when industrialists address the problems of farming because industrialists tend to oversimplify. The author presents an example in which industrialists separate the problems of water retention and water drainage and choose to solve them separately instead of viewing them as related functions. This strategy of separation and simplification ultimately creates more problems than it solves. The correct answer should capture the idea that farming problems should not be oversimplified.

A. No. Madden never states that water drainage and retention are the most important parts of good farming.

B. Yes. This goes along well with the argument. Madden states that industrialists should not simplify problems in farming because that strategy usually leads to oversimplification. Thus, problems in this area should be viewed in all their complexity.

C. No. The argument compares only farmers and industrialists.

58

D. No. The argument states that industrialists usually oversimplify things and therefore create more farming problems, but this does not mean that such techniques are always bad.

E. No. The argument states only that the typical approach of industrialists is usually flawed in relation to farming.

17. **D** | **Necessary Assumption**

The critic concludes that it is impossible for a contemporary work of literature to be a tragedy because this age no longer takes seriously the belief that human endeavors are governed by fate. The critic states that the only way a work of modern literature can be viewed as a tragedy is if the protagonists are seen as possessing nobility. There is a missing link between viewing protagonists as having nobility and taking the idea of fate seriously.

A. No. If anything, the argument actually suggests the opposite of this.

B. No. The critic never presumes that the belief that human endeavors are governed by fate is false.

C. No. The critic never discusses whether any plays were misclassified.

D. Yes. This choice establishes a link between taking the idea of fate seriously and viewing the protagonist as possessing nobility. If you negate this answer choice, you will see that it is indeed necessary to the conclusion. If those whose endeavors are not regarded as governed by fate are seen as possessing nobility, then works of modern literature may still be tragedies, which is contrary to the critic's conclusion.

E. No. While a work containing an ignoble character may not be considered a tragedy given the critic's criteria, this choice is not necessary to the argument.

18. **E** | **Flaw**

The author concludes that the graduate students should not unionize. The author supports his statement by stating that the majority of graduate students disapprove of the attempt. However, it is not clear that the majority of graduate students disapprove; rather, the majority of graduate students were unaware of any unionization attempt. Thus, the feelings of the majority of graduate students toward unionization are unknown, which casts doubt on the validity of the author's conclusion.

A. No. The argument never mentions any long-standing practice.

B. No. The argument is focused on whether graduate students disapprove, not on why they do or don't disapprove.

C. No. The author bases his conclusion on the belief that the majority of graduate students disapprove of the attempt, not that the majority of them are unaware of the attempt.

D. No. The author doesn't really discuss the reasons for unionizing; the argument is focused on whether to do so.

E. Yes. The author assumes that the majority of graduate students disapprove of unionizing from a premise stating that the majority of graduate students are unaware of unionizing efforts. Thus, he is confounding this lack of awareness, which is akin to lack of approval (you can't approve if you aren't aware), with active disapproval.

19. **B**

The author concludes that Griley does not believe in democracy. The author supports this claim by stating that Griley is an elitist who believes that popular artwork is unlikely to be good. The problem with the conclusion is that the author never explains what characteristic Griley has that makes him a non-believer in democracy. The only thing you know about those who do believe in democracy is that they have a high regard for the wisdom of the masses. If you could link together those who believe popular artwork is not likely to be good to those who do not have a high regard for the wisdom of the masses, then the conclusion would work.

A. No. The author never suggests that this is a requirement to be an elitist.

B. Yes. If this statement is true, then the conclusion is true. Griley believes that if an artwork is popular it probably won't be good. And if everyone who holds such a belief does not have a high regard for the wisdom of the masses, then that would mean Griley does not have a high regard for the wisdom of the masses. By virtue of the premise, this would mean he does not believe in democracy.

C. No. The argument states that Griley is an elitist.

D. No. This choice would not help explain why Griley does not believe in democracy.

E. No. This choice treats having a high regard for the wisdom of the masses as sufficient for believing in democracy, whereas the argument treats having a high regard for the masses as necessary for believing in democracy. This choice does not explain why Griley does not believe in democracy.

20. **E**

Fact 1: Salt intake tends to increase blood pressure. Fact 2: During a study some people who had very high salt intake before and during the study maintained low blood pressure levels. You need to figure out why these people had low blood pressure despite having high salt intake.

A. No. You must figure out how some people had high salt intake but low blood pressure. You are not concerned with those who have high blood pressure.

B. No. Like (A), this choice concerns itself with those who have high blood pressure.

C. No. Like (A), this choice concerns itself with those who have high blood pressure.

D. No. The paradox at hand involves those with low blood pressure and high salt intake. Knowing more information about those with very high blood pressure and very low salt intake does not help.

E. Yes. This choice explains how salt intake could be very high while blood pressure remains low. If people with abnormally low blood pressure eat salty foods, it could raise their blood pressure to a level that is higher but still relatively low compared to others' levels.

21. **D**

The author concludes that many people greatly overestimate the odds of winning a major jackpot. However, the premises never mentioned overestimating jackpots. Rather, the premises simply stated that few people win major jackpots and those who do win receive a lot of media attention. The author also says that most people come to have some awareness of events that receive extensive media coverage.

58

You must link the idea of overestimating the odds of winning to being aware of events receiving extensive media coverage.

A. No. The argument never states that media coverage of those who have won a major jackpot downplays the odds against winning.

B. No. Those who receive media attention without winning jackpots are not relevant.

C. No. There could be other reasons that people overestimate their chances of winning the lottery.

D. Yes. This choice links one's awareness of media coverage of jackpot winners to overestimating one's chances of winning. If you negate this answer choice ("Becoming aware of individuals who have won a major jackpot does not lead people to incorrectly estimate their own chances of winning such a jackpot."), the conclusion is no longer valid.

E. No. The argument never mentions people who are heavily influenced by the media but do not overestimate their chances of winning the lottery.

22. **C** Parallel Flaw

The argument states that there are two things sufficient to bring about a successful book tour: It must be well publicized and the author must be an established writer. The conclusion, however, assumes that just because you have an established writer and a successful book tour, the tour must have been well publicized. The argument essentially commits a necessary-sufficient error by flipping the necessary component and one of the sufficient components.

A. No. Unlike the original argument, which had two factors sufficient to bring out a single outcome, this argument has a single factor sufficient to bring out two outcomes.

B. No. This choice incorrectly assumes that what is true of this year was true of last year, which does not match the flaw in the original argument.

C. Yes. This operates just like the original argument. In this argument, watering cacti more than twice a week is a sufficient factor to bring about the plant's death. In the conclusion, however, the plant's death is presented as one of the factors sufficient to know the plant was watered more than twice a week. In other words, the argument switches the necessary and sufficient terms.

D. No. This argument is not flawed.

E. No. This argument is not flawed.

23. **B** Strengthen

The author concludes that eight linear craters were probably caused by volcanic events and not meteorites. The author supports this by stating that all of the craters are different ages and cannot be from both sources due to the craters' linearity. To strengthen the conclusion, you need either a choice that shows that meteorites cannot cause linear craters from different time periods or a choice that states that volcanic activity can.

A. No. You are trying to strengthen the idea that volcanic activity can cause craters of different ages, whereas this choice is discussing craters of the same age.

B. Yes. This choice supports the conclusion that volcanic activity probably caused the eight linear craters by questioning the likelihood of meteorite craters of different ages forming a straight line.

C. No. This would only weaken the idea that volcanic events caused the craters.

D. No. If anything, this choice weakens the conclusion by questioning whether volcanic events can produce craters similar to those produced by meteorites.

E. No. While this choice may seem appealing at first since it questions the ability of meteorites to create linear craters, it is ultimately concerned with a single meteor shower, implying that the craters created would thus be from the same time period. However, the argument is concerned with the cause of linear craters of different ages, so this choice doesn't strengthen the conclusion.

24. **B**   **Sufficient Assumption**

The author concludes that rare innovators tend to anger the majority. The author supports the conclusion through a long chain of reasoning: 1) Such innovators are dissatisfied with merely habitual assent to widely held beliefs; 2) those who are dissatisfied with habitual assent to widely held beliefs tend to seek controversy; and 3) those who seek controversy enjoy demonstrating the falsehood of popular viewpoints. What's missing, though, is the final link: the idea that those who enjoy demonstrating the falsehood of popular viewpoints tend to anger the majority.

A. No. This choice considers a single person who is both angered and dissatisfied with merely habitual assent to widely held beliefs. In the argument, the person who is angered and the person who is dissatisfied are two separate people.

B. Yes. This links the new information in the conclusion to the premises as discussed above.

C. No. The argument does not discuss people who hold beliefs not held by a majority of people.

D. No. What you're looking for is a choice that states that those who demonstrate the falsehood of popular viewpoints anger the majority. This choice flips around the necessary and sufficient terms.

E. No. Like (D), this choice flips around the necessary and sufficient terms.

25. **A**   **Principle Match**

Claude considers salting one's food before tasting it a negative trait in job candidates; in Claude's view, such a decision is based on inadequate information. Larissa responds to Claude's statement with two analogies, each of which demonstrates that taking an action beforehand based on a general rule is sound policy.

A. Yes. This perfectly describes the principle used by Larissa. In both the supermarket and credit card examples, Larissa shows that sometimes performing an action before ascertaining whether it is the best decision is reasonable since previous experiences have shown it to be so.

B. No. Larissa never states that one should not use observations of job-related behavior to judge a person's character.

C. No. Although the type of behaviors discussed by Claude and Larissa do not appear to be job related, this choice does not match up with the idea underlying Larissa's examples, which is that there may be a reasoned policy behind one's actions even if they are taken prior to establishing a need for them.

D. No. Larissa never discusses social norms.

E. No. Larissa never mentions excusing a person for possible lapses of rationality.

Chapter 9
PrepTest 59:
Answers and
Explanations

ANSWER KEY: PREPTEST 59

Section 1:
Games

1. C
2. A
3. C
4. D
5. C
6. C
7. E
8. D
9. B
10. D
11. D
12. E
13. C
14. A
15. D
16. A
17. A
18. E
19. D
20. E
21. E
22. B
23. B

Section 2:
Arguments 1

1. A
2. D
3. A
4. E
5. E
6. C
7. E
8. B
9. C
10. D
11. B
12. C
13. C
14. D
15. A
16. E
17. E
18. D
19. C
20. D
21. C
22. A
23. D
24. B
25. B
26. B

Section 3:
Arguments 2

1. A
2. A
3. C
4. C
5. C
6. B
7. A
8. B
9. D
10. E
11. B
12. A
13. D
14. C
15. C
16. E
17. A
18. D
19. E
20. D
21. E
22. D
23. B
24. E
25. B

Section 4:
Reading
Comprehension

1. C
2. C
3. E
4. B
5. C
6. B
7. A
8. E
9. C
10. E
11. B
12. A
13. E
14. B
15. A
16. C
17. D
18. D
19. C
20. E
21. B
22. A
23. B
24. D
25. D
26. C
27. D

EXPLANATIONS

Section 1: Games

Questions 1–5

This is a spatial 1D order game with some distribution requirements in which you have to assign seven departments—F, H, I, L, P, S, and T—to three floors—bottom, middle, and top, with a maximum of four departments per floor. Your diagram should have three rows, labeled B, M, and T, with spaces for four letters on each floor.

Clue 1: $\boxed{\text{PT}}$

Clue 2: $\boxed{\begin{array}{c} \text{H} \\ \text{I} \end{array}}$

Clue 3: L must be alone.

Deductions: From clue 2, you know that H can't be in B and I can't be in T. Because that block can go only in two places (T and M or M and B), you know that L can go only in T or B. Because L must be all by itself, the PT block can go only with H or I. The two unrestricted elements, F and S, also will be with H or I. Overall, there are only two ways the HI block and L can be arranged: Either the HI block is in T and M, respectively, with L in B, or the HI block occupies M and B, respectively, with L in T.

Here's the diagram:

			Scenario 1	Scenario 2
FHILPST	~I	T	H _ _ _	L
	~L	M	I _ _ _	H _ _ _
	~H	B	L	I _ _ _

1. **C** [Grab-a-Rule]

   Use the clues to eliminate answer choices. Clue 1 eliminates (B). Clue 2 eliminates (A) and (E). Clue 3 eliminates (D). Therefore, the credited response is (C).

2. **A** [Specific]

   Put I and P in M. From clue 1 you know that T will also be in M. From clue 2 you know that H will be in T. This forces L into B, with F and S either in T or M. Only (A) could be true.

~I	T	H $^F/_S$
~L	M	I P T $^F/_S$
~H	B	L

3.   **C**   **General**

Use your clues, deductions, and past work to eliminate answer choices. You're looking for a choice that must be false.

A.   No. This could be true. If F, H, P, and T are all on one floor, that leaves I and S for another floor, and then L by itself on the remaining floor. This doesn't violate any clues, so it's possible.

B.   No. Your work from question 2 shows that this is possible.

C.   Yes. From your deductions, you know that one of H, I, or L occupies a space on each floor. Since this choice doesn't contain any of those elements, you'll either have too many elements on a floor or violate clue 2. Therefore, this choice must be false.

D.   No. This could be true. Because F and S are essentially interchangeable, this is the same as (A).

E.   No. Your work from question 2 shows that this is possible.

4.   **D**   **Specific**

Draw the FS block and see where it can go. F and S will have to be with either H or I, taking up three spaces out of four, so the PT block must also be with either H or I, as you know from clue 3 that L must be by itself. Since both of the possibilities from your deductions are feasible, try them both out, making sure you allow for some flexibility in placing the blocks.

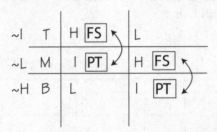

A.   No. If there's only one department on a floor, it would have to be L, and you know from your deductions that L can't go in M.

B.   No. Both H and I will have three departments each on their floors. L will be by itself.

C.   No. There are either one or three departments per floor.

D.   Yes. This is possible in the second arrangement in your diagram.

E.   No. There are either one or three departments per floor.

5.   **C**   **Specific**

From clue 1 and your deductions, you know P is always with T and one of either H or I. Since L must be alone, F and S must be on the same floor as each other with one of either H or I. From your deductions, you know there are only two way to arrange H, I, and L, so you can map out both scenarios on your diagram.

```
~I   T   | H  FS  | L
~L   M   | I  PT  | H  PT
~H   B   | L      | I  FS
```

A.   No. This is never true.

B.   No. This is never true.

C.   Yes. This is true in both cases.

D.   No. This could be true, but you're looking for what must be true.

E.   No. This could be true, but you're looking for what must be true.

Questions 6–10

This is a 1D order game with a 1:1 correspondence between elements and spaces. Your task is to order seven photographs—F, G, H, I, K, L, and M—on a wall. The columns of your diagram should be numbered 1 through 7 across the top.

Clue 1: $\boxed{GK}$

Clue 2:   H ≠ 1; H—K

Clue 3: $\boxed{IL}$ / $\boxed{LI}$

Clue 4:   M = 1/2/3

Clue 5:   F = 1/7

Deductions: Link the first two clues together to get H—$\boxed{GK}$. Now you know H can't go in 1, 6, or 7. Furthermore, G can't go in 1, 2, or 7, and K can't go in 1, 2, or 3. From clue 4 you know that M can't be in 4, 5, 6, or 7. From clue 5 you know that F can't be in columns 2 through 6.

Here's the diagram:

```
          ~G    ~G                          ~H    ~H
          ~K    ~K    ~K    ~F    ~F    ~F    ~G
          ~H    ~F    ~F    ~M    ~M    ~M    ~M

          1  |  2  |  3  |  4  |  5  |  6  |  7
FGHIKLM   ___|_____|_____|_____|_____|_____|_____
```

6. **C** Grab-a-Rule

Use the clues to eliminate answer choices. Clue 1 eliminates (A). Clue 2 eliminates (B). Clue 3 eliminates (D). Clue 5 eliminates (E). Therefore, the credited response is (C).

7. **E** Specific

If I is immediately before G, you can link your clues together in one big chain: H—|LIGK|. Since the LIGK block takes up so much space, it can only go in either 3/4/5/6 or 4/5/6/7. Try each scenario on your diagram. In the first instance, if the block takes up 3/4/5/6, both M and H would have to come before it, with M in 1 and H in 2, leaving F in 7. If the block is in 4/5/6/7, however, F would have to be first, followed by either M or H in slots 2 and 3.

~G	~G				~H	~H
~K	~K	~K	~F	~F	~F	~G
~H	~F	~F	~M	~M	~M	~M
1	2	3	4	5	6	7
M	H	L	I	G	K	F
F	M/H	H/M	L	I	G	K

A. No. This does not occur in either scenario.

B. No. This does not occur in either scenario.

C. No. This does not occur in either scenario.

D. No. This does not occur in either scenario.

E. Yes. This is possible in the second scenario.

8. **D** Complex

Unfortunately, you have to try each choice to see whether it tells you where everything else goes.

A. No. This tells you only that K is fifth.

B. No. The GK block could be just about anywhere after that, so this doesn't tell you much.

C. No. You don't know whether L is before or after it.

D.

					~H	~H
~G	~G				~F	~G
~K	~K	~K	~F	~F	~F	~G
~H	~F	~F	~M	~M	~M	~M
1	2	3	4	5	6	7
L	I	M	H	G	K	F

Yes. If L is in 1, then I is in 2 (clue 3), putting M in 3 (clue 4) and F in 7 (clue 5). The only slots left for H, G, and K are 4, 5, and 6, respectively, so this choice allows you to determine the placement of all seven elements.

E.   No. This doesn't tell you where anything else goes definitively.

9.   **B**   [Specific]

Put M in 2. However, this doesn't lead to many more definite placements. Four of the choices will be possible, but one must be false, so try the choices until you find one that doesn't work. Start with (A), which tells you that M is in 2 and H is in 3. You actually have already seen this in question 7, in which both elements are in identical spaces, so eliminate this choice. Choice (B) tells you that M is in 2 and H is in 4. This means the GK block will have to follow H, but what about the other block with I and L? This arrangement leaves no room for both blocks to fit, so it's not possible. Therefore, (B) is the credited response; there is no need to try the other choices.

					~H	~H
~G	~G				~F	~G
~K	~K	~K	~F	~F	~F	~M
~H	~F	~F	~M	~M	~M	~M
1	2	3	4	5	6	7
	M					

10. **D**   [Complex]

You need to find a rule that would replace H—[GK] and have the same overall effect on the game.

A.   No. This is more restrictive than the original rule, which places H anywhere before the GK block.

B.   No. The first half seems to come close, but the second half is too restrictive and doesn't leave open the possibility of I or L coming first.

C.   No. This is less restrictive than the original, leaving open the possibility that the GK block comes before H.

D.   Yes. Cross off "unless" and replace it with "if not." Now you can diagram it as ~H$_2$ → M—H—GK; the contrapositive is ~M—H—GK → H$_2$. This means that either H is in 2 and GK will have to follow it at some point (remember that if H is in 2, there's no way for G to come before it because of G's attachment to K), or H comes somewhere before G and after M, which can be only in 1, 2, or 3. So no matter what, H can't be first and has to be before the GK block. Therefore, this choice has the same overall effect as the original clue.

E. No. The second part of this choice doesn't allow F to be in 7, so it's more restrictive than the original.

Questions 11–16

This is an In-Out game. In this game, you're deciding which four courses Alicia will take and which four she won't. Her options are G, J, M, P, R, S_3, S_9, and W. Your diagram should be two columns, In and Out, with four spaces in each column. The setup tells you she can take a course only once per semester, so the fact that there are two sections of Statistics means she can't take both S_3 and S_9. Be sure to diagram that and put a placeholder in the Out column.

$S_3 \rightarrow \sim S_9$; $S_9 \rightarrow \sim S_3$

Clue 1: $\sim R \rightarrow J$; $\sim J \rightarrow R$

Clue 2: $M \rightarrow \sim J$; $J \rightarrow \sim M$

Clue 3: $S_9 \rightarrow \sim W$; $W \rightarrow \sim S_9$

Clue 4: $P \rightarrow S_9$; $\sim S_9 \rightarrow \sim P$

Clue 5: G/W; $G \rightarrow \sim W$; $W \rightarrow \sim G$

Deductions: The setup gives you a S_3/S_9 placeholder in the Out column. Clue 1 gives you a J/R placeholder in the In column. Clue 2 gives you a J/M placeholder in the Out column. Clue 5 gives you G/W placeholders for both the In and Out columns. Also, you can link clues 1 and 2 ($M \rightarrow \sim J \rightarrow R$ and $\sim R \rightarrow J \rightarrow \sim M$) to get $M \rightarrow R$ and $\sim R \rightarrow \sim M$. Link clues 3 and 4 ($P \rightarrow S_9 \rightarrow \sim W$ and $W \rightarrow \sim S_9 \rightarrow \sim P$) to get $W \rightarrow \sim P$ and $P \rightarrow \sim W$.

Here's the diagram:

$$GJMPRS_3S_9W$$

IN	OUT
$J/_R$ $G/_W$ _ _ _	$J/_M$ $W/_G$ $S_3/_{S_9}$ _

11. **D** Grab-a-Rule

Use the clues to eliminate answer choices. Clue 1 eliminates (B). Clue 2 eliminates (C). Clue 4 eliminates (A). Clue 5 eliminates (E). Therefore, the credited response is (D).

12. **E** General

The answer choices give you three out of the four courses. Keep track of what the fourth course would be and eliminate any choices that violate clues.

A. No. This violates clue 5.

B. No. This violates clue 2.

59

C.   No. If P is In, then S_9 must be In, but S_9 and W can't both be In (clue 3).

D.   No. If P is In, then S_9 must be In, but S_9 and W can't both be In (clue 3).

E.   Yes. The fourth course could be J or M.

13.   **C**   Complex

Unfortunately, you have to try each choice to see whether it tells you where everything else goes. Start with (A). If R and W are In, you know that G and S_9 are Out; S_9 Out means P is also Out. That's as far as you get, though, so you can eliminate this choice. Choice (B) tells you that R and S are In, but since you don't know which S is In, you can eliminate this choice as well. Choice (C) places R and P in the In column, which means that S_9 is In and W is Out. If W is Out, then G is In, which fills the In column. Therefore, (C) is the credited response; there is no need to try the other choices.

IN	OUT
R P $\underline{S_9}$ G	W $\underline{S_3}$ J M

14.   **A**   Specific

Look at your clues; both clues 3 and 4 have restrictions relating to S_9. Cross out any choice that mentions P or W. Choices (B), (C), (D), and (E) can all be eliminated, leaving you with (A).

15.   **D**   Specific

If Alicia takes S_3, then S_9 is Out along with P (clue 4). If she takes G, then W is Out, too. You can't have both J and M In, so one will be In and the other will be Out. Looking at the placeholders you created when making deductions, you know that either J or R must be In. So you'll have either M and R or J and R; either way, R must be In. Therefore, (D) is the credited response.

IN	OUT
R G $\underline{S_3}$ $\underline{}^{M/J}$	$\underline{}^{J/M}$ W $\underline{S_9}$ P

16.   **A**   Complex

This question changes clue 4; you now have P → S_3 or S_9. All other clues remain the same, though, so use those in addition to the new clue above to eliminate choices.

A.   Yes. This conforms to all the clues, old and new.

B.   No. This violates clue 1.

C.   No. This violates your new clue.

D.   No. This violates both your new clue and clue 5.

E.   No. This violates clue 5.

Questions 17–23

This is a 1D order game with a 1:1 correspondence between elements and spaces. This game asks you to order six meetings in six cities—L, M, N, T, V, and W. Your diagram should have six columns numbered 1 through 6.

Clue 1: T—L

Clue 2: $\boxed{V\ W}\ /\ \boxed{W\ V}$

Clue 3: $\boxed{T\ \_\ \_\ M}\ /\ \boxed{M\ \_\ \_\ T}$

Clue 4: $\boxed{V\ \_\ \_\ L}\ /\ \boxed{L\ \_\ \_\ V}$

Deductions: From clue 1 you know T can't be in 6 and L can't be in 1. If T can't be in 6, M can't be in 3. If L can't be first, then V can't be fourth. While you can see that clues 1, 3, and 4 are connected by T and L, you can't tell with certainty how they will influence each other.

Here's the diagram:

LMNTVW

	~L		~M	~V		~T
	1	2	3	4	5	6

17. **A**   Grab-a-Rule

Use the clues to eliminate answer choices. Clue 1 eliminates (B). Clue 2 eliminates (D). Clue 3 eliminates (E). Clue 4 eliminates (C). Therefore, the credited response is (A).

18. **E**   General

Save this question for later and use your prior work to eliminate answer choices.

A. No. Your work from question 21 shows that this is not always true.

B. No. Your work from question 21 shows that this is not always true.

C. No. Your work from question 21 shows that this is not always true.

D. No. Your work from question 21 shows that this is not always true.

E. Yes. This is true from all your prior work on questions 17, 19, and 21, so it must be the correct answer.

19. **D** `Complex`

Unfortunately, you have to try each choice to see whether it tells you where everything else goes. Start with (A). If L is in 5, then V is in 2, but you don't know anything else for certain. Eliminate (A). Choice (B) tells you that M is in 6, so T must be in 3, but again, you can't determine anything else, so cross it out. Choice (C) puts N in 5, which tells you nothing about the other elements. Eliminate it and move on to (D). If V is in 1, then L is in 4. W must be in 2 and T must go in 3, which means M must be in 6, leaving N in 5. Therefore, (D) is the credited response; there is no need to try (E).

	~L		~M	~V		~T
	1	2	3	4	5	6
	V	W	T	L	N	M

20. **E** `General`

Use your prior work. From questions 17, 19, and 21, you learned W could be in 2 and 3, which eliminates (A) and (D). Since you still have three choices remaining, you'll need to try W in another spot. Place W in 1; doing so puts V in 2 and L in 5. This means you'll have to put T in 3 and M in 6 in order to satisfy clue 1 and clue 3, leaving N in 4. This scenario works, so you can cross out (B) and (C). Choice (E) is the credited response.

	~L		~M	~V		~T
	1	2	3	4	5	6
	W	V	T	N	L	M

21. **E** `Specific`

If M is in 1, then T is in 4 (clue 3). Clue 1 tells you L has to be in 5 or 6. Try out both scenarios. If L is in 6, then V is in 3 and W is in 2, leaving N in 5. If L is in 5, then V is in 2 and W is in 3, leaving N in 6.

	~L		~M	~V		~T
	1	2	3	4	5	6
	M	W	V	T	N	L
	M	V	W	T	L	N

A. No. This is true in the second scenario.

B. No. This is true in the first scenario.

C. No. This is true in both scenarios.

D. No. This is true in the first scenario.

E. Yes. This is not true in either scenario.

22. **B** General

Use your deductions and past work to eliminate choices.

A. No. Your initial deductions show that this cannot be true.

B. Yes. This is possible.

C. No. Your initial deductions show that this cannot be true.

D. No. Your initial deductions show that this cannot be true.

E. No. Your initial deductions show that this cannot be true.

23. **B** General

Use your deductions and past work to eliminate choices.

A. No. Your work from questions 19 and 21 shows that this could be true.

B. Yes. If L is next to W, W can't be next to V; it would be impossible to satisfy both clues 2 and 4.

C. No. Your work from question 21 shows that this could be true.

D. No. Your work from question 21 shows that this could be true.

E. No. Your work from questions 19 and 21 shows that this could be true.

Section 2: Arguments 1

59

1. **A** Strengthen

This is a classic causal argument. The researcher's conclusion is that eating certain fruits causes atypical Parkinson's disease. Her evidence is a research study in which those with atypical Parkinson's regularly ate certain tropical fruits, whereas those without Parkinson's were less likely to eat the fruit. In order to strengthen this argument, you need to prove that correlation equals causation and that there are no other possible causes.

A. Yes. This is one solid way to prove causation: Remove the cause and the effect goes away.

B. No. If anything, this goes in the wrong direction, showing that some people can eat the fruits without developing Parkinson's.

C. No. Again, this weakens the argument somewhat, showing that there may be other causes.

D.   No. The quantity of the fruit may or may not be relevant to the argument, and this choice somewhat weakens the causal relationship.

E.   No. While this may be interesting information and explain why the fruits might be good to eat, it doesn't have anything to do with atypical Parkinson's.

2.   D   Point at Issue

Price's point is that a corporation's primary responsibility is to its shareholders because they take the greatest risks. Albrecht, on the other hand, concludes that a corporation's primary responsibility should be to its employees because their livelihood is at stake. Price and Albrecht disagree both about the point of their arguments (to whom a corporation should be primarily responsible) and about their central premises (who takes the greatest risks).

A.   No. This may be tempting, but the argument is about "primary" responsibility. Albrecht would probably agree that there is some responsibility to shareholders, too.

B.   No. This is one of Albrecht's ideas, but you have no evidence that Price would disagree with this entirely, only about the "primary" responsibility aspect.

C.   No. This choice is irrelevant to both arguments, neither of which mentions recouping losses.

D.   Yes. Albrecht would disagree with this statement, whereas Price would agree because, as he notes, the shareholders take the greatest risk.

E.   No. Neither of the two says this. Price says it's the investment of the shareholders that is at risk, while Albrecht says it's the livelihood of the employees.

3.   A   Strengthen

The argument's claim is that it is extremely unlikely that a large accidental credit will not be detected, despite the large number of transactions processed daily. In other words, it's likely that the bank will catch the accidental credit. In order to support this, you need strong evidence of how the bank will catch the error.

A.   Yes. Another set of computer programs to double-check is strong evidence that there's a system in place to detect errors, especially those made by the first set of programs.

B.   No. While this might reduce errors on the part of bank tellers, this doesn't explain how an error will be detected after it happens.

C.   No. This might explain how a customer will find mistakes, but not the bank itself (reread the conclusion).

D.   No. This choice addresses only the first sentence of the argument, but doesn't support the conclusion.

E.   No. This choice isn't relevant to the conclusion, which is about detecting errors. This explains why hacking is less likely to happen, which has nothing to do with accidental credits.

4. **E**   `Flaw`

The scientist concludes that "in this case" (the 1500s), atmospheric pollution was the cause of global warming. His only evidence is that the pollution coincided with a period of relatively high global temperatures. This is a clear "correlation equals causation" flaw.

A. No. This is irrelevant. No mention is made in the argument as to whether global warming is harmful.

B. No. Reread the conclusion. He's making a claim only about one specific instance, not about all cases involving a rise in temperatures.

C. No. Reread the conclusion; it says "in this case," indicating that the scientist is not making a universal claim.

D. No. While the scientist does take the reliability of the data collection for granted, this is not the central flaw in the conclusion.

E. Yes. This is exactly the flaw as stated above.

5. **E**   `Strengthen`

Gilbert says that the food label, which claims "only natural ingredients," is mistaken, because the food in question contains chemically synthesized ingredients. Sabina, on the other hand, is claiming that the label is not a mistake, that the ingredients are natural. Her evidence is that alphahydroxy acids occur naturally in sugarcane. She makes one major assumption: Things that occur naturally somewhere else are natural, even if they're synthesized. You're looking for a choice that supports her assumption.

A. No. This choice address the time period after the label was written, not this particular batch of cookies.

B. No. This is irrelevant. This doesn't address whether alphahydroxy acids are natural.

C. No. Like (A), this doesn't address this particular batch of cookies.

D. No. Other foods are irrelevant to whether this label is true. Perhaps the other food labels are mistaken as well.

E. Yes. This choice clearly bridges the gap in Sabina's argument and, if true, proves that alphahydroxy acids are natural.

6. **C**   `Flaw`

The author is trying to prove that Jaaks's review of Yancey's book is wrong and that Yancey's book is accurate. The only evidence is the book's similarity to Yancey's other books, all of which have been very popular. The flaw here is a clear appeal to popular opinion in lieu of providing actual evidence that Yancey's book is indeed accurate.

A. No. This goes in the wrong direction. The argument is disagreeing with a respected scholar, not relying on her word to advance his argument.

B. No. No attack on either Jaaks's character or motives is made in the argument. In fact, the author calls her a "respected historian."

C. Yes. This matches the prediction noted above.

D. No. There is no "sample that is likely to be unrepresentative" given in this argument.

E. No. This doesn't match what the author does. There is no reference to Yancey's methods as being the only methods that could yield accurate results.

7. **E** Reasoning

The question asks for the role of the first sentence, which states that attending a live musical performance is a richer experience than is listening to recorded music. The columnist notes that some people say that the reason live music is richer is that we do not see the performers in recorded music. The columnist then disagrees with this explanation and says that there must be another reason, drawing an analogy to people reading stories to support this point. Therefore, the role of the first sentence is to provide a fact that some people explain with one cause, with which the columnist disagrees.

A. No. The first sentence is what the columnist is trying to explain; it is not the point of the argument.

B. No. The reason is in the second sentence, not the first.

C. No. The columnist disagrees with a possible explanation of the phenomenon stated in the first sentence; he doesn't, however, provide his own explanation for it.

D. No. The columnist is refuting the explanation, not the fact itself.

E. Yes. Unfriendly though the wording may be, this is exactly the role of the first sentence. The position that the columnist tries to undermine (live music is richer because you see the performers) is an attempt to explain the phenomenon in the first sentence (attending a live musical performance is a richer experience than is listening to recorded music).

8. **B** Flaw

The author notes that there has been a drop in sales of ice cream, an excellent source of calcium, and a rise in sales of cheddar cheese. His conclusion is that people are choosing to increase their calcium through cheddar cheese rather than ice cream. This is a causal argument, and the central flaw, as in every causal argument, is a failure to consider other causes.

A. No. This is not the flaw in the conclusion. If you take the premises to be true, which you must do on the LSAT, then you don't need more statistics.

B. Yes. There could be any number of other reasons, unrelated to the increase in sales of cheddar cheese, for the decline in sales of ice cream.

C. No. While the dairy farmers do report their sales, this is not the sole source of evidence. This argument makes no appeal to their authority.

D. No. No mention is made of which product is a better source of calcium.

E. No. The author never describes ice cream and cheddar cheese as being mutually exclusive.

59

9. C Parallel Flaw

Diagram this in order to see the pattern. No member can be both a performer and an administrator: P → ~A and A → ~P. Leon and Marta are not administrators, so they must be performers: ~A → P, which is a clear violation of the contrapositive. Look for a choice with exactly the same pattern.

A. No. This doesn't match the original argument. The first sentence should set up two things as mutually exclusive, and this choice does not.

B. No. This choice doesn't contain a flaw. The first sentence tells you that T → ~A/~C, and the second sentence gives you the contrapositive, A&C → ~T.

C. Yes. This contains the same flaw as the original argument. C → ~M and M → ~C. Dumone and Tedenco are not headquartered in Mexico, so they must have headquarters in Canada: ~M → C.

D. No. This choice doesn't contain a flaw. This one tells you that D → ~T. Ms. Tseung represents Dumone, so therefore she doesn't represent Tedenco: D → ~T.

E. No. This choice doesn't contain a flaw. Also, the second sentence gets into stuff about numbers, which doesn't parallel the original argument.

10. D Main Point

The conclusion here can be found in the second sentence; all the stuff in the first and last sentences is evidence to prove the recommendation that the use of chemical fertilizers should be avoided. Use the "Why Test" to be sure you've correctly identified the conclusion.

A. No. This is a premise.

B. No. This is a premise.

C. No. This is a premise.

D. Yes. This is the conclusion as stated above. Note the clue here: The phrase "for this reason" tells you that the prior sentence acts as a premise, so what follows is likely to be the conclusion.

E. No. While this part of the sentence begins with "thus," it isn't the main conclusion of the argument. If you apply the "Why Test," you'll see that only part of the rest of the argument explains why this statement is true.

11. B Resolve/ Explain

Fact 1: The Beta Diet is, overall, a healthier diet. Fact 2: People who follow the Beta Diet for a long time are more likely to be in poor health. You're looking for something to explain both sides of this. How can a diet be healthier, yet the people who follow it more sickly? There has to be some other factor that makes these people have poor health.

A. No. While this accounts for the first fact, it doesn't account for the second one.

B. Yes. If many of the people following the diet for a long time were in poor health to begin with, then that explains why people following the diet are in poorer health even though the diet is better.

59

C. No. Again, this accounts for the first fact, but not the second one.

D. No. This choice splits the group of Beta dieters, but doesn't explain why on average they're in poorer health.

E. No. Other diets are irrelevant.

12. **C** Main Point

Your job is to fill in the conclusion. The argument starts by stating that a theoretical framework is a good thing, and that many historians argue that historical analysis should use a theoretical framework. The author, however, argues that the past is too complicated for all of its main trends to be captured within a theoretical framework. If you fill in your own conclusion, you might say something such as "Therefore, a theoretical framework won't allow for a thorough historical analysis."

A. No. This is close, but too extreme. No benefit, ever? The argument is about the "best" analysis, which doesn't preclude an incomplete one.

B. No. This is irrelevant. You don't know anything about their value in other disciplines.

C. Yes. This matches the idea that a theoretical framework won't be sufficient for a complete historical analysis.

D. No. This choice leads you in the wrong direction; the author suggests that using a theoretical framework may impose some limitations.

E. No. The point is that a theoretical framework won't be enough for a complete historical analysis; therefore, there might be a big difference between the two analyses.

13. **C** Principle Strengthen

Bethany's conclusion is that psychologists should direct their efforts toward identifying nightmare-prone children so the children can be taught to replace their nightmares with pleasant dreams. Her evidence is that adults can be taught a technique to do this and that children who have nightmares are likely to have nightmares as adults. There are several assumptions at work here (that you can teach children the same technique that you teach adults, that this is worth the psychologists' time, and so forth). But mostly, you're looking for a choice that supports the notion that psychologists should direct their efforts toward identifying nightmare-prone children.

A. No. Why children have nightmares is irrelevant; Bethany is concerned only with identifying these children and teaching them techniques to have better dreams.

B. No. This does bridge one of the gaps in the argument, but it's going in the wrong direction (child to adult) and doesn't support the main point about psychologists.

C. Yes. This is the only choice that supports the point that psychologists should direct their efforts toward helping nightmare-prone people.

D. No. The difficulty inherent in either identifying children or teaching adults is irrelevant. And, if anything, this choice weakens the argument.

E. No. The argument is about people who are likely to suffer from nightmares, not people who are unlikely to suffer from nightmares.

59

14. **D** Necessary Assumption

The author concludes that people who eat doughnuts and people who eat bagels consume almost the same number of calories per sitting. The evidence for this is that doughnut eaters consume about 680 calories per sitting and that while bagel eaters consume only 500 calories in bagels, they can add extra calories in the form of spreads. This argument assumes that all factors in the comparison are the same and that there are no other factors that would make the calorie counts different.

A. No. This is a tempting answer, but if you reread the conclusion, you'll see it is only about total calorie content. Therefore, fat and health impact are both irrelevant.

B. No. Bagel eaters' awareness is irrelevant to the argument, which is about the number of calories consumed.

C. No. This is irrelevant; health benefits are not part of the argument.

D. Yes. This is the "no other factors" answer you were looking for. Use the "Negation Test" to be sure: If the doughnut eater does add other substances, then the doughnut eater is going to consume a lot more calories than the bagel eater will.

E. No. The argument does not set up doughnut eaters and bagel eaters as mutually exclusive groups. If you negate this choice, it doesn't have any effect on the number of calories consumed in one sitting and therefore does not invalidate the conclusion.

15. **A** Flaw

Bowers disagrees with the view of some theorists, who believe that society could flourish in a condition of anarchy. However, while the theorists define anarchy as merely the absence of government, Bowers defines anarchy as a social philosophy that countenances chaos. Therefore, the flaw in Bowers's argument is this shift in meaning.

A. Yes. The key term, anarchy, is defined in two different ways.

B. No. The argument is about anarchy, not laissez-faire capitalism.

C. No. Bowers never mentions the number of people who hold a particular view as grounds for rejecting that view.

D. No. Whether a peaceful society will flourish is irrelevant to the argument.

E. No. Bowers doesn't reject the view because it's extreme; he rejects it based on his definition of anarchy.

16. **E** Parallel Reasoning

Start by diagramming the statements. Poet and ~ only epigrams → wit. Lyrical composer → poet, which means, if he doesn't write epigrams, he'll have wit. Then apply this rule to specific case: Azriel is a lyrical composer, which means he's a poet. He doesn't write epigrams, so therefore he has wit. You need to find an answer choice with this same logical structure.

A. No. While this choice contains many of the same elements, the conclusion doesn't match that of the original argument.

B.   No. The original argument has only one exception; this choice starts off with two exceptions, so it can't be parallel.

C.   No. While this choice starts off with the right elements, it ultimately confuses the rule (assigned by this office) with the exception (diplomatic channels) and is therefore not correct.

D.   No. The last sentence in this choice reverses the rule. To match the original argument, it would need to be winter garment → sale, not the other way around.

E.   Yes. Bloom House is a townhouse, which means it's a residential building. It wasn't built last year, so therefore it's subject to the original fire code.

17. **E**   Sufficient Assumption

The argument concludes that a teacher who doesn't know the answer to a question shouldn't pretend to know the answer. The support for this conclusion is that teachers should not cause students to lose respect for them and that students can sense when someone is trying to hide his or her ignorance. There seems to be a big shift in language between the first two sentences of this argument and its conclusion—namely, that if a teacher tries to hide his or her ignorance, students will lose respect for that teacher.

A.   No. Effectiveness is irrelevant.

B.   No. Honesty is irrelevant.

C.   No. The amount of knowledge students attribute to a teacher is irrelevant; the argument is focused on how teachers act when they don't know the answer to a question.

D.   No. The argument is not concerned with whether teachers are able to tell when students respect them.

E.   Yes. This is a clear expression of the language shift in this argument.

18. **D**   Reasoning

This question asks you to determine the role played by the statement "human food-producing...population." This fact is contrary to one of Malthus's arguments, but the overall conclusion agrees with Malthus's prediction. So, what's the role? It's a fact, but it's one that won't be true anymore in the future, when a lack of biodiversity will erode humans' capacity to produce food.

A.   No. It is currently a true statement.

B.   No. There is no well-known view in this argument, only Malthus's prediction, which the argument's conclusion agrees with.

C.   No. The statement actually contradicts Malthus's arguments.

D.   Yes. It's true now, and the argument predicts that this fact won't be true in the future.

E.   No. There is no mention in the argument as to the quality of the evidence supporting this statement.

59

19. **C** **Inference**

Diagram all the facts and see what you know. All bankers are athletes: B → A; ~A → ~B. So you know that at least one of the athletes is a banker, but there might be other non-banker athletes, too. You also know that no lawyers are bankers: L → ~B; B → ~L. Put it all together, and you know that at least one athlete (the one who is a banker) is not a lawyer.

A. No. This is a clear violation of the contrapositive.

B. No. The lawyers could all be athletes, just not banker athletes.

C. Yes. This matches your prediction and must be true. You know there's at least one banker there and that he must be an athlete, but because he's a banker, he cannot be a lawyer.

D. No. This contradicts the end of the sentence.

E. No. As noted in (B), it's possible to have lawyer athletes.

20. **D** **Flaw**

The investigator concludes that the supplier has violated its contractual obligation to limit the rate of defects to 5 percent. The investigator's evidence is that 20 percent of the products sampled were defective. The investigator is assuming that the sample was representative and that there are no additional factors that would make the sample unrepresentative.

A. No. This does address the sample, but not how the sample might be unrepresentative.

B. No. This does address the statistical nature of the flaw. However, if this were the case, then the results would be 50 percent defective, not 20 percent defective.

C. No. Whether only a few of the sites are responsible for the defective products doesn't affect the overall percentage of defective products.

D. Yes. If the inspectors are choosing only samples that they suspect are defective, then the sample is clearly unrepresentative of the whole.

E. No. The number of visits made to each site is irrelevant to the percentage of defective products.

59 21. **C** **Weaken**

The essayist's conclusion is that microorganisms were the main cause of all the extinctions, given that it is implausible that the hunting done by humans at the time could have had such an effect. The central assumption of every causal argument is that there are no other causes or factors that could explain the phenomenon at issue. So to weaken the argument, you need another clear cause of the extinctions.

A. No. This strengthens the argument by showing how the disease-causing microorganisms could have caused the extinctions.

B. No. Whether humans have immunity is irrelevant to the argument, which is focused on animals.

C. Yes. By showing that most of the animals that later became extinct were those hunted by humans, this choice gives a clear alternative cause: hunting.

D. No. This doesn't provide an alternative cause for the extinctions.

E. No. This is outside the scope of the argument, which focuses on the animals that became extinct 2,000 years after the first migrations.

22. **A** Strengthen

The argument's conclusion is that nutritious breakfasts help workers to be more productive. The evidence is a study about workers at two plants, Plant A and Plant B. In order for this argument to be true, you need to prove that the nutritious breakfast was the only cause of the difference in productivity and that the only difference between the groups was their breakfasts.

A. Yes. If Plant B workers didn't consume nutritious breakfasts, then it helps prove the causal relationship (no cause, no effect).

B. No. Starting at the same time of day doesn't have any significance for the workers' productivity or the quality of their breakfasts.

C. No. This establishes that the two groups are comparable, but not that the nutritious breakfast was the cause of the difference in productivity.

D. No. This shows that there's another factor, which would hurt the argument.

E. No. This shows that the two groups were different and therefore hurts the overall argument.

23. **D** Principle Match

A small river town gets flooded, and Hollyville, another town that's been through a disaster, gives out a whole lot of aid, more than it gave to a different town that had been shaken by an earthquake prior to Hollyville's being hit by a tornado last year. What does this show? It seems to suggest that people give more when they've gone through some kind of trouble themselves.

A. No. There's no indication as to whether the people of Hollyville know the victims in the small river town.

B. No. Government relief programs are irrelevant.

C. No. You don't know how much this disaster (the flood) has been publicized.

D. Yes. This is most supported by the situation. Review the timeline—they gave more because they'd been through a disaster recently, too.

E. No. Though Hollyville is a river town, it experienced a tornado, not a flood, so this choice doesn't match.

24. **B** Main Point

You need to supply the conclusion here, so put the premises together. The first premise is that many consumers anticipate paying off their credit card balances before interest charges accrue. The second premise is that in order to win business, credit card companies tend to focus on improving the services that their customers are most interested in. So you might expect, then, that they would focus less on the interest rates they charge and more on other things.

A. No. They would probably care about some things, particularly the services offered by the card.

B.   Yes. If customers expect to pay off their card balances before the interest kicks in, they won't care too much about the advertised interest rates.

C.   No. Borrowing money from banks is irrelevant, and most consumers don't intend to pay the interest anyway.

D.   No. If they anticipate paying off the balance before interest accrues, they'll probably pay attention to the length of time they have before said interest kicks in.

E.   No. The number of places that accept a given credit card is irrelevant.

25.   **B**   [Weaken]

The argument concludes that the level of carbon dioxide in the atmosphere 3 billion years ago was higher than it is today. The evidence is that water, rather than ice, filled the oceans at that time. The only way that could have been possible is if there were a higher level of greenhouse gases, gases such as carbon dioxide and methane, in Earth's atmosphere than there is today. To weaken this, you need to show that something other than carbon dioxide was responsible for keeping the oceans from freezing.

A.   No. This says that volcanic activity was not the cause. In other words, this choice would strengthen the argument.

B.   Yes. If there was a lot of methane around 3 billion years ago, then methane, rather than carbon dioxide, could have been responsible for warming the oceans.

C.   No. This choice also eliminates another potential cause and would therefore strengthen the argument.

D.   No. The increasing complexity of life forms is irrelevant.

E.   No. This choice explains how Earth got warmer, but not why the oceans were warm enough to be full of water 3 billion years ago.

26.   **B**   [Sufficient Assumption]

The conclusion is that the auto repair industry is not a free market. The central premise is that a free market allows each buyer to contact a large number of sellers to figure out what an item is worth. The new idea introduced in the conclusion, but not mentioned in the premise, is the auto repair industry, so the commentator must be assuming that the auto repair industry doesn't allow people to assess what an item is worth.

A.   No. This is irrelevant; the fact that people go to a regular repair shop out of habit doesn't mean that it's impossible to assess what an item is worth.

B.   Yes. This choice links the premise (what these repairs are worth) to the conclusion (auto repairs).

C.   No. Written estimates aren't essential to determining the worth of a repair.

D.   No. This wouldn't matter if the auto repair industry were a properly functioning free market.

E.   No. Regulation of the industry is irrelevant.

Section 3: Arguments 2

1. **A** | Resolve/Explain |

Your job is to explain two seemingly contradictory facts. Investing in new technologies that extend life and decrease pain is very risky because the extensive research and capital needed are unlikely to provide a return on the investment. On the other hand, some people are willing to invest. So you need a choice that explains why some people are willing to take the risk.

A. Yes. If the return is that big, then some people might be willing to gamble with the chance of getting a big payback.

B. No. This is an interesting fact, but it does nothing to explain why people take the risk of investing.

C. No. Other technologies are irrelevant.

D. No. This suggests why people shouldn't take risks, but it doesn't explain why some do.

E. No. This is irrelevant and doesn't help explain why some people invest.

2. **A** | Weaken |

The department chair's position is that a particular textbook was chosen for purely academic reasons, even though the textbook company gave the department a large donation after the book was chosen for a large introductory course. Her evidence is that the department's textbook committee gave this book its highest rating. She's assuming that the rating was based on the academic quality of the book, not on the prospect of a donation. To weaken this argument, you need to prove that they chose the textbook because of the donation, not because of the textbook's academic merit.

A. Yes. This choice clearly shows that the committee was influenced by the donation.

B. No. If anything, this choice strengthens the argument, but it doesn't tell you anything about the quality of the rating.

C. No. The previous year is irrelevant, and you don't know whether last year's textbook was chosen for academics or money.

D. No. This might weaken the argument slightly, but it doesn't prove that anyone was influenced by the donation. Perhaps the department chair was honest, too.

E. No. The fact that this isn't a common practice doesn't prove the department was influenced by the donation.

3. **C** | Inference |

You need to figure out what must be true based on the given facts. Hemoglobin picks up oxygen molecules. With every molecule it picks up, it gets more effective at picking up more molecules. The greatest number of oxygen molecules any hemoglobin molecule can pick up is four.

A. No. You only know that the hemoglobin molecule has become more effective at picking up additional oxygen molecules, not that it's "probably" going to pick up another one.

B. No. This is too extreme. You know that shape is a factor, but not that it's the only factor.

C. Yes. The argument says that as a hemoglobin molecule picks up oxygen molecules, it gets more effective at picking up additional oxygen molecules.

D. No. The last sentence states that each new oxygen molecule changes the shape.

E. No. There's no indication in the argument as to where this process takes place.

4. **C** Resolve/ Explain

On a short trip, a passenger makes an accident more likely. So why, on a long trip, does a passenger make an accident less likely? What could the passenger do on a long trip to prevent accidents?

A. No. This choice doesn't address why accidents are more or less likely.

B. No. This would explain why there are fewer accidents on long trips, but it doesn't address the role of the passenger.

C. Yes. On a long trip, if a passenger is there to keep you awake, you'll be less likely to fall asleep at the wheel and have an accident.

D. No. The facts are about only one passenger, so the number of passengers is irrelevant.

E. No. This has nothing to do with the role of the passenger.

5. **C** Flaw

The question asks you to describe the flaw in the mayor's argument. The mayor's challenger is arguing that although the mayor claims an 8 percent increase in the number of jobs since she took office, the 8 percent increase comes from a national office relocating to the city; all of those supposedly new jobs were actually retained by the original outside staff. The mayor responds to this by citing the 8 percent increase again, completely ignoring the challenger's assertion that all the jobs went to outsiders.

A. No. Both the challenger and the mayor state this explicitly, so neither of them takes this for granted.

B. No. The 8 percent figure has to do with the number of newly employed people, so the number of unemployed people is irrelevant.

C. Yes. The mayor completely fails to address her challenger's evidence.

D. No. The influx of newcomers affected the number of employed people, not the size of the voting public.

E. No. The mayor is addressing the challenger's argument, but ignoring the challenger's evidence; she is not misinterpreting the challenger.

6. **B** Principle Match

An editorial criticizes psychologists for not trying to establish the order in which areas of the brain are activated. The author calls this criticism unfair because the technology to do this doesn't exist. You're looking for a choice in which someone gets unfairly criticized for not doing something that can't be done yet.

A. No. They're being unfairly criticized for using advanced technology, not for failing to do something that can't be done.

B.   Yes. The utility companies are being criticized for not using nuclear fusion, but the technology for harnessing fusion doesn't exist yet.

C.   No. The cost of the food is irrelevant.

D.   No. The technology exists, so sacrificing other subjects is irrelevant.

E.   No. The theory exists, so this isn't about not using a technology that doesn't exist.

7.   **A**   Inference

Put the facts together to see what you know. Although most people know what their bad habits are, they have a tough time quitting because quitting will be painful in the short run, while the long-term benefits are hard to perceive. So what do you know about someone who manages to end a bad habit? The chances are good that that person can perceive the long-term benefits of giving it up.

A.   Yes. If you can perceive the long-term benefit, you'll be more likely to see past and get over the painful short-term effects.

B.   No. This would make it a lot harder to quit.

C.   No. You don't know anything about the quitter's past.

D.   No. The first sentence states that most people are aware of their bad habits.

E.   No. This doesn't explain how they can get past the difficult short-term pain.

8.   **B**   Flaw

The conclusion of this argument is that the Mayan people in general had a strong grasp of sophisticated mathematical concepts. The author's evidence for this is that the writings of the Mayan religious scribes show that they were good at math. The underlying flaw is a sampling flaw; the author assumes Mayan religious scribes are representative of the Mayan people overall.

A.   No. This isn't a flaw in the argument.

B.   Yes. This is exactly what you predicted.

C.   No. Other civilizations are irrelevant.

D.   No. "Scientific" is used only once in the argument; there is no shift in the term's meaning.

E.   No. This isn't a causal argument.

9.   **D**   Main Point

The manager's main point seems to be the first sentence: "There is no good reason…" Why? Because jobs require little to no creativity, and there's no evidence creativity can be taught.

A.   No. This is a premise, not the conclusion.

B.   No. This is too strong. And this functions more as evidence than as a conclusion.

C.   No. This is a premise.

D. Yes. This is in line with the discussion above.

E. No. This is a premise. It's also more strongly worded than the actual argument, which doesn't actually say that creativity is in demand.

10. **E** **Sufficient Assumption**

The producer is arguing that boycotting the advertisers of shows that promote violence amounts to censorship. His reason is that boycotting would result in a restriction of the shows the public can watch. His argument assumes that whatever restricts what the public can view constitutes censorship.

A. No. You need to demonstrate that boycotting is censorship.

B. No. The effect of public boycotts on shows that do not promote violence or erode values is irrelevant.

C. No. This is irrelevant to the conclusion.

D. No. Public agreement is irrelevant.

E. Yes. This links the premises to the conclusion in a manner strong enough to prove that boycotting is censorship.

11. **B** **Strengthen**

The author's point is that books in electronic formats will probably not replace printed books. His evidence is that bookstores and libraries will continue to stock printed books, which is the format desired by the general public. The right answer will prove that printed books will continue to exist.

A. No. This choice favors electronic formats.

B. Yes. As long as publishers continue to print books, they'll continue to be around.

C. No. This also favors electronic formats.

D. No. This choice weakens the argument by suggesting that printed books are on the way out.

E. No. This choice also shows that electronic formats might win out.

12. **A** **Necessary Assumption**

The argument concludes that a decrease in humidity can make people ill. The evidence is a high school's new air-conditioning system, which decreased humidity by 18 percent; this in turn was followed by a 25 percent increase in the number of visits to the school nurse. There are several gaps here, so you need to prove at least one of them: that this particular incident of decreased humidity is representative of what generally happens when humidity is lowered, that the decrease in humidity was the only cause of the increase in visits to the school nurse, or that those visits were actually ill students.

A. Yes. This choice addresses the shift in language between the conclusion and premises. You can also apply the negation test. If none of the visits were due to illness, then the conclusion falls apart.

B. No. This strengthens the conclusion, but isn't necessary to the argument (only 25 percent more went to the nurse). Use the negation test.

C. No. Viruses are irrelevant.

D. No. Try the negation test. Even if this choice weren't 100 percent true, the conclusion could still be true.

E. No. Cost is irrelevant to the conclusion.

13. **D** Weaken

This argument has a statistical flaw; you can spot it from the use of the words "percent" and "likely." The author concludes that one is much less likely to be injured in an automobile accident if one drives a large car rather than a small one. The evidence is a study showing that of people involved in accidents, a higher percentage of people driving small cars were injured. However, the author assumes that similar numbers of large and small cars were involved in accidents. If there were a lot more accidents involving large cars, then the conclusion is weakened. Look for a choice that shows you're more likely to get injured when driving a large car.

A. No. High speed limits are irrelevant.

B. No. This doesn't have anything to do with the likelihood of accidents.

C. No. Medium-sized cars are irrelevant to the comparison of large and small ones.

D. Yes. If a large car is far more likely to be involved in an accident, this skews the relative numbers of injured people toward those who drive large cars.

E. No. This has nothing to do with the relative numbers of injured people who drive large or small cars.

14. **C** Reasoning

The economist's conclusion is that a trade deficit is only an indicator of a weak economy, so a country shouldn't restrict imports to reduce a trade deficit. He supports this conclusion by drawing a comparison to sticking a thermometer in a glass of cold water to relieve a fever.

A. No. He may or may not imply this, but he doesn't claim it outright.

B. No. He uses an analogy to support his point. He doesn't claim the analogy is wrong.

C. Yes. He does use an analogy, as noted above.

D. No. There is no mention of authority.

E. No. He merely demonstrates the futility of a course of action; he never claims it would be disastrous.

15. **C** Parallel Flaw

The first premise is that it's sometimes moral to make threats. The second premise is that it's sometimes moral to ask for money or a favor. The conclusion is that there are circumstances in which it's moral to do both. Look for a choice that combines two premises in this flawed manner: Sometimes one thing is okay. Sometimes another thing is okay. Therefore, it's sometimes okay to do both.

A. No. The first half seems as if it's going to match, but the second half is about "neither," not "both."

B.   No. This choice doesn't combine two premises the way the original argument does.

C.   Yes. This is a clear match of the original argument's flawed structure. Taking A is good. Taking B is good. Therefore, taking A and B at the same time is also good.

D.   No. The first premise states something is good, but the second states that something is bad.

E.   No. The second half of this choice contains a necessary-sufficient error, which doesn't match the flaw in the original argument.

16.   **E**   Necessary Assumption

The author concludes that we will be able to eliminate periodontitis altogether. His evidence is that researchers are developing a way to restore an individual's levels of a particular enzyme, the absence of which is one of the causes of periodontitis. His assumption is that the missing enzyme is the only cause of periodontitis, that there are no other causes.

A.   No. Use the negation test. If restoring the enzyme is not the only way to eliminate periodontitis, that doesn't mean it won't work.

B.   No. The conclusion is about eliminating periodontitis, so this isn't really relevant.

C.   No. The argument merely stated that researchers are developing methods, but it made no claims about when or how soon they will succeed.

D.   No. This is irrelevant. There may be other causes of gum disease unrelated to the genetic mutation.

E.   Yes. Cross off the "not" to negate this choice, and you'll find that the conclusion is no longer valid.

17.   **A**   Resolve/ Explain

Four of these choices will explain why people like to see several new movies a year despite the fact that a majority of movie plots are variations on ones that have been used before. The right answer will either not explain anything or will account for only part of the discrepancy.

A.   Yes. This is the exception. This choice explains why plots might be reused, but not why people enjoy going to several new movies each year.

B.   No. This explains why, despite many similar elements, people enjoy seeing different movies.

C.   No. This shows that, despite the fact that a majority of movies are variations on earlier plots, people who go to many movies probably won't see the same plot used twice.

D.   No. This explains why people would go to see several movies that had very similar plots.

E.   No. This explains how someone could go to several movies in a year and not see the same plot; they're all recycled from decades ago.

18.   **D**   Principle Match

Try to generalize from the author's overall argument. The conclusion is that the government should continue to devote resources to space exploration. The evidence is that many beneficial technologies have been unexpected consequences of space exploration. The overall principle is that the government should continue to devote resources to something that yielded unexpected positive consequences.

A. No. This choice doesn't address unexpected positive consequences.

B. No. This doesn't support the main point.

C. No. This is too strong, and this also doesn't address the argument's conclusion.

D. Yes. This choice is in line with both the conclusion and the premises of the argument.

E. No. While this choice supports the main point, it doesn't address the unexpected beneficial consequences.

19. **E**   Inference

If understanding a word always involves knowing its dictionary definition, then understanding requires knowing the words in the definition. The second sentence tells you that some people, such as all babies, don't know the dictionary definitions of some of the words they utter. What does this suggest? Either babies don't understand the words they're using, or it's false to claim that understanding a word requires understanding its dictionary definition.

A. No. You don't know whether babies understand the words they utter, so you don't know whether this is true.

B. No. This is too strong.

C. No. This one is tempting, but notice that the first sentence begins with "if," which means that the definition it provides for understanding a word is not necessarily true. Since you don't know for certain whether this definition is true, this choice is too strong to be correct.

D. No. You don't know whether babies understand the words they utter, so you don't know whether this is true.

E. Yes. This is the contrapositive of the first sentence. If some babies understand all the words they utter, then that means it's possible to understand a word without knowing its dictionary definition, which means you don't always need the dictionary definition of a word to understand it.

20. **D**   Flaw

The author concludes that the darkest peppered moths were the least likely to be seen and eaten, based on the premise that the lightest ones were the most likely to be seen and eaten. The author assumes that there were no other shades of moth in between the lightest and the darkest that might have been able to blend in better with their backgrounds.

A. No. The number of predators is irrelevant to whether the moths blend in with their background.

B. No. The argument makes no claims about whether moths can control the degree to which they blend in.

C. No. This is too strong. The author addresses only relative likelihoods in general; there is no claim about all moths with the same coloring having the same likelihood.

D. Yes. This is exactly what you predicted above.

E. No. Moths may have other defense mechanisms, but they are irrelevant to this argument.

21.   **E**   **Inference**

The original reason for designing the QWERTY keyboard was to slow down the typist and make it harder to type, because early typewriters would jam if someone typed too fast. Keyboard configurations other than QWERTY have been shown to be more efficient, but the expense and inconvenience of switching to a new keyboard configuration prevent these from attaining widespread use.

A.   No. You don't know anything about most people who have tried non-QWERTY keyboards.

B.   No. According to the historian, the early ones were more likely to jam.

C.   No. This is far too speculative. The early designers still needed to slow down the typists of their day, no matter what was going to happen in the future.

D.   No. The argument says nothing about the benefits to society of switching to a non-QWERTY keyboard configuration.

E.   Yes. If there were no need to prevent jams, then the keyboard would probably have been designed differently.

22.   **D**   **Flaw**

The first sentence of this argument contains a necessary/sufficient flaw; that is, while making an agreement creates an obligation, it is not necessarily the case that someone who has an obligation to act has agreed to perform that action. The second sentence contains a language shift from obligations in general to legal obligations. You need to find a choice that contains both of these flaws.

A.   No. There is no discussion of an action with good consequences in the argument.

B.   No. Other obligations and other reasons are irrelevant to the argument's major flaws.

C.   No. This is not a circular argument.

D.   Yes. The first part matches the necessary/sufficient flaw in the first half of the argument. The second part describes the shift from obligations in general to legal obligations.

E.   No. There's no shift in meaning for the word "action," which is used in the same sense throughout.

23.   **B**   **Reasoning**

The first sentence explains how to predict that something will be invented. But then the author's point is that this cannot happen, because the definition of invention is developing a detailed conception and one can't predict what has already taken place.

A.   No. There's no specific example or counterexample in the argument.

B.   Yes. The "occurrence" is predicting that something will be invented, which the author argues is impossible. The "definition" is the definition of invention.

C.   No. This is a tempting answer, but there's no hypothesis here, only an explanation of how to predict that something will be invented.

D.   No. This has no relevance to the argument.

E.   No. This choice has some of the words from the argument, but it doesn't address the conclusion, which is focused specifically on predicting an invention, not predicting any event in general.

24.   **E**   Flaw

The argument concludes that there can be no complete theory of aesthetics. The support for this conclusion is that while there used to be a relatively complete theory in the eighteenth century, art from the 1960s falls outside the bounds of that aesthetic theory. The flaw here is that the author assumes that aesthetic theory can't be modified to include the rebellious artists of that period.

A.   No. The importance of what the theory should account for is irrelevant to its completeness.

B.   No. The author never discusses what motivated the rebellion or whether it was guided by knowledge of eighteenth-century theory, so this isn't the flaw.

C.   No. Where the theory was developed is irrelevant.

D.   No. The point of the argument is that eighteenth-century theory cannot account for 1960s art, but the author doesn't claim that this is the only art that is not adequately addressed by that theory.

E.   Yes. The author never explains why it's not feasible to update the theory to make it complete.

25.   **B**   Necessary Assumption

The science writer concludes that any slanted interpretations of data in a serious scientific paper will be removed before that paper gets published. The science writer's evidence is that all such papers are reviewed by other scientists who are likely to notice and object to biases they do not share. The assumption here is that the scientists reviewing a given paper wouldn't share the same beliefs and values from which any bias present might derive.

A.   No. Depending on whether the biases are the same as those of the original author, this choice could either help or hurt the argument.

B.   Yes. Negate this choice: If they do all share the same biases, then those biases won't get removed before publication, rendering the conclusion invalid.

C.   No. The value of the papers is irrelevant.

D.   No. Whether the interpretation of data is the only part of a serious scientific paper that can be affected by bias is irrelevant.

E.   No. Negate this choice. Even if there were other ways to remove biases, this doesn't weaken the science writer's conclusion.

59

Section 4: Reading Comprehension

Questions 1–8

Passage A

This passage discusses the difficulties of running computer simulations of large-scale climate trends. The first paragraph notes that while the computer models are accurate, all the variables in the model have a wide range of values and it's important to know what happens when those values change even slightly. The second paragraph explains that the only way to make reliable predictions is to run many calculations and simulations using all the possible combinations of values. The problem is that currently no individual computer is capable of doing all those calculations. The third paragraph describes a solution. If all the necessary calculations are divided up among individual desktop computers connected via the Internet, privately owned computers can work simultaneously to run climate simulations. This kind of public computing project has been successful before, but only when the public has been interested enough to participate.

Passage B

This passage further explores a kind of computing model known as parallel computing. The first paragraph explains that researchers are learning that many of the problems of science are "parallel" and can be solved using parallel methods. The second paragraph gives an example of a parallel system: A large number of similar simple elements function together to comprise a highly complex system. Each ant in an anthill is similar and follows a small, simple set of rules, but the overall system of an anthill is a vastly complex, almost intelligent system. The last paragraph describes how the field of computing is shifting from the use of sequential computing (running one calculation at a time) to the use of parallel computing (using thousands of computers to run calculations simultaneously) to solve computation-intensive problems. Because the problems of science are parallel, the computing used to solve those problems should be parallel, too.

1. **C**   Big Picture

   The main point of passage B is that computing is shifting from sequential computing to parallel computing.

   A. No. This is too narrow. This presents the reason for the shift, not the shift itself.

   B. No. This doesn't even mention parallel computing, and it goes beyond the passage in stating that sequential computing is no longer useful.

   C. Yes. This expresses the overall main point.

   D. No. This choice doesn't mention parallel computing.

   E. No. The human mind is irrelevant.

2. **C**   Reasoning

   Go back to the first paragraph of passage A. The large-scale climate trends are complex systems with lots of variables. In passage B, the only complex system discussed in detail is the anthill.

   A. No. This is the solution to the problem, not the system itself.

B.   No. One ant is not the overall complex system.

C.   Yes. This is a similarly complex system with lots of smaller variables.

D.   No. Climate trends aren't going through a paradigm shift.

E.   No. Speed limits are not a complex system.

3. **E**   Extract
              Infer

Both authors state that the best way to run calculations relating to big complex systems is to use parallel computing rather than sequential computing.

A.   No. The first half of the choice is correct, but the second part is wrong. Parallel computing systems do use brute force; see the second paragraph of passage A.

B.   No. Parallel computing systems might be able to do this.

C.   No. Only passage A mentions this, and they are in fact feasible if the public participates.

D.   No. Individual computers are capable of running simulations, but no single computer can run them sequentially.

E.   Yes. This is consistent with the main points of both passages.

4. **B**   Structure

The author mentions public participation because it's the only way to currently solve the problems of modeling large-scale climate systems.

A.   No. This goes further than the passage's intent; the author doesn't try to encourage anybody.

B.   Yes. The projects have been successful only when the public was sufficiently interested and willing to participate, so public participation is a factor in determining the feasibility of the proposed computing model.

C.   No. The government is irrelevant.

D.   No. The support has existed for other projects in the past, but you don't know whether it currently exists.

E.   No. It's feasible if the public gets interested.

5. **C**   Structure

Both passages describe new ways of thinking about the use of computers to run calculations for scientific problems. Passage A describes one scientific problem and the kind of computing needed to solve it. Passage B further elaborates on the reasons that a computing system will work.

A.   No. Passages A and B are closely related.

B.   No. Passage B agrees with passage A.

C.   Yes. Passage B explains why parallel computing works better.

D.   No. "Brute force" isn't referred to in passage B.

E.   No. Passage B agrees with passage A.

6.   **B**   Big Picture

Both passages describe new ways of thinking about the use of computers to run calculations for scientific problems.

A.   No. This doesn't mention the new approach.

B.   Yes. The new approach is parallel computing.

C.   No. There are no skeptics in either passage.

D.   No. Neither passage claims that it has supplanted the traditional paradigm yet.

E.   No. This choice doesn't mention the new computing systems.

7.   **A**   Extract Infer

The author describes the ant population as a complex whole that works together.

A.   Yes. This is a direct paraphrase of what the author states.

B.   No. This relates to a different paragraph.

C.   No. The question is about ant populations, whereas this choice is about computers.

D.   No. The question is about ant populations, whereas this choice is about computers.

E.   No. The question is about ant populations, whereas this choice is about computers.

8.   **E**   Extract Infer

Passage B is all about how and why such parallel computing systems work, so the author would agree that using many computers simultaneously would be faster than using just one computer working sequentially.

A.   No. The ant colony, not the parallel computing system, is a live computer.

B.   No. The author is in favor of this kind of system.

C.   No. The system would allow for many calculations of all the variables.

D.   No. Passage B doesn't mention the role of the public.

E.   Yes. The author of passage B would favor this system.

Questions 9–15

This passage is advocating for law schools to give more attention to the study and analysis of statutory law. The first paragraph describes how, currently, law students spend a great deal of time on case law, studying cases and judicial decisions. The second paragraph notes that lawyers often learn once they're out of law school that their practice has more to do with interpreting relevant statutes, not prior cases. In the third paragraph, the author states that studying statutory law would improve students' synthesis skills—seeing how statutes form a coherent whole. This would aid their ability to synthesize in other areas of statutory law. The last paragraph addresses a possible objection to the proposal, which is that statutes vary so much from region to region that mastery of one group of statutes would be inapplicable elsewhere. The author answers this objection by stating that it's not the actual statutes that are important, but rather the skills acquired in mastering a given set of statutes.

9. **C** **Big Picture**

This passage is advocating for law schools to give more attention to the study and analysis of statutory law.

A. No. There is no mention of a standard national curriculum in statutory law.

B. No. The author never states that one is more important than the other, just that more emphasis should be placed on studying statutes.

C. Yes. This matches the overall main point, including the author's refutation of the objection.

D. No. This choice doesn't mention statutes.

E. No. This is more extreme than the author's point; the author never claims that law schools fail to impart the necessary skills.

10. **E** **Extract Fact**

Go to the last paragraph, which is where the major objection is raised. The objection is that statutes vary so much from region to region that mastery of one group of statutes would be inapplicable elsewhere.

A. No. Diverting resources isn't mentioned in the passage, so this choice is irrelevant.

B. No. See the first paragraph, which states that currently law students study mostly cases.

C. No. There is no mention in the passage of other means.

D. No. The author does not claim that such training would be irrelevant for those who do not specialize.

E. Yes. This is a direct paraphrase of the objection raised in the beginning of the final paragraph to the teaching of statutes.

11. **B** **Reasoning**

You need an answer choice that suggests that studying statutes would be unproductive or unnecessary and that therefore there is no need to change what students study in law school.

A. No. This strengthens the author's point.

59

B. Yes. If lawyers can learn about statutes quickly and easily, then statutory law doesn't need to be taught in law school.

C. No. The passage addresses this objection by stating that the skills acquired in mastering statutes are what's important, not the statutes themselves.

D. No. This strengthens a fact stated in the first paragraph.

E. No. The author addresses this objection in the last paragraph.

12. **A**   Structure

Why does the author mention synthesis? According to the third paragraph, studying statutory law would improve students' ability to synthesize, which they could in turn apply to other areas of statutory law within their specializations.

A. Yes. The skill of synthesis is a clear benefit of studying statutory law.

B. No. This is the function of the first paragraph, not the third.

C. No. This is an important skill, but the author does not claim it is more important than others.

D. No. Studying statutory law helps you learn the skill of synthesis; the skill is a benefit, not a requirement.

E. No. The author provides an example in the second paragraph, not the third.

13. **E**   Extract Fact

Go back to the passage as needed to verify or disprove each choice.

A. No. The author never discusses synthesis as it relates to the analysis of cases and judicial decisions.

B. No. You know that law schools focus on case analysis, but not why.

C. No. The passage makes no mention of what they have in common.

D. No. The author mentions an objection to including training in statutory law as a standard part of law school curricula; however, the passage doesn't discuss any objections to including it in regionally oriented law schools.

E. Yes. This is answered in the second half of the first paragraph.

14. **B**   Extract Infer

You know from the passage's main point that the author believes that studying statutes is a good thing.

A. No. The passage never states that regionally oriented law schools have been deficient in the teaching of case law.

B. Yes. This is supported by the last sentence of the second paragraph.

C. No. There is no mention of how training in statutory law helps you get better at analyzing cases.

D. No. The author advocates mastering sets of statutes from particular regions.

E. No. The author advocates the study of statutory law for everyone.

15. **A** `Reasoning`

Look for the one that doesn't agree with the author's main point, which is that law schools should give more attention to the study and analysis of statutory law.

A. Yes. This is not addressed in the passage.

B. No. This is consistent with the discussion of statutes in the third paragraph.

C. No. See the first sentence of the passage.

D. No. This is consistent with the discussion of statutes in the fourth paragraph.

E. No. See the first sentence of the passage.

Questions 16–22

This passage is about the sculptor Isamu Noguchi. The first paragraph introduces Noguchi as an unconventional and creative artist who departed from well-known traditions of sculpture. The second paragraph narrates his development as a young sculptor and his work under the sculptor Brancusi. It also discusses his realization that most sculpture uses negative light to communicate. The third paragraph details his initial contact with R. Buckminster Fuller, whose suggestion introduced Noguchi to the materials he would use to create a positive-light sculpture. The fourth paragraph describes the reflective nature of Noguchi's resulting sculpture of Fuller. The fifth paragraph highlights the favorable reaction to Noguchi's work and notes that Noguchi continued to evolve even after such success.

16. **C** `Extract` `Infer`

The author seems to be drawing a distinction between materials that make use of negative light and materials that permanently give off positive-light reflections.

A. No. The passage states that gold can be relied upon generally, not only in certain applications.

B. No. All metals appear to be suited for sculpture, but only gold gives off positive-light reflections.

C. Yes. Brass and bronze can be made reflective (Noguchi polished them) but only nonoxidizing gold can be relied upon to give off positive-light reflections.

D. No. Bronze and brass are metals; nonmetals are never discussed.

E. No. There is no evidence that gold was acceptable to both types of sculptors; all you know is that it is expensive. The experimental metal, chrome-nickel steel, is mentioned in the next paragraph.

17. **D** `Extract` `Fact`

Go back to the passage as needed to verify or disprove each choice.

A. No. This is not addressed anywhere in the passage.

B. No. Art forms other than sculpture are not addressed anywhere in the passage.

C. No. The passage discusses only his use of metal.

D. Yes. This is answered in the second sentence of the last paragraph.

E. No. This is not addressed anywhere in the passage.

18. **D** **Extract Infer**

Go back to the passage as needed to verify or disprove each choice.

A. No. There's no evidence that Brancusi or other sculptors sought to overcome the problems of negative light, only Noguchi.

B. No. Go back to the second sentence of the passage. He might have become a scientist, but there's no information about his training.

C. No. Noguchi's realization about negative light occurred while he was working for Brancusi, not Fuller.

D. Yes. According to the last paragraph, Noguchi was an idea-driven conceptual sculptor who evolved constantly.

E. No. Science is mentioned only in the second sentence of the first paragraph. In this passage, Noguchi is important mostly for his exploration of light.

19. **C** **Reasoning**

Ford developed a material that Noguchi used for art. Find an answer choice in which a material developed for commerce or industry is used for something else entirely.

A. No. The material isn't used for an alternative purpose.

B. No. In Noguchi's case, Ford (the developer) didn't suggest using the material—Fuller did.

C. Yes. In this choice, a new type of strapping material developed for commerce is used for a recreational sport.

D. No. In this case, the new software is actually rejected for a better alternative.

E. No. You're looking for an alternative use of one material, not an exploration of several similar materials.

20. **E** **Extract Infer**

Go back to the passage for each choice.

A. No. The passage makes no mention of whether Fuller himself had ever used the material.

B. No. The end of the third paragraph suggests that Noguchi used the material because of its reflective properties and its availability, not its commercial value.

C. No. This is a misinterpretation of the fourth paragraph; the sculpture doesn't appear to have the shape and dimensions of surrounding objects.

D. No. You don't know this. Perhaps it would reflect negative light and therefore be more like a traditional sculpture (see the end of the second paragraph).

E. Yes. This is supported by the fourth paragraph, the first sentence of which notes that Noguchi's sculpture was an alternate model of traditional, negative-light sculptures. If the perception of the shape and dimensions of Noguchi's sculpture depends on its reflections of the shapes in its surrounding environment, then this wouldn't be the case for traditional, negative-light sculpture.

21. **B**   Extract
              Infer

The sculpture of Fuller is discussed in the third and fourth paragraphs. You know that it was a portrait of Fuller and that it was made with highly reflective material.

A. No. The third paragraph seems to suggest that Noguchi was the first to use this material for sculpture. Other sculptors are not mentioned in connection with the new material.

B. Yes. This choice is supported by the first sentence of the second paragraph.

C. No. There's no description of either Fuller's reaction to the sculpture or Noguchi's reaction to Fuller's response.

D. No. Noguchi offered to sculpt the portrait, but there's no mention of it being a personal favor.

E. No. Brancusi's art did depend on contrasts of light and shadow—see the end of the second paragraph.

22. **A**   Reasoning

The main thesis is that Noguchi was the first person to use positive-light reflections and was therefore creative and revolutionary. Look for a choice that downplays Noguchi.

A. Yes. This suggests that Noguchi may have been copying Brancusi and was therefore not innovative.

B. No. This agrees with the point of the last paragraph, which states that Noguchi continued to evolve.

C. No. This doesn't reveal anything about Noguchi's creativity.

D. No. This agrees with the point of the last paragraph, which states that Noguchi continued to evolve.

E. No. While this appears to relate to the second sentence of the first paragraph, that sentence provides the author's opinion of Noguchi, not Noguchi's opinion of himself. This also doesn't tell you anything about the originality of Noguchi's artistic efforts.

Questions 23–27

This passage provides an evolutionary explanation for the results of an experimental scenario about sharing money known as the Ultimatum Game. The first paragraph describes the game, in which one person—the "proposer"—decides how to split $100 and the second person—the "responder"—decides whether to accept the offer. If the responder doesn't accept the offer, neither person gets any money. The second paragraph details the results researchers have garnered. Most of the time, the proposer offers between 40 and 50 percent of the money and the responder accepts this offer. However, if the proposer offers too small an amount, the offer is often rejected, even though the responder loses out on whatever money he or she would get. The third paragraph describes one possible, albeit incomplete, explanation for such high and fair offers: our prehistoric ancestors' need for group strength. The fourth paragraph gives a more compelling reason: the fact that we have evolved emotionally as members of small groups where it is hard to keep secrets. People reject offers that are too low in order to preserve their self-esteem and reputations; this in turn allows them to benefit in future encounters within their group.

23.   **B**   **Big Picture**

The main idea is that there's an evolutionary explanation for the unexpected results of the Ultimatum Game.

A.   No. This is only about the second paragraph.

B.   Yes. This encompasses the passage as a whole and summarizes the main point.

C.   No. This summarizes only one point of the last paragraph.

D.   No. This mixes up the points made in the last two paragraphs—maintaining group strength is cited as an explanation for why proposers offer fair or large amounts.

E.   No. The need to outcompete rivals is discussed only in the third paragraph and the author does not claim that it is the main driver of participants' behavior.

24.   **D**   **Extract Infer**

Go back to the passage for each choice.

A.   No. "Trust" is never mentioned in the passage.

B.   No. This is too extreme. It contradicts an expectation, but doesn't completely overturn the theory.

C.   No. While the passage does suggest that the results were unexpected based on the assumptions of traditional theoretical economics, it doesn't claim that they were unpredictable.

D.   Yes. There is evidence for this in the last paragraph. The third-to-last sentence notes that we can't distinguish between one-shot and repeated interactions, implying that the Ultimatum Game is a one-shot interaction.

E.   No. The author is claiming that our evolution explains the results of the Ultimatum Game, not the other way around.

25. **D** **Big Picture**

The author's primary purpose is to explain the unexpected results of the Ultimatum Game.

A. No. The passage doesn't survey multiple interpretations; it focuses on just an evolutionary explanation.

B. No. The author gives one incomplete explanation and then moves on to a more compelling one, so the point isn't to show how they complement each other.

C. No. This doesn't mention the explanation.

D. Yes. This nicely summarizes the author's purpose.

E. No. There's no criticism of the experiment in the passage.

26. **C** **Reasoning**

Add your own sentence to the end of the passage based closely on the last sentence. If we want to maintain our reputation for future encounters, this explains why we would both reject low offers and make fair offers.

A. No. This contradicts the point of the explanation, which is that human beings are acting out of (future) self-interest.

B. No. This is irrelevant.

C. Yes. This choice is closely related to the last sentence and ties together the main point of the passage.

D. No. Other benefits are irrelevant.

E. No. This choice isn't closely related to the last sentence of the passage.

27. **D** **Reasoning**

Find the major objection at the end of the third paragraph, which is that the group strength hypothesis doesn't explain why people reject low offers. You need a choice that addresses this inadequacy.

A. No. The size of the groups is irrelevant.

B. No. The presence of hierarchies does not help to explain why people reject low offers.

C. No. This is relevant to the explanation in the last paragraph, not the third one.

D. Yes. If it's counterproductive to be outcompeted by one's rivals, this would explain why someone would reject a low offer.

E. No. This doesn't explain why someone would reject a low offer.

Chapter 10
PrepTest 60:
Answers and
Explanations

ANSWER KEY: PREPTEST 60

Section 1:
Arguments 1

Section 2:
Games

Section 3:
Arguments 2

Section 4:
**Reading
Comprehension**

	Section 1		Section 2		Section 3		Section 4
1.	D	1.	B	1.	A	1.	D
2.	E	2.	D	2.	B	2.	C
3.	B	3.	A	3.	A	3.	D
4.	D	4.	A	4.	B	4.	B
5.	C	5.	E	5.	D	5.	D
6.	B	6.	C	6.	D	6.	E
7.	C	7.	E	7.	C	7.	A
8.	E	8.	C	8.	C	8.	C
9.	D	9.	D	9.	C	9.	A
10.	D	10.	A	10.	C	10.	D
11.	C	11.	C	11.	D	11.	D
12.	A	12.	C	12.	E	12.	C
13.	C	13.	E	13.	D	13.	C
14.	D	14.	D	14.	D	14.	E
15.	B	15.	E	15.	D	15.	A
16.	C	16.	A	16.	E	16.	D
17.	A	17.	B	17.	D	17.	D
18.	E	18.	A	18.	C	18.	C
19.	*	19.	B	19.	D	19.	C
20.	D	20.	B	20.	A	20.	B
21.	B	21.	D	21.	E	21.	B
22.	A	22.	E	22.	A	22.	A
23.	E	23.	C	23.	C	23.	E
24.	C			24.	B	24.	C
25.	C			25.	C	25.	B
						26.	D
						27.	B

EXPLANATIONS

Section 1: Arguments 1

1. **D** | Flaw

Jim concludes that the substance he was examining contained iron. He concludes this on the basis of the fact that magnets attract iron, and the substance became attached to the magnet. Jim confuses a necessary factor (all iron is magnetic) with a sufficient factor (only iron is magnetic). If the substance does contain iron, then it will behave in this way; however, knowing that it behaves this way doesn't prove that it contains iron. It could contain something else that magnets attract (another metal, for example).

A. No. This is not possible because according to the argument, "magnets attract iron."

B. No. This is irrelevant. The attractive object used here was definitely a magnet, so even if iron is attracted to other things, that would have no bearing on what happened.

C. No. Even if this were true, it is not clear what orientation has to do with anything. The argument says that magnets attract iron, but it does not make clear whether they do so in every possible orientation or only in some, so it is impossible to know what bearing this has on the argument.

D. Yes. A magnet attracted this substance. If magnets attract substances other than iron, then the fact that this magnet attracted this substance does not prove that the substance is iron.

E. No. The strength of the attraction is irrelevant. The issue at hand is whether the substance contained iron or not, not how best to attract it.

2. **E** | Reasoning

The argument concludes that the book Horatio wants was either misplaced or stolen. It does so on the basis of the facts that it is not in its proper place, no one is using it, it is not checked out, it is not awaiting shelving, and it is not part of a special display. That is, it rules out the alternatives to being misplaced or stolen.

A. No. There is no general conclusion about the status of similar objects. The only object mentioned is the book that Horatio wants.

B. No. The conclusion is not that there is a deficiency in the library's system for keeping track of books. While a possible next step for this argument would be to say, on the basis of the fact that a book could be misplaced or stolen in this fashion, that the system is deficient, the argument never actually takes this next step.

C. No. There is no generalization that applies to most such objects but not to this one. The only generalization in the argument is that all the books have their proper shelf locations recorded in the catalog, but this appears to apply to Horatio's book, too, since the librarians know that Horatio's book is definitely not where it is supposed to be.

D. No. There is no generalization that fails to hold in one particular instance. Just as in (C), the only generalization is the one in the first sentence, but it applies to Horatio's desired book just as well as to any other book.

E.   Yes. The other possible explanations ruled out are that it is in its proper place, someone is using it, it is checked out, it is awaiting shelving, or it is part of a special display.

3.   **B**   Inference

The last sentence says that if the regulations had been followed, the level of sulfur dioxide would have decreased. The first sentence says that the level of sulfur dioxide did not decrease. Combining these statements, we know that the regulations have not been followed.

A.   No. All of the statements given are about the past. No predictions about the future are logically justified on the basis of generalizations solely about the past.

B.   Yes. The contrapositive of the third sentence is that if the level of sulfur dioxide did not decrease, then the regulations were not followed, and the first sentence says that the level of sulfur dioxide did not decrease. The regulations have not been followed, so there have been violations.

C.   No. All of the statements given are about the past. No predictions about the future are logically justified on the basis of generalizations solely about the past.

D.   No. This might be true based on outside knowledge, but the statements do not mention whether these emissions are significant as sources of air pollution or not.

E.   No. All of the statements given are about the past. No predictions about the future are logically justified on the basis of generalizations solely about the past. The word "never" makes a prediction about the future in this answer choice.

4.   **D**   Reasoning

The argument is structured to disagree with the particular part that the question asks about. The unstated conclusion, signaled by the "However," is that it is not inevitable that there will be a crisis in landfill availability. Thus, the role of the claim asked about is to put forward a point of view that the rest of the argument tries to refute.

A.   No. The ecologist appears to believe that the first sentence is true, since it is stated without any attribution to anyone else or contradicted anywhere. However, the next sentence does not follow from that, because the ecologist does not believe that it is true.

B.   No. The main conclusion is unstated and disagrees with the claim asked about.

C.   No. It is not evidence that supports the argument's conclusion.

D.   Yes. This is indicated by the fact that the ecologist says that "Some people" think this, opening the possibility that he might not, and this possibility is confirmed by the "However" that follows.

E.   No. It is something the argument disagrees with. An intermediate conclusion would be direct support for the main conclusion, not an opposing point of view.

5.   **C**   Resolve/ Explain

The first sentence indicates that disease P does not occur very often in Country X, and the second sentence adds that when it does occur, it causes death more often in Country X than in other countries. The credited response should explain that the few cases of disease P in Country X are much worse than the many cases elsewhere.

A. No. This does not address the fatality rate; even if some forms are more contagious that just means that certain forms are more likely to spread from one person to and does not explain why people die in Country X.

B. No. Even if the people who die of disease P in Country X are from other countries, still does not explain why they die of the disease primarily when they're in Country X their own countries.

C. Yes. If this is true, then the high death rate comes as a natural consequence of diagnosi most severe cases. It connects the low incidence rate—they diagnose only the most seve perhaps they are not diagnosing the less severe cases and are undercounting the actua of the disease—and the high fatality rate—they diagnose only the most severe cases, so are diagnosed are very likely to die.

D. No. This does not address the fatality rate.

E. No. Even if there are other fatal illnesses, this answer still does not explain why this disease, disease P, has this fatality rate. Other illnesses are out of scope.

6. **B**   Weaken

The argument concludes that the effort to save sea otters by removing oil from them was not worth-while. The evidence is that they were not able to save a very high percentage: 18 percent of the otters that were physically seen and counted were saved, and only a fifth of the affected otters were ever found. Since the question stem specifically says to attack the integrity of the evidence, it is likely that this last part—the number of otters never found was estimated somehow—is going to be attacked.

A. No. If sea otters in other areas existed, they would not be relevant to this argument, because this argument is only about this effort for these otters.

B. Yes. The argument claims to estimate the total number of otters, including those that were never found, and it uses this as evidence for its conclusion.

C. No. Even if the process did involve trapping some unaffected otters, it is not clear how that would affect the worth of the effort. The effort still saved some otters and failed to save others.

D. No. The effort did not involve other species of wildlife, so this answer is irrelevant.

E. No. Knowing the costs associated with saving otters would not address the evidence offered in the argument.

7. **C**   Necessary Assumption

The conclusion is that cancer-patient support groups may have genuine therapeutic value. The evidence involves a language shift: The author assumes that the group's reduction in stress levels is connected to a weakened immune system and a vulnerability to cancer. This is the missing link in the chain from support groups to stress levels to immune systems to vulnerability to cancer.

A. No. This answer makes support groups less necessary, because if they can function well under ex-treme stress, then the stress-reducing effects of the support groups are not needed. This hurts the argument instead of helping it.

60

This is not required by the argument, as can be seen from the Negation Test: If disease is a ~~chemical~~ phenomenon at least in part, these groups could still reduce stress, and stress reduc~~tion could~~ still help strengthen the immune system, provided that there is some biochemical reac~~tion to~~ stress reduction.

~~This~~ connects the premises to the conclusion. Use the Negation Test: If stress can't weaken ~~the immune~~ system, then stress reductions won't help the weakened immune system problem ~~raised~~ in the first sentence, which means that the stress reductions no longer necessarily have ~~anything~~ to do with helping cancer victims. The argument falls apart.

~~This is~~ not necessary to the argument. Even if discussing the condition only reduces but does ~~not eliminate~~ the stress of the condition, the stress reduction could help the immune system.

~~This is backwards:~~ If stress is a symptom of a weakened immune system, then stress reduction ~~won't help the~~ immune system, because it will alleviate only a symptom of the problem, not the ~~cause of~~ it.

particul

~~This is the~~ first sentence. The second sentence is a fact about adobe, and the third sentence ~~explains~~ why this feature of adobe is useful in deserts, which justifies that adobe is good for building in deserts. The third sentence also makes a contrast with other building materials to justify that adobe is special in this regard. The other three sentences support the first, and the credited response should match the first sentence as closely as possible.

A.   No. This is not what the first sentence says.

B.   No. This is not what the first sentence says.

C.   No. This is not what the first sentence says.

D.   No. This is not what the first sentence says.

E.   Yes. This is almost exactly the same wording as the first sentence.

9.   **D**   Resolve/
     Explain

The apparent discrepancy is that two studies found different percentages for patterned stems, one 70 percent and the other 40 percent. The credited response should give some reason that the two studies would have found different percentages of plants with patterned stems.

A.   No. This doesn't address the patterned stem percentage.

B.   No. Other plant species are out of scope.

C.   No. This doesn't address the patterned stem percentage.

D.   Yes. If this is true, then both studies were looking at the same plants, but some of the plants that the first study saw as patterned were not seen as patterned by the second study.

E.   No. The primary or secondary focus of each study does not address why they found different rates of patterns.

10. **D** **Flaw**

The conclusion is the second sentence. The evidence is the third, which is an appeal to popular opinion. The fact that many people of unknown nature oppose the plan is not evidence that the plan is bad, just that it is not universally popular.

A. No. The argument does not distort the editor's view. It presents the editor's proposal accurately.

B. No. The argument does not need to establish that the alternative is viable. The conclusion is not that the alternative is better, just that the proposal would be damaging.

C. No. The letter writer's self-interest is not involved in this argument.

D. Yes. The argument appeals to the opinions of 20,000 people, but there is no evidence that they are correct.

E. No. The argument does not take this for granted, because even if a third option were available, the conclusion could still be true: The proposal could still be damaging.

11. **C** **Strengthen**

The conclusion is that students are offered a more in-depth and cosmopolitan education than they have been before. The evidence is that the university's history textbooks include a broader discussion of African, Asian, and indigenous American cultures than they once did. The credited response should connect cultural inclusivity (from the premises) and an in-depth and cosmopolitan education (from the conclusion).

A. No. How interesting the courses are is irrelevant to the conclusion, which is about how in-depth and cosmopolitan they are.

B. No. Innovative study-abroad programs do not necessarily make for an in-depth and cosmopolitan education so this does not support the conclusion.

C. Yes. This suggests that the evidence, that the history course textbooks are more culturally inclusive, leads to the conclusion, that the educations are more in-depth and cosmopolitan.

D. No. This would weaken the argument by saying that the history courses may be the exception, not the rule, and as a result, the educations are not in general in-depth and cosmopolitan.

E. No. Textbooks that cover only a single culture are irrelevant to the conclusion about multicultural textbooks leading to an in-depth and cosmopolitan education.

12. **A** **Flaw**

The conclusion is that the disclosures reduce the public's ability to be informed about the safety of airlines. The evidence is that airlines will not give complete reports under the proposed policy. The flaw is that the argument assumes that these incomplete reports will not increase the public's information about airline safety.

A. Yes. If incomplete reports still give important information about airline safety, then the conclusion may no longer follow. The argument is neglecting this possibility.

60

B. No. Whether the public has a right to know is irrelevant to the conclusion about whether the proposal will help the public to know.

C. No. Other ways to learn information are irrelevant to the conclusion about whether the proposal will help the public become informed about airline safety.

D. No. The responsibility for accuracy is irrelevant to this argument's conclusion, which is about whether the information would be accurate, not whose responsibility it is.

E. No. The revenue of airlines is irrelevant.

13. **C** Weaken

The conclusion is the final sentence, suggesting that the economists in the first sentence are wrong. The economists, according to the first sentence, think that financial rewards are the most important factor in choosing a job. The reason that the argument claims that this is wrong is the second sentence, which shows that high salary is not named as the most important factor. There is a language shift from the first sentence to the second: The financial rewards of a job and the salary may not be identical.

A. No. This answer provides a disadvantage of high wages, and the argument argues that high wages are not a decisive factor, so this would not weaken the argument.

B. No. If people prefer high wages over low wages in otherwise identical situations, then this shows that people care about wages somewhat, whereas the argument is concerned about it being the strongest incentive.

C. Yes. If this is true, then evidence about salaries is completely inadequate for drawing a conclusion about overall financial rewards, because salary is only one part of financial benefits. This says that the evidence provided is not sufficient to draw the conclusion given.

D. No. This is in the wrong direction. If this is true, and further, if this enjoyment is more important than financial rewards, then this answer choice strengthens the conclusion.

E. No. Information about what some people know about jobs does not impact the argument about motivations for choosing a job.

14. **D** Necessary Assumption

The researchers concluded it is questionable to reason that small classes sizes lead to greater time devoted by the teachers to each student and in turn to greater student engagement. They concluded this because in reduced-size classes, students' grades were similar to how they had been beforehand. This argument is assuming that students' grades are related to engagement.

A. No. Try the Negation Test: Even if other schools are also appropriate for study, the sizes of the schools studied in the argument are not specified, so it is not clear how this affects the argument.

B. No. Whether teachers devote more time to some students than others or equal amounts of time to each student does not impact whether being able to devote more time to students overall will increase student engagement.

C. No. The author's argument about smaller class sizes does not discuss the number of teachers. In fact, for a given number of students to have smaller class sizes, there would necessarily be more teachers.

60

D.   Yes. The reason that the argument doubted that the smaller class sizes led to increase student engagement was that their grades did not increase, which assumes that grades are a good proxy for student engagement.

E.   No. The reasons for parental support for the proposed law are irrelevant to whether the law will work.

15. **B**   Flaw

Rebecca's conclusion is that the manufacturers' claims about cost savings are not exaggerated. Her evidence is that she personally has had lower water bills since she installed the type of faucet in question. She does not mention whether she has saved as much as the manufacturer of the faucet claimed she would, however, which means that it is not clear whether the claims were exaggerated in her case.

A.   No. This does not directly address the conclusion about the manufacturers' claims.

B.   Yes. While Rebecca does indicate that her bills are lower, she never indicates whether it is as much as the manufacturer claimed.

C.   No. All claims do not need to be consistent in order to be correct. Rebecca's argument is that her bills are lower so the manufacturers' claims about her water-saving faucet are not exaggerated.

D.   No. Consumer satisfaction is not relevant to the conclusion about the manufacturers' claims.

E.   No. This does not address the issue of how much the manufacturer claimed would be saved.

16. **C**   Weaken

The company spokesperson's conclusion is the final sentence. The evidence is that automobiles that predate 1980 account for considerably more of the local air pollution than the company's plant does. The credited response that weakens this argument should indicate that there is some problem with the plan to buy old cars to reduce air pollution.

A.   No. Even if this is true, these automobiles still account for much more pollution than the plant does.

B.   No. This doesn't address the issue of whether the plan will work. Indicating that buying old cars will save the company money doesn't provide enough information to determine which will reduce air pollution more.

C.   Yes. If this is true, then the non-running cars that the company is going to purchase aren't going to be the cars that are contributing to the pollution mentioned anyway, so buying these non-running cars is unlikely to affect air pollution much, if at all.

D.   No. Even if this is true, it doesn't address the comparison between buying old cars and redesigning the plant, since the old cars would still account for much more pollution than the plant.

E.   No. This does not address whether the car-buying plan is better than redesigning the plants.

60

17.   **A**   **Parallel**

The argument gives a conditional statement, that if our ancestors had not been motivated by a certain desire, then humanity would not have survived. It denies the "then" part of the conditional, saying that humanity has survived. It identifies one part of the conditional, the desire, with another concept, altruism, and then concludes something regarding the "if" part of the conditional and the additional concept, that the ancestors were at least partly altruistic.

A.   Yes. This argument gives a conditional statement, denies the "then" part, identifies one part of the conditional with another concept, and concludes something to do with the "if" part of the conditional and the additional concept, just as the original argument does. Students raising their grades can be identified with humanity surviving, increasing study time with the desire to sacrifice themselves, and good time management with altruism.

B.   No. This argument gives a conditional statement but never denies the "then" part. It's missing a statement that organisms are not capable of manufacturing their own carbohydrate supply, to match that humankind has survived in the original argument.

C.   No. This argument gives a conditional statement but never denies the "then" part. It's missing a statement that their endemic species will not perish, to match that humankind has survived in the original argument.

D.   No. This argument gives a conditional statement but never denies the "then" part. It's missing a statement that the natural resources will not be depleted, to match that humankind has survived in the original argument.

E.   No. This argument has an either/or in its conclusion, which doesn't match the original argument's conclusion. Furthermore, it needs to say in the premises that public buildings do harmonize with their surroundings, to match that humankind has survived in the original argument, but it does not say this.

18.   **E**   **Principle Strengthen**

The bus driver concludes that the company should not reprimand him for the accident.

His evidence is that the garbage truck was exceeding the speed limit, while he was abiding by all traffic regulations. The credited response needs to say that the premises lead to the conclusion: If a bus driver is abiding by traffic regulations, then he should not be reprimanded, even if he is involved in an accident.

A.   No. Who is responsible does not directly determine whether the bus driver should be reprimanded.

B.   No. The police report did not confirm who was at fault, so this conditional does not give any information about the issue at hand.

C.   No. This tells when the bus driver should be reprimanded but not when he shouldn't be reprimanded.

D.   No. This tells when the bus driver should be reprimanded but not when he shouldn't.

E.   Yes. This collision did not result from the bus driver's violating a traffic regulation, so this principle says that the bus driver should not be reprimanded.

19. **N/A** Item removed from scoring.

20. **D** `Necessary Assumption`

The conclusion says that today's generation of television viewers exercises the imagination less frequently than radio listeners did. The evidence is that radio was the dominant form of entertainment previously, and it requires listeners to exercise their imaginations. Since no evidence is given about television or the present generation, one assumption has to be about the present generation. Specifically, the argument assumes that television does not exercise the imagination as much as radio, nor does anything else that the present generation does.

   A. No. This does not address the conclusion, which was about exercising one's imagination.

   B. No. This goes against what the argument said about radio: It was a dominant form of entertainment, but it caused people to exercise their imaginations regularly.

   C. No. The desirability of this type of entertainment is not addressed in the passage, nor is it relevant to whether television does in fact cause people to exercise their imaginations less.

   D. Yes. Try the Negation Test: If something did fill the gap for exercising the imagination, then today's generation would exercise the imagination as often as the previous generation did, which would make the argument fall apart.

   E. No. Try the Negation Test: If television drama does require its viewers to think about what they see, this may or may not constitute exercising the imagination, and it may not require them to think about what they see as often as radio required them to think about what they heard. The conclusion could still be true.

21. **B** `Parallel Flaw`

This argument depends heavily on conditional and quantity statements, so consider analyzing them as such. The first sentence says that if someone is a candidate in this year's mayoral election, that person is a small-business owner ("candidate → smallbusiness"). The second sentence is a quantity statement directly ("most small-business owners are competent managers"). The third sentence says that if a person is a competent manager, then that person does not lack the skills to be a good mayor, or equivalently, has the skills ("competent manager → has skills"). The final sentence, the conclusion, is a quantity statement (most candidates have the skills). The problem is that even though all the candidates are small-business owners, they might happen to be in the minority of small-business owners who aren't competent managers and as a result may not have the skills. Thus, it is illicit to conclude that most of the candidates have the skills.

   A. No. The "most" statement in the premises aligns being in the company's management with being a small-business owner in the original argument and working in the sales department with being a competent manager in the original argument. However, if being in management is like being a small-business owner, then to match the first premise in the original argument, being in management should be on the right side of a conditional somewhere (all people of some sort or other are in management). No such premise exists in the argument. This does not match. This argument is actually valid: Combine the second premise with the third and you get the conclusion.

   B. Yes. If being on the menu at Maddy's Shake Shop is like being a candidate in the mayoral election, being fat-free is like being a small-business owner, being sugar-free is like being a competent manager, and being low in calories is like having the skills to be a good mayor, this argument matches the original perfectly (even in order, which is more than it has to do).

60

C. No. The conclusion does not match. It contains a "never" when it should contain a "most."

D. No. This argument draws a weaker conclusion than is justified by the premises. The first sentence might diagram as, "film at film festival → less than an hour long," and the third might diagram as, "less than an hour long → ~intermission." These should combine to the conclusion, "film at film festival → ~intermission." The premises justify the conclusion that none of the films at the film festival has an intermission, but the conclusion actually drawn is that most of them do not.

E. No. This argument, while convoluted, is valid. If all the bike helmets have plastic, and most have rubber, then most of the bike helmets that have plastic have rubber, too.

22. **A** `Sufficient Assumption`

The argument establishes in the premises that money exists across all societies and that money is a human invention. It concludes that the invention of money occurred in more than one society independently. The one aspect of this that it has not justified in the premises is the "independently" part; the credited response should say that the cultures were independent of each other at least to the necessary extent for this argument.

A. Yes. If this is true, then the money used there—which had to have been invented at some point—was invented independent of other inventions of money, which is good enough for the conclusion to be true.

B. No. If this is true, it does not affect the conclusion, which is about money, not language.

C. No. The premises already establish that money is an invention, so other features of society are not relevant to the conclusion about money.

D. No. This justifies a conclusion that money is useful, but that has nothing to do with the argument's actual conclusion about its multiple, separate inventions.

E. No. The premises already establish that money is universal, so societies cannot have abandoned it anyway.

23. **E** `Principle Strengthen`

The argument concludes that libel laws can prevent anyone from having a good reputation. The evidence is that libel laws prevent people from saying anything bad about public figures. There is a language shift from people not saying anything bad about public figures to no one having a good reputation, so the credited response should indicate that no one saying anything bad about public figures leads to no one having a good reputation.

A. No. The conclusion is about the effect of the presence of libel laws, not the absence of them.

B. No. The conclusion was stronger than this, that no one would have a good reputation, so the "even if" doesn't make sense.

C. No. Whether something is libel or not is irrelevant to the issue of what the effect of strong libel laws is.

D. No. This does not address the issue of why no one would have a good reputation when there are strong libel laws.

E. Yes. The contrapositive of this is that if no other public figures have bad reputations, then public figures cannot have good reputations. If libel laws result in no one saying anything bad about public figures, and if that in turn results in no public figures having bad reputations, then no public figures will have good reputations (according to this conditional).

24. **C** **Inference**

A. No. The argument says that mammals cannot digest cellulose, but they might get beneficial health effects without digestion.

B. No. The argument says that beta-glucans do this, but it does not say that they are the only things that do this.

C. Yes. The last part of the argument says, "the antitumor activity of beta-glucans increases as the degree of branching increases," and, "These extracts prevent tumor growth...by increasing immune cell activity." Putting those two together, when the degree of branching increases, the antitumor activity of beta-glucans increases, which happens because they increase immune cell activity.

D. No. Immune-cell activity in general was not discussed.

E. No. Mushrooms can do this, but the argument does not say or imply that any organism can.

25. **C** **Reasoning**

The comparison that is utilized is marked with the phrase "just as...so." Paraphrase the comparison: Societal laws are like manners in that both are obeyed because obedience to such rules is what's normal, not because there are penalties for lack of obedience.

A. No. Varying from society to society was not the basis of the comparison.

B. No. The basis to consider when adopting something was not the comparison made, though this answer may be tempting because "custom" was definitely part of the comparison. It was not the basis for adoption.

C. Yes. This paraphrases the comparison effectively. The reason for compliance was custom both for manners and for law.

D. No. The argument did not actually say that either laws or manners do not prescribe behavior that is ethically required.

E. No. The nature of the penalties was not the basis of the comparison. Whether the penalties were strict or not was not the issue here.

60

Section 2: Games

Questions 1–6

The Wednesday through Friday order should constitute the core of the diagram, and there is a morning/afternoon aspect that should be represented with rows.

This game has a one-to-one correspondence between elements and spaces in the diagram: Each space has one element and each element has one space.

Clue 1:

J
K

or

J
Q

Clue 2:

N
R

or

S
R

Clue 3:   Q $\Big\langle$ K
                   N

Deductions: By clues 1 and 2, J is somewhere in the morning and R somewhere in the afternoon. By clue 3, neither K nor N can happen on the first day, and Q can't be on the last day. Q is heavily restricted: It appears in two of the three clues, which means that it should draw attention whenever answer choices need to be tested.

Your diagram should look like this:

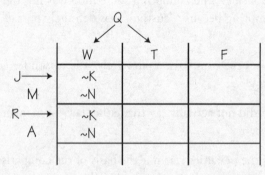

1. **B** | Grab-a-Rule |

   Clue 1 eliminates (E), because J is in the afternoon. Clue 2 eliminates (D), because R is in the morning. Clue 3 eliminates (A) and (C), because in (A), K is on the day before Q, and in (C), Q and N are on the same day.

2. **D** | General |

   Use previous work and the Process of Elimination.

   A. No. The arrangement could be W: S, R; T: J, Q; F: K, N.

60

B. No. The arrangement could be W: Q, S; T: J, K; F: N, R.

C. No. The arrangement could be W: Q, S; T: N, R; F: J, K.

D. Yes. If Q is on Thursday morning, then K and N must be on Friday (clue 3). Since J needs to be in the morning (clue 1), it would be Wednesday, but it needs to be on the same day as Q or K, which are on Thursday and Friday, respectively.

E. No. The arrangement could be W: J, Q; T: S, K; F: N, R.

3. **A** General

Neither N nor K can be on Wednesday (clue 3). Choice (A) shows K on Wednesday. Since this cannot be true, it is the answer.

4. **A** Specific

If K is on Friday morning, then clue 1 forces J to be with Q either on Wednesday or Thursday. The other day that is not filled with the J/Q block has the R block from clue 2, either S/R (if it is on Monday, since N cannot be on Monday) or S/R or N/R (if it is on Tuesday).

A. Yes. This is possible if, for example, the arrangement is W: S, R; T: J, Q; F: K, N.

B. No. Either R or Q is on Thursday afternoon. N is either on Thursday morning as part of the N/R block or on Friday afternoon to be after Q.

C. No. Wednesday morning is either J or S. Q is either on Wednesday afternoon or Thursday afternoon, either way as part of the J/Q block.

D. No. This violates clue 2.

E. No. Wednesday afternoon is either Q or R. S is either on Wednesday morning as part of the S/R block, Thursday morning as part of the S/R block, or Friday afternoon to occupy the last remaining space.

5. **E** Specific

If Q is in the morning, then J must be in the morning on the same day as K (clue 1). Since Q must come before the J/K block and N (clue 3), the arrangement must be W: Q, S; T: J, K; F: N, R or W: Q, S; T: N, R; F: J, K.

A. No. This could be done in the arrangement W: Q, S; T: J, K; F: N, R.

B. No. This could be done in the arrangement W: Q, S; T: J, K; F: N, R.

C. No. This could be done in the arrangement W: Q, S; T: N, R; F: J, K.

D. No. This could be done in the arrangement W: Q, S; T: N, R; F: J, K.

E. Yes. If Q is on Monday morning and S is on Thursday, then the J/K block goes on Friday, S must be part of the S/R block on Thursday, and as a result, the only space left for N is on Wednesday, violating clue 3.

6. **C**   General

Wednesday morning cannot have K or N (clue 3) or R (clue 2). Use previous work to confirm J, Q, and S, could be on Wednesday morning.

Questions 7–12

There are six elements and six spaces in the diagram, and there is a one-to-one correspondence between elements and spaces in the diagrams.

Clue 1:
$$L \diagup \!\!\! \diagdown \, \begin{array}{c} \\ H \\ \end{array} \diagdown \!\!\! \diagup M$$

Clue 2:
$$\begin{array}{c} L \\ \diagdown \!\!\! \diagup P \end{array} \!\!\! \diagdown J$$

Clue 3: M—P → H—G
        G—H → P—M

Clue 4: G ≠ 6

Deductions: Combine the first two range clues and build a large web. From clues 1, 2, and 3, H and J are the only things that can appear last. H and J cannot be first or second (clues 1 and 2). L cannot be fifth (clues 1 and 2).

$$\begin{array}{c} M \\ \diagdown \, H \\ L \diagup \!\!\! \diagdown \\ \diagdown \, J \\ P \diagup \end{array}$$

Your diagram should look like this:

GHJLMP	1	2	3	4	5	6
	~H	~H			~L	H/J
	~J	~J				

7. E **Grab-a-Rule**

Rule 1 eliminates (C), which has H before L. Rule 2 eliminates (A), which has J before P. Rule 3 eliminates (B), which has M before P but G before H. Rule 4 eliminates (D), which has G last.

8. C **General**

A. No. This is possible if the order is, for example, M, L, H, P, G, J.

B. No. This is possible if the order is, for example, P, M, L, G, J, H.

C. Yes. This is impossible because L has to have both H and J after it, according to clues 1 and 2.

D. No. This is possible if the order is, for example, P, M, L, G, J, H.

E. No. This is possible if the order is, for example, L, P, M, G, J, H.

9. D **General**

Only H or J could appear sixth, so the answer is (D), 2.

10. A **Specific**

If J is earlier than M, then L and P are earlier than J, which in turn is earlier than M, which in turn is earlier than H. G can fit anywhere in there except last.

A. Yes. The order G, L, P, J, M, H is permissible.

B. No. H and L are in the wrong order, violating clue 1.

C. No. H and P are in the wrong order. See above.

D. No. This puts G last, violating clue 4.

E. No. This puts G last, violating clue 4.

11. C **Specific**

This now fits an LG block into the larger web, putting G, H, and J after L.

A. No. This could be false if the order were, for example, P, M, L, G, H, J.

B. No. This could be false if the order were, for example, P, M, L, G, H, J.

C. Yes. If G, H, and J are after L, then L can't be any later than third.

D. No. This could be false if the order were, for example, P, L, G, M, H, J.

E. No. This could be false if the order were, for example, L, G, P, M, H, J.

12. **C**

If M is first, then clue 3 is active: M is before P, so H is before G. That means that L and P are before J, and L is also before H, which is before G. Since clue 4 says that G can't be last, and since everything other than J must have something after it, J is last.

A. No. P could be fifth.

B. No. P could be third.

C. Yes. J is the only element left that can be last, so it is last.

D. No. P could be second.

E. No. P could be second, third, or fifth.

Questions 13–17

This is a 1D Order Game with a twist. There are three M's and four S's. The twist is the cleaning of the cargo bed when switching between M and S elements. It may be useful to indicate this information in the clues.

Clue 1: Clean ≤ 3

Clue 2: M = 5

Deductions: Because of the small number of clues, deductions will be limited. Include clue 2 in the diagram and keep in mind that clue 1 means that load switching can occur at most 3 times.

Your diagram should look like this:

```
MMM
SSSS    |  1  |  2  |  3  |  4  |  5  |  6  |  7  |
        |     |     |     |     |  M  |     |     |
```

13. **E**

Since the fifth load must be mulch (clue 2), the two remaining mulch loads in the answer choices constitute all of the other mulch loads. Use previous work to see that S, S, S, M, M, M, S, is a possible arrangement.

A. No. This would create an M, S, M, S, M, S, S order, which has too many cleanings.

B. No. This would create an S, M, M, S, M, S, S order, which has too many cleanings.

C. No. This would create an S, M, S, S, M, M, S order, which has too many cleanings.

D. No. This would create an S, S, M, S, M, M, S order, which has too many cleanings.

E. Yes. This would create an S, S, S, M, M, M, S order, which has only two cleanings.

14. **D** Specific

Use previous work to eliminate answers that are not always true.

A. No. The second load could be M if the order were M, M, S, S, M, S, S.

B. No. The first and second loads could be different if the order were, for example, M, S, S, M, M, S, S.

C. No. The second and third loads could be the same if the order were, for example, S, S, S, M, M, M, S.

D. Yes. If the M's were all non-consecutive, then there would need to be at least four cleanings.

E. No. There could only be pairs of stone loads if the order were, for example, M, M, S, S, M, S, S.

15. **E** General

If M is the third load as well as the fifth load (clue 2), the arrangement must be S, S, M, M, M, S, S to limit the number of cleanings to no more than 3.

MMM
SSSS

	1	2	3	4	5	6	7
					M		
	S	S	M	M	M	S	S

16. **A** Specific

If there are exactly two cleanings, the elements could be arranged as S, S, S, M, M, M, S, or S, S, M, M, M, S, S.

MMM
SSSS

	1	2	3	4	5	6	7
					M		
	S	S	M	M	M	S	S
	S	S	S	M	M	M	S

17. **B** Specific

If no more than two of the same element appear consecutively, and there are no more than three cleanings, the order must be M, S, S, M, M, S, S or M, M, S, S, M, S, S.

MMM SSSS	1	2	3	4	5	6	7
					M		
	M	M	S	S	M	S	S
	M	S	S	M	M	S	S

Questions 18–23

The core of the diagram should be arranged around R, S, and T (as the Grab-a-Rule shows). The photographer/writer aspect should be represented as rows.

There are six elements and six spaces in the diagram, with a one-to-one correspondence between elements and spaces in the diagram.

Clue 1: ⬛ G | L ⬛ or ⬛ G — L ⬛

Clue 2: ⬛ F/K ⬛ and ⬛ F̸—K ⬛

Clue 3: H = P

Clue 4: J = T

Clue 5: K ≠ S

Deductions: Clues 3, 4, and 5 can be put into the diagram, but there is little else to deduce.

Your diagram should look like this:

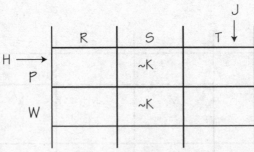

18. **A** **Grab-a-Rule**

Even though the answer choices are missing the W row, this question can be done like a Grab-a-Rule. Clue 1 eliminates (B), since G is in the row but L is not. Clue 2 eliminates (C), because neither F nor K is in the P row, so they are both in the W row. Clue 3 eliminates (D), because H is nowhere in the row. Clue 5 eliminates (E), because K is in S.

19. **B** `Specific`

If F is in R, it could be in either the P row or the W row. K is in the other row, according to clue 2. Clue 3 puts H in the P row, and the G/L pair must be in the W row, because there is not enough space anywhere else. J then fits in the P row. Thus, the P row contains either F or K, H, and J. According to clue 4, J is in T, and according to clue 5 and the question stem, F and K can't be in S, so H must go in S.

A. No. G could be assigned to T.

B. Yes. H is in S.

C. No. K is assigned to R.

D. No. L could be assigned to T.

E. No. L could be assigned to S.

20. **B** `Specific`

Since clue 4 has H in P, F is in W. By clue 2, K is in P. This pushes the G/L pair into W, because there isn't enough space in P, and then J must go into P. In P, J must be in T (by clue 4), and K must be in R (by clue 5), so H is in S, and, in the W row, so is F (according to the question stem). G and L are in the W row in R and T, though it's not clear which is which.

A. No. F is in S.

B. Yes. G can be in R or T.

C. No. H is in S.

D. No. K is in R.

E. No. L is in R or T.

21. **D** `Specific`

If F is in W, then K is in P (by clue 2), and H is always in P (by clue 3). This sticks the G/L pair in W, because there's not enough space in P, and J is in P. In the P row, J is in T and K in R (by clues 4 and 5) and H is in S. Thus, the answer is K and any one of G, L, or F.

A. No. K is in R.

B. No. K is in R.

C. No. K must be paired with G, L, or F. H is in the P row.

D. Yes.

E. No. K is in R.

22. **E** `Specific`

If there is a GK vertical block, it must be in R, because J is in T, and K can't be in S.

A. No. G and K are assigned to R.

B. No. G and K are assigned to R.

C. No. G and K are assigned to R.

D. No. G and K are assigned to R.

E. Yes. G and K are assigned to R, but L can be anywhere.

23. **C** `General`

This is a fairly subtle deduction, so testing answers may be necessary. Previous work should eliminate a few answers. H might look like an interesting one to try because of clue 3's restriction.

A. No. F can be assigned to T in the following arrangement: in the P row, in R, S, and T, respectively, K, H, J, and in the W row, in R, S, and T, respectively, G, L, and F.

B. No. G can be assigned to T in the following arrangement: in the P row, in R, S, and T, respectively, K, H, J, and in the W row, in R, S, and T, respectively, F, L, and G.

C. Yes. If H is in T, and so is J by clue 4, then the G/L block occupies the rest of either P or W, which leaves the last two spaces (in the same row, whichever it is) to be occupied by F and K. But this violates clue 2.

D. No. K can be assigned to T in the following arrangement: in the P row, in R, S, and T, respectively, F, H, J, and in the W row, in R, S, and T, respectively, G, L, and K.

E. No. L can be assigned to T in the following arrangement: in the P row, in R, S, and T, respectively, F, H, J, and in the W row, in R, S, and T, respectively, K, G, L.

Section 3: Arguments 2

1. **A** `Resolve/ Explain`

The discrepancy is that the goal was to reduce traffic, but the result was that traffic actually increased. The credited response should give some reason explaining how widening and extending highways would lead to increased, not reduced, traffic.

A. Yes. If there are more motorists, then there can be more traffic, despite the wider roads.

B. No. If the population increase had already taken place before the road project, and if the population had leveled off by the time of the project, then the population was constant during the road project. This makes the discrepancy worse by eliminating a possible reason (population increase) for the traffic to increase.

C. No. The number of accidents is irrelevant to the discrepancy involving the amount of traffic.

60

D. No. The types of vehicles are irrelevant to the discrepancy involving the amount of traffic.

E. No. The fact that urban traffic is worse than traffic in other areas does not, by itself, explain why widening the road doesn't at least improve it, even if it is still bad.

2. **B** Strengthen

The argument concludes that in-store advertisements over a store's audio system were effective. The evidence was that more people bought the product shortly after the ads were aired than bought it before. The argument contains a causal flaw: It's assuming that there is no other cause for people to purchase the product.

A. No. This would explain why there were more purchases after the ad than before, but not (as the argument indicates) why a higher percentage of the customers bought the relevant items.

B. Yes. This suggests that the ad actually was responsible for their behavior, because it eliminates the possibility that a large percentage of people just showed up to the store to buy the products at the same time right around the time the ad was being played.

C. No. Even if a handful of customers report something, it doesn't necessarily account for the behavior of many.

D. No. Even if they could not remember the ads, they might have been affected by them.

E. No. Even if they buy the product only occasionally, the answer choice does not explain why they purchased it at this time.

3. **A** Sufficient Assumption

The argument concludes that the library will not be completed on schedule. The premises are that if the building permit is not obtained by February 1 of this year or if the other necessary activities are not completed in less time than originally planned, then the library will not be completed on schedule, and the building permit isn't going to be obtained by February 1. The missing piece is the other half of the "if" statement, the other necessary activities. The credited response should say that the other necessary activities will not be completed in less time than originally planned.

A. Yes. If the other activities will take at least as much time as originally planned, then they will not be completed in less time than originally planned.

B. No. Even if they've admitted that it "probably" won't be completed on schedule, it could still be completed on schedule, so this is not enough.

C. No. This just further specifies the premise that the building permit cannot be obtained by February 1, which we already know is true.

D. No. What happened the first time is irrelevant to this time.

E. No. Even if this is true, it doesn't address the issue of the other necessary activities.

4. **B** Weaken

The conclusion is that inhaling the scent of peppermint makes insomnia worse. The evidence is that a study showed that people who inhaled the scent of peppermint had a harder time falling asleep than people who inhaled the (apparently sleep-neutral) scent of bitter orange. The argument assumes, among other things, that the two groups of people being compared were the same in every respect except the kind of scent they inhaled when trying to go to sleep, so it could be weakened by pointing out that that assumption is not true.

A. No. The conclusion is about people who do suffer from insomnia, so the effects of peppermint on other people are not relevant.

B. Yes. If this were true, it wouldn't be the peppermint that accounted for the difference in how easily the two groups could fall asleep; it would be the severity of their insomnia.

C. No. This would affect both groups of patients equally, since they would both know that they were undergoing a study, and would not account for the difference between the peppermint and bitter orange groups.

D. No. The argument's conclusion is about the impact of the scent on falling asleep, not the amount of time they were able to stay asleep.

E. No. If this were true, it would strengthen the argument. If these scents can affect the degree to which a patient suffers from insomnia, they could worsen it, as the conclusion indicates.

5. **D**   Reasoning

The statement asked about is the conclusion of the argument. The evidence begins with "After all," and it involves a study.

A. No. It's the conclusion, not a premise.

B. No. It is stated in the argument as the conclusion.

C. No. The issue in the argument is whether this statement is true, so this is not background information to help understand the issue; it is the issue.

D. Yes. The study is a premise in support of this conclusion.

E. No. There is no other conclusion.

6. **D**   Parallel

The conclusion is the second sentence, and the premise is the first. The argument assumes that the particular pilot tomorrow will have the same reaction to flying the plane as all the previous pilots have, or more generally, that the pattern that has continued up to this point will continue with a specific event in the future as well.

A. No. The average reader in the conclusion introduces an additional shift from the book reviewers in the premise that was not in the original argument.

B. No. Many of the book reviewers thinking something does not match none of the test pilots finding something.

C. No. Two book reviewers do not match many test pilots. This answer choice creates a survey flaw that is not in the original argument.

60

D. Yes. This is assuming that what has happened with many reviewers up to this point will happen with a specific book reviewer in the future as well, just as the original argument assumed about test pilots.

E. No. This argument introduces an additional shift from book reviewers in the premise to the general public in the conclusion.

7. **C** | Reasoning

The question task is asking for the role played by the mention of astrology. The argument claims that affecting perception of the world is a necessary but not sufficient condition for taking a theory seriously. The role of astrology is to see that it is not sufficient. If astrology is to prove that affecting perception of the world is not sufficient reason to take a theory seriously, then astrology must affect perception of the world but should not be taken seriously.

A. No. According to the argument, astrology affects our perception of the world.

B. No. According to the argument, astrology is a theory.

C. Yes. According to the argument, astrology is a theory that affects perception of the world but should not be taken seriously.

D. No. According to the argument, astrology should not be taken seriously.

E. No. According to the argument, astrology is a theory that affects perception of the world but should not be taken seriously.

8. **C** | Flaw

The argument concludes that Michaela must be a critically acclaimed playwright. The evidence is that critical acclaim is one of the main factors considered in deciding which play to perform, and her play is going to be performed. The flaw is that it is neglecting the other, unnamed factors that are used to determine the selection of plays.

A. No. There is no condition in this argument that is necessary for a playwright's being critically acclaimed.

B. No. There are no different effects.

C. Yes. A main factor in the selection of plays is critical acclaim, and the argument assumes that a play must be critically acclaimed to be performed.

D. No. There is no reason to doubt the reliability of any source in this argument.

E. No. The argument argues that being critically acclaimed is the cause of the play being selected, so it does not need to provide evidence that being critically acclaimed is the result of being selected.

9. **C** | Principle Strengthen

The conclusion is that governments should not be allowed to use diaries as evidence. The premises are that writing in a diary is for oneself (not others), and that this is similar to keeping one's thoughts to oneself. The credited response should indicate that such things, which are intended for oneself and not others and are like keeping thoughts to oneself, should not be allowable evidence.

60

A. No. Other types of evidence that should not be used by governments are not relevant to whether diaries should be used.

B. No. This answer choice is irrelevant and is in the opposite direction of the original argument, which was trying to limit what the government could do.

C. Yes. This answer choice could be paraphrased to say that if the remarks were not intended for other people, they should not be acceptable for the government's prosecutorial use, which connects the premise to the conclusion.

D. No. The individual's personal correspondence—which is different from a diary in that it is clearly intended for others—is not at issue here.

E. No. This goes in the opposite direction to the argument, which was trying to limit such government efforts.

10. **C** **Inference**

The argument says that there is a gas ring maintaining an orbit close to a black hole, and the gas ring could not maintain an orbit close to a black hole unless the black hole was spinning. Combining these statements, the credited response is likely to say that the black hole is spinning.

A. No. There is no information given about rings of gas greater than 49 kilometers.

B. No. There is no information given about other rings of gas.

C. Yes. If the gas couldn't be where it is unless the black hole is spinning, then the black hole must be spinning.

D. No. Whether the X-rays cause the spinning or something else does is not given.

E. No. It is never stated that black holes must have gas rings.

11. **D** **Necessary Assumption**

The conclusion is that there has not been a black water phenomenon at last year's intensity any time in the past two centuries. The evidence is that the black water wiped out some species of coral that were more than two centuries old. The line of reasoning argues that even if there were black water before, the coral survived it, so it must not have been as bad. This assumes, however, that the black water's intensity is the only factor relevant to its effect.

A. No. The argument does not assume that there was or was not a black water phenomenon in the past two centuries, because the conclusion is conditional: If there was such a phenomenon, then it must have had a lower intensity.

B. No. Try the Negation Test: Even if a few were not seriously harmed, that would have no impact on the conclusion about the history of black water.

C. No. Try the Negation Test: Even if it did decimate other species, this still does not affect whether there were black water phenomena earlier. Indeed, if it decimated other old living things, then the negation of the answer choice supports the argument, instead of destroying it.

D. Yes. Try the Negation Test: If the mounds were especially fragile before the black water, then they might have been wiped out by coincidence, not by the severity of the black water.

E. No. Even if everything were equally vulnerable, the black water might still have been of higher intensity than it had been before.

12. **E**   Inference

The argument gives two facts: In the last sentence, it says that if a fruit tree can't be grown in a tub or pot, then it can't correctly be labeled "miniature." In the preceding sentence, it says that some Stark Sweet Melody nectarine trees are labeled "miniature" at some nurseries and not so labeled at others.

A. No. It is not clear in the argument whether any trees labeled "miniature" are not suitable for growing in a tub or pot (which would make them mislabeled).

B. No. The only labels that are mentioned in the argument are ones that would be inappropriate if the variety is unsuitable for growing in a tub or pot.

C. No. It is not clear whether Stark Sweet Melody nectarine trees are suitable for growing in a tub or pot, so it is not clear whether they can correctly be labeled "miniature."

D. No. If they are not labeled "miniature," they may not be labeled anything, which would make it impossible for them to be labeled incorrectly.

E. Yes. If these trees are not suitable for growing in a tub or pot, they cannot correctly be labeled "miniature," so they are mislabeled.

13. **D**   Weaken

The argument concludes that many inclinations are genetic and not environmentally influenced. The premises are that identical twins have the same genes, but when they are brought up in different environments, they have the similar ethics, dress styles, and careers. This argument is assuming, very broadly, that the genes cause the similarities and nothing in the environment. A problem with this is that it may be possible to have two different environmental stimuli that lead to the same effect. The credited response should address this causal flaw, although it is hard to predict from the argument what exactly it will say.

A. No. Even if this were true, those changes could have been genetically programmed. The argument doesn't address what is causing these changes.

B. No. A few differences are completely compatible with the many similarities suggested in the conclusion.

C. No. Genes might lead to inclinations even if it is not clear which ones lead to which at the current level of scientific development.

D. Yes. If this is true, then beliefs, tastes, and careers can be influenced by the environment, but the conclusion indicated that they could not.

E. No. These twins have different genes, so it is reasonable for them to develop different beliefs, tastes, and careers even if their genes are completely responsible for their behaviors.

14. D Main Point

The argument says that human beings can live happily only in certain circumstances. It also says that economic needs can be satisfied without those circumstances. Combining these statements, it should conclude that satisfying economic needs does not necessarily make people happy.

A. No. Economic utility can be a motivator. The problem is that fulfilling economic needs doesn't guarantee happiness, not that it prevents happiness.

B. No. The argument just says that economic needs depend on different things than happiness, not that happiness depends on more than economic needs.

C. No. The argument says that economic needs can be satisfied in one way, but it doesn't say that it's the only way.

D. Yes. The argument says happiness depends on one thing, but economic needs can be satisfied even without that. Thus, economic needs can be satisfied without obtaining happiness.

E. No. The argument says the opposite of this, namely that economic needs can be satisfied even without that which is required for happiness.

15. D Main Point

The conclusion is the third sentence, which says that the infrastructure is likely to appear and grow rapidly. The first two sentences are background for the third, since they clarify the kind of infrastructure under discussion and point out facts about its nonexistence. The final sentence is support for the third sentence by means of an analogy.

A. No. This is a premise (the first sentence).

B. No. This is a paraphrase of part of a premise (the second sentence).

C. No. This is a broader generalization than the conclusion. This argument is only about hydrogen fuel infrastructure.

D. Yes. This paraphrases the third sentence, which is the conclusion.

E. No. This is an assumption underlying the analogy in the fourth sentence, not the conclusion.

16. E Flaw

The argument concludes that wildlife management experts should not interfere with the natural habitats of creatures in the wild. It concludes this because interfering to help out endangered species hurts nonendangered species. It's assuming that this is not worth doing, that it is bad to help endangered species at the cost of harming nonendangered species.

A. No. Even if they do, this does not address the problem with nonendangered species.

B. No. Harming nonendangered species is the very problem that the argument raises, so endangering a species is not something the argument fails to recognize.

C. No. The argument suggests that helping an endangered species survive invariably makes it harder for nonendangered species to survive, so the possibility that it is not possible to save an endangered species and also preserve species diversity is implied, not overlooked.

D.   No. This does not address the problem with nonendangered species. Even if the endangered species were not at all equal, the argument's conclusion that none should be helped could still hold, so this argument does not presume this.

E.   Yes. If preserving endangered species were of higher priority than preserving nonendangered species, then it might be a good idea to help endangered species even at the cost of some harm to nonendangered species, so the argument would no longer work.

17. **D**   **Inference**

The argument gives a large number of facts about food preservation and sterilization. These facts do not clearly combine to lead to a specific conclusion so the credited response will likely be the inverse of one of the facts in the paragraph.

A.   No. The third sentence says that some acceptable food-preservation techniques involve slowing the growth of disease-causing bacteria, so the food is not necessarily free of the bacteria.

B.   No. The techniques mentioned in the final sentence, which destroy enzymes, may be part of the former or latter category in the previous sentence, a sterilizing method or a slowing-growth method. If they are part of the former category, this answer choice is untrue.

C.   No. It is not made clear in the information given whether sterilization involves destroying the food enzymes mentioned in the final sentence.

D.   Yes. The first sentence says that any food that is not sterilized and sealed can contain disease-causing bacteria. The answer choice describes food that is not sterilized, so it can contain disease-causing bacteria according to the first sentence.

E.   No. The argument says that sterilization causes a food to contain no bacteria and that preservation can involve sterilization, but it does not say that food is sterilized only for preservation. If the food were sterilized for some other reason, it would contain no bacteria but would not have been preserved by an acceptable method.

18. **C**   **Principle Match**

The principle created an absolute identity between acceptable activities posing risks to life and gaining a benefit that cannot be had without the risks or bearing the risks voluntarily. If either of the two criteria is met, then the activity is acceptable, even though it poses risk to life.

A.   No. It is not clear whether this poses risks to life.

B.   No. No benefit is gained that cannot be had without such risks, and the risks are not borne voluntarily by the people who must suffer them.

C.   Yes. This is a risk to life, and it is judged acceptable because the person who bears it bears the risk voluntarily.

D.   No. This answer choice does not specify that there is no other way to get the benefit without the risk.

E.   No. The principle did not involve whether policies were acceptable, only risks.

60

19.   **D**   **Flaw**

The argument concludes that compounds are not responsible for butterflies' ability to avoid preda-tion. The evidence is that the compounds were separated out and each individual one does not cause predators to avoid eating. The assumption is that there is no difference between the compounds taken individually, as in the premises, and the compounds taken together, as in the conclusion, on the actual butterfly.

A.   No. Incompatibility of the theories is not the issue. One theory could still be wrong even if both could have been true.

B.   No. There is no statistical correlation. There is a lack of a predicted effect, and the argument con-cludes lack of causation on those grounds.

C.   No. There is no condition in this argument that is definitely sufficient for sea butterflies' ability to avoid predation.

D.   Yes. The argument concludes, from the claim that no individual compound has the effect of avoid-ing predators, that the compounds together do not have that effect. The answer describes this.

E.   No. The premises do not state that the compounds are not responsible for the ability to avoid pre-dation. They state that one compound at a time is not responsible for the ability.

20.   **A**   **Strengthen**

The principle says that if criticism will harm the person criticized or if one does not criticize in the hope or expectation of benefiting someone other than oneself, one should not criticize the works or actions of another person. (That is, harm or ~hope to benefit other → ~criticize.) The application gives a situa-tion in which the criticism did not benefit anyone, and it concludes that the criticism should not have happened. It is not clear, in this example, whether the criticism was offered in the hope or expectation of benefiting someone (and just failed to do so) or was offered even though it would not benefit anyone. In the latter case, the application is legitimate.

A.   Yes. In this case, Jarrett did not criticize in the hope or expectation of benefiting someone other than himself (or anyone, in truth), so he should not have criticized as he did.

B.   No. It is not clear whether Jarrett knew this or not, so even if this were true, he still might have been hoping to benefit Ostertag.

C.   No. Even if this were true, he might have been hoping to benefit Ostertag.

D.   No. Even if this were true, he might also have been hoping to benefit Ostertag.

E.   No. Even if this were true, he might have been hoping to benefit someone other than himself and Ostertag (someone else in the class, perhaps).

21.   **E**   **Strengthen**

The argument concludes that minivans have a good safety record because they are driven by low-risk drivers and not because they are inherently safer. The evidence is that the number of injuries per vehicle is lowest for minivans (out of all vehicles), but they don't appear in crash tests to be inherently safer.

The argument assumes that other factors outside of the actual mechanics of a collision are no more important than the crash itself.

A. No. Minivans don't perform better in crash tests, so if this were true, low-risk drivers would not necessarily select minivans.

B. No. The safety record of minivans is not at issue in this argument, rather the conclusion is concerned with the cause of the low injuries per licensed vehicle.

C. No. If this were true, it would make the number of injuries per licensed vehicle statistic more impressive (more people, but fewer injuries), but it does not address why there are so few injuries

D. No. This weakens the argument by saying that it is the inherent safety, not the type of driver, that makes the minivans so safe.

E. Yes. If this is true, then not only are the minivans no safer when they're actually in a collision, but they also are no safer in preventing a collision, so they cannot be inherently safer than other vehicles. This strengthens the conclusion (that it is the low-risk drivers that are the cause) by eliminating a possible alternate cause.

22. **A** Necessary Assumption

The conclusion is that the government is responsible for the increased cost of gasoline. The evidence is that the government's policies have increased demand, and as a result of increased demand, the price has risen. The argument is assuming, broadly speaking, that this is enough to assign the responsibility solely on the government.

A. Yes. Try the Negation Test: If the government could not bear responsibility for that which it indirectly causes, then the government could not bear responsibility for the gasoline price increase, since it only indirectly caused it.

B. No. Whether the consequences were unforeseen is unknown, so this may not even be relevant.

C. No. Try the Negation Test: Even if consumer demand could increase without causing gasoline prices to increase, it did not in this case, so this does not matter.

D. No. The issue in the argument was not the government's obligation, but whether the government was responsible.

E. No. The government did pursue policies that increased the demand for fuel, so this answer choice describes a situation that is not relevant to the argument.

23. **C** Parallel Flaw

This argument commits a necessary/sufficient flaw by reading a conditional statement backwards. One could diagram the premises as "mutations → evolutionary adaptations" and "survive changes → evolutionary adaptations." The conclusion might be represented as "mutations → survive changes." The problem is the argument assumes these two statements are linked, which would require one of them to be reversed. The credited response should likewise flip a conditional improperly.

A. No. This is logically valid. Take the second conditional first and the first second: "sturdy → properly built" and "properly built → stone supports stone." This does lead to the conclusion, which is "sturdy → stone supports stone."

B. No. This likewise is valid. It gives that different audience will give different reactions, and it says that there are always different audiences, so there will always be different reactions.

C. Yes. Being "honest" matches "mutations frequently occurring," "telling the truth" matches "developing new evolutionary adaptations," and being "morally upright" matches "surviving dramatic environmental changes." Then this argument matches the original, as the premises would diagram as follows: "honest → truth" and "moral → truth." The conclusion would diagram as follows: "honest → moral." This again reads the second conditional backwards.

D. No. This is logically valid. It takes the contrapositives of both conditionals in the premises and combines them to create the conclusion. That is, the premises are "productive → well drained" and "well drained → good soil," which would lead to the contrapositives "~good soil → ~well drained" and "~well drained → ~productive," which can be combined to form the conclusion, "~good soil → ~productive."

E. No. This answer choice introduces a language shift at the very end. It takes a contrapositive of both conditionals in the premises and combines them to create the conclusion. However, the conclusion also involves a language shift from not eating a healthful diet to not being healthy, while no such language shift was present in the original argument.

24. **B** **Principle Strengthen**

The conclusion of the argument is that sales are not a mark of a rock group's success as an underground group. The evidence is that strong sales may be the result of being too trendy, and weak sales may be the result of incompetence. The credited response should connect the premises (being trendy or incompetent) with the conclusion (not successful as an underground group).

25. **C** **Point at Issue**

Graham and Adelaide are arguing about how to interpret the defeat of the world chess champion by a computer. Graham says that it shows that the computer mastered the principles of chess and indicates the potential for intelligence someday. Adelaide says that the computer was just doing what the people who created it programmed it to do. They disagree about whether the computer or the humans were responsible for the computer's success in playing against the world chess champion.

A. No. Neither compares this to other intellectual activities governed by fixed principles.

B. No. Neither says this. Whether chess is typical or atypical is not addressed.

C. Yes. Graham attributes the player's defeat to the computer. Adelaide attributes it to the humans who programmed the computer.

D. No. Adelaide does not address the issue of intelligence at all, so while Graham would agree with this statement, Adelaide may not disagree with it.

E. No. Graham seems to agree with this, since he says that machines can master such activities, but Adelaide does not disagree, since she says that the computers were extensions of the people who programmed them (i.e. tools).

60

Section 4: Reading Comprehension

Questions 1–7

The passage describes New Urbanism, which disapproves of suburban sprawl and proposes instead mixed-income and mixed-use neighborhoods, on the basis of the effects that these neighborhoods have on communal interactions and the values that they represent. The first paragraph introduces New Urbanism, which argues that the separation of homes, stores, businesses, and schools into separate spaces damages the communal nature of town life. The second paragraph explains some of the harm that suburban sprawl does and indicates that New Urbanists favor neighborhoods that are economically mixed and build different types of buildings (homes, stores, etc.) near each other. The third paragraph gives a criticism of New Urbanism, that people legitimately desire what suburbs offer, and provides a rebuttal, that people have the right to their own values but those values should be examined.

1. **D**   **Big Picture**

   The author's main point is, briefly, that New Urbanists think that suburban sprawl is bad and propose mixed-income and mixed-use neighborhoods instead.

   A. No. The author says that opponents of New Urbanism say that New Urbanists neglect this, but the author never expresses agreement with the opponents.

   B. No. This attempts to summarize the second paragraph, which makes it too narrow in scope.

   C. No. The "generally more gratifying" comment is limited to a single sentence in the second paragraph.

   D. Yes. The corrosive effect on community life is described in the first and third paragraphs, and the alternative is described in the second.

   E. No. This answer choice focuses on the traffic policies and not zoning laws in general.

2. **C**   **Extract Fact**

   The detrimental results of automobile travel are described in the second paragraph. The passage says that people lose the time they would spend interacting pleasantly and instead engage in competitive and antisocial behaviors when they do interact while in cars.

   A. No. Financial burdens are not mentioned in this part of the passage.

   B. No. Devoting the time in other ways is not mentioned in this part of the passage.

   C. Yes. The extra time spent in the car, where people engage in antisocial behavior, is described in the middle of the second paragraph as a consequence of this need.

   D. No. Air pollution is not mentioned in the passage.

   E. No. Parents spending time with their children is not mentioned in the passage.

3. **D**   **Extract Infer**

   New Urbanists, in general, think that suburban sprawl has negative effects on communities, that mixed neighborhoods would be better, and that the values that generate suburban sprawl need to be examined critically.

A. No. While the passage indicates that New Urbanists think that car travel, as opposed to pedestrian travel, is one reason that people are less civil to each other in suburbs, the passage does not indicate that it is the most important factor.

B. No. Whether the private citizens can influence the zoning effects is not discussed in the passage.

C. No. In the second paragraph, the passage indicates that people are required to drive to get more or less anywhere, so this contradicts the passage.

D. Yes. The spatial configuration of suburbs influencing attitudes of those who live in them was mentioned in the first and second paragraphs (making people more antisocial, among other things). The spatial configuration of suburbs being influenced by the attitudes of those who live in them is in the third paragraph.

E. No. The New Urbanists don't say that valueless design is necessary (or even possible). The third paragraph argues that the values need to be examined critically.

4. **B**   Extract
             Infer

In the first reference, the word "communities" means a place where a group of people live, whereas in the second reference, the word means the more abstract sense, a group of people who share living space and have social connections.

A. No. They are not meant identically.

B. Yes. This matches the description of the terms above.

C. No. The first term does not mean that groups are defined in terms of the interests of their members. They just live in the same area.

D. No. The first term does not mean that the people have professional or political ties. They just live in the same area.

E. No. The first term does not mean that the people have informal personal ties. They just live in the same area.

5. **D**   RC Reasoning

The critics say, in the beginning of the third paragraph, that the expansion of suburban sprawl is the result of people's legitimate desire to have what the suburbs offer due to the automobile. This could be weakened by suggesting that it is the result of something else.

A. No. The answer choice does not weaken the claims of the critics; it weakens the New Urbanists claims that suburban life leads to greater travel times.

B. No. This might weaken the New Urbanists' claim that people in suburbs spend a lot of time driving and this time influences their interactions with each other, but it does not weaken the critics of the New Urbanists.

C. No. The critics claim that the suburbs offer the enjoyment and personal mobility afforded by the automobile, but this is not necessarily the same as easy access to shopping and entertainment. This access is irrelevant to the critics' argument.

D. Yes. This suggests an alternate reason that people might choose to live in the suburbs: price. They do not desire the advantages of the automobile; they just can't afford anything else comparable.

E. No. Even if there are other important issues in municipal elections, this issue of zoning could agree or disagree with the critics.

6. **E** Extract Infer

Duany and his colleagues suggest building mixed neighborhoods at the end of the second paragraph.

A. No. Zoning laws would enforce Duany's proposals anyway, so zoning laws would remain in place.

B. No. The number of such buildings might change, but this is not mentioned in the passage.

C. No. The goal was to put grocery stores and other work and shopping facilities within walking distance of everyone, so the amount of time spent traveling to get to these would likely decrease rather than increase.

D. No. The coordination of zoning policies is not discussed in the passage.

E. Yes. The grocery stores and schools were described as "corner grocery stores" and "small neighborhood schools," indicating that they would be small. To service the same areas and numbers of people, there would need to be more of them.

7. **A** Extract Infer

A. Yes. At the beginning of the second paragraph, Duany and his colleagues point out that subdivisions contain identically priced houses and conclude that the financial statuses of the families that inhabit them must be similar (resulting in economic segregation). If most people who bought suburban houses did pay drastically less than they could afford, then the housing prices would not be a good way to approximate the incomes of the resident families, so the areas might not be economically segregated.

B. No. This is the opposite of what the New Urbanists say actually happens. The suburban sprawls are usually economically segregated because of zoning.

C. No. The hostilities are between motorist and motorist in the second paragraph, not between nommotorist and motorist.

D. No. Awareness of potential health benefits is not discussed in the passage.

E. No. The passage indicates that people typically do this in suburban sprawl, but it does not indicate that people prefer this.

60

Questions 8–12

Passage A

The passage describes several investigations into the honeybee's dance, which allows bees to communicate the location of food, and concludes that sound plays a role in the communication in addition to the visual aspects of the dance. The first paragraph describes the honeybee's dance and the original attempts to study it and figure out how bees locate food from it. The second paragraph presents evidence that vision is not the sole component of the dance and says that some proposed that smell was part of the communication as well. The third paragraph indicates that smell is not a component of the communication, but sound is.

Passage B

The passage discusses the problem of animal communication in general and how it applies to bees in particular. The first paragraph indicates that bee communication is a subset of the larger problem of animal communication. The second paragraph says that bees communicate food location via their dance. The third paragraph says that bees don't automatically follow the information in the dance and somehow can determine whether the location indicated will be likely to contain flowers.

8. **C** **Big Picture**

Both passages mention the dance of the honeybee, passage B in the more general context of animal communication in different species.

A. No. Neither argues for human-like intelligence in animals.

B. No. Passage A is not about primates. It's about bees.

C. Yes. Passage A describes Wenner and Esch, Gould, and several others studying the communication of honeybees. Passage B describes Seyfarth, Cheney, and Marler, Karl von Frisch, Wenner, and others studying the communication of vervet monkeys, bees, and other animals.

D. No. The function of the honeybee's dance is known: It communicates the location of food. The controversy in passage A is whether sound or smell is involved. It would be hard to describe passage B as focusing on a central controversy in the first place, since disagreements are contained within a single sentence not about the function of the dance.

E. No. No conditions to meet are mentioned in either passage.

9. **A** **Extract Fact**

A. Yes. Passage B talks about ants, fish, and vervet monkeys in addition to honeybees, while passage A talks about honeybees only.

B. No. This description of passage B is inaccurate. In the third paragraph, passage B presents some of the evidence for Gould's claims.

C. No. While passage A mentions Aristotle in the first sentence, it does not outline the historic development of the theories any more than passage B does. Both start with von Frisch and work up to Gould.

D. No. Passage B does not explain the distinction between symbolic and nonsymbolic communication. It mentions symbolic communication in the second paragraph, but nonsymbolic communication is not described.

E. No. Passage B does not discuss human communication.

10. **D** **Extract Infer**

In the third paragraph of passage A, Gould's research showed that "foragers can dispatch bees to sites they had not actually visited," and in the third paragraph of passage B, Gould's research showed that bees "do not automatically follow just any information," since they did not go to a boat in the middle of a lake.

A. No. Forager honeybees never communicate olfactory information to their nestmates, according to the third paragraph of passage A and the second paragraph of passage B.

B. No. This is contradicted by passage B, which says in the third paragraph that the foragers would give instructions to the hive members, but the hive members would ignore them. The forager honeybees do not instinctively know where pollinating flowers usually grow; the nestmates do.

C. No. No comparison is made between experienced and inexperienced foragers.

D. Yes. Passage A mentions that the foragers can draw honeybees to sites that the forager has not visited, and passage B mentions that foragers can fail to draw other honeybees to sites that the forager has visited.

E. No. A trail does not appear to be involved, since passage A indicates that they don't have to have been to the food source to draw honeybees to it.

11. **D**   **Extract Infer**

The credited response should be something supported both by passage A and by passage B, but the passages have many similarities.

A. No. Honeybees ignoring forager's instructions were mentioned only in the third paragraph of passage B, and being unable to detect odors is irrelevant in both.

B. No. The third paragraph of passage A and the second paragraph of passage B say that odor is not the way in which the foragers communicate to other bees.

C. No. Passage A does not discuss animals other than honeybees. Passage B says that all animals communicate in some sense, but whether that communication is symbolic is not mentioned.

D. Yes. Passage A describes the pattern that von Frisch discovered in the dance and mentions that he deciphered it. Passage B mentions that von Frisch cracked the code of the honeybee's dance.

E. No. Neither passage compares experienced bees and inexperienced bees.

12. **C**   **Structure**

The most notable difference between the two passages is that passage A just talks about bees, whereas passage B talks about bees and other animals.

A. No. Passage A does not reject any position from passage B. Passage A rejects the idea that bees use smells to communicate about food, but passage B did not put forward this idea. Passage B mentions that Wenner put forth this idea and then mentions that it is wrong.

B. No. This is the opposite of what is seen in the passages: Passage A gives only one example of animal communication (bees), whereas passage B gives many (ants, fish, etc.).

C. Yes. Passage A is concerned exclusively with bee communication, which passage B talks about as part of animal communication in general.

60

D. No. There is nothing that passage B says cannot be explained.

E. No. The primary concern of passage B is animal communication. Passage A does not provide a historical account of the origins of animal communication.

Questions 13–20

The passage says that the Chicano theater of the 1960s and 1970s that was epitomized by the *actos* genre was created in a large part by Luiz Valdez in conjunction with the Teatro Campesino. The first paragraph begins the explanation of the Chicano Theater movement, which Luis Valdez and the Teatro Campesino began together in the context of unionizing farm workers. The second paragraph describes the invention of *actos*, which are small sketches or skits that present problems and a solution in a brief comic statement, in satirical fashion. The third paragraph says that while the invention of *actos* was a collective accomplishment, Valdez deserves a large portion of the credit.

13. C **Big Picture**

The passage says that the Chicano theater of the 1960s and 1970s that was epitomized by the *actos* genre was created in a large part Luiz Valdez in conjunction with the Teatro Campesino.

A. No. There is no evidence in the passage that there was once a widely accepted view that Luis Valdez was uninfluenced.

B. No. César Chávez was mentioned in only a small portion of the passage so this answer is too narrow in scope.

C. Yes. The first paragraph discusses the creation of the early material of the Teatro Campesino, and the second and third paragraphs talk about Luis Valdez's contributions relative to the other members.

D. No. This goes in the wrong direction. The passage indicates in the third paragraph that Valdez was crucial, but this puts emphasis on the contributions of the others.

E. No. Valdez's academic connections bringing the Teatro Campesino recognition is not an aspect of the history that is discussed in the passage.

14. E **Structure**

In context, the word "immediacy" is referring to the fact that these performances reflected people's daily lives and their experiences, so there was little emotional distance between the audience and the work.

A. No. The physical distance is not what immediacy expresses; the sentence describes the emotional distance.

B. No. Addressing lines directly to the audience is not mentioned in the passage.

C. No. Ease is not the idea expressed by "immediacy." It might not have been easy; it was just closely related to their lives.

D. No. Collaboration is not the aspect of the performance that "immediacy" emphasizes.

E. Yes. Vividness is the sense that "immediacy" is expressing. The viewers felt as though there was no emotional distance between themselves and the performers' work, so the work was vivid.

15. **A** Structure

The second sentence describes a move made by the United Farm Workers, who were politically organizing around the themes that Valdez's group portrayed in performance.

A. Yes. They were motivated by attempting to improve farm working conditions and performed about such topics.

B. No. There is no reason to believe that the boycott represented an obstacle for Valdez.

C. No. There is no objection being countered.

D. No. There is no evidence that scholars of Mexican American history have excluded theater history.

E. No. It has nothing to do with Valdez being single-handedly responsible for the *actos*; this comes later.

16. **D** Extract Fact

Both were satirical, according to the middle of the third paragraph.

A. No. The *carpas* may or may not have had roots in European theater; this is not mentioned.

B. No. This is true of neither; Valdez was in the San Francisco Mime Troupe, but this was an influence on *actos*, not vice-versa.

C. No. The *carpas* were performed in tents.

D. Yes. Both were satirical.

E. No. The carpas were not part of union activities. They were before Chavez.

17. **D** Extract Infer

Valdez created the *actos* out of improvisation with striking farm workers.

A. No. The *carpas* were quite similar, not unsuited.

B. No. Chavez did enough, in the first paragraph, and there is no evidence that Valdez wished for him to do more.

C. No. Valdez was influenced by the European tradition, according to the third paragraph.

D. Yes. According to the second paragraph, the actors in *actos* were not formally trained; there were merely striking farm workers.

E. No. The political ramifications seemed to have been a substantial part of the point of the actos anyway, and there is no evidence that Valdez wanted to separate the two.

18. **C** Extract Infer

The third paragraph mentions that Broyles-González thinks that Valdez did not completely invent *actos* by himself out of nothing; the other actors and the *carpas* genre contributed.

60

A. No. Nothing in the passage describes the influences that shaped *carpas*; the *carpas* helped to shape *actos*.

B. No. The motives of the theater historians are not discussed.

C. Yes. Broyles-González "traces especially the *actos*' connections to a similar genre…known as *carpas*."

D. No. The passage says that "[m]any participants" in the *actos* had some connection to carpas, but not necessarily Valdez himself.

E. No. Broyles-González does not address this issue.

19. **C** Extract
Infer

A. No. Winning acceptance of farm owners is not mentioned.

B. No. Valdez is the only one mentioned who belonged to the San Francisco Mime Troupe.

C. Yes. The earliest efforts by the United Farm Workers Union were no later than 1965, according to the first paragraph, and the Teatro Campesino got going late in the same year. The Teatro Campesino could not have played a role in something that happened before it began.

D. No. The language of the performances is not mentioned.

E. No. Critics in Mexico are not mentioned.

20. **B** Extract
Infer

A. No. The only historian mentioned who analyzed *carpas* was Broyles-González.

B. Yes. The second paragraph mentions that the *actos* was the quintessential form of Chicano theater at the time, and it was a brief comic statement.

C. No. There is no evidence of recreating the *carpas*, just being influenced by them, according to the third paragraph.

D. No. The second paragraph indicates that there were no scripts; they were improvised.

E. No. Valdez's later experiences are not mentioned in the passage.

Questions 21–27

The passage describes the recommendations of the LRCWA for contingency lawyer fees based on successfully trying a client's case and critiques the recommendations, bringing up several negative aspects of them. The first paragraph mentions that the LRCWA made recommendations for contingency fees. The second paragraph defines the uplift fees and says that there were certain limitations recommended on their use. The third paragraph indicates that investigating clients' financial statuses, as would be necessary under the recommendations, would be burdensome. The fourth paragraph gives other negative side effects of the recommendations.

21. **B** `RC Reasoning`

The LRCWA recommends that the lawyers be paid a special uplift fee if the cases they argue for certain clients are argued successfully. The credited response should be a similar performance bonus for success in some other context.

A. No. This shares risk. There is no bonus for success; indeed, the success will be split among them.

B. Yes. The consulting firm gets a bonus for success. This is like the uplift fee.

C. No. This shares risk. There is no bonus for success; indeed, the success will be split among them.

D. No. There is no bonus for success. This is a cost based on a predicted outcome, not based on an actual outcome.

E. No. There is no bonus for success. In this case, there is a failsafe in case of problems arising.

22. **A** `Extract Fact`

A. Yes. In the middle of the third paragraph, the second listed point indicates this.

B. No. The second paragraph mentions that the plaintiffs should get just compensation, but what the lawyers deserve is not mentioned.

C. No. The first paragraph mentions that these recommendations are buried. It is not clear how likely to be incorporated they are.

D. No. The last sentence of the passage indicates the opposite of this, that the contingency-fee arrangements would like increase the lawyers' diligence and commitment to their cases.

E. No. The beginning of the second paragraph says that the uplift fee is an "agreed-upon percentage of that fee" (the regular fee before the uplift), not a percentage of the damages.

23. **E** `Big Picture`

The primary purpose was to describe the recommendations about contingency fees in the report and also describe some issues with them.

A. No. The author offers criticism of the proposed reform rather than defend it.

B. No. These are not the current shortcomings of a legal system but the shortcomings of a proposal to reform the legal system.

C. No. The change is described as burdensome and unfair in the third and fourth paragraphs, but "worsen" goes beyond this. The author does not oppose uplift fees altogether.

D. No. The changes are not indicated to be insignificant.

E. Yes. The author explains the suggested reform, uplifts fees, and critically evaluates it, indicating some shortcomings of the reform.

60

24. **C** `Extract Fact`

At the end of the third paragraph, the author points out that the requirement would be onerous because "the final cost of litigation depends in large part on factors that may change as the case unfolds."

A. No. While the length of time that a trial lasts may be related to what the author mentions, the final cost of litigation varying, it is not necessarily the same as the final cost of litigation and therefore is not exactly what the passage said.

B. No. Prospective clients' wishes are not mentioned in the passage.

C. Yes. This is indicated at the end of the third paragraph.

D. No. The passage says that uplift agreements should be entered as a last resort, but it may be difficult to determine when they are necessary, making the "last resort" requirement burdensome.

E. No. Taking time away from investigating legal issues was not mentioned in the passage.

25. **B** `Extract Infer`

The phrase refers to lawyers getting more than they properly should from the result of a case (and therefore, the client getting less).

A. No. This is too general. It's not just a payment of any sort that is at issue here. It's a payment as a portion of the awards from a case.

B. Yes. This is a reasonable paraphrase of the sentence in the second paragraph.

C. No. What the client considers fair is not mentioned or relevant.

D. No. The uplift fees make this situation possible (receiving higher payment than what would have been received without a successful case), but uplift fees were supposed to prevent what the phrase describes.

E. No. What the judge or jury intended the lawyer to receive is not mentioned and irrelevant.

26. **D** `Extract Fact`

The recommendations are in the second paragraph. The first is that the contingency fees be used only as a last resort. The second is that the lawyer verify that the client cannot pay the fee if sufficient damages are not awarded.

A. No. Increasing the lawyer's diligence and commitment is a happy side-effect that the author proposes will always happen. It is not part of the recommendations.

B. No. The size of the damages is not involved.

C. No. This is close to the second recommendation, but it is exact. The lawyer must be satisfied that the client is unable to pay without the damages.

D. Yes. This is the first requirement.

E. No. Whether the client will win is not a consideration.

27. **B**   **RC Reasoning**

The author's criticism is in the last two paragraphs. The criticisms are as follows: first, that the lawyers would have to investigate the clients' financial circumstances, and this is likely to be burdensome; second, that limiting the uplift fees to clients who are unable to pay otherwise may bar certain other clients from being able to enter into certain types of litigation; and third, that the reasons for uplift fees hold for all clients.

A. No. This supports the author's criticism that uplift fees advantage the least well-off and disadvantage the most well-off.

B. Yes. The author indicates that evaluating clients' financial circumstances would be excessively onerous. If they do this already on a regular basis, then the author's criticism is not a fair one.

C. No. Whether the recommendations will be implemented is irrelevant to whether they are good recommendations.

D. No. The amount by which the fees increase is not relevant to the author's criticisms.

E. No. It is not clear why there would be a difference in usage; perhaps they are worse than other types of arrangements, but perhaps there is some other reason. This might strengthen the author's criticism or might be totally irrelevant. It is inadequately specific.

Chapter 11
PrepTest 61:
Answers and
Explanations

ANSWER KEY: PREPTEST 61

Section 1:
Reading
Comprehension

1. D
2. B
3. B
4. D
5. E
6. A
7. C
8. A
9. E
10. C
11. B
12. E
13. B
14. B
15. A
16. D
17. D
18. C
19. B
20. D
21. E
22. A
23. E
24. E
25. B
26. A
27. B

Section 2:
Arguments 1

1. D
2. E
3. C
4. D
5. A
6. C
7. D
8. A
9. E
10. A
11. A
12. A
13. B
14. D
15. B
16. C
17. A
18. A
19. D
20. C
21. E
22. C
23. D
24. B
25. D

Section 3:
Games

1. A
2. E
3. A
4. C
5. D
6. A
7. C
8. A
9. C
10. B
11. D
12. D
13. D
14. B
15. A
16. E
17. B
18. D
19. C
20. D
21. B
22. B
23. A

Section 4:
Arguments 2

1. E
2. B
3. A
4. D
5. C
6. C
7. E
8. E
9. D
10. A
11. A
12. C
13. A
14. A
15. B
16. C
17. D
18. A
19. E
20. A
21. C
22. C
23. D
24. E
25. B
26. B

EXPLANATIONS

Section 1: Reading Comprehension

Questions 1–6

The passage discusses the Universal Declaration of Human Rights (UDHR), the reasons for its creation, and some of its strengths and weaknesses. The first paragraph provides background information about some limits of the original UN Charter that led to the commissioning of the UDHR. The second paragraph outlines the process by which the UDHR was drafted and approved, and it lists the fundamental rights it sets forth. The third paragraph addresses both a weakness of the UDHR and a reason it is worthy of recognition.

1. **D** **Extract Infer**

   The second sentence of the final paragraph comments on the weakness of the UHDR mentioned in the first sentence of that paragraph. "Purely programmatic" refers to the "nonbinding legal status" of the UHDR.

   A. No. "Purely programmatic" does not refer to the inspiring nature of the document. The sentence describes a weakness.

   B. No. In emphasizing a weakness, "purely programmatic" does not refer to the translation of ideals into standards.

   C. No. There is no mention of compromises that may have been necessary to gain approval.

   D. Yes. "Unenforceable" describes the nonbinding legal status of the UHDR to which "purely programmatic" refers.

   E. No. The passage contains no evidence of stubborn resistance within the UN hierarchy.

2. **B** **Structure**

   These quotes are attached to the discussion in lines 12–18 about how strong the basic human rights guarantee put forth by the UN should be. The UN Charter "encourage[s] respect for human rights" while the proposal requires members "to take separate and joint action" to promote human rights.

   A. No. The quotes have a similar definition of human rights.

   B. Yes. The UN charter is "not strong enough" but the proposal "implied an obligation for member states to act."

   C. No. The quotes set up a comparison in language but there is no mention of a bureaucratic vocabulary.

   D. No. The important points of the proposal are not highlighted in the first paragraph.

   E. No. The quotes do not compare stylistic differences between the documents.

61

3. **B**

Extract
Infer

The final paragraph argues that the UHDR "deserves recognition" despite its weaknesses.

A. No. By acknowledging a weakness, the author's enthusiasm is not "unbridled."

B. Yes. The author approves of the UHDR as a "standard-setting piece of work," but qualifies that approval by discussing a weakness.

C. No. The final paragraph indicates that the positives of the UHDR outweigh its negatives.

D. No. The author does not reject the UHDR.

E. No. The author recognizes a weakness but is not hostile.

4. **D**

Extract
Fact

This is an EXCEPT question, so eliminate the answer choices that are true of the UDHR.

A. No. The author mentions that the UHDR asserts a right to rest and leisure at the end of the second paragraph.

B. No. The passage indicates that the UHDR was produced from 1946 to 1948 after the UN Charter was approved in 1945.

C. No. The UN Commission is shown to be charged with producing the UHDR in line 28.

D. Yes. The passage discusses some consequences of the UHDR in the third paragraph.

E. No. The passage mentions that the UHDR "was the first international treaty to expressly affirm universal respect for human rights" in lines 3–4.

5. **E**

Extract
Infer

A. No. Though the author sees weaknesses in the charter, "wholly ineffectual" is too strong.

B. No. The third paragraph indicates that the document's strengths overcome its weaknesses.

C. No. The second paragraph discusses the challenging nature of the UHDR's passage.

D. No. There is no mention of important rights that are missing from the UHDR.

E. Yes. The third paragraph indicates that the UHDR would be stronger if it were a legally binding document.

6. **A** RC Reasoning

The delegates and representatives in the first paragraph believe that the language of Article I was "not strong enough" and proposed a stronger guarantee to basic human rights. The credited response should incorporate a requirement for separate and joint action to promote human rights.

A. Yes. The delegates and representatives would advocate for joint (UN authenticates) and separate (remedial action) action to promote human rights.

B. No. The delegates would not advocate a policy that did not require member states to take action and cooperate with the organization to promote human rights.

C. No. The delegates would not advocate a policy that did not require member states to take action and cooperate with the organization to promote human rights.

D. No. The delegates would not advocate a policy that did not require the UN to take action to promote human rights.

E. No. The delegates would not advocate a policy that did not require the UN to take action to promote human rights.

Questions 7–13

The passage discusses the aesthetic merits of van Meegeren's forged painting *The Disciples at Emmaus*. The first paragraph introduces a common assumption about the merit of art forgeries and introduces van Meegeren's painting as an example of a forgery that attracted praise before it was found to be a forgery. The second paragraph poses questions about well-crafted forgeries that may challenge the common assumption discussed in the first paragraph. The third paragraph provides answers to these questions from Alfred Lessing who argues that originality be used to judge artistic works. The final paragraph concludes that van Meegeren's art, and forged art in general, is inferior because it lacks originality of vision.

7. **C** Big Picture

The main point of the passage is that van Meegeren's art, and forged art in general, is inferior to original art because it lacks the innovation that makes an artwork artistically great.

A. No. The author does not categorize *The Disciples of Emmaus* as a failure. Instead the author acknowledges the aesthetic success of the painting in the third paragraph.

B. No. The author does include both aesthetic value and originality in the value of art but does not compare the relative weight of each in the overall value.

C. Yes. The author believes forged artworks are artistically inferior.

D. No. The author is primarily concerned with the artistic value of forged and orginal paintings, not the deception of art experts.

E. No. The passage does not discuss the reliability of art critics as judges of art.

8. **A** Extract Fact

The passage discusses the views of Lessing in the third paragraph in order to answer questions posed in the second paragraph.

A. Yes. Lessing argues that forged paintings can be both aesthetically superb and artistically inferior because they lack originality.

B. No. The author does not discuss Lessing's views on the financial value of artworks.

C. No. Lessing's argument is not concerned with who would be best to determine a work's authenticity.

61

D.   No. Lessing does not compare van Meegeren's painting to artists less significant than Vermeer.

E.   No. Lessing discusses art that has aesthetic value but is inferior artistically, not works that have no aesthetic value but do have artistic value.

9.   **E**   **Structure**

The author mentions art critic's beliefs in order to show that almost perfect forgeries can be mistaken for an original.

A.   No. The author is not attacking the inflexibility of critics.

B.   No. The author is not attacking the critics knowledge about art.

C.   No. The author is astonished by the persistence of the beliefs of some art critics so does not believe the painting to be an original.

D.   No. The problem posed by skilled forgeries is how closely they resemble the original, not the concept of forgery itself.

E.   Yes. The art critic's belief shows how art experts have been "duped" by an almost perfect forgery.

10.   **C**   **RC Reasoning**

The first paragraph shows that the critics lavished praise on *The Disciples of Emmaus* and were embarrassed when van Meegeren announced that it was forged.

A.   No. The music lovers rejection of imitation is not consistent with the art critics praise of a forgery.

B.   No. The discovery would not be embarrassing since the artist created original works.

C.   Yes. The diners praise the food until they realize it was not created by the chef they thought prepared the food.

D.   No. The critics' enthusiasm for a mistaken interpretation of an original work is different than the art critics' praise for a forgery.

E.   No. The fans' bias for an actor is different from the art critics' praise for an imitation.

11.   **B**   **Extract Infer**

The author discusses Lessing's views regarding the artistic value of an artwork in the third paragraph.

A.   No. The author does not mention Lessing's views about art forgeries in museums.

B.   Yes. Lessing argues that Vermeer's painting should be acclaimed for "pioneering techniques" in the seventeenth century.

C.   No. The author does not discuss Lessing's views about the importance of an artist's influence on others.

D.   No. Lessing's argument that artistic value includes both aesthetic and innovative judgements does not vary over time.

E.   No. Lessing regards innovation as an originality of vision that is distinct from the individual techniques an artist uses to accomplish this new way of seeing.

12. **E** `Extract Infer`

    A.   No. The author does not discuss a changing definition of what constitutes a "forgery."

    B.   No. The author does not argue that an artist using another artist's techniques is a forger. A forger is one who imitates another artist.

    C.   No. The author does not discuss the steps necessary to become a successful forger.

    D.   No. The author does not compare early and late periods of artists.

    E.   Yes. In the first paragraph, *The Disciples at Emmaus* is shown to be an example of a forged painting that is not a copy of another work.

13. **B** `RC Reasoning`

Lessing's argument in the third paragraph is that a painting can be aesthetically brilliant but lack originality of vision so would be artistically inferior.

    A.   No. Forgers who have succeeded as painters of original works would not support Lessing's argument about the artistic value of a painting.

    B.   Yes. Reproductions that are beautiful but not valued as great art provide more evidence for Lessing's argument that art can be aesthetically pleasing and artistically inferior.

    C.   No. The challenges forgers pose to art critics do not support Lessing's claims about the importance of both aesthetics and originality.

    D.   No. Unsuccessful attempts at a forgery are irrelevant to Lessing's argument about the artistic value of an artwork.

    E.   No. Changing aesthetic judgements do not support Lessing's argument about including originality of vision in the artistic value of artwork.

Questions 14–19

Passage A

The author claims that while animal and human vocalization both alter the listener's behavior, they differ in that animal vocalizations alter this behavior without intending to do so. The first paragraph introduces the topic and discusses one function of language in humans. The second paragraph uses multiple examples to show how animal vocalizations can produce effects without intending to do so and concludes that these vocalizations "are not as purposeful as they first appear."

Passage B

The author questions the beliefs of many scientists who argue that animal communication is a mechanical response to stimuli, whereas human communication is made with understanding and intent. The first paragraph introduces this commonly held belief that animals communicate without intent. The second paragraph describes the logic that is often used to prove the theory that animals communicate as a conditioned reflex. The third paragraph points out a flaw in this reasoning and introduces new studies that may indicate that the gap between animal and human communication may be smaller than is perceived.

14. **B**   **Big Picture**

Both passages compare human and animal communication and the degree to which that communication is purposeful.

   A.   No. Passage A does not address this question.

   B.   Yes. Both passages discuss the intent behind animal vocalizations.

   C.   No. Passage B argues that animal vocalizations are not simply response to mechanical stimuli.

   D.   No. The passages argue the differences between animal and human communication. There is no contrast among animal species in the passages.

   E.   No. Passage A does not discuss the opinions of other scientists, and so does not address this question.

15. **A**   **Structure**

The author discusses the philosopher in the second paragraph in order to provide an example of the view that "conscious intention" is "uniquely human," which the author argues is a view based on flawed logic.

   A.   Yes. In the third paragraph, the author's argument that Maritain's belief that animals do not have a conscious intent is flawed.

   B.   No. The Maritain example does not provide evidence for a conscious intent.

   C.   No. The Maritain example does not indicate that animal communication is spontaneous or creative.

   D.   No. The author does argue that Maritain's view is flawed, but there is no evidence in Maritain's view that could be used as evidence against this theory.

   E.   No. The author believes Maritain's view is flawed.

16. **D**   **Extract Infer**

The author of passage B argues that the views held by people like the author of passage A are flawed because they make fundamental assumptions about communication that have not been studied scientifically.

   A.   No. The author of passage B does not discuss the mental states of human listeners.

B.   No. The author of passage B does not attack the credibility of these scientists in arguing that their views are based on flawed logic.

C.   No. The author of passage B does not discuss evidence of animals that deceive.

D.   Yes. The author of passage B argues that recent studies point out assumptions held by the views of many scientists that agree with the position put forth in passage A.

E.   No. The author of passage B does not discuss the impact of evolution on animal communication systems.

17.   **D**   **Extract**
                Infer

The Maritain example argues that animal communication is "merely a conditioned reflex."

A.   No. "Influencing behavior" does not match the "conditioned reflex" in Maritain's view.

B.   No. The behavior-altering ability of communication does not support the "conditioned reflex" in Maritain's view.

C.   No. Chimpanzee's ability to detect mental states in others does not support the "conditioned reflex" in Maritain's view.

D.   Yes. This kind of call without intent supports Maritain's view that animal communication is a "conditioned reflex."

E.   No. Macaques' calls do not directly support the "conditioned reflex" in Maritain's view because we do not know if they are purposeful.

18.   **C**   **Extract**
                Infer

The authors hold different views on the purposefulness of animal communication.

A.   No. The author of passage B does not discuss the ability of humans to perceive mental states.

B.   No. Both authors discuss this issue as something scientists should consider. They do not disagree about the importance of this question, only its answer.

C.   Yes. The author of passage A argues that animal vocalizations "are not as purposeful as they first appear" but the author of passage B argues that recent studies indicate a problem in the assumption that "animal and human communication is qualitative rather than merely quantitative."

D.   No. The author of passage A does not address this ability in chimpanzees.

E.   No. The author of passage B does not address the role of evolution in animal communication.

19.   **B**   **Big Picture**

The attitude of passage B is more negative in that it argues about flaws in the approach many scientists are using to argue about animal communication.

A.   No. The author of passage B does not argue that science will find answers, only that studies have recently cast doubt on the beliefs of many scientists.

61

B. Yes. In the third paragraph, the author of passage B states that the arguments of many scientists are flawed.

C. No. The author of passage B does not accept the validity of the opinions of the many scientists who use flawed reasoning.

D. No. There is no evidence that the author of passage B supports ongoing research.

E. No. The author of passage B is not cautious nor is he or she waiting for research to settle the issue before calling out the flawed reasoning of many scientists who believe animal communication is without intent.

Questions 20–27

The passage explains why some African American historians adopted a transnational perspective and how that perspective may be considered within the nationalist historiographical context of mainstream U.S. historians. The first paragraph introduces the contrast between mainstream historians and some early African American historians. The second paragraph explains how the "problem of citizenship" played into the transnational perspective of African American historians. The third paragraph discusses the mainstream nationalist approach to historiography during the period. The final paragraph discusses the similarities between the transnational approach and the mainstream nationalist approach. The author argues that the transnational approach was actually a kind of nationalism.

20. **D**   Big Picture

The passage explains why some African American historians adopted a transnational perspective and how that perspective may be considered within the nationalist historiographical context of mainstream U.S. historians.

A. No. The article is concerned with approaches of African American historians. The discussion of citizenship is limited to the second paragraph so it too narrow.

B. No. In the second paragaraph, the author argues that African American historians were involved in a debate about citizenship and emigration, but that is too narrow to be the main idea of the whole passage.

C. No. The author does not argue that there was a conflict between mainstream and African American historians. Instead the passage argues that African American historians attempt to adopt a transnational approach contrasted the mainstream but was actually consistent with mainstream nationalist historiography.

D. Yes. In their attempt to counter mainstream U.S. historiography, the author argues, African American historians adopted a transnational approach that could be viewed as a form of nationalism.

E. No. The author views African American historians through the lens of mainstream nationalism but does not argue that the transnational approach adopted by African American historians converted any mainstream historians.

21. **E** `Extract Infer`

As it is used in the passage the word "reconstructing" means recreating in order to overturn old views and establish a new identity.

A. No. Historians were not trying to correct a misconception in creating a new "shared identity."

B. No. The author does not discuss a sequence of events in the fourth paragraph.

C. No. Investigating implications is not consistent with the author's argument that historians were creating a new "shared identity."

D. No. Historians were not "rewarding the promoters" in order to overturn degrading representations.

E. Yes. Historians were attempting to shape a new "shared identity."

22. **A** `Extract Infer`

A. Yes. In the second paragraph, the author argues that emigrationist sentiment was a result of a "profound pessimism" regarding the citizenship of African Americans.

B. No. The author does not discuss scholars who write about the history of diasporic communities.

C. No. The author does not argue that nationalists overstated the greatness of their nations.

D. No. The author does not mention foreign policy in his definition of nationalism.

E. No. The author does not discuss the number of African Americans who embraced the "inevitability of the dominance of the nation-state."

23. **E** `RC Reasoning`

The transnational approach employed by African American historians is discussed in the final two paragraphs. The credited response should show an example of how this approach unified African Americans within a cultural nation.

A. No. This study would not discuss African American culture.

B. No. This study would not discuss African American culture.

C. No. This study would not discuss African American culture.

D. No. This study would not discuss African American culture.

E. Yes. This study would show how traditions of Africa unified an African American "nation."

24. **E** `Extract Fact`

A. No. There is no mention of specific African nations.

B. No. There is no mention of languages spoken by African American's ancestors.

C. No. There is no mention of specific territories upon which the United States attempted to exert influence.

D. No. While the argument acknowledges that the question of citizenship for African Americans was not resolved, it does not argue that "textual ambiguities" caused this situation.

E. Yes. The author answers this question in the second paragraph by discussing the emigrationist policies of some black leaders.

25. **B** Structure

A. No. The author discusses the diasporic community as a group of people who "saw themselves as an oppressed 'nation' without a homeland" in the fourth paragraph.

B. Yes. The author argues that African American historians, while not having a territory of their own, maintained a nationalist perspective by unifying African American culture as "a history that began in Africa."

C. No. The author does not argue that African American transnationalists did not engage in myth-making.

D. No. The author mentions that "some black leaders" promoted emigration but does not discuss their level of prominence in the field of history.

E. No. The author acknowledges some differences in the approaches of the different historians but does not indicate that they focused "on entirely different events."

26. **A** Extract Infer

The second paragraph details the reasons African American historians adopted a transnationalist approach that the author mentions in the first paragraph.

A. Yes. The author uses the second paragraph to explain why African Americans adopted a transnational perspective.

B. No. The author does not discuss the desired effects of governmental actions in the second paragraph.

C. No. The author does not discuss criticism of U.S. imperialism by African Americans in the second paragraph.

D. No. The author does not indicate that emigrationist beliefs were an alternative to "fighting for the benefits of U.S. citizenship."

E. No. The author does not argue that the Fourteenth Amendment is too limited in the discussion of the questions that were left unresolved.

27. **B** RC Reasoning

Mainstream U.S. historians adopted a nationalist approach that consisted of a "glorification of the nation and a focus on the nation-state as a historical force" and resulted in the creation of a shared identity among members of the nation.

A. No. Repeating past actions is not an example of the nationalist perspective adopted by mainstream U.S. historians.

B. Yes. The innate talents of the novelist leading to early achievements is consistent with the nationalist approach that incorporated "the inevitability of nations, their 'temperaments,' their destinies."

C. No. Mainstream U.S. historians did not argue that nationalism was the best approach because it was expressly created to explain the history of the United States.

D. No. The newspaper series' attempt to inform the public is not consistent with the mainstream U.S. historians' attempt to glorify the nation-state or a common identity.

E. No. Mainstream U.S. historians did not believe in nationalism because it had consistently provided the same result in analyzing history.

Section 2: Arguments 1

1. **D**   Flaw

Mary's argument concludes that Jamal's reasoning is absurd. Jamal's statements that Mary has a "legal right to sell" her business but has no "right to do so" involve a shifting meaning in the use of the word "right." The flaw in Mary's argument is her failure to recognize that shift in meaning.

A. No. Mary's conclusion does not overlook this possibility because Jamal's statement indicates that Mary may sell whenever she wishes.

B. No. The rights of the employees are not relevant to the argument.

C. No. This was Jamal's claim, not Mary's.

D. Yes. Mary's argument fails to recognize that Jamal may refer to different kinds of right—a legal right versus a moral right.

E. No. Mary makes no mention of Jamal's character.

2. **E**   Parallel

The argument concludes that the evolution of organs to not greatly outlast other organs is a result of natural selection. Evidence is presented that there is no survival value for the animal to have an organ that does greatly outlast the body. The principle in this argument is that it is inefficient for parts to outlast the whole.

A. No. The comparison of price does not match the part-whole comparison made in the argument.

B. No. One organ that compensates for another deficient organ does not match the part-whole principle.

C. No. The comparison drawn between two whole car models does not match the part-whole comparison made in the argument.

D. No. Rather than compare the survival of individual parts within a system, this answer considers how the parts impact each other.

E. Yes. Like the body, if the parts of an automobile outlast the whole, it does not increase the overall quality of the whole and is therefore not cost-effective (efficient).

3. C   Inference

The first sentence is a conditional statement: The combination of economic success and success at protecting individual liberties leads to overall success. The second sentence says that environmental protection is not necessary for success at protecting individual liberties. The third sentence acknowledges the present administration's success at protecting individual liberties and its lack of care for the environment. Combining these sentences leaves open the question of whether the present administration is a success since we are missing information about the present administration's economic success.

A. No. While it is possible for this to be true, there is no evidence that it must be true.

B. No. There is not enough information to know whether the present administration is an overall success or not.

C. Yes. If the present administration is an economic success, we know it must be an overall success, since the final sentence of the argument states that it has successfully protected individual liberties. These two successes are sufficient to know the present administration is an overall success.

D. No. There is no evidence of a link between economic success and caring for the environment.

E. No. There is no evidence that environmental protection would be sufficient for overall success.

4. D   Reasoning

The argument concludes that the bill prohibiting fishing should be enacted despite the potential impact on the industry. The author cites a study that found toxin levels in fish that exceed standards. The author indicates that continuing to allow fishing in the bay could have negative effects on public health. The argument proceeds by explaining a negative impact of failing to pass the ban.

A. No. The evidence presented does not state the economic effects of toxic contamination in fish, but rather the health effects.

B. No. There is no evidence about moral principles.

C. No. The study put forth as evidence does not attack opponents of the ban.

D. Yes. The study and its conclusion indicate that the toxic contamination in the bay's fish would have "grave effects on public health."

E. No. There is no evidence that the ban will be successful in reducing toxins in fish.

5. A   Principle Strengthen

Vandenburg argues that the small size of the museum's contemporary art collection goes against the museum's purpose—devoting as much attention to contemporary art as to the art of earlier periods. Simpson argues that the size of the museum's contemporary collection is appropriate because the art museum does not need to collect every style of art, and the small size of its collection is a product of few high-quality contemporary art pieces. Simpson's argument could be helped by connecting the premises about high-quality art pieces with the conclusion about the size of the collection.

A. Yes. If museums should collect only high-quality art pieces and there are few high-quality pieces of contemporary art, then Simpson's conclusion would be true.

B. No. Art that violates the founder's purpose is not relevant to Simpson's conclusion.

C. No. This is a premise of Simpson's argument.

D. No. The purpose of an ethnographic museum is not relevant to Simpson's conclusion.

E. No. The intentions of the art museum's curators are not relevant to Simpson's conclusion.

6. **C** **Strengthen**

The argument concludes that corporate actions to discourage alternative-energy projects influenced the government's funding decisions. The author provides evidence that funding for alternative-energy projects has been reduced from initial reserves. The author also indicates that large corporations discourage alternative-energy projects. The author's argument attempts to establish a causal relationship between the government's actions and the corporation's actions from evidence that indicates only that these actions are correlated. The argument can be strengthened by bolstering the causal link between the two actions or by removing other possible causes.

A. No. The fact that projects do not receive funding does not strengthen the argument about why projects do receive funding.

B. No. Changes in funding levels do not help connect corporate actions with government decisions.

C. Yes. If this is true, it suggests a connection between specific corporate actions and government funding decisions.

D. No. If this were true, it would weaken the argument by showing that large corporations encourage some projects that receive reduced funding.

E. No. This does not demonstrate a connection between corporate actions and government funding decisions.

7. **D** **Point at Issue**

Talbert argues that chess is beneficial for school-age children because it promotes mental maturity. Sklar argues that chess diverts attention from other things that have societal value.

A. No. While Talbert would agree with this, Sklar does not take a side on the issue.

B. No. Neither argument discusses other activities that may promote mental maturity.

C. No. Talbert provides no evidence regarding the social value of either science or chess.

D. Yes. Talbert argues that teaching chess would be beneficial, while Sklar voices an objection to teaching chess to children.

E. No. Neither argument discusses the mental maturity of children who do not play chess or study science.

8. **A** **Flaw**

Theodora argues that Marcia is wrong to claim "that vegetarianism cannot lead to nutritional deficiencies" because switching to a vegetarian diet may cause some people working in meat-based industries to have a nutritionally poor diet. The problem with Theodora's conclusion is that Marcia's argument is that "not all vegetarian diets lead to nutritional deficiencies," which is a different conclusion than the one Theodora argues against.

A.   Yes. Theodora's argument is disproving a different conclusion than that made by Marcia.

B.   No. Theodora's argument provides an alternative consideration to the research in Marcia's argument.

C.   No. By stating a situation that would occur if most people became vegetarians, Theodora does not make any assumptions about other factors that could lead to the collapse of meat-based industries.

D.   No. Theodora's argument does not use "diet" in a different sense to that in Marcia's argument.

E.   No. Theodora does not assume that people that lose jobs would become vegetarians, only that they would not be able to "afford a nutritionally adequate diet."

9.   E   **Main Point**

The musicologist argues that the piano is properly called a percussion instrument. The author provides evidence that musical instruments are classified based on the mechanical actions that produce music and that piano strings vibrate because of the impact of hammers.

A.   No. The argument is concerned primarily with the classification of the piano, and this statement is used as a premise in the musicologist's argument.

B.   No. The argument does not refer to the "way musicians interact with" instruments.

C.   No. There is no evidence that people refer to the piano as a stringed instrument.

D.   No. This it the opposite of the argument's conclusion.

E.   Yes. This correctly paraphrases the musicologist's conclusion.

10.   A   **Inference**

A.   Yes. Combining the first two sentences in the passage shows that agricultural runoff has doubled the phosphorus level, which has stimulated the growth of plankton.

B.   No. There is no evidence in the paragraph to indicate whether fish could have survived in the area in the time before the past few decades.

C.   No. There is no evidence in the paragraph about what is occurring in the ocean region at present to support this hypothetical, future situation.

D.   No. The first sentence does not indicate a change in the quantity of agricultural runoff during the past few decades.

E.   No. Phosphorus leads to a lack of oxygen in this particular area because it stimulates the growth of plankton and the use of oxygen by bacteria that feed on decaying plankton. This situation may not be the same in other bodies of water.

11. **A** Weaken

The argument concludes that drivers are possessive of parking spaces especially in situations where another driver wants the space. A study is used to support the argument. The author assumes that there is no other reason for the time difference among drivers in the study than their level of possessiveness. The argument can be weakened by providing evidence for considerations that could explain the time difference other than a driver's possessiveness or by attacking the integrity of the study.

A. Yes. If other drivers that are waiting for a space put pressure on a driver, that pressure could reduce the speed at which he or she is able to leave a parking space. This provides an alternative explanation for the time difference mentioned in the study.

B. No. The length of time spent entering a space does not weaken the claim about possessiveness, which is based on a study regarding the length of time leaving a space.

C. No. This does not address why it is more difficult and time-consuming to leave a space. It does not directly attack the conclusion since the difficulty could be be caused by the increased possessiveness drivers feel.

D. No. The differences between the mall parking spaces and other parking spaces is irrelevant to the conclusion about whether people are possessive of those spaces when other drivers are waiting to enter them.

E. No. While anger at impatient honking may be a factor in the length of time drivers leave a space, the study indicates that drivers delayed even in situations when there was no honking. Since the answer choice does not address the entire argument, it does not adequately weaken the conclusion.

12. **A** Resolve/
Explain

The paragraph says on one hand that shark teeth are the most common fossils but that shark skeleton fossils are comparatively rare.

A. Yes. While the teeth of sharks are likely to fossilize, the skeletons of sharks are not. Thus, shark teeth fossils should be more common than shark skeleton fossils.

B. No. The location of fossils that are found does not explain why shark teeth fossils are so much more common than skeletons.

C. No. The paragraph says shark teeth fossils are more common than the skeleton fossils. That it is difficult to distinguish shark teeth from other teeth fossils is irrelevant.

D. No. Information about sharks that live today does not explain why shark teeth fossils are more common than shark skeleton fossils.

E. No. This makes the situation worse by arguing that skeletons and teeth fossilize by the same process.

13. **B**   Sufficient Assumption

The critic argues that photographs are interpretations of reality. The evidence for this argument is that photographers express their own views by choosing a subject. There is a language shift between photographers expressing a view and photographs interpreting reality.

A. No. This gives us only the possibility that photographs are interpretations, whereas the question task asks for something that will make the conclusion logically sound based on the evidence provided.

B. Yes. If this is true, then photographs expressing a view would make photographs an interpretation of reality.

C. No. All art may express a view but there is a missing connection between this view and the interpretation of reality.

D. No. This is the opposite of what is needed. It argues that interpretations of reality (the conclusion) express a view (the premises) and an answer is needed that says that to express a view is to interpret reality.

E. No. All photographs may express a view but there is a missing connection between this view and interpreting reality.

14. **D**   Weaken

The argument concludes that the track marks are likely due to a geological process instead of worms. It provides evidence that the marks were made many years before the existence of the earliest known traces of multicellular animal life. The author assumes without providing any evidence that geological processes could have made the marks and could be weakened by providing additional evidence pointing to an alternate consideration or otherwise stating that geological processes were not responsible for the marks.

A. No. The age of sandstone is irrelevant. The argument states that the marks in this piece of sandstone were made "more than half a billion years" before known animals could have made the tracks.

B. No. By providing additional evidence that geological processes made other marks in sandstone, this answer choice strengthens the argument.

C. No. The argument provides evidence that the marks in this piece of sandstone were made "more than half a billion years" before known animals could have made the tracks. "Life forms" other than worms that existed would not weaken the claim that the geological processes caused the marks without additional evidence that those "life forms" made the marks.

D. Yes. If geological processes could not have caused the marks, the conclusion is not valid.

E. No. The answer indicates that worms could have existed earlier than is known but does not indicate that they could have been alive "more than half a billion years" before known animals could have made the tracks.

15. **B**   Main Point

The passage provides evidence that different species are likely to develop similar types of organs or body structures since that organ or body structure is the only way to accomplish a task. To conclude, the argument indicates that since animals have similar needs, that they will have similar ways to accomplish those needs. The credited response should match the information provided in the argument.

A. No. The argument provides no information about animals living in the same environments.

B. Yes. The argument says that animals have similar organs to perform similar tasks so animals are likely to adapt similar ways to satisfy the needs of the last sentence.

C. No. The argument attempts to compare different animals with similar needs so this answer choice is inconsistent with that comparison.

D. No. There is no evidence that animals with different needs will have similarities.

E. No. While the passage makes an example out of eyes and wings, there is no indication that all animals with similar needs will develop them.

16. C **Necessary Assumption**

The argument concludes that steel plants could save money as a reduction in their electrical bills by installing thermophotovoltaic generators if there is a way to feed the heat produced into the generators. Evidence is provided that steel plants generate a lot of heat as waste and thermophotovoltaic generators convert heat into electricity. There is a gap between the conversion of heat to electricity and saving money.

A. No. The author does not argue that thermovoltaic cells are the most cost-effective option available to steel plants. Other options are irrelevant.

B. No. The conclusion is explicitly predicated on the ability to convert the heat waste from steel plants into electricity.

C. Yes. This links the ability to convert heat to electricity with saving money. Use the negation test: If the electrical bills are not reduced enough to cover the costs of installation, then steel plants will not save money.

D. No. The argument does not require electricity to be the primary source of energy as long as electricity is a source of energy.

E. No. Other ways to save money are irrelevant to the conclusion.

17. A **Reasoning**

The argument concludes that herbal remedies are more likely to retain effectiveness against new and different strains of bacteria than do standard antibiotics. The herbalist provides evidence that standard antibiotics usually have only one active ingredient whereas herbal remedies have several. The herbalist also uses an analogy that compares the resistance of a bacteria to multiple ingredients (herbal remedies) or one ingredient (standard antibiotics) to the challenge of cooking for several guests or only one guest.

A. Yes. The single guest is easier to prepare for in the same way that a it is easier to resist an antibiotic with only one ingredient.

B. No. The author uses the several dozen guests to correspond with herbal remedies.

C. No. The challenge of pleasing a guest corresponds with the ability of a bacteria to resist a treatment.

D. No. The cook in the analogy corresponds to the bacteria.

E. No. There are no ingredients mentioned in the analogy.

18. **A**   Flaw

The argument concludes that barn owls cease to use vision to locate sounds once they have developed a scheme for estimating that location. It provides a study done on barn owls as evidence of the conclusion. The credited response will hurt the argument by describing a way the study does not necessarily lead to the author's conclusion.

A. Yes. If this is true, then it is possible that the owls continue to use a distorted vision in their estimation of a sound's location.

B. No. The hypothesis is specific to barn owls so the scientists do not make assumptions about other owls.

C. No. The hypothesis does not assign human reasoning to owls.

D. No. The hypothesis is specific to barn owls so the scientists do not make assumptions about other types of birds.

E. No. The experimental results about barn owls is relevant to the scientists' conclusion about barn owls.

19. **D**   Resolve/ Explain

The passage indicates that, on one hand, journalists are using more quotations to report the unsupported or false claims of newsmakers but, on the other hand, are "less likely to openly challenge" the truthfulness of those claims. The credited response will be the one answer choice that does not explain this situation.

A. No. The possibility of losing a subscriber could explain why journalists are less likely to challenge the views of newsmakers.

B. No. The likelihood of journalists reporting on a topic about which they are not especially knowledgeable could explain why they are less likely to challenge the views of newsmakers.

C. No. If journalists are more likely to report claims by people with whom they agree, it makes sense that they are less likely to challenge the views of these newsmakers.

D. Yes. The basic principle of journalism established here would seem to indicate that journalists should be more likely to draw attention to a debate over an unsupported claim. This does not explain why journalists are less likely to challenge the views of newsmakers.

E. No. The criticism associated with challenging the views of newsmakers could explain why journalists are less likely to do it.

20. **C**   Weaken

The argument concludes that interpreting EKG data should be left to computer programs because a computer program performed better in a study than a highly skilled cardiologist. The argument assumes that there were not drawbacks to the computer program that were not mentioned by the study.

A. No. The computer program correctly diagnosed a higher proportion of cases regardless of the number of mistakes made by the cardiologist.

B. No. The inability to make subjective judgements is not at issue in the argument about whether a computer program should interpret EKG data.

C. Yes. The answer points to a negative impact associated with computer programs interpreting EKG data. If a computer program incorrectly diagnoses heart attacks, it may not be the best option to interpret EKG data.

D. No. The argument is specifically discussing the interpretation of EKG data so other information is irrelevant to the conclusion of whether a computer program should interpret EKG data.

E. No. If the very experienced, highly skilled cardiologist is not representative of cardiologists in general, then the average cardiologist is less experienced and not highly skilled. This does not weaken the argument that a computer program should interpret EKG.

---

21. **E**   **Principle Strengthen**

The author concludes that the speed limit on straight stretches of high-speed roadways should be set to 75 miles per hour, the average actual speed on those roadways. The author provides a study that indicates speed limits that reflect the actual average speeds of traffic reduces the accident rate to support the conclusion. The credited response should help the argument by providing more evidence that speed limits should be set to this speed or that bolsters the integrity of the evidence provided.

A. No. Uniform speed limits only on straight stretches of high-speed roadways would not justify the conclusion that it should be set at 75 miles per hour on all straight stretches of such roadways.

B. No. Uniform traffic laws across the nation would support the idea that speed limits across the nation should be the same but would not justify the conclusion that the speed limit should be set at 75 miles per hour.

C. No. Since the actual average speed on all the roadways is unknown, this would not justify the conclusion that a uniform speed limit of 75 miles per hour be set on all such roadways.

D. No. Laws that are frequently violated are not discussed in the argument and would not help our conclusion about adjusting the speed limit on straight stretches of high-speed roadways to 75 miles per hour.

E. Yes. If any measure that reduces traffic accidents should be implemented, then the speed limit on straight stretches of high-speed roadways should be set to the average actual speed on those roadways.

---

22. **C**   **Strengthen**

The psychiatrist argues that some first-year students could reduce spending on recreation without increasing anxiety or depression. Evidence is provided that those students that report the highest levels of spending on recreation have the same levels of anxiety and depression as those with the lowest levels of spending. The argument contains several common flaws that could be improved. The credited response in this EXCEPT question will not strengthen the conclusion.

A. No. The psychiatrist assumes that the first-year students at this university are representative of other first-year students. Information that the pattern holds at other universities would strengthen the argument.

B.   No. If students with moderate spending have lower levels of anxiety and depression than both groups discussed in the argument, then students with high levels of spending may actually reduce anxiety and depression by spending less.

C.   Yes. Information about adults between 40 and 60 has no bearing on a conclusion about first-year university students.

D.   No. Information about the accuracy of the screening tools used by the psychiatrist bolster the integrity of the evidence cited in the argument thereby strengthening the conclusion.

E.   No. This provides additional evidence that students could reduce spending without increasing anxiety or depression thereby strengthening the conclusion.

23.   **D**   **Parallel Flaw**

The argument concludes that most brick houses on River Street have two stories because every brick house on River Street has a front yard and most houses on River Street with front yards also have two stories. The argument is flawed because it fails to recognize that the evidence provided does not directly connect brick houses with those houses that have two stories. It is possible, for instance, that there are many homes on River Street with front yards but few of them are brick houses. In this situation, it is possible that all of the brick houses have only one story even while most homes with front yards have two.

A.   No. This does not match the original argument. It argues that legislators are politicians and most legislators have run for office so most politicians have run for office. The flaw in this answer choice is a matter of degree: The evidence would support the claim that some politicians have run for office but it is unknown if in fact most have. In the original argument it is possible that no brick house has two stories.

B.   No. This does not match the original argument. It argues that since most legislators have run for office and most politicians who have run for office are public servants that most public servants are legislators. This answer choice assumes legislators are politicians whereas the original argument did not involve a language shift.

C.   No. The answer choice argues that since every legislator is a public servant and not all public servants are legislators that some public servants have not run for office. The flaw here is that there is no evidence connecting legislators or public servants with running for office.

D.   Yes. This matches the original argument. It argues that since all legislators are public servants and most public servants have never run for office that most legislators have never run for office. It fails to recognize that the evidence provided does not directly connect legislators with the public servants who have not run for office. It is possible that both premises are true and yet all legislators have run for office.

E.   No. This answer choice does not match the original argument. It argues that since most public servants have not run for office and most legislators have, that most legislators are not public servants. The flaw here is that the data points about most legislators and most public servants may not overlap. The original argument provided evidence about all brick houses, so an argument about most legislators would not match.

24. **B** **Sufficient Assumption**

The argument concludes that increased knowledge of history reduces the chance a person will view history as the working out of moral themes. The historian provides evidence that says people who do not hold clear and unambiguous moral beliefs are unlikely to see history as the working out of moral themes. Also, people are less likely to morally judge human behavior as knowledge of history increases. There is a missing link between morally judging people and holding clear and unambiguous moral beliefs.

A. No. Whether historical events elicit moral approval or not is irrelevant to the argument about individuals who judge and hold moral beliefs.

B. Yes. If this is true, then increasing knowledge of history would lead to a decrease in the inclination to morally judge people and a comparable decrease in the likelihood to hold clear and unambiguous moral beliefs.

C. No. The moral significance placed on an event is different from the idea that these events worked out a moral theme. This does not confirm the conclusion that people with greater knowledge of history will be less likely to consider that history is the working out of moral themes.

D. No. This is the reverse of the premise from the first sentence. The author argues that holding clear and unambiguous moral beliefs is necessary for seeing history as the working out of moral themes and does not assume that it is sufficient.

E. No. A connection between objectivity and knowledge of history would not help the author's conclusion about viewing history as the working out of moral themes.

25. **D** **Resolve/ Explain**

The passage establishes that students at the university would prefer a new president with extensive experience, but most students chose someone who has never served as a university president from the list of leading candidates.

A. No. The inability to use experience as the sole criteria does not explain why students who prefer experience as one criteria chose a candidate who lacks experience.

B. No. This does not explain why students at the university did not choose one of the candidates with experience.

C. No. That there were few candidates to choose from does not speak to the issue of experience as a criteria students prefer but did not select.

D. Yes. If students prefer experience but were unaware of the experience offered by the candidates, the students were unable to choose by using that criteria.

E. No. The fact that someone without experience may be well-suited does not explain why students prefer experience but did not choose a candidate with experience.

Section 3: Games

Questions 1–5

Assign six workers—F, G, H, J, K, and L—to one of two cars. This is a two-group game in which each car must have at least two and at most four workers. One worker in each car will be the driver.

Clue 1: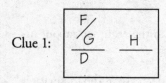

Clue 2: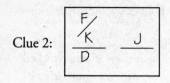

Clue 3: $\boxed{GL}$

Deductions: The block clues do not combine to create many useful deductions about the cars. We do know that either F or G must drive one of the cars.

Your diagram should look like this:

FGHJKL $\underline{\hspace{1cm}}$ 1 $\underline{\hspace{1cm}}$ | $\underline{\hspace{1cm}}$ 2 $\underline{\hspace{1cm}}$

                — — | — —

                D   D

1. **A**   **Grab-a-Rule**

Clue 1 eliminates (D) because K is driving the car with H. Clue 2 eliminates (B) because L is driving the car with J, and (E) because J is driving. Clue 3 eliminates (C) since G and L are in different cars. Choice (A) is the credited response.

2. **E**   **General**

Use previous work and POE to eliminate answer choices that contain workers that CAN be the two drivers.

A. No. Both F and G can drive as long as J is in the car with F (clue 2) and L is in the car with G (clue 3).

B. No. F and K can drive if H is in the car with F (clue 1).

C. No. Use past work. When L drives one car, G will be a passenger (clue 3) so F will drive the car with H and J (clues 1 and 2).

D. No. Use past work. When F is a passenger, the two drivers will be G (clue 1) and K (clue 2).

E. Yes. K and L cannot both drive because either F or G must drive the car with H (clue 1).

3. **A** Specific

L driving requires G as a passenger in the same car (clue 3). Clues 1 and 2 combine to force F as the driver of the other car with H and J as passengers. K could be in either car so (A) is possible.

$$
\begin{array}{c|c}
1 & 2 \\
\hline
\underset{D}{\underline{L}} \quad \underline{G} \quad \underline{(K)} & \underset{D}{\underline{F}} \quad \underline{H} \quad \underline{J} \quad \underline{(K)}
\end{array}
$$

4. **C** Specific

The question task requires two groups of three workers each. F rides as a passenger in one car. Clues 1 and 2 require the two drivers to be K and G with J riding in the car with K and H riding in the car with G. Clue 3 also requires L to ride in the car with G. One car will be K (driving), F, J, while the other is G (driving), H, L. Choice (C) lists J as the other passenger in the car with F.

$$
\begin{array}{c|c}
1 & 2 \\
\hline
\underline{K} \quad \underline{F} \quad \underline{J} & \underline{G} \quad \underline{H} \quad \underline{L}
\end{array}
$$

5. **D** General

Use past work to eliminate answer choices that are possible.

A. No. G can ride in a car with L driving, while the other workers ride in a car with F driving.

B. No. H can ride in a car with F driving, while the other workers ride in a car with K driving.

C. No. J can ride in car with K driving, while the other workers ride in car with G or F driving.

D. Yes. If K were to ride as a passenger, K would ride in a car with F driving and J as a passenger (clue 2) or in a car with G driving and L as a passenger (clue 3).

E. No. L can ride in car with G driving, while the other workers ride in a car with F driving.

Questions 6–11

The ranking from first (oldest) to sixth (most recent) should constitute the core of the diagram. There is a one-to-one correspondence between the elements and spaces: Each element is in exactly one space and each space has exactly one player.

Clue 1:

$$F \left\langle \begin{array}{c} J \\ H \end{array} \right.$$

Clue 2:

$$\begin{array}{c} N \\ \diagdown \\ J \diagup \end{array} T$$

Clue 3:

$$P \left\langle \begin{array}{c} H \\ N \end{array} \right. \quad \text{or} \quad \begin{array}{c} H \\ N \end{array} \right\rangle P$$

Deductions: Combine Clues 1 and 2 to make a larger branching range clue like this:

$$\begin{array}{c} \quad\quad\quad N \\ \quad\quad\quad \diagdown \\ F—J—T \\ \quad\diagdown \\ \quad\quad H \end{array}$$

Clues 1 and 2 combine to limit five of the six players so that F cannot be in 4, 5, or 6 because it has at least H, J, and T that must be to the right of it, and T cannot be in 1, 2, or 3 because at least J, F, and N must be to the left of it. Neither H nor J can appear in space 1 or 6 (clue 1). N cannot be in space 6 (clue 2).

Your diagram looks like this:

	~H					~H ~N
	~J					~J ~F
	~T	~T	~T	~F	~F	
FHJNPT	1	2	3	4	5	6
						T/P

6. **A** **Grab-a-Rule**

Clue 1 eliminates (D) because F is listed after J. Clue 2 eliminates (B) and (E) because N is after T. Clue 3 eliminates (C) since P is between H and N. Thus, (A) is the credited response.

7. **C** **General**

The deductions show that H, J, and T cannot be first so eliminate (D) and (E). The grab-a-rule question has F first, and past work has used P first, so the number must be at least two, eliminate (A). Try using N first. N, F, H, J, T, P is a valid order so the correct answer is (C).

8. A General

Since H, J, and T must all come after F according to clues 1 and 2, F cannot be fourth.

9. C Specific

F in space 3 must be followed by J—H—T or H—J—T based on clues 1 and 2. Since P must now come before H, it must also come before N. Clue 3 forces P into space 1 and N into space 2.

```
 ~H                          ~H  ~N
 ~J                          ~J  ~F
 ~T     ~T      ~T     ~F    ~F
  1  |   2   |   3  |   4  |  5  |  6
  P  |   N   |   F  |  H/ |  J/ |  T
     |       |      |   /J|   /H|
```

10. B Specific

If P is space 1, F is limited to either space 2 or space 3, from your deductions. F in space 3 forces N into space 2. This can be seen in the previous question. Thus, space 2 is limited to only F or N.

```
 ~H                          ~H  ~N
 ~J                          ~J  ~F
 ~T     ~T      ~T     ~F    ~F
  1  |   2   |   3  |   4  |  5  |  6
  P  |   F   |      |      |     |  T
     |       |      |      |     |
  P  |   N   |   F  |  H/ |  J/ |  T
     |       |      |   /J|   /H|
```

11. D General

This question asks which answer choice would replace clue 2 with the same result. The credited response will force T to come after N and J.

A. No. This would put T between F and H, but it would not force it to be after N and J.

B. No. This would put T after both F and N, but it leaves open the possibility that T is before J.

C. No. This would create a situation in which T comes either before or after both N and J in the same way clue 3 describes the relationship among P, H, and N.

D. Yes. This would force T to come after N, J, and F, which is the effect of clue 2.

E. No. This would not force T to come after J.

Questions 12–17

This is a 1D ordering game with an additional space for the runner that is not chosen. The sequence 1–4 and the out column should constitute the core of the diagram. Once an out column is added, this game has a one-to-one correspondence of players and spaces but it is important to distinguish those players that are chosen to run from those that are not.

Clue 1: $Q \rightarrow$ $\boxed{QT}$

$\overline{\boxed{QT}} \rightarrow \sim Q$

Clue 2: $S \neq 2, 4$

Clue 3: $U \rightarrow R = 2$
$R \neq 2 \rightarrow U$

Clue 4: $R = 2 \rightarrow \sim U$
$U \rightarrow R \neq 2$

Deductions: It is helpful to indicate the information from clue 2 in the diagram. Also, the contrapositive of clue 1 tells us that Q cannot run fourth. Also, clues 3 and 4 combine to indicate that U running and R = 2 are linked in both directions.

Your diagram should look like this:

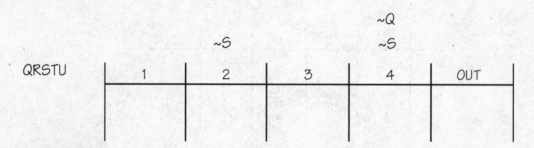

12. **D** | General

Clue 1 eliminates (C) because Q must run immediately before T. Clue 2 eliminates (B) since S cannot run in 2 or 4. Clue 3 eliminates (E); because U is not running, R must be in 2. Clue 4 eliminates (A); because R is in 2, U cannot run. The answer is therefore (D).

13. **D** | General

Use previous work to eliminate (A), (B), (C), and (E). Clue 1 requires T to follow Q if Q runs in the race. The contrapositive would result in Q as the one runner that does not race which would force T to run in the race somewhere.

14. **B** General

Try the answers. Since clues 3 and 4 involve R, it would be best to try (B) first.

A. No. If R is 1, the QT block could fill 2 and 3 or 3 and 4. The question is not completely resolved.

B. Yes. If R is second, U does not run the race. This forces the QT block to fill spaces 3 and 4 and S to be 1.

C. No. If R is 3, T could be 1 or 2. The question is not completely resolved.

D. No. If R is 4, T could be 2 or 3. The question is not completely resolved.

E. No. If R does not run, Q could be 1 or 2. The question is not completely resolved.

15. **A** General

Use previous work to eliminate (B), (C), (D), (E).

A. Yes. If R is immediately before S, R would be 2 and S in 3. This would require U to not run (clue 4). Q and T would be split in 1 and 4, which would violate clue 1.

B. No. The order could be S, Q, T, U.

C. No. The order could be R, U, S, T.

D. No. The order could be U, Q, T, R.

E. No. The order could be U, T, S, R.

16. **E** Specific

If U is first, R cannot be 2. Since clue 2 says S must not be 2 either, it follows that either Q or T must be in 2. If Q is 2, T must be 3 and R must be in 4 since S cannot. If T is 2, Q must not run the race which forces S to be 3, and R to be 4.

	~S		~Q ~S	
1	2	3	4	OUT
U	T	S	R	Q
U	Q	T	R	S

17. **B** Specific

If S runs, it must be in 1 or 3 (clue 2). If S is 1, then the QT block could start in 2 or 3. If S is 3, then the QT block must start in 1. Thus, S or Q must be in 1 and the credited response is (B).

| | ~S | | ~Q ~S | |
1	2	3	4	OUT
S	Q	T	U	R
S	R	Q	T	U
Q	T	S	U	R

Questions 18–23

This is a 1D ordering game and the seven days should constitute the core of your diagram.

The seven nurses are the players. This gives the game a one-to-one correspondence of players and spaces with one nurse conducting a session on each day.

Clue 1: H __ __ + M or M __ __ + H

Clue 2: GK

Clue 3: M—J

Clue 4: L—F—K

Clue 5: L ≠ 2

Deductions: Clues 2, 3, and 4 provide ordering deductions that indicate that J, K, and F cannot be on the 1st; L cannot be on the 5th; F and L cannot be on the 6th; and F, L, M, and G cannot be on the 7th. Clue 5 should be indicated in the diagram. Clues 3 and 4 can be combined to form a larger ordering rule seen here:

$$L—F— \boxed{GK}$$

Your diagram should look like this:

FGHJKLM

| | ~K ~F ~J | ~L | | | ~L | ~F ~L | ~F ~M ~G ~L |
| | 1 | 2 | 3 | 4 | 5 | 6 | 7 |

Grab-a-Rule

Clue 1 eliminates (E) since at least 2 sessions must be between M and H. Clue 3 eliminates (C) because J must occur after M so cannot be 1. Clue 4 eliminates (A) since F must be between K and L. Clue 5 eliminates (B) since L cannot be 2. Therefore, the answer is (D).

19. **C** **General**

Use previous work to eliminate sessions that J could conduct; then try any remaining answer choices.

A. No. The order could be M, J, L, F, H, G, K.

B. No. The order could be L, M, J, F, H, G, K.

C. Yes. If J were 5, G and K would be in 6 and 7. For M and H to be separated by at least 2 sessions, they would be 1 and 4 which would require L to come before F in 2 and 3. Because L cannot be in 2, this sequence is not possible.

D. No. The order could be L, M, F, G, K, J, H

E. No. The order could be L, H, F, G, K, M, J.

20. **D** **Specific**

If J is 3, L and M must be in 1 and 2. The diagram below shows the possible sequences.

							~F
	~F					~F	~G
	~K	~L			~L	~L	~L
FGHJKLM	1	2	3	4	5	6	7
	L	M	J	F	H	G	K
	L	M	J	F	G	K	H

21. **B** **Specific**

If K is before M, then K, M, and J must be in 5, 6, and 7, respectively. The diagram below shows possible assignments of the remaining players. Since either F or H must be third, the answer is (B).

							~F
	~F					~F	~G
	~K	~L			~L	~L	~L
FGHJKLM	1	2	3	4	5	6	7
	L	F/H	H/F	G	K	M	J

If G is 5, K must be 6. Since L cannot be in 2, it must be in 1 or 3 (clues 3, 4, and 5). M and H must be separated by at least 2 sessions (clue 1) and M must be before J (clue 3) so H must be in 7. Thus, the answer is (B).

FGHJKLM	1	2	3	4	5	6	7
	~F ~K	~L			~L	~F ~L	~F ~G ~L
	L	F/M	M/F	J	G	K	H
	L	M	J	F	G	K	H
	M	J	L	F	G	K	H

23. **A** General

Use previous work. L has been used in spaces 1 and 3 so the answer is (A).

Section 4: Arguments 2

1. **E** Principle Match

The passage states that while male guppies with large spots are more attractive to female guppies than males with small spots, only guppies with small spots live to maturity in waters where predators are abundant.

A. No. The passage does not discuss the dangers of large spots in a comparison between male and female guppies. This does not match.

B. No. There is no information in the passage regarding the number of offspring among male guppies with large spots. This does not match.

C. No. There is no information in the passage regarding the number of offspring relative to life span of guppies. This does not match.

D. No. The passage does not discuss the dangers of large spots in a comparison between male and female guppies. This does not match.

E. Yes. Guppies with large spots cannot live to maturity in certain environments where predators are abundant.

2. **B** Except

The programmer argues that the pay difference between the average salaries of technical writers and computer programmers at Mytheco is unfair. The executive counters that the pay difference is acceptable since many technical writers have greater seniority than many programmers.

A. No. The previous jobs of the technical writers are irrelevant to the executives' conclusion connecting salary with seniority.

B. Yes. While many writers have more seniority than many writers, the executives' counter argument is concluding that the pay difference in the average salary is fair. It would be important to know the relationship of the seniority of the average writer and the average programmer.

C. No. The programmer and executive include both salary and benefits in their arguments so it is unnecessary to consider the benefits separately.

D. No. The work history of the executive is irrelevant to the conclusion connecting salary with seniority.

E. No. The executive's salary is irrelevant to the conclusion regarding the pay difference between programmers and writers.

3. **A** `Inference`

A. Yes. There is no information in the passage to support a statement about where stations can be viewed.

B. No. The passage states that cable TV stations can charge lower rates for advertising than broadcast stations because cable stations charge subscriber fees.

C. No. The passage mentions the lower rates cable TV stations can charge as an advantage cable stations have over broadcast stations.

D. No. The final sentence mentions the worldwide expansion of some cable TV stations as an advantage cable stations have over broadcast stations.

E. No. The passage mentions targeted audiences, specifically those of 24-hour news, as an advantage cable stations have over broadcast stations.

4. **D** `Strengthen`

The argument concludes that air pollution likely eradicated plant diseases which are presented as diseases that disappeared in English cities during the Industrial Revolution. This causal argument assumes that no other factors were present during the time that could have caused these diseases to disappear.

A. No. That plants can develop a resistance is irrelevant to the conclusion about the disappearance of two specific plant diseases.

B. No. The difficulty of eliminating the two diseases does not address the cause of their disappearance during the Industrial Revolution.

C. No. The effect of air pollution on some plant species is not directly linked to the conclusion about two specific plant diseases.

D. Yes. This bolsters the causal link between pollution and the disappearance of the two diseases and strengthens the conclusion.

E. No. Whether other plant diseases disappeared or not is not relevant to the conclusion about the causes of the disappearance of these two specific plant diseases.

61

5. **C**   Inference

The passage states that while the author of the seventeenth-century abridgment of Hamlet is unknown, there are two facts about the author that are known: The author did not have a copy of the original play when he or she wrote the abridgment and the author wrote one character's speeches accurately but not the speeches of other characters. The credited response should match this description.

A. No. Shakespeare himself would likely have had a copy of the play and knowledge of the speeches of all characters equally. The facts in the passage do not indicate that Shakespeare wrote the abridgment.

B. No. The passage does not indicate that the abridgment was drafted so that the play would be easier to produce.

C. Yes. An actor who had played a role would likely have knowledge of the play generally and the speeches of one character more accurately than others.

D. No. A spectator may have knowledge of the play as a whole but would have equal knowledge of the speeches of all characters.

E. No. There is no information in the passage that the abridgment was attempting to improve the play.

6. **C**   Main Point

The musicologist disagrees with critics who complain of disproportion between text and music in the arias written by Handel. The musicologist provides evidence that the repetition serves a vital function by allowing the audience to focus on the music rather than the text.

A. No. The author argues that the disproportion between text and music in Handle's *da capo* arias serves a vital function.

B. No. The author does not compare Handel's *da capo* arias to other arias.

C. Yes. The author argues that the complaints of many critics can be refuted.

D. No. The author argues that the repetitions in Handel's *da capo* arias serve a vital function.

E. No. The author does not discuss most criticism in the argument about a specific criticism of Handel's *da capo* arias.

7. **E**   Inference

A. No. There is no information in the passage to support the claim that there are other large design companies besides Baxe.

B. No. There is no evidence in the passage regarding categories other than corporate interiors.

C. No. There is no information in the passage comparing the quality of most work produced by small companies with that of Baxe.

D. No. There is no information in the passage indicating the level of awareness of quality of those soliciting design proposals.

E.   Yes. Despite the fact that other companies have won awards and Baxe has not, it continues to have a near monopoly in the corporate market.

8.   **E**   **Weaken**

The argument concludes that while the asteroid that created the Chicxulub crater in Mexico likely resulted in the extinction of some nearby species, it is unlikely to be responsible for the extinction of most dinosaurs worldwide. Evidence is provided that larger craters exist at times when there were no known extinctions.

A.   No. This would strengthen the claim that the asteroid that produced the Chicxulub crater did not cause most dinosaurs to become extinct.

B.   No. This size of the asteroid is irrelevant to the claim that it did not cause most dinosaurs to become extinct.

C.   No. The author acknowledges that some species may have become extinct as a result of the asteroid impact. This does not weaken the claim that the asteriod impact did not cause most dinosaurs to become extinct.

D.   No. Other asteroids are irrelevant to the claim that this asteroid did not cause most dinosaurs to become extinct.

E.   Yes. If most dinosaurs lived in or near the region of the impact, then it is likely the asteroid was responsible for the extinction of most dinosaurs.

9.   **D**   **Parallel**

The passage argues that infection is more widespread in lot B than in lot A because more samples from lot B contained *Aspergillus* than from lot A. The argument assumes the samples are representative of the infections in each lot.

A.   No. The comparison is between the parts of a machine and the whole machine. Since there is no direct comparison between groups, it does not match.

B.   No. There is no comparison between groups so this does not match.

C.   No. There is no comparison between groups so this does not match.

D.   Yes. The passage compares the results of a survey among samples from two different groups and assumes that what is true from each sample will be true among the greater groups.

E.   No. There is no comparison between groups so this does not match.

10.   **A**   **Inference**

A.   Yes. The author states that it is correct to believe that losing a job is a result of impersonal social forces and that a widespread knowledge of this belief would lead to economic disaster.

B.   No. The author does not mention protections against impersonal social forces.

C.   No. The author states that in this situation increased governmental control would lead to economic disaster, but there is no indication that there should never be government interference.

D.   No. The author offers a prediction for events that have not yet occurred. There is no direct evidence that societal demand for government control is in fact growing.

E.   No. The author does not discuss the level of responsibility people should feel for military invasions or economic disasters.

11.   **A**   Flaw

The argument concludes that it is unlikely Dalton will build an airport. Evidence is offered that a majority of residents in favor of building an airport would be sufficient for its success. The author then states that this sufficient condition is unlikely to be met. The conclusion assumes that majority support is also a necessary condition.

A.   Yes. The argument assumes that majority support, which is stated to be a sufficient condition, is necessary by stating that since majority support is unlikely, the airport is unlikely to be built.

B.   No. The author does not argue that anything must be true.

C.   No. The conclusion states that the event is unlikely to occur since the majority support is unlikely. The author does not argue that the event will definitely not occur.

D.   No. The author does not consider what people near Dalton believe because those people are not relevant to the argument.

E.   No. The author overlooks the economy because it is not relevant to the argument about residents' favoring the airport proposal.

12.   **C**   Resolve/ Explain

The passage states that when rush-hour speed limits were reduced on a motorway, rush-hour travel times decreased. One might expect travel times to increase when speed limits drop and the question task asks for an answer choice that explains this difference.

A.   No. It is expected that speeds would decrease when the speed limit was reduced. This does not explain why the travel times also decreased.

B.   No. What occurred outside of rush-hour does not explain why travel times during rush-hour decreased even as the speed limits were reduced.

C.   Yes. If the reduced speed limits also caused a reduction in accidents that caused lengthy delays, it is possible that the lower speeds would lead to reduced travel time.

D.   No. Enforcement of the reduced speed limits does not explain why travel times were reduced.

E.   No. The number of drivers may remain the same or decrease. Since there is no direct connection between the number of drivers and travel times, this does not explain why travel times were reduced.

13.   **A**   Sufficient Assumption

The author concludes that the artistic merit of an artwork can depend on both the creator of the work and those who evaluate it. Evidence is provided that indicates that the pleasure one takes in an artwork can be increased or decreased based upon the criticism or praise given by art critics. There is a missing link between pleasure and artistic merit.

A. Yes. If the pleasure one gets from a work of art determines the artwork's merit, the conclusion follows logically.

B. No. The confidence necessary for the evaluation is irrelevant to the author's argument about the merits of an artwork depending on the evaluation of critics.

C. No. The author argues that art critics determine merit as well as artists but does not argue that one does so more than the other.

D. No. Whether people seek out reviews is irrelevant to whether evaluation of a work in part determines its artistic merit.

E. No. The author indicates that the evaluation of artwork can alter the pleasure one receives from viewing artwork. This does not add anything substantive to the original argument.

14. **A** **Resolve/ Explain**

The passage indicates that the number of thefts has declined during the past five years. At the same time, it is more likely that someone who steals a car will be convicted.

A. Yes. This provides information that there are fewer people who steal cars and that they are more likely to maintain possession of the car after it is known to be stolen. It explains both issues discussed in the passage.

B. No. The frequency of car alarms may explain why there are fewer thefts, but the fact that many people ignore them does not explain why more criminals are convicted of theft.

C. No. The diversion of resources to investigate home burglaries does not explain why more criminals are convicted of theft.

D. No. The quick disassembly of cars does not explain why more criminals are convicted of theft.

E. No. Lenient punishment on younger offenders does not explain why there are fewer of them, nor does it explain by itself why they are more likely to be convicted.

15. **B** **Flaw**

The legislator concludes that the constituents would support a bill to reduce corporate income taxes based on a survey that asked whether they favored high taxes. The legislator's argument assumes that corporate income taxes would be considered part of the question asked in the survey.

A. No. The legislator's argument is about the constituents specifically, so their representation of the country as a whole is irrelevant.

B. Yes. There is no evidence that the current corporate income tax is "high" and so there is no evidence about the constituents' feelings toward the newly introduced bill.

C. No. The legislator provides evidence in the study that constituents oppose high taxes and assumes they would be in favor of reduced taxes for corporations. Confusing the results of the survey is not the same as failing to provide evidence.

D. No. The argument is not circular. The legislator assumes the results of the survey indicate a support for a bill that may not be represented by the question asked in the survey.

61

E. No. This the opposite of what is needed. The legislator's survey is consistent with support for a bill but does not prove support for the bill.

16. **C** **Main Point**

The author concludes that prohibitions against having pets in nursing homes should be lifted since animals can reduce stress and provide health benefits.

A. No. The author's argument is about how animal companions can make a home more rewarding. This is a premise.

B. No. The author does not compare nursing home residents to other people.

C. Yes. This is a paraphrase of the author's conclusion.

D. No. This is a premise in support of the conclusion that residents in nursing homes should be allowed to have pets.

E. No. The author's conclusion is specific to the residents of nursing homes being allowed to have pets.

17. **D** **Reasoning**

The author concludes that water is among the biggest polluters of water. Evidence is provided that rainwater runoff contributes more to the contamination of bodies of water than industrial discharge.

A. No. The statement in question is a premise not the conclusion.

B. No. The statement is evidence for a different conclusion, specifically that water itself is among the biggest water polluters.

C. No. The statement is a fact used to support the conclusion. The second sentence explains why this statement is true.

D. Yes. The statement is evidence for the conclusion that water itself is among the biggest water polluters.

E. No. The argument is concerned with water as a polluter of water. It does not discuss typical city pollution.

18. **A** **Point at Issue**

Wong argues that some countries may need an autocratic government as they transition to a democracy, which is better for all countries. Tate argues that some countries are better off as autocracies.

A. Yes. Wong says all countries are better off as democracies, whereas Tate says some may be better off as autocracies.

B. No. Wong does not speak to this issue.

C. No. Neither argues that some countries may not be able to become democracies.

D. No. Both seem to agree to this point.

E. No. Wong does not speak to this issue.

19. **E** **Principle Match**

The rule is to hire the most productive candidate when none of the fully qualified candidates currently works for the company. The application argues for hiring a fully qualified candidate over the other, but information about who is most productive and whether either currently works for the company is missing.

A. No. This would still leave open the question of which candidate would be most productive.

B. No. This would not use the rule since it applies when none of the fully qualified candidates currently works for the company.

C. No. This would not use the rule since it applies when none of the fully qualified candidates currently works for the company.

D. No. This would not use the rule since it applies when none of the fully qualified candidates currently works for the company.

E. Yes. Since Delacruz is fully qualified and none of the candidates works for the company, the company should hire the candidate who is most productive. This confirms the application of the rule was correct.

20. **A** **Necessary Assumption**

The argument concludes that important types of medicine will never be developed if tropical rain forests are not preserved. Evidence is provided that many important types of medicine have been developed by substances found in plants that live in the tropical rain forests. There is a missing link between many previous medicinal discoveries and future development of important medicines.

A. Yes. Use the negation test: If there are no substances in rain forests that have not already been discovered, then future development based on previous discoveries is likely and the conclusion is invalid.

B. No. The author assumes the opposite, that these substances cannot be found in other environments.

C. No. Use the negation test: If the majority of plants do not contain substances of medicinal value, it is still possible that some will and the conclusion could be valid.

D. No. The author does not assume that plants that can be discovered will be; instead, the author argues that plants cannot be discovered if the rain forests are not preserved.

E. No. This paraphrases the conclusion of the argument and is stated in the passage, not assumed.

21. **C** **Weaken**

The argument concludes that ichthyosaurs were deep divers because, like modern deep-diving marine mammals, the outer shell of their bones was porous. The argument assumes that a characteristic common to many modern deep-diving mammals is sufficient evidence to know that prehistoric reptiles were also deep-diving animals. The credited response will weaken the conclusion by providing more evidence that indicates ichthyosaurs were not deep divers or an alternative consideration to the one discussed in the argument.

61

A.   No. This states that the porous outer shell may not have been necessary for the ichthyosaurs to be deep divers but does not indicate whether this type of shell was sufficient so it does not weaken the conclusion that the ichthyosaurs were deep divers.

B.   No. This does not discuss deep-diving reptiles so this does not weaken the claim about ichthyosaurs, which are reptiles who had bones with porous outer shells.

C.   Yes. If this is true, then a porous outer shell in reptiles is not sufficient to know that the reptile is a deep diver since some reptiles with porous outer shells are not deep divers.

D.   No. While this establishes the possibility of a difference between whales and the ichthyosaurs, it does not provide evidence that the ichthyosaurs may not have been deep divers.

E.   No. This states that the porous outer shell may not have been necessary for the ichthyosaurs to be deep divers but does not indicate whether this type of shell was sufficient so it does not weaken the conclusion that the ichthyosaurs were deep divers.

22. **C**   Reasoning

The librarian concludes that the preservation grant should not be used to restore the town's charter. The argument is structured to disagree with some people who argue that the town's charter should be restored using the grant money since the charter will soon deteriorate beyond repair without such restoration. The librarian argues that since the charter has no scholarly value and copies are readily available, the money should be spent on other projects.

A.   No. The librarian does not argue with the point that the charter will deteriorate beyond repair if it is not restored.

B.   No. The librarian rejects the claim that the grant should be used to restore the charter but does not argue with the point that the charter will deteriorate if it is not restored.

C.   Yes. Some people argue that the grant should be used to restore the charter since it will deteriorate if it is not restored, and the librarian disagrees with the conclusion of those people.

D.   No. The statement in question is evidence used by some people, not the librarian, to argue for the use of the grant to restore the town charter.

E.   No. The statement in question is evidence used by some people to argue for the use of the grant to restore the town charter. It is not required by the librarian's argument that claims the money should be spent on other projects.

23. **D**   Principle
             Strengthen

The columnist argues that we should preserve the most species possible if there is a goal to preserve any. Evidence is provided that states that we are ignorant of the interrelationships among species and that allowing some species to die may impact the viability of other species, presumably the ones that we care about.

A.   No. This would strengthen the claim that some species be preserved but would not justify the columnist's argument that the preservation be directed at the maximum number of species.

B.   No. The columnist's argument indicates that action should be taken precisely because all the relevant information is unknown.

C. No. The columnist's argument does not make exceptions for flourishing human populations so this does not justify the claim that animal preservation be directed at the maximum number of species.

D. Yes. If this principle is true, it would be important to maximize animal preservation to avoid potentially undermining the viability of a species that is important since the important species may be connected to species to which humans are indifferent.

E. No. The columnist's argument does not state that maximizing animal preservation would have the best future consequences in the immediate future.

24. **E**   Flaw

The author concludes that long-term friends are likely the same age since most of these friendships resulted from someone feeling comfortable to speak to a stranger and people are likely to feel comfortable speaking to a stranger who is the same age. The argument fails to provide evidence about other things that may make people feel comfortable approaching a stranger.

A. No. The author does not indicate that people would not feel comfortable approaching someone that was not a stranger.

B. No. The author does not make a comparison between a situation and other similar situations.

C. No. The author does not compare the comfort levels of people approaching strangers versus non-strangers.

D. No. The author's argument allows for the possibility that there are exceptions by stating that the probable conclusion is based on a situation that is more likely.

E. Yes. There may be other factors that are related to approaching strangers. If people are comfortable approaching people who are not of the same age, then long-term friendships may be present regardless of age.

25. **B**   Sufficient Assumption

The argument concludes that there can be no individual freedom without the rule of law. The premises indicate that individual freedom requires social integrity and pursuing the good life requires social integrity. There is a language shift from social integrity in the premises to the rule of law in the conclusion and assumes that social integrity requires the rule of law.

A. No. This is the opposite of what is needed. Use the negation test: If there could be a rule of law without social integrity, it is still possible that the rule of law is required for individual freedom.

B. Yes. Use the negation test: If there could be social integrity without the rule of law, then it would be possible for individual freedom to exist outside the rule of law as well and the conclusion would be invalid.

C. No. The author does not argue that the pursuit of the good life is connected to the rule of law. Use the negation test: If one could pursue the good life without the rule of law, it is still possible that individual freedoms require the rule of law.

D. No. The author states as a premise that social integrity is required by individual freedoms but does not indicate that individual freedoms are necessary for social integrity.

E. No. The conclusion states the opposite: The rule of law is necessary for individual freedoms. The author does not assume the individual freedoms are necessary for the rule of law.

26. **B** Parallel Flaw

The economist's argument concludes that a nation that commits to public education will avoid economic and political weakness. The premises state that an uneducated population will lead a country to be weak economically and politically and that an educated population requires a commitment to public education. The author assumes the presence of a necessary factor (an education) to avoid economic and political weakness is sufficient, ignoring the possibility that there may be other necessary factors.

A. No. This argument assumes that a broader diet is a diet that is more flexible when the traditional food supply is removed. The language shift that applies in this argument does not match the necessary/sufficient flaw in the original passage.

B. Yes. This mistakes a necessary factor (empathy) for a good candidate to be a sufficient factor. It is flawed because it is possible that some people who can manipulate others may not be good candidates despite their having one of necessary characteristics of a good candidate.

C. No. This argument has a related structure but its conclusion incorrectly creates a contrapositive by negating but not flipping the premise. This argument does not match because the conclusion lacks the presence of a necessary characteristic in defining one that can give orders.

D. No. The argument assumes that a situation that is unlikely to happen is a situation that will not happen. It does not have a necessary/sufficient flaw that matches the original argument.

E. No. The argument assumes that people who like to eat are unable to curtail their food intake in order to lose weight. The argument provides two options and argues that one option is not possible and concludes that the other option is not possible.

NOTES